INDOC

التلقين

(Indoctrination)

Ideology, Propaganda and Conflict in the Corps and al-Qaida

K2

INDOC

التلقين

(Indoctrination)

Ideology, Propaganda and Conflict in the Corps and al-Qaida

Karl D. Klicker

Captain of Marines, Ret.

B.A., MSED, MSEAT, EdD

© 2013

Vade Mecum Publishing Group

Indispensable

Designed in-house by VMPG, Inc.

Library of Congress Cataloguing-in-Publication Data has been applied for.

ISBN 978-0-9856335-4-7

For

US Marine Major Megan McClung
&
US Army Captain Travis Patriquin
KIA 6 December 2006; Ramadi, Anbar Province, Iraq

In the months before Megan and Travis were killed by an IED in Ramadi, my team and I met with Travis periodically at Forward Operating Base (FOB) Fallujah, in the plywood-walled shack that housed many of the State Department civilians and Marine Reservists who worked on the Provincial Reconstruction Teams in Anbar Province. Travis was a polyglot – an impressively talented self-trained linguist and *Foreign Area Officer* who spoke fluent Arabic with an Arabic accent. Travis brought my team a clearer picture, from first-hand interviews, of the *Anbar Awakening* and Sheikh Abdul Sattar Ftikhan al-Rishawi al-Dulaimi – Sheikh Sattar.

What Americans who read think of as "The Sons of Iraq" owe their thanks to Travis. He had been providing my intelligence team with invaluable insights into the birth of Sahawa al-Anbar (SAA) – the Anbar Awakening Council – and its genuine intentions in the Summer and Autumn of 2006, and thus to my briefings to the general staff. What Iraqis who read need to understand is that Sahawa al-Anbar was not created to topple the Shi'ite dominated government of Iraq, but to rid Iraq of al-Qaida. SAA turned Anbar's Sunni majority against al-Qaida because al-Qaida, like the US earlier on, had failed to understand Anbar's tribal customs. Sattar had determined, and convinced fellow sheikhs from neighboring tribes to understand, that throwing their lot in with the Americans would bring peace to Iraq. Sheikh Sattar, killed by an attacker with a roadside bomb at the gates to his own home compound during Ramadan, in September 2007 – six months after I left Iraq – is a hero. No matter how he's judged, he saved some Marines' lives. Travis Patriquin's debriefs allowed my team to accurately advise the general staff at Multi-National Forces–West headquarters of Sattar's intentions.

Travis saved Marine lives. Travis is a hero.

Megan is another story. We intersected both as Marines and as marathoners. I arrived in Iraq in the first days of September 2006 with 2d Intelligence Battalion; Megan was serving as a public affairs officer on a year-long assignment with the Marine Expeditionary Force headquarters. Before Megan and I would meet in Fallujah, I had wrapped up business in Virginia Beach, headed for Camp Lejeune. In my final scan of e-mail, I spotted an invitation from the Houston Marathon to sign up for the coming race in January 2007. I had run the Houston Marathon five years straight before a recall to active duty in the Marine Corps in 2005. I fired off a note to the race organizer that I would be deployed but would be happy to run a "Houston Marathon in Iraq" so I could move toward Houston Marathon veteran status (10 races). I was kind of joking. I had no idea they would accept.

By the time we got settled in Fallujah weeks later and I was able to log in to those precious e-mails from home, the race organizer had taken me up on the offer:

> Karl, greetings from the Chevron Houston Marathon. We have discussed the issue and are fine with your participating in the "Camp Fallujah Houston Marathon" (we'll even customize a T-shirt for you...and any of your buddies you can recruit to run with you). All that we ask is that you are able to provide us with some verification that you actually do complete the run (all 26.2 miles of it). Is it possible for you to have a superior act as course referee? He/she could provide us

with a letter of sorts confirming your completion.

Regards,
Steven Karpas
Director of Marketing
Director of Race Development, Chevron Houston Marathon

From a Public Relations point of view – good for the Marine Corps; good for the Houston Marathon. In the scant spare minutes a day I had to scout the possibilities of how to organize a marathon in a combat zone, I was time and again sent off in search of Marine Major Megan McClung, a public affairs officer (a cute redhead from the Naval Academy, class of '95). As it turned out, the Public Affairs Office (the PAO) was a two-minute walk from the Intelligence Fusion Center where I would spend the coming 189 days.

Megan served as my mentor at first, and offered me a binder full of helpful forms and letters to request support: first aid, security, water, MWR (Morale/Welfare and Recreation) assistance, time-keepers, approvals from the general staff, etc., and some verbal advice about the uphill battle I would face trying to convince combat-focused colonels and generals that running a marathon on a Sunday morning at FOB Fallujah would be good for morale. Megan had already fought that battle and had organized the Marine Corps Marathon mirror race (run in full in Washington, DC) for October 2006, but it had been moved from Fallujah to al-Asad Air Base for security reasons.

Fallujah, a smaller FOB, was taking rockets and mortars until I left Iraq. With four or five other runners based at Fallujah, I hopped on a Blackhawk helicopter to al-Asad and ran that race in late October. We had about 110 runners from bases all over Iraq. More than 200 had signed up, but some couldn't make connections. Megan was the first woman across the finish line. She also beat most of the men. She was awesome.

By then – late October 2006 – I was well on the way to hosting the Houston Marathon at Fallujah. Megan had transferred to Community Relations duties in Ramadi before the race at al-Asad. Fact is...Megan's final e-mails from Ramadi expressed an opinion that she thought I was trying to get her to organize "my" race. We didn't talk much through November. No ill will. I pressed on, with impossibly helpful work from Erin McGowan at the Houston Marathon office in Texas, and Crystal Nadeau, a civilian contractor with the MWR offices in Fallujah and al-Asad. And then –

Megan and Travis, traveling together in a HUMVEE, were killed by a coward with an IED, a roadside bomb, in Ramadi, December 6, 2006. Megan never had a chance to run the Houston Marathon in Iraq.[i]

Megan had been working with the Women's Engagement Program, talking with Iraqi women, including the women in Sheikh Sattar's extended family, about how the US could assist in security and reconstruction programs, what their children needed, what their communities needed. The Iraqi women loved her. Megan was, as generations of Marines before, a peacekeeper. I made sure Megan's Dad and Mom, Mike and Re, received Megan's honorary finisher's medal and T-shirt from the 35th Houston Marathon, at Forward Operating Base Fallujah, Anbar Province, Iraq, which we dedicated to Megan in January 2007.

Megan is a hero.

(Megan's Father, Dr. Mike McClung, passed away on July 2, 2013, at his home in Coupeville, WA. Mike and Megan are survived by Megan's Mother, Dr. Re McClung, who remains active with the Megan McClung Memorial Scholarship Foundation.)

Acknowledgements

My original dissertation in 1990, upon which this book is based, was dedicated to my parents: Staff Sergeant Marvin L. Klicker, USMC, Ret., and Shirley Isabelle Klicker, and that dedication stands. As of 1994 and 1996, my parents have gone to fill in the blanks from a line in the Marines' Hymn:

> If the Army and the Navy
> Ever looked on Heaven's scenes,
> They would find the streets are guarded by
> United States Marines.

Throughout my doctoral studies and on through completion of my dissertation, Dr. James H. McElhinney served as my committee chair. Jim, born in September 1926, was just two months younger than my own father. After my Dad died – Jim, more than a favorite professor and mentor – was like my *spare* Dad, and his wife Sondra is Sondra-Mom. Jim retired from Ball State University in 2003. Jim died on July 1, 2011. As a professor, Jim speaks through this book in many ways.

My sincere thanks to Christopher R. Rate, Doctor of Philosophy in Psychology (Yale University), Colonel, United States Air Force, serving as the HQ US Special Operations Command Senior Strategic Behavioral Scientist and Planner, for suffering through the manuscript and offering solid advice on better ways to express technical topics in social psychology. I owe a note of thanks also to Adam, an exceedingly rare Marine non-commissioned officer, and Harry C. who both served our country with finesse in pursuit of peace in Iraq. And because the bubbas will be forever entertaining…a nod to High Pockets, Dave, Pete, John and Todd.

Never last nor least important: My love to Teresa, Marina, Erik & Allison with thanks for support and the time to write and edit.

Also by Karl D. Klicker

MERATHON

MERATHON is part memoire, part social psychology, part science fiction. *MERATHON* explores the causes and impact of the December 2001 collapse of ENRON, the once-powerful Fortune 7 energy and commodities-trading company. *MERATHON* runs through unemployment and the grief cycle, leadership, and the philosophies of Quality – with marathons as both metaphor and therapy. *MERATHON* is a resource for the unemployed, the entrepreneur, the MBA student, and men and women in leadership positions in any industry.

Tested by Fire:
Recipes for Leaders, With Metaphors on the Grill

TESTED BY FIRE presents the arts, sciences and intuition of backyard grilling as a metaphor for instructing new leaders in any industry. Combining theory and real-world experience from 40 combined years in military leadership, industrial training, organizational psychology and backyard grilling, the author presents 13 fundamental, thought-provoking scenarios for middle and senior leaders who own the responsibility for training and educating their organization's next generation of leaders. Examples include tales from the combat zone of Anbar Province in Iraq to life post-ENRON; comparing Santa Claus and jihad; and managing the challenges inherent in The 2nd Law of Social Thermodynamics - wrapped around the arts and sciences of spare ribs, potato salad, beer can chicken, and more.

Contents

Tables

Foreword

by Dr. Tawfik Hamid

Indoctrination: Ideology, Propaganda and Conflict in the Corps and al-Qaida by Karl D. Klicker is a brilliant contribution to the literatures about Islamic Radicalism. The author not only discusses issues related to radical Islam but also explains in discerning ways the culture of the Marine forces and their conflict with radical Islamists. His hands-on experience in this field is invaluable. The author makes a clear distinction between those who use Islam as a violent tool to kill others and those Muslims who just want to live a conservative life style.

One of the greatest points of the book is the honesty and factuality in addressing the problem of Radical Islam. The author does not shy away from explicitly identifying *ideology* as the main cause of the problem and at the same time acknowledges the criminality part of radicalism.

Dr. Klicker's ability to see the need of a multidisciplinary approach to solve the problem deserves respect. Additionally, I am impressed with the author's observation that *dehumanization* of non-Muslims is one of the vital steps that creates the radical mindset. In this complex but very readable book, the author describes eloquently the causes and effects of cultural changes and conflicts in the Marine Corps during an approximately 30-year period (from the mid-1950s to the mid-1980s), with a balanced, rational analysis of the cultural challenges facing the Corps today, and illustrative, effective parallels and examples to explain the Islamists' mindset and culture to the western audience.

Overall, this well-referenced book offers a great input to understanding Islamic radicalism and the US Marine Corps culture. I strongly recommend this book to those who want deep and truthful understanding of the conflict between Radical Islamists and our civilization.

Dr. Hamid is an Islamic thinker and reformer, and one time Islamic extremist from Egypt. He was a member of a terrorist Islamic organization, with Dr. Ayman Al Zawahiri who was the second in command of Al-Qaeda before becoming its leader following the death of Osama Bin Laden. Some thirty years ago, he recognized the threat of Political and Radical Islam and the need for a reformation based upon modern peaceful interpretations of classical Islamic core texts. Dr. Hamid provided a fresh and theologically valid interpretation for the Quran to counterbalance the radical teaching by others of this holy text. As the Daily Express (UK) mentioned "Dr. Hamid predicted the attacks on the twin towers, Madrid and London."

After September 11, Dr. Hamid boldly decided to speak out through western broadcast and print media. He appeared on shows spanning the spectrum from CNN to Fox News, and his articles and op-ed pieces have appeared in publications such as the Wall Street Journal, the New York Daily News, the Washington Times, and the Jerusalem Post. Dr. Hamid's exceptional knowledge of the jihadi mindset led him to be a guest speaker at many reputable private and governmental fora - both within the US and internationally such as the US Congress, Director of National Intelligence, the Pentagon, United States Special Operations Command (USSOCOM), National Prayer breakfast, JINSA (Jewish Institute for National Security Affairs), Princeton University, Defense Academy of the United Kingdom, and the European Parliament.

Dr. Hamid also appeared on ABC News 20/20 and was quoted by the Associated Press, the Washington Post, and several other world media voices. Dr. Hamid is also a qualified Medical Doctor (Internal Medicine Specialist) and has a Masters degree in Cognitive Psychology and Effective Educational Methodologies as well. Currently, Dr. Hamid is a Senior Fellow and Chair of the Studies of Islamic Radicalism at the Potomac Institute for Policy Studies-Washington, DC.

Prologue

The following text addresses one conclusion, through four stories. The conclusion, supported by personal experience and 30 years of primary academic research and secondary sources: the social psychology of recruitment to war, to *jihad*, is basically the same from organization to organization, state to state, generation to generation.

This book focuses mainly on United States Marines and radical Islamists. The book is a map, a trail of bread crumbs describing how I arrive at this conclusion. The reader will discover this is not a new concept, but the guts of this argument must be applied to the strategic solutions that will defeat the radical Islamists who seek to destroy the United States – both from without and within.

While the social psychology of attracting recruits to and indoctrination in a military cause is common across cultures or societies; the cultures themselves diverge widely. *All* organizations seeking to recruit new employees create cultural narratives – internally as the collective mythology; externally viewed as a corporate reputation. This is true for Wal-Mart, the FBI, Starbucks or NASA as much as for the Marine Corps or al-Qaida.

We acknowledge that cultural change or evolution is inevitable, but those engaged in the *purposeful* change of a given culture must also accept that those who own the original culture will do all in their power to fight organizational entropy... what they view as organizational decay. This is true in Islam, in the fight to prevent "innovation" as much as it is true in the Marine Corps where senior Marines seek to prevent what they see as a hostile takeover through social experimentation. All sides need to read this text with an open mind and get to the conclusions in this book.

The four stories, or four parallel premises supporting this conclusion, are the recruiting and indoctrinating *processes* and *messages* of the Marine Corps and the radical Islamists, and the internal cultural conflict evident in each organization. And truly the fifth story is the conflict between the two organizations. Acknowledging that the United States has, over the past century, stepped away from the term *propaganda* (propaganda is what the bad guys do; *we* use strategic communication, military influence support operations, advertising, and public affairs), this book applies the term *propaganda* to both organizations from Jacques Ellul's clinical definition:

> *Propaganda is a set of methods employed by an organized group that wants to bring about the active or passive participation in its actions of a mass of individuals, psychologically unified, through psychological manipulation and incorporated in an organization.*[ii]

Bytwerk, footnoted above, observes that Ellul "sees propaganda [is] not something done by evil propagandists to ignorant citizens:"

> *[But in order] for propaganda to be so far-ranging, it must correspond to a need. The State has that need: Propaganda is obviously a necessary instrument for the State and the authorities. But while this fact may dispel the concept of the propagandist simply as an evil-doer, it still leaves the idea of propaganda as an active power vs. passive masses. And we insist that this idea, too, must be dispelled: For propaganda to succeed, it must correspond to a need for propaganda on the individual's part. One can lead a horse to water but cannot make him drink; one cannot reach through propaganda those who do not need what it offers. [One cannot sell a Ford truck to one who does not want, desire or need (attitude) to buy (behavior) a new Ford truck.]*

> *The propagandee is by no means just an innocent victim. He provides the psychological action of propaganda, and not merely leads himself to it, but even derives satisfaction from it. Without this previous, implicit consent, without this need for propaganda experienced by practically every citizen of the technological age, propaganda could not spread. There is not*

just a wicked propagandist at work who sets up means to ensnare the innocent citizen. Rather, there is a citizen who craves propaganda from the bottom of his being and a propagandist who responds to this craving. Propagandists would not exist without potential propagandees to begin with. To understand that propaganda is not just a deliberate and more or less arbitrary creation by some people in power is therefore essential. It is a strictly sociological phenomenon, in the sense that it has its roots and reasons in the need of the group that will sustain it. (Ellul, p. 121)

To put this in perspective: propaganda, by definition, applies to advertising, religion and education. The million-dollar commercials for beer, or Ford trucks, during a Super Bowl halftime blitz for example, are aimed at viewers with needs. On the surface, this appears to be people who need beer or trucks. Beneath the surface, the need is the perception of social belonging that comes with drinking a particular beer or the status that comes with owning a new vehicle and the perceived prestige of a particular truck or owning a *new* truck. The influence campaign, seeking to persuade viewers to buy a particular brand of beer or truck, is artfully crafted to convince viewers that their product responds to that need better than other options (other brands of beer or trucks; other drugs or status symbols). Embedded in the advertising are symbols, distilled through the analysis of market demographics, designed to appeal to the deeper need: sex, manhood, social status, etc. (Thus red cars and trucks, and attractive women in car commercials.)

Service in a military organization provides rewards that respond to a range of attitudes and needs for young men and women: the need to belong, the need for a sense of relevance or purpose, the need for a job or an education, the response to patriotism or ideology and a few others, to be discussed in the book. Marine Corps advertising applies symbols, such as manhood, images of tough training and others, designed to convince (mostly) males in the 17- to 25-year old demographic that the Corps can fulfill these needs better than other options, like the Army, Navy, or Air Force, college, entry-level civilian jobs and so on.

Al-Qaida goes through the same *process*, but with other symbols based on the radical Salafist narrative – which will also be discussed in following chapters. Some of those options, outside of the First World, include unemployment in a destitute, dysfunctional country. The recruiters of radical Islam may be college-educated and *not* unemployed – but many of their recruits are the marginalized, destitute, angry youth of both First World and barely governed Third World nations. The symbols may include the lion, the sun, the moon, blood spilled in the desert, or Osama bin Laden as an icon, but not beer or Ford trucks.

Religion responds to a need. Education responds to a need. Recruiting propaganda – advertising – responds to a need. A small percentage of Americans will become Marines, just as a small percentage of Muslims will fight jihad as "terrorists." And some of those will say they're fighting jihad but are really just murderers, or drug runners and money launderers, or both murderers and drug runners who justify illicit financing as a way to further Allah's cause. Note also in Ellul's definition that he accounts for both active and passive participation. Public civilian, taxpayer, support for the Marine Corps has never been higher; many Muslims who will never carry a rifle still offer financial or other support for those who claim to be protecting the name of Allah or rebuilding the Caliphate.

As young men and women respond to the call to war, as touted in the recruiting pitch, *Social Identity Theory* suggests they take on the identity characteristics of their adoptive organization (Marine Corps or al-Qaida for example), creating part of their personal identities or personal narratives based on the identity of the whole.[iii] Tajfel and Turner's work in this area further explains that this process of categorizing oneself in an in-group establishes boundaries – and therefore out-groups. Other Marines are more like me; US soldiers are less like me; radical Islamist fighters are not like me.

As for internal conflicts: the symbols, rituals and myths which form the cultural narrative of any of these organizations are subject to internal and external evolutionary pressures. Cultural elements change; change foments conflict – between ideologically different camps within an organization, between generations, genders, races and other subdivisions. So while radical Islamists and United States Marines are locked in deadly conflict with each other, each organization expends some energy policing its own internal conflicts. Salafist Sunni Islamists and Shi'a alike see Sufism as outside Islam; Sunni and Shi'a are doctrinally divided and Salafist Sunnis see the Shi'a as apostate. Western scholars and moderate Muslim clerics alike identify murderous Salafist Islamists as irhabi (terrorists) and takfiri – those who excommunicate fellow Muslims because their beliefs are not in accord with a specific brand of ultra-conservative Salafist Islam. Veteran Marines in the late 1970s and through the 1980s, particularly combat veterans, came to view the incoming crop of Marine recruits as the "Coca-Cola generation." Soft. Undisciplined. Today's veteran Marines see the incoming generation as the "Nintendo" generation. Soft. Undisciplined. But today's veteran Marines were the Coca-Cola generation recruits of the 1980s. And in 20 years, today's lieutenants, privates, privates-first class and lance corporals who are veterans of Iraq and Afghanistan will see the incoming recruits of 2033 as soft and undisciplined.

Muslim leaders have remained irksomely silent, for the *most* part, since 9/11. Various groups such as the Council on American-Islamic Relations (CAIR) and the Muslim Brotherhood proclaim the *peaceful* intent of Muslims to install shariah over all the earth. Through *peaceful* means. Everyone will live in *peace* and be happy. Muslim happy. Islam has no police save world opinion. There is no "pope." There is neither caliphate nor central governing body with a senate and house of representatives. Most takfiri and irhabists have forsaken their homes and are stateless warriors and criminals.

Yet: for the *least* part:

There are in fact moderate Muslim voices, both in America and abroad. There aren't enough. Among these are this book's Foreword author, Dr. Tawfik Hamid (Tareg abdelHamid), whose own provenance reads thus:

A self-described former member of the militant al-Gama'a al-Islamiyya, Tawfik Hamid advocates a peaceful understanding of Islam that is compatible with universal human rights and intellectual freedom. He says that he started to preach in mosques to promote his message of and, as a result, became a target of Islamic militants, who threatened his life. Hamid then migrated to the West where he has lectured at UCLA, Stanford University, University of Miami and Georgetown University - against Islamic fundamentalism. He currently serves on the Advisory Council of The Intelligence Summit, an annual conference on security. Hamid has also appeared on television programs, including Fox's *Glenn Beck* Show, Fox News Channel, and the BBC's *Religion and Ethics.*

Hamid, also known as Tarek Abdelhamid, has a medical degree in internal medicine and a master's degree in cognitive psychology and educational techniques.[iv]

Dr. Hamid self-reports that he is an Islamic thinker and reformer, and one time Islamic extremist from Egypt. He was a member of a terrorist Islamic organization with Dr. Ayman Al Zawahiri who was the second in command of Al-Qaeda before becoming its leader following the death of Osama Bin Laden. Some thirty years ago, he recognized the threat of Political and Radical Islam and the need for a reformation based upon modern peaceful interpretations of classical Islamic core texts.[v]

Hamid's website (with access to his books) is located at: <http://www.tawfikhamid.com/>.   Hamid's Facebook page is available at:

https://www.facebook.com/ModernQuranInterpretation?ref=hl

The link to the Facebook page, in Arabic, is:

ال كريم   ل ا قرآن   ال ع صرى   ال ت ف س ير

(The Facebook site is in Arabic.)

Contrast Hamid's imagery at this web site to the images discussed in Chapter Five (butterflies and flowers versus AK47s and blood spilled in the desert). At his personal web site, the banner reads: "I am a Muslim by faith...Christian by the Spirit...a Jew by heart...and above all I am a human being."

In contrast to those *not* so moderate, Marines operate in a republic with civilian control of the armed forces. From time to time, the Marine Corps and other armed forces face the imposition of new policies that serve to disrupt the cultural status quo. The integration of minorities, particularly Blacks (or African-Americans), more than a generation ago was a challenge. Racial tensions were high in the United States broadly as well as in the Marine Corps specifically through the years of Vietnam and into the 1970s. I enlisted in 1973 and have seen the changes of 40 years. Mostly positive. It's not perfect but the Marine Corps of 2013 is much more an organization where everyone's blood runs green.

Opening previously all-male domains to women has led to a different range of challenges. Rape and sexual harassment, fraternization, and pregnant warriors have served as *distractions* from the missions of the armed forces. As women move into fighter jets, submarines, counter-intelligence, infantry and other previously all-male domains, the ground truth seems to be that when women prove themselves, like men have to prove themselves, they are accepted by the majority of their peers, generally speaking. My findings with today's 20-year veterans suggest that age and maturity play significant roles: senior enlisted Marines and majors and lieutenant colonels see their female counterparts doing their Marine Corps jobs, birthing babies and raising families, performing in professional military education programs, going in harm's way in Iraq and Afghanistan...and they get it: these women are Marines too. If anything, there are latent concerns about "girls coming home in body bags," something no parent ever wants to endure. And yet – women are blazing trails in combat zones where men have been culturally forbidden: interviewing women in Muslim countries.

The doors to the next two social experiments have just been opened: gays serving openly in the military and women in the infantry, and possibly special forces. Chaplains may now perform "civil unions." Select few hard-core homophobe "anti-fag" Marines and Soldiers will have a problem with this, particularly in the infantry. Battalions of lawyers will be working on the social experiments for a generation. Studies on women in direct combat are under-way. Results are due the Secretary of Defense in 2016. Proponents of a more inclusive Armed Forces declare that diversity will enrich the military services, or that opening the doors to gays serving openly, or women in ground combat, will be more fair to all citizens who want to serve. The other camp protests: gays in uniform and women in the infantry are distractions, and dilute the culture of the Army, Navy, Air Force and Marine Corps we once knew. The Epilogue wraps this up in the metaphysics of Quality.

Balance

The reader will discern an imbalance in the following discussion of "what is Marine Corps" and "what is radical Islam." This is an artifact of the genesis of this book. The first two chapters explain this in more detail, but the general idea is that the core of this text was my doctoral dissertation in 1990. I retired from the Marine Corps in 1995 and was recalled in 2005, in my military intelligence field. When I re-entered the "retired from the Marine Corps" world in 2008, I saw an opportunity to bring the ethnographic analysis of Marine Corps propaganda and cultural evolution current by 20 years – as well as compare these views with radical Islam. There is therefore more information about Marines and the Corps' culture in this book, but enough discussion of radical Islam to make the case for my conclusions. Portions of the book are technical, yet readable, in the sense of applying theories from social psychology to explain much of what we already discuss in conversational language.

What this book is not

This is not a history book, tho' cultural meta-narratives are certainly rooted in history. (And one must be realistic: the data I collected between 1983 and 1989 might now be considered historical in context.) While many academic disciplines overlap, we need enough historical reference to illustrate the source of the Shi'a–Sunni split: one explanation for the takfiri narrative; enough historical reference to guide discussion on the Marine's individual narrative that he is elite among the nation's armed forces. The original work does provide a historical snapshot of the enlisted Marine anthropology from the 1980s, but my work is focused on human motivation rather than historical analysis.

This is not a book about Islam. We have libraries full of both Western and mostly Arab Islamic scholars more authoritative than I. My goal has been to draw *from* a range of sources to arrive at mutually supporting explanations for why young men and a considerable number of young women are drawn to war. I will have provided references to religious scholars and historical sources.

This book does not contain classified information. Drawn to the field of military intelligence in 1985, initially as a Navy officer analyzing North Korean threats to the stability of Northeast Asia, my intersection with radical Islam evolved gradually, like many in the intelligence community. Read in that context, *The Looming Tower*,[vi] by Lawrence Wright, is a window to the broader intelligence-law enforcement community that needed to be kicked, hard, with the evidence that radical Salafist Islam was a threat.

While Sayyid Qutb was forming his opinions about America as well as the failings of modern Islamic states in 1948, American intelligence officers were focused on the dangers of Communism. When Osama bin Laden first entered Afghanistan, ostensibly to wage jihad against the Soviets in 1984, most Western intelligence analysts were still focused on the Cold War and the dangers of Communism. The ample supply of unclassified material related to radical Islam and conflict in the Middle East and Southwest Asia – I've studied since my first assignment in the Persian Gulf Theater in 1988-89, both in and out of my assignments as an intelligence officer. Even then, on the USS NIMITZ, our mission had everything to do with the security of American-flagged oil tankers transiting the Strait of Hormuz and comparatively little to do with Islamist radicals directly.

This is not a military order of battle analysis. The brass ring in the intelligence community is *predictability*. During World War II, intelligence analysts and operational planners gleaned as much as possible from the intelligence sources of the day in order to assess where Rommel might strike next in North Africa, for example. Those assessments were often drawn out on huge paper maps, with estimated numbers of tanks and troops, availability of fuel, ammunition, food and water, weather and terrain.

This War on Terror is a different kind of war, referred to variously as *irregular warfare*, *unconventional warfare*, or *counter-insurgency*. We do seek to predict where our adversaries will strike, where they will live and bank and build bombs; but ones and twos are more difficult in the extreme than armies and corps. Predictability in any of these is a chimera. The orders of battle today are lopsided, so our adversary – a stateless creature not feeling bound to the Geneva Conventions and laws of armed conflict, and without fleets of ships, aircraft, tanks or other "heavy weapons" – seeks unpredictability with unconventional weapons. My premise is: we are not fighting an army; **we are fighting an ideology**. It will take guns and bullets *and* an ideology to defeat an ideology. Bush, Rumsfeld and Cheney didn't get it and Obama and crew are even farther from the mark.

In Cold War terms, our "order of battle" analysis turns to defeating improvised explosive devices (IEDs), ideology, propaganda and counter-narratives. Inasmuch as unconventional war is a *population-centric* endeavor, "order of battle" might stretch to which Pashto tribe in a particular valley in Afghanistan has accepted American-led international assistance in learning to defend itself from the Taliban, and in concert – supports the elected government in Kabul. The current and coming generation of intelligence and operations professionals (the "G2 and G3") will need to understand human motivation – the human domain – through sociology, anthropology, ethnography and psychology on par with their knowledge of military aircraft, ships and submarines, tanks and artillery...and don't forget space and cyberspace.

Finally, this text offers far too little space to the contributions of women in uniform, to our sister services: the Army, Navy and Air Force, and to allied governments' military, law enforcement, academic and other <u>US</u> inter-agency government partners. I've not "corrected" all of the gender-specific pronouns left over from the

1990 text, and a few other elements of the text will read as politically incorrect. As I am not running for political office, that doesn't cause me sleepless nights.

In addition to not containing classified information or military orders of battle, this text does not represent the views or opinions of US Special Operations Command, the United States Marine Corps, or the US Department of Defense.

With regard to salty language: There are naughty words in this book. These are not words I use on a daily basis, and certainly not in my home, with three teenagers at home. The language is an accurate reflection of what I recorded of how Marines talk in their *native language*. Accordingly this is not a book I would buy for a 13-year-old girl, but at the same time I can be personally disgusted with 19-year old women Marines swearing "like sailors." (That's almost amusing in a book about Marines.) Today's reality is – the whole country is going through a rather uncivil phase, and that too is a reflection of the national cultural narrative that both divides the nation and serves to recruit young men and women for combat to defend the nation. More internal conflict.

*Perspective. This is IMPORTANT. This book is wrapped around a study begun in 1979 and completed in 1990. A portion of this book's purpose is to compare Marine Corps culture and folklore of today – 2013 – with the assessment of the Corps' culture in 1990. The reader is cautioned to make note of which decade a given paragraph is written in. Proclamations from 1989-'90 will seem outrageous today – but no more outrageous than the notion of married gay couples serving openly in the military and women in SEAL platoons, MARSOC or Ranger regiments would have seemed to the broader readership in the late 1980s. Readers of **all** persuasions seeking open-mindedness need to accept this. Headline in the Marine Corps Times: "UNISEX DRESS BLUES." (July 20, 2013)*

(Style note: Rather than a "glossary" to explain the differences between Osama bin Laden and Usama bin Laden, or al Qaida and al-Qaeda, and other such aberrations dealing **primarily** with Arabic language translations – I've left the original language intact in each quotation. Some other terms are in quotations; others in **bold**. The reader is left to fend for oneself.)

Chapter One

<u>Genesis</u>

How does one define a terrorist? A jihadist? To define is to limit.
Everything that is – is. Everything that isn't – isn't. Too absolute for
defining terrorists. Trying to define "radical" or "fundamentalist" or
"terrorist" will increasingly yield a definition, and to define is to limit.

For all its flaws, the 9/11 Commission report delivered one observation that continues to echo: America's failure to *read the tea leaves, connect the dots* or act on what we did know, before the September 2001 attacks, amounted to "a failure of imagination." Getting stuck in single-discipline definitions limits the imagination. Before a "first chapter," I offer this introduction much more to put this book into perspective than to tell my story, but as my story has been on a collision course with jihad for 30 years, that story explains the roots of this book.

Those roots begin in 1979 with the start of my master's degree and a thesis titled *Propaganda Cycles in the United States Marine Corps* (USC, 1982), followed by doctoral research in the same question, and a dissertation titled *The Edifice Complex: a Study of the causes and effects of conflict between generations of Marines and cultural changes in the United States Marine Corps* (Ball State University, 1990). That was 23 years ago and literally on the eve of Desert Storm – Saddam Hussein's bid to annex Kuwait. Saddam Hussein was a Sunni Muslim; does that make him a *jihadist?* History rather clearly shows his aims were political and economic, not "holy war." Saddam Hussein had too much of an ego to be on a real jihad, greater or lesser.

So that this concept of "jihadist" is *not* buried in a footnote: American and coalition partner nation's armed forces are fighting multiple wars on countless fronts. Not "Iraq" and "Afghanistan," but a global war against terrorists and terrorism in all their forms, and incidental wars against true mujahidin – more or less legitimate jihadis who are pissed off because we invaded their countries correctly or incorrectly on the hunt for terrorists (*irhabists*) and they want us out.

Among the most respected voices in this domain are Marine General James Mattis (recently retired Commander of US Central Command), Jim Guirard (truespeak.org) and Dr. David Kilcullen (Royal Australian infantry reserve lieutenant colonel). We will address this concept in a bit more detail in the coming chapters, but what Kilcullen, Guirard and Mattis have expressed is the need to *not* provide the criminals, thieves and murders the legitimacy they crave by referring to their war as a jihad. They are not *jihadis* but irhabists. Terrorists. Criminals. If the majority in the US intelligence community (the IC) are still using "jihadi," and we need to wean them – I'm game. That's not the mission of this book, but we can communicate to all, broadly, with "jihadi" and slip "irhabi" and "takfiri" into the dialogue. Kilcullen's book *The Accidental Guerilla* addresses this topic superbly.

US Marines like to operate with a mission – a *why are we here?* Broadly, that may be to *support and defend the Constitution of the United States against all enemies – foreign and domestic.* We typically start from a "commander's intent." In Iraq and Afghanistan, it may be viewed as *Clear, Hold, Build* or *Village Stability Operations* or *Foreign Internal Defense.* At least for a time it was. The former mission, "support the Constitution," is enduring; the latter are temporal. My goal is to bring that <u>cultural</u> understanding of Marine missions current, refresh our understanding of the process of recruiting in the Marine Corps, and compare and contrast. Those comparisons include conflict within

Islam, conflict between generations of Marines, and on both sides –
the resulting political, social, economic and especially cultural
foundations that provide content to recruitment propaganda.

January 2007:
Forward Operating Base (FOB), Fallujah
- and a week in Dubai

As a retired intelligence officer, a 50-year-old Captain of
Marines recalled to active duty in 2005 and now in Iraq, and
erstwhile adjunct professor for a dozen universities over 30 years, past
industrial training manager at General Motors, NASA and Enron,
independent consultant in leadership and organizational psychology,
veteran social psychologist and ethnographer, I am by default an
inveterate people watcher. I'm all about locations, people,
motivations and *meanings*. The menageries of personalities in
subways and shopping malls are particularly interesting, for example.
In the confined spaces of subway cars, with little mobility, less dialog,
and usually no social connection between people – individual attire,
mannerisms and facial expressions are the primary means of
communication. I read them. The Metro back in the international
city of Washington DC, as a case in point, communicates with the
silent cacophony of an international library. Everyone is screaming
intellectually or visually. What we have in common: we're all going
somewhere. They're reading newspapers and text messages and I'm
reading their faces and body language.

Shopping malls are another matter. We've all already arrived;
there is endless mobility in a mall compared to a subway car; and the
vast array of shops and stores discriminates one set of purposes from
another. Walking through Dubai's Mall of the Emirates this January
2007, in search of souvenirs for my family back in the US, I pass a
shop one wouldn't find in most malls in the States – from the looks of
it, a high-end "Rodeo Drive quality" shop (this is, after all, Dubai's
Mall of the Emirates) – specializing in hijabs and burqas, chadors and

niqabs. As two apparently Arab women in tight denim jeans and high heels, but no head scarves, cruise past the entrance of this shop, one pushing an infant in an expensive stroller, two other women, dressed in black burqas (only their eyes are visible), are window-shopping. They cast disapproving glances toward the women in Western dress...and continue chatting. I'm off to the side, observing. The two with the stroller may be Arab Christians, or *not* Arab, but there is no way to know. They may have been from London, Lebanon or Cleveland...or Riyadh. One shows off a midriff with a "belly-button" piercing.

It struck me then and I shared it when I returned to my battalion at Camp Fallujah in Iraq at the end of the week – one of the women at that "Rodeo Drive" burqa shop would likely ask her husband later the same day, "Does this burqa make me look fat?"

I lived that husband's dilemma (...a long time ago), but it wasn't in reference to a burqa (it was blue jeans). What if her husband replied, "It's not the burqa that makes you look fat, it's the *fat* that makes you look fat." He'd probably get the same treatment I got. What if that woman's husband and I have at least that experience – the broader experience not limited by the blue jeans or the burqa – *and* something else in common? What if he's a jihadi...on a week's respite from the war, like I was? Doesn't matter where we live, what our cultures are... we go through common experiences.

Dubai, one of the seven United Arab Emirates, is emblematic of the world at war with itself. Contrasts and conflicts are ubiquitous. The Mall of the Emirates has an indoor snow skiing park; outside it's 86 in January. Summer temperatures will surpass 120°F on the Arabian Peninsula. Islam's shariah law guides marriages, divorces, child custody and other litigations in a principality where a traveling Western businesswoman or businessman can find a shot of tequila, an ice-cold Corona beer and a cigar at the bar in a hotel run by Australians and Pakistanis and owned by Arab Muslims who supposedly don't drink or smoke. Emiratis drive Jaguars, Porsches, Mercedes and Bentleys; migrant workers from South Asia (Pakistan, Bangladesh, the Philippines), laboring on the construction of billion-dollar office towers and real estate complexes live in poverty, in slums, out of sight of the commercial public. And women wear burqas...or blue jeans...or bikinis at the beach.

What we all have in common in this world at war with itself is that we're all going somewhere. We just have different views of how to get there. My business in Dubai complete, I too need to go somewhere...back to the occasional incoming rockets and mortars at FOB Fallujah, Anbar Province; back to the Intelligence Fusion Cell...back to the sand, palm trees and Marines.

Summer 2010:
Tampa, FL

In *War, Memes and Memeplexes*[vii], Christopher Coker's essay summons another writer to ponder the affinity of young men for war:

The Darwinian still wants to know why young men are so susceptible to what the writer Luis Borges called 'the moral and ascetic charms of war,' and therefore open to exploitation by priests and politicians who still send them off to war.[viii]

Well now, *that's* poetic. I take Darwin as an anachronistic curiosity, and take metaphors from Darwinian concepts, as do those who write in the field that grabs Coker's interest. But – I take Coker's words also as the prose that starts this conversation.

Coker's hook, the notion that "those rare individuals who invite [death] do so because they believe they owe their life a good death, and that a good death makes life meaningful..." is explicable in part through the science of *memetics*. The concept is that war is a *meme*, a cultural imperative spread like a virus, from culture to culture over eons, as a *gene* is passed from generation to generation.[ix]

The challenge with war, as a meme, is that the newly digital generation has allowed cultural imperatives to spread at the speed of light, globally, through web sites, Google, Facebook, Twitter, YouTube, e-mail and text messages....The fall of Hosni Mubarak and the role of Egyptian activist (and Google employee) Wael Ghonim, is the living example of a cultural imperative, freedom as a meme, gone viral.[x] More on memes, memetics and the viral spread of al-Qaida's brand: the meme of jihad...war...in following chapters. Coker writes in 2008, but I'm interested in his question, why young men are susceptible, now.

Backspace 27 years to 1981 and I was a staff sergeant in the United States Marine Corps serving as Community Relations Chief for the Marine Corps Recruit Depot public affairs office at Parris Island, South Carolina. Half of the men and all of the women who enlist in the Marine Corps each year go through basic Marine Corps training here. Around duties as a journalist and base newspaper editor during that three-year assignment, I spent a month as military advisor to a film crew from the National Film Board of Canada (NFB). Their mission was to shoot enough footage on recruit training at Parris Island to be edited into a one-hour film as part of a six-hour documentary in the Public Broadcasting Service (PBS) television series: *WAR*.[xi]

The title of the one-hour film depicting US Marine Corps recruit training, *Anybody's Son Will Do*,[xii] introduces script author Gwynne Dyer's premise that training young men for war is a universal constant. The broad cultural themes, the psychology, the mechanics and themes of indoctrination, and the subjects (martial discipline, physical fitness, first aid, instruction in weapons and tactics, uniforms and rank insignia, military history and culture) are common to any culture. Dyer emphasizes his premise in the film's opening sequence, filmed in Moscow's Red Square in 1981 with soldiers of the Soviet Army marching in the background: *ANYbody's*

Son Will Do. A parallel to memetics, which had its first modest appearance in 1976,[xiii] via Richard Dawkins' *The Selfish Gene*.

Rewind to June 1979, two years before I met Dyer and the NFB film crew. I had started that 10-year journey through my master's and doctoral studies in Marine Corps social psychology, organizational culture and recruitment advertising two years earlier, understood through the principles of *propaganda*. I majored in Adult Education, but wrote both my master's thesis and doctoral dissertation in "educational psychology," meaning – propaganda. As of June 1979, I had been a Marine for six years. Although classified these days as a Vietnam *Era* veteran, I did not serve "in country" in Vietnam.

And finally, backspace a few more years and I had early on served in the 3rd Marine Division headquarters on the island of Okinawa from December 1974 through January 1976. When Saigon fell on April 30, 1975, absolutely and totally finishing American military presence in Vietnam, I was on guard duty at the 3rd Marine Division headquarters, at Camp Courtney, Okinawa, about 1700 miles from Vietnam. I was then a corporal. I was 20. I was a pup.

After Vietnam, other than comparatively smaller engagements in Haiti, Beirut and Somalia – police actions and peace-keeping operations by comparison – there was no overt evidence we would be involved in war as Marines know wars on the scale of WWI, WWII and Korea, between 1975 and 1990.

As it turned out, I returned to Okinawa in 1979, four years after Saigon fell, as a staff sergeant with an avocational interest in folklore and social psychology. Days – I worked in the Camp Butler Base Education Office. Evenings – I worked on my master's degree, and returned to the US in the summer of 1980, spending the following two years putting the finishing touches on my master's thesis[xiv] as I moved into the field of Marine Corps Public Affairs.

During my first assignment as a print journalist, I found an intersection with my original thesis – that *the social psychology of recruiting and indoctrinating for war is a universal construct*. That master's thesis investigated the concept of Marine Corps culture as a behavior-shaping tool, folklore as propaganda. The intersection: Gwynne Dyer's script, director Paul Cowan's film – *Anybody's Son Will Do* – two years later. Three months after contributing my small part to NFB Director Paul Cowan and crew's success in 1982, I graduated from the University of Southern California (meaning – I finally got my completed thesis approved).

My trek to understand "why young men are so susceptible to...'the moral and ascetic charms of war,'" had started in 1979.

What few of us could have seen in 1979 was a world without the Soviet Union or a world at war against Islamic extremists. Walking back through the decades, numerous other catalytic events predicted the world of 2010: the US CIA's role, with the British SIS, in the overthrow of Iran's prime minister Mossadegh in favor of British Petroleum (BP) in 1953; the division, sub-division and re-division of Middle East lands by fading colonial powers "Great" Britain, the Soviet "Union," France, and Germany during the first half of the 20th century; the fall of the Ottoman empire in 1924; and the British Government's imputed policy on Israel stated through the Balfour Declaration of 1917 and eventual Israeli declaration of Independence from the British Palestine Mandate and marginalization of the Palestinians in 1948. There are others, but 1979 stands as a landmark year. In 1979, most of these are isolated, apparently unrelated events:

January, 1979: Shah Mohammad Reza Pahlavi departs Iran for exile, in the US, then Panama, and ultimately Egypt. In a diplomatic coup, one-term Democratic President Jimmy Carter pisses off anti-Shah Iranians with a New Year's Day toast to the ailing Shah.

February: The Ayatollah Khomeini leaves Paris for Iran, now a revolutionary state. A national referendum at the end of March redefines the country as an Islamic Republic with a theocratic constitution.

March: US-backed peace accord between Egypt and Israel is signed in Washington, DC. (Ultra-conservative takfiris will soon see Egypt as an apostate government.)

July: Saddam Hussein consolidates power in Iraq. Saddam will invade Iran in September 1980, miscalculating Iran's turmoil and resolve. The US will support Iraq against Iran in this eight-year conflict.

4 November: Iranian revolutionaries seize the US Embassy in Iran; 53 Americans will be held captive 444 days.

20 November: Islamic apocalypticists take over the Grand Mosque in Mecca, Saudi Arabia - the holiest city in Islam.[xv]

25 November: Ayatollah Khomeini accuses the US and Israel of complicity in the Grand Mosque seizure, further inflaming the Islamic "community" – the ummah.

27 December 1979: The Soviet Army begins the invasion and nine-year occupation of Afghanistan. Osama Bin Laden and fellow anti-Soviet Afghan mujahidin fighting the Soviets in Afghanistan will eventually receive American and Saudi funding through both Carter and Republican President Ronald Reagan administrations; although bin Laden's *real* contribution to pushing out the Soviets is miniscule.[xvi]

Ten years later – 1989 – and the Berlin Wall was coming down. The Soviet Union was dismantling. The US-backed mujahidin, *freedom fighters*, in Afghanistan are emboldened by the collapse of the godless communists and their withdrawal from

Afghanistan, certain of their role in the fall of the other super power. And by the dawn of the 1990s...they were *unemployed* mujahidin. Were there any other infidels around they could go to work on? How about corrupt apostate dictators in historically Muslim countries? The jihadis – mujahidin – take meaning from the fall of the Soviets in Afghanistan. They are emboldened. Osama bin Laden ponders this question from Sudan, while the Saudis revoke his passport and bin Laden is disowned by the Saudi dictators and members of his own family.

Saddam Hussein invades Kuwait and threatens Saudi Arabia in 1990; Osama bin Laden offers the mujahidin to repel the attack. The Kingdom of Saudi Arabia and the Kuwaiti Emir, Al-Sabah, instead accept American forces – based in and launching from Saudi Arabia, the land of the two mosques (Mecca and Medina). Osama is incensed, pissed off at the infidel Americans for basing on holy lands, pissed off at the house of al-Saud for allowing it. Writing on al-Qaida's racist views on African Muslims and those African jihadi groups that seek to buy into the Al-Qaida franchise, French professor Jean-Pierre Filiu observes:

"A homogenous nucleus of Arab jihadis secretly founded al-Qaida in Pakistan in August 1988. At first the group took little notice of Africa, focusing [instead] on Afghanistan and the Arabian Peninsula. Osama bin Laden, the groups' founder, grew incensed in August 1990 when the Saudis requested a massive U.S. military deployment to deter the Iraqi threat to Kuwait. He was even angrier when American troops stayed in his country after Kuwait was liberated."[xvii]

From 1982 through 1989, I worked on the footnote to my master's thesis, a doctoral dissertation more fully exploring the processes of proselytizing the Marine Corps message and converting slovenly civilians to the ways of US Marine Corps culture.[xviii] (I had been commissioned as a Navy Intelligence Officer in 1985; I was awarded my doctorate in May 1990. I had completed my written exams in the bowels of the aircraft carrier USS NIMITZ in 1989 while on station at the Strait of Hormuz near the end of the Iran-Iraq War.) Working as a Navy Intelligence officer at the advent of Operation Desert Shield/Desert Storm later in 1990-'91, teaching electronic warfare at "the intel school" in Virginia Beach, I felt irrelevant (in Coker's terms) and in November 1990 requested an inter-service transfer back to the Marine Corps. My focus on Islam – radical Islam – as a Marine journalist or intelligence officer, had been on the fractures in Lebanese politics in 1983-'84 and on the Persians and Arabs fighting the Iran-Iraq War in 1988-'89. With 18 years in uniform, I was accepted back in the Corps in April 1991…but by the time the paperwork found its way through "the system," the short-lived war was over. I spent four more years in the Corps and retired in November 1995 with 22 years, 3 months in uniform.

The year *after* I retired: it didn't exactly command banner headlines in major US newspapers, but Osama bin Laden declared war on the United States in 1996. His rationale, al-Qaida's rationale, was based on the religiously unacceptable American/infidel presence in the land of the two holy cities, Mecca and Medina, which amounted to foreign military, or *Crusader*, domination of Islamic people – which facilitated American exploitation of Saudi oil wealth. These and other bin Laden complaints continue to fuel jihadi propaganda, radicalization and recruitment today.[xix]

By 1996: instead of in desert camouflage, the opportunity to apply my doctoral major, adult education, and minors in curriculum and educational psychology (social psychology and organizational propaganda) played itself out in khaki trousers and steel-toed shoes or in coat and tie through the coming seven years. By way of Hughes Aircraft, General Motors' culture was interesting. Raytheon bought huge chunks of Hughes, and with Raytheon I transferred from Detroit to Houston in 1997, immersed in developing, selling and managing elements of astronaut training; NASA's culture was fascinating. I left Raytheon and Houston's Johnson Space Center in August 2000 for Enron. From a social psychologist's retrospect, Enron's culture was a bacterial laboratory.

Although this essay is not about Enron, or Raytheon's business unit at NASA's Johnson Space Center, or General Motors, each organization has failed, in quiet or spectacular ways; those corporate failures inform this study, in part, and confirm a range of principles or theories about organizational psychology, recruiting, indoctrination and institutional propaganda. My personal goal is that violent Islamic extremism fails in *both* quiet and spectacular ways. With additional lessons from that earlier career in the Marine Corps, lessons from corporate America contributed to my teaching points in a range of college courses with more than five thousand students over more than 30 years (years before and years after Enron), from abnormal psychology to strategic management, to the most recent courses in organizational dynamics and consulting skills with George Washington University from 2006 to 2008.

Yes – I am painfully aware of the danger of applying a newfound principle to explain everything. This is the picture of the little boy who finds a hammer...and everything becomes a nail. But while there are indeed exact parallels from, say, Iraq or Afghanistan to the US at the *Maslow's Hierarchy* level (*all* people have physiological needs, security, friendship and self-esteem needs); there are also stark differences. If you ask an Iraqi if the light stays on when you close the refrigerator door, he may respond, "inshallah." If God wills it. And so, organizational or social psychology is one methodology, one hammer, with which to decipher the recruiting, indoctrination and radicalization of fundamentalist Islamists, but there are other methods.

Apocalyptically (apoplectically?), Enron's dynamic money engine ground to a halt in December 2001, some 90 days after 9/11. If investigating al-Qaida through the lens of contemporary business or organizational psychology models, why not explore "why businesses fail" – as in "why did Enron fail?" in business terms for example, through the lesson of brand corruption and dilution, loss of faith in what AQ has to sell, leadership failures and similar models. And why not evaluate radicalization and indoctrination to jihad in terms of adult education? And what about that *memetics* thing and the impact of the Internet on the spread of jihadist propaganda? And when we get to individual motivations, for either US Marines and Soldiers *or* Insanely Radical Islamist Fundamentalist Terrorists, what about chemistry or neuropharmacology...Do thrill-seekers – drawn to combat – have a different endorphin package?

There are many ways to understand the draw to the hell of war. My executive analysis is that despite all of our efforts to understand *the enemy*, we still end up with narrow analyses. Reports are out there... and the reality looks like a Rubik's Cube of Rubik's Cubes, but the policy makers are not prone to accepting details. (How many congressmen or senators are former intelligence officers? Anthropologists? Ethnographers? Sociologists? Psychologists? Most of them are attorneys.) Most of them are intelligent – but are they "people-smart?"

Some of these solutions and analyses are metaphors; some must be viewed as solutions. Solvents.

While anticipating an inevitable recall to active duty, I wrote on Enron's collapse,[xx] and pulled in many of these principles. I worked toward building a business as an independent consultant from 2002 through 2004 and into 2005, and lived as close to an ascetic lifestyle as I can ever remember for more than three years. Unemployment and under-employment were a different kind of combat. Shortly after 9/11, the US invaded Afghanistan in 2001, then Iraq in 2003, and by the Summer of 2005, ten years after "retirement," I accepted a recall to active duty in the Marine Corps.

Those three years back in uniform, from 2005 through 2008, offered ample opportunity to compare notes from 1990 to the recent present. That wasn't my mission, of course – recording changes in the culture – (I am that inveterate people watcher), tho' one can't help but notice, for example, 20 women Marines in an infantry headquarters intelligence battalion in Iraq. In flak jackets and Kevlar helmets and teeny-tiny combat boots, and a Mary Kay Cosmetics shrine in the Tactical Intelligence Fusion Center.[xi] Or (male)(that's *straight* male) majors and lieutenant colonels commenting on some inane higher headquarters requirement – "wear reflective belts while running" – with comments like: "That's too gay." Those women would not have been there in 1979; even *use* of the word "gay" among Marines in the 1990s and before was culturally off the table. "Gay" is "icky." Let's just focus on war, 4X4 pickup trucks, gun collections, beer brands, NFL football and the right way to grill ribs or steaks.

The chapters that follow offer multiple views to the eschatology of that earlier question: "why young men are so susceptible to…the moral and ascetic charms of war," or the questions imbedded in the notion that "those rare individuals who invite [death] do so because they believe they owe their life a good death, and that a good death makes life meaningful…." For ultimately, there is an element of the "Я" word (in *radical* or *religion*), as the foot soldiers on both sides fight their individual Armageddons and the battlefields of Iraq and Afghanistan offer very personal experiences in death, judgment, heaven and hell.

The Book

Ultimately this kind of book must have some kind of *aboutness*. That 30-year parallax of my academic and military careers with jihad focuses on:

- The social psychology of attraction to and indoctrination in a cause, through Conformity and Justification theories;

- The actors – principally real and wannabe American GI's and mujahidin. Jihadis. And the false jihadis – the terrorists;

- The environment in which this takes place – the external cultural, religious, social and inevitably political dynamics, and the internal individual and group psychology of recruits for any army or organization. Included are observations of women in previously all-male domains; the penchant for a liberal US President and Senate to engage the armed forces in social experiments; the increasing professionalization and higher educational standards of career enlisted Marines; and the impact of technology – broadly;

- The chaos of war and *Strange Attractors*: The Internet and the increasing reach of satellite communications, for example. One could blame *CNN* (as much as Qatar-based *al-Jazeera*) and the New York Times and Washington Post for fanning the flames of al-Qaida's propaganda, and (with tongue in cheek?) blame Al Gore for the hundreds of jihadist web sites on the Internet.

My primary goal is to inform; secondarily to influence. The sum of this text will generally follow the artificial format of my original study: An Introduction, Review of Related Literature, Research Methods, Findings, Conclusions and Recommendations. The first view of the text is the original study, rooted in an ethnographic analysis of the Marine Corps, with data collected, written and polished from 1979 through 1989. My goal will be to leave the original text intact as much as possible, abbreviated where I can omit lists or taxonomies of data collected in fieldwork, and with **Perspectives** added to clarify a 20-year-old point of view or acknowledge significant events or recent changes to clarify the older text. (There are many *Perspectives*, generally separated or identified by offset italics.)

Changes in Marine culture since 1990 that I can document

based on personal observation from 2005 through 2013, without too much editorializing, are the second view. Current interviews (in 2010 through 2013) with active duty Marines and updated market demographics from JWT (previously J. Walter Thompson, the Marine Corps' recruitment advertising agency) will add to the validity and reliability of this portion. Additional content in this area derives from printed literature and the range of television, Internet and other media devoted to Marine Corps and other military topics. My working hypothesis was, in 1990, and in 2013 remains:

> Organizational culture, expressed in folklore's *symbols, rituals and myths*, serves as a behavior-shaping tool. Internal folklore is the foundation of an organization's propaganda.

Since the unHoly War began in 2001 (or with bin Laden's illegitimate fatwa in 1996, or realistically with the overthrow of the Shah in Iran in 1979), the question on many researchers' minds seems to be "What factors and processes radicalize and recruit Muslim youth?" What causes someone to become a "terrorist?" The same kind of question, a generation ago, focused on those "nice," blond-haired, blue-eyed farm boys in Germany who bought in to Hitler's propaganda. How *could* they??!!! Or…the thousands of kamikaze pilots of the Japanese Imperial naval air forces. Thus the birth and evolution of military social psychology as a discipline over the past 70 years.

And my reply, based on 30 years of observation, is that the same kinds of factors and processes that radicalize and recruit Muslim youth also "radicalize" and recruit US Marines. Not the same factors… the same kinds of factors.

So, the third view – in comparison and contrast – are parallels from the jihadi perspective, but the reader must accept that:

- We are at war, and that

- □ Some of the warriors on the other side of the conflict are soldiers (fighters, combatants) who believe *they* are at war;

- □ But some are illegal combatants who rob their religion for legitimizing names – like mujahidin or jihadi – and wage war on innocents, including Muslim women and children.

This third view derives from the existing and growing body of unclassified research on the roots of radicalization. Some of this unclassified material includes documents captured in Iraq and other locations, translated, declassified, and made available for scholars, offering a unique insight into what the radicals are thinking. This view will be introduced in the following chapter and amplified in the remaining chapters. In line with the review of related literature in the original *EDIFICE COMPLEX* second chapter, I will provide ample unclassified references to who's doing what in the domain of jihadi and *irhabist* (terrorist) propaganda, recruiting and radicalization research. The first decade of the millennium has spawned hundreds, if not thousands, of individual and corporate books and papers on terrorism and radicalization; entire organizations devoted to counter-terrorism have sprouted like academic mushroom clouds.

Changes: The 1990 *EDIFICE COMPLEX*, an ethnography, portrays the Marine Corps as an *ethnic group* and for a variety of reasons focused mainly on the majority ethnic group of enlisted, male Marines – avoiding lengthy discussion of women Marines, officers, other services (Army, Navy, Air Force) or formerly subterranean issues like gays in the military. Confident in the generalizability of my findings from 1990 to other military services, this updated text will occasionally refer to "Marines and Soldiers," or "servicemen and women." Women have been integrated into virtually all occupations in the armed forces, save direct infantry roles.

As of 24 February 2010 the Navy started the process of eliminating its prohibition of women on submarines. Later in 2010, the Marine Corps started admitting women to the formerly restricted counter-intelligence/human intelligence (CI/HUMINT) career field. In contrast to 1990, we have female fighter pilots – even as air forces move to an unmanned vehicle, joystick generation.

And, as of January 2013, out-going Secretary of Defense Leon Panetta announced plans to scrap the 1994 law that keeps women out of direct combat roles. The services had until May 2013 to write plans to integrate women into 180,000 combat arms positions currently closed to them, and until 2016 to implement those plans. Deadlines have since been extended. The services will have an opportunity to justify continued exclusions. Debates continue, but one side of the argument is that combat arms positions typically produce the majority of senior leadership positions – leading to general officer promotions, and women have been excluded from promotions because most senior billets go to officers in combat arms.

The close proximity of officers and enlisted Marines in combat suggests a discussion on officers; and the question of gays in the military is topical in 2010 through 2013.

Interestingly, and sadly, the godfathers of military sociology, Charles Moskos and Morris Janowitz, writing in *Armed Forces & Society*, had foreseen the coming of a generation in which there are no front lines, a generation in which the threats of nuclear war and terrorism threaten everyone, everybody's back yard. Leaders in the Inter-University Seminar on Armed Forces and Society for decades, Janowitz died in 1988; Moskos died in 2008.

According to the web site of the Inter-University Seminar on Armed Forces and Society, during the Clinton administration, Moskos had:

[...] coined the term, "Don't Ask, Don't Tell," as a name for the policy he proposed, the policy eventually adopted, that steered between punishing members of the military because they were gay and allowing gays

to serve openly. It was a compromise criticized by those on both sides. Charlie believed that was a sign of success and liked to call it "the policy everyone hates."[xxii]

As *Indiana Jones* famously said, *"Archaeology is the search for fact...not truth. If it's truth you're looking for, Dr. Tyree's philosophy class is right down the hall."* As an intelligence officer, an ethnographer, a businessman, a teacher and an anthropologist/archeologist, my quest is facts, empirical evidence, and objectivity. In this quest, however, I don't have a problem with inserting editorial comments, for I am also a story-teller, and I already earned an "A" on my report card 23 years ago for the dissertation upon which this is based. The stringent academic requirements for pure objectivity are passed, and I cannot make recommendations for strategic change without offering opinion. I promise the reader to do my best to signal fact from opinion. This manuscript will have opinions as well as science.

But before we launch this assessment – let's all be realistic. Nations and empires have been defeating nations and empires for thousands of years.[xxiii] Four hundred and some years ago, Western European (white) "settlers" had yet made almost no impact on what we today call "the Americas." According to varying sources, 400 to 700 indigenous tribes or nations once inhabited the Americas. Most are dead; their languages are gone; some of their descendants now run gambling casinos. Those who remain struggle to retain their languages and cultures. The Black Africans who became slaves in America were sold to European and American slave traders by Black Africans who were slave traders. That's objectively where we are.

Looking *way* back...Egypt's pharaohs are gone; the Mongol horde was assimilated, absorbed; Attila and the Huns left their name on Hungary. The greater ancient Rome is now Italy – a smaller state in a larger (bankrupt) European Union with a value-added tax and fungible carbon dioxide credits – and the Mayans, Incas and Aztec succumbed to their own internal wars and European diseases. Few

Mayans exist who know their own legacy. The Hebrew / Jewish caste who call Israel home have a documented, checkered history of wins and losses.

Some of the most pressing problems the world will face in the coming century date to the most powerful colonizing nations of the 17th through the 20th Centuries: Great Britain, France, Italy, Portugal, Germany, Spain and the Dutch. Each of these erased tribal boundaries and redrew the maps of South America, Africa and South Asia with excellent views of commerce and little regard for populations, cultures, local laws and traditions. Elements of those colonial maps remain today, as do *also* the tribal boundaries – many of them nomadic – (which existed for centuries before colonization), and they don't line up. Consider the Tuareg of North Africa, or the Kurds of Southwest Asia. There are many more.

The people who built China, Korea and Japan over millennia spent millennia waging war on each other. Japan's modern Showa Emperor – Hirohito – and Germany's Hitler spent their imperialistic sperm in the blood of tens of millions in the middle of the 20th century, their empires stillborn; and the rising tide of Communist-Socialist ideology found its footing in the fall of the Russian Czar in 1917 only to decline late in the 20th century and reinvent itself in Washington through the Obama administration beginning in January 2009. Ideologies have battled ideologies for thousands of years. That Islam lost its caliphate in 1924 is a blip on the historical radar. No one worth a damn gives a damn. And the United States is as susceptible to falling as any other empire. If it falls, and if humankind survives…in the year 2929, the "united states of america" will be a couple of ones and zeroes in some kid's "textbook."

Chapter Two: Context

Mujahidin "я" Us

All snakes are creepy. Not all snakes are poisonous.

September 1983: In Billings, Montana, 'Jason' is born into the family of Hank Jr. and Carrie. Their home is Park City, 25 miles west of Billings. Hank Jr. once worked the mines in Montana and now works snow removal in the winter, heavy equipment in the summer, when he can find work. They're near the bottom end of middle class in America; more like working poor. Jason is the third son; he will have a younger sister in three years. Jason's mom grew up in Park City and was baptized and confirmed at St. Paul's Lutheran Church in Park City. She never left the small town. Hank Jr. knew the Baptist church where he came from, used to go...doesn't go much anymore. When the family goes to church, Carrie takes them to St. Paul's in a ten-year-old Chevy station wagon. Hank Jr. goes to church with the family on Christmas Eve and Easter, when Carrie insists. "Church" is generally reserved for Sundays.

Carrie was working at the Park City Café alongside Interstate 90 West (still works there) when Hank Jr. came into town in 1973. By the time the draft ended in 1973, he had just barely skirted the war in Vietnam. Traveling west in Montana, Hank Jr. was looking for a job in the mines; he was looking for "silver and gold." He found both in Carrie. She was 18; he was 22. The animated *Rudolph the Red-Nose Reindeer* was a favorite from both of their childhood memories; *Yukon Cornelius* is forever seeking "gold and silver, silver and gold." Hank Jr. and Carrie were in love.

When the United States invades Iraq in 1991, Jason has recently turned 7. Operation Desert Storm doesn't register on his

Richter Scale, tho' mom and dad watch Bernard Shaw, John Holliman and Peter Arnett reporting live from Baghdad on CNN's satellite-fed, 24-hour news cycle explosion into world consciousness. Jason plays "army" with his two older brothers, two cousins on his mother's side, and their friends, in the hills well east of the Rocky Mountains. The boys have .22 rifles and BB guns. Jason has a GI Joe. His oldest brother harasses Jason and calls the GI Joe "a doll." Jason's dad can't remember an ancestor in a military uniform…maybe a great uncle in World War I.

Combat for Jason is fighting for relevance in a family dominated by alpha males – his two older brothers and his borderline alcoholic father, who more than often dines on Budweiser after work. His dad drives a Ford F-150. He voted for George H.W. Bush and before that, Ronald Reagan. Jason's oldest brother, 16, who plays football in high school, and next older brother, 14, who plays football in junior high, both give Jason a healthy ration of shit when their mom drives him to soccer practice. Soccer is new to Montana. Sissies play soccer; real men play football. Ask Jason about his affiliations and he will give you, in order, his family name, the local school – Park City Panthers – and tell you he is an American from Montana. If you ask the right question, he'll add that he's Lutheran. He probably won't say he's a Christian; but if he's Lutheran – he is.

August 1983. 'Salim' is born to Ahmed al-Assad albu-Nimr al-Dulaimi in Fallujah, Anbar Province, Iraq. Ahmed was 26; his wife, Nada was 17. Their marriage was more or less arranged. Nada's midwife delivers Salim's twin brother, 'Salam,' twelve minutes later. As Salim is the first child and oldest son, and will be pushed toward an eventual engineering degree at the University of Baghdad, he is favored by his father. There will be another brother and a sister in the coming years. The family's heritage is Sunni Islam, but Iraq – particularly Anbar Province – is largely secular in 1983 under Saddam Hussein, and Salim's father, a civil engineer working on the expansion of the University of Baghdad, visits the European-style saloons in Ramadi, west of Fallujah, for a couple of shots of Johnny Walker whiskey and a few Marlboro cigarettes before his trek back to Fallujah in his Toyota Hilux pickup truck.

Salim's father, Ahmed, is a minor sheikh in the albu-Nimr clan of the Dulaimi tribe, the largest tribe in Iraq, which numbers in the millions. Ahmed has the option to take more wives, but his finances are cut short by the war and he's not able to maintain another wife, an apartment in Baghdad, and more mouths to feed. Salim's allegiance is first to his family, then to the albu-Nimr clan, then to the Dulaim tribe. *Dulaim*, the historic name for the modern al-Anbar Province, translates to "granary" or warehouse in Arabic. Anbar's expansive desert lands were once used as a storehouse for the ancient Persian and Arab traders and smugglers who used the wasteland to hide the booty from their camel caravan raids on the Silk Road to China, long before Islam. T.E. Lawrence would find friends here in a later generation. *After* the family, clan and Dulaimi tribe, Salim thinks of himself as Sunni Muslim, but doesn't give it much thought. Islam dominates how he eats, how he goes through the motions of praying (but not necessarily five times a day), what he eats and how he cleans himself when he goes to the toilet. Islam is always there, but not. It's just a way of life. It's a given. *After* family, clan, tribe, Islam, Salim is Iraqi. His lineage has been degreed engineers for three generations, builders and architects before that.

When the United States invades Iraq in 1991, Salim has recently turned 7. He is immune to the war, at first. He plays soccer in his village near Fallujah. When the war starts, his father continues his daytime job, when he can drive into Baghdad. When Ahmed can't negotiate the American roadblocks on the highway into Baghdad, and returns home in the afternoon, he dons the *dishdasha* – the ankle-length *thawb* common to Arab men – as he heads to the teahouse near the souk, to smoke the *shisha* with his fellow tribesmen and curse the occupation forces of the United States. Ahmed will dole out favors and work to the rest of the clan. Some of Ahmed's cousins are still smugglers, now moving oil illegally to Syria. The money for jobs and favors comes from the coffers of Saddam Hussein, who has favored the Sunni tribes. The war is over quickly, and the disruption begins to impact Salim's life. The United Nations (read: U.S.)-imposed oil-for-food program provides milk, food, medicine and basic necessities for Salim and his siblings; but also sets the stage for his uncles to tap into the black market for oil and other commodities, including surreptitious sales into neighboring countries.

March 2003: The U.S. once again invades Iraq – under questionable pretense. Jason, from Montana, is 19. Salim, and his twin, Salam, are 19. In late 2004, Salim and Jason will meet on the urban battlefield called Fallujah in Operation *Al-Fajr*. *Al-Fajr* – the dawn, in Arabic. It's the Second Battle of Fallujah, and both Salim and Jason are snipers. Salim has been called to combat and trained by al Qaida; Jason was called to combat by his country and trained by the Marine Corps. More than half of the US Marines in the infantry battalions – about 800 warriors per battalion – will be awarded Purple Hearts after *Al-Fajr*. Many of these are posthumous. Salim's twin, Salam (*peace* in Arabic; the parallel in Hebrew is shalom, both with roots in ancient Aramaic) will seek paradise as a suicide bomber in the coming year. On the way to his 72 virgins in paradise, Salam kills 36 people and himself; two are American soldiers; two are Iraqi National Police and most of the rest are Shi'a Muslims – unarmed women and children – at a market near a Shi'a mosque. Salam believes he is defending Islam from apostates, threats to pure Islam. Salim believes he is defending Fallujah from occupation forces.

Jason believes he is defending America.

Why?

And why, back in Montana, do Jason's older brothers have

two different points of view – one absolutely opposed to the war, one indifferent? In the quest to understand "why young men are so susceptible to…'the moral and ascetic charms of war,'" I think back to Cowan's film. The title is not *Every*body's Son Will Do. And on memetics, Coker does not ponder why *all* young men are so susceptible to the moral and ascetic charms of war.

The "Я" War: Generalities

Welcome to America's first unHoly War: Capitalism vs. Insanely Яadical Islamist Fundamentalist Terrorism. Presidents won't use the "Я" word; (most) generals certainly won't use the "Я" word, but while we are embroiled in a war of Яeligion,[xxiv] a Holy War, it is also a war of business, a war of technology, a war of education and propaganda, and most importantly, a war of freedoms. And because each of these – business, technology, education, propaganda and freedom – are concepts you can't hold in your hand, this is a war of *ideas* and the human dimension in parallel with the kinetic war of improvised explosive devices, M-4 carbines and Predator drones; snipers, exploding heads and suicide bombers. Whereas the previous chapter outlined the historical roots of this text, this chapter illustrates the broad contemporary context of the remainder of the book. As Islam (via shariah law) is described as universally applicable to all elements of the social, cultural, religious, economic and political life of those who fight with violent Muslim extremist groups – understanding the broader context of what calls young men and women to war is essential.

Bear with me as I seek to condense an opaque, complex phenomenon to a digestible concept. The coming chapter relies on unclassified information, knowledge adopted and adapted over more than two decades in military intelligence and the scholarship of a wide variety of other authors. This chapter's goal is to introduce that social, cultural, religious, economic and political environment which serves to recruit young men and women to war. The emphasis in *this* chapter is weighted more to the overview of that environment on the Islam side of the equation. A more in-depth analysis of US Marine Corps culture follows in subsequent chapters.

Why an unHoly War? A war of "Яeligion?"

A discussion of religion's role in recruiting and indoctrination to jihad has to be part of the solution. To deny we are engaged in a Holy War is naïve. To define al-Qaida and the Taliban (and the Haqqani Network and Lashkar e-Taiba (Army of the Pure), and Hamas and Hezbollah, and al-Shabaab in Somalia, and on and on) merely as criminals is overly simplistic, denies the distorted religious underpinnings, and caters to Arab and Islamic dictators who wish to distance their foundations from terrorists. Yet to deny that al-Qaida, the Taliban, Lashkar e-Taiba, the Haqqanis and others have devolved to principally criminal motivations and the financial excesses that now fund their Islamist insurgencies misses the point as well. It is that murderous religious ideology that guides and informs their recruiting efforts. No jihadi web site is going to reveal that certain jihadi leaders have gotten rich by skimming proceeds from heroin, cocaine, oil, diamonds, cigarette smuggling, kidnapping, bank robbery, piracy or extortion; it's "all for Allah…"

Terminology – the correct terminology – is essential. I don't follow in lockstep with either, but my word choices are *informed* by David Kilcullen[xxv] and Jim Guirard (truespeak.org).[xxvi] Kilcullen's book *The Accidental Guerilla* discusses the phenomenon of the US fighting multiple wars – one against terrorists and terrorism, and the others against those insurgents who pop up as enemies while we're hunting terrorists. An example is Iraq's 1920 Revolution Brigade in Anbar Province – a Sunni militia group. Like al-Qaida, they have Sunni roots, but their fight with the US is not the same as al-Qaida's fight with the US. Some breakaway elements fight *against* al-Qaida.

Guirard's point is that we should stop using terms like "jihadi" because such terms reflect the legitimacy that terrorists crave. I get it. And I care. But I am concerned principally with the culture, on both sides, and how culture supports the recruiting and indoctrination process. All evidence points to a reality that jihadis and terrorists (irhabists) *believe* they are at war, and that theirs is a holy war. I even agree with Guirard that the bad guys have hijacked Islam. Guirard's prologue chides:

PART 1 – The al Qaeda, Taliban and Communist Narratives

The late, great linguist and rhetorician George Orwell of "1984" and "Animal Farm" fame would surely have agreed with what US Marine Corps General James Mattis (then head of the Joint Forces Command at Norfolk) meant three years ago when he sharply condemned al Qaeda-style Terrorism as "tyranny in false religious garb."

In this context, both of these wise men would seem to agree that we should stop calling these genocidal haters and assassins by the self-sanctifying "false religious" labels they have so cynically chosen for themselves via their all-too-familiar, self-canonizing narrative of:

1. Jihad (alleged holy war) by supposed

2. mujahideen (holy warriors) and bin Laden-anointed

3. shahideen (martyrs) destined for a promised 72-virgin

4. Jennah (Paradise) as reward for killing us alleged

5. kuffr (infidels) and, in time, destroying the alleged

6. Shaitan al-Akbar (the Great Satan, America), as well.

Those among us who use these terms routinely fall into three main categories: first, those who repeat them without regard as to whether they are objectively true; second, those who believe that they represent only the deviant and "false religious garb" of the Terrorists and; third, those who believe (as Osama bin Laden claims) that this narrative represents the heart and soul of Islam itself, rather than a sinful and criminal deviancy from it.

As for the Holy War, or unHoly War, as this text will explore, there are interesting and important parallels and contrasts in the personal and group psychology (between "them" and "us") that help us understand <u>why</u>. *Occam's Razor* cuts too fine; radicalization and jihad are too complex. We cannot shave off phenomena that do not explain radicalization...to be left with what does. Radicalization and terrorism do not beg simple solutions. What we need is Occam's Hammer...a broader set of models, metaphors and solutions...to think our way out of this while we fight to establish security in the Middle East, Afghanistan and at home.

Bandura's *Mechanisms of Moral Disengagement in Terrorism*[xxvii]offers more than one model for understanding part of the "why" or "how" in terrorist behavior. *Dehumanizing* the victim allows the terrorist to justify murder by casting the enemy in less-than human terms. Available literature reviews discussed below indicate that ultra-conservative imams teach that the Jews are apes; Christians are swine. Literally. *Displacing* responsibility allows the radical Muslim ideologue to preach that killing infidel Jews and Christians falls within the dictates of Allah, based on carefully chosen passages in the Quran or Sunnah. Another disengagement mechanism is *diffusion*, whereby the lone terrorist doesn't see or care that the five or six people he's murdered are just numbers in the tens of thousands of civilians and military killed by terrorists in the past 10 years.

Dehumanizing names are just the start of this process, and returns to Tajfel's notes on in-groups and out-groups. American soldiers have done the same since at least World War II: japs, nips, slopes, wops, krauts, gooks.[xxviii] I'm not saying it's right; I'm just reporting that it's true – and probably in all militaries. Try Google or Bing searches on "what do British/French/Russian/Iraqi/other) military think of American military?" This broad concept will be addressed again in the discussion on the documentary film *Anybody's Son Will Do*, below.

If failed, captured, wannabe suicide bomber statements clearly indicate that they seek <u>personal</u> honor in martyrdom, in the name of Allah, and combat Marines and Soldiers commonly reflect that they are in the fight, and death, <u>for their brothers in arms</u>...in light of the words of Jesus Christ: "This is my commandment, that you love one another, even as I have loved you. Greater love has no man than this, that he lay down his life for his friends,"[xxix] is the American soldier fighting for a higher ideal? Do all Marines and Soldiers sign up for this esoterica? Do *all* jihadis seek personal honor in martyrdom? I'd love to be able to answer those questions (there *are* philosophically, metaphysically right answers), but since we can't crawl around inside their almost impenetrable heads we are left with what they say and what they do to inform our inferences of social psychology. More on this later – and the broad answer is that motivations for going to war run from the radical to the lukewarm for *both* US Marines and Islamist radicals.

Why a Holy War: In Coker's terms, young men and a substantial and growing number of young women respond to the call of priests and politicians – to defend what they believe they believe in. What they have *faith* in. Gallup polls echo concepts presented in undergraduate psychology: humans are becoming aware of their personal political, religious or ideological convictions while they are in the same age group – 17 to 25 – targeted by both Marine Corps and jihadist-irhabist recruitment advertising.[xxx] In the US, people tend to identify themselves as liberal or moderate when they're younger (70 percent combined in the 18-29 age group, and 30 percent conservative); with those who self-identify as conservative gradually increasing to nearly 50 percent in the 65 and older age group (with 35 percent moderate and 16 percent liberal in the older age group). A recent Pew Research poll indicates Marines are more conservative than liberal, and tend toward Republican; 70 percent identify some religious affiliation.[xxxi] There is no poll that tells us what percentage of specifically 17- to 25-year-old Muslim males believe in liberal democratic institutions versus what percentage of the same demographic may be conservative...fundamentalist...or radical Islamists, and those views vary from country to country.

But what we do know is: some 20,000 young men and women answer the call to enlist in the Marine Corps each year (closer to 30,000 during the "surge"); another few thousand are commissioned as officers, some from the enlisted ranks, many out of Reserve Officer Training Corps (ROTC) and other college programs, or upon graduation from the service academies – the Air Force Academy, Naval Academy and the US Military Academy at West Point. Freshly minted Marines back-fill normal attrition: battlefield casualties, the end of enlistments, and retirements, and maintain the Corps' *end-strength* at around 200,000, or about .06 percent of the US population. As Marines are wont to say, *We are the Few. The Proud.*

As for the jihadis – no one seems to have a solid answer to the question of how many hard core jihadis (or Salafist/irhabists) there are either, and as noted in the musing at the start of the previous chapter – *GENESIS* – to define is to limit. Like Marines as a percentage of the US population, those jihadis on the battlefield are a small percentage of the whole of Islam, and *Islam* is not a monolithic whole. Those who commit acts of terror – suicide bombings, beheadings – a smaller percentage. In generalities, some of the remainder of "the whole of Islam" support violent jihad; some do not. Some offer financial support; others ideological support. Ideological support is like "I don't like the United States and its hegemonic goals, its Western decadence and its arrogance, so I'm rootin' for the Islamic jihadis – but I'm not necessarily going to send them my charitable donations. Charity begins at home. In Detroit, or Minneapolis, Karachi or Dubai."

The parallel in American culture is the continuum of: citizens who *hope* someone will be elected; those who actually vote; those who send in campaign donations and vote; and those who do all of this and hit the street, knocking on doors to campaign for their candidate. Our goal is to understand what calls young men and women to the other side of the war – violent jihad.

Holy War: Capitalism; Radical Shi'a and Radical Salafist Islam:

In order to get through the remainder of this chapter expeditiously, we need to introduce the concepts of recruiting – media and messaging based on culture and ideology; the arts and sciences of persuasion and the resulting individual and social psychology that influences young men and women to respond to the call of the priests and politicians; and the clarification of what distinguishes a foot soldier jihadi who answered the call to get the Americans out of their country from a terrorist. And they are mostly *young* men and women – in both camps. We don't find 65-year-old jihadis in either Marine boot camp or al-Qaida training camps. War is generally a young man's game.

The Truth

The March 1, 2010, issue of *FORBES* magazine carries the cover story: *Is Al Qaida Bankrupt?"* Never mind the subtitle (*Desperate for funds terrorists are changing their business model* – which provides its own fodder for later discussions), my initial reaction is: Sure. Al-Qaida is bankrupt. Morally bankrupt. I'm not the only American to have this reaction. Truth is…this is the point at which I could write about the morally bankrupt jihadis and the superior United States Marines. That would be too easy, comparing *our* morals to *their* morals. Truth is…at least some of the jihadis believe they are fighting for something worth dying for and they think their morals are pure and ours are decadent. Truth is…United States Marines believe *they* are fighting for something worth dying for, and the *bad guys'* morals are impure and decadent. But such a comparison would give you my opinion and fail to get at the commonalities in recruiting propaganda.

Whether one motivation is more pure than the other will not necessarily win the war. Some wars, jihads, are lost on financial backing, logistics or choice of allies.[xxxii] Some are won or lost on tactics and strategies – the plans and decisions of captains and generals. Some wars are won or lost on training, small unit leadership and morale, or the ability to win the hearts and minds of the hometown population in a Counter-Insurgency. Or on patience. Or resolve. Determination. Technology. Faulty business models. Military history offers endless possibilities. In this war, we cannot quantify the possible end results, especially by comparing relative orders of battle – who has more tanks, planes, ships, troops or money. And, this is not "Dr. Tyree's philosophy class." Truth is…the truth isn't handy at this point. We need facts.

More useful is the process of analyzing what jihadis and Marines have <u>in common</u>, how they are attracted to the fight, how they are indoctrinated and how they internalize the message of that motivation. Part of this process includes the discovery of why Marines and jihadis leave the fight, which is a fraction of the process of preventing or dissuading fundamentalist Islamists from seeking jihad in the first place.

Since 9/11 I've read tens of thousands of pages of classified and unclassified raw intelligence reports and finished analytical assessments on terrorism, jihad and Insanely Radical Islamist Fundamentalism, hundreds and hundreds of monographs and books. Many have pointed to our (US) lack of knowledge of "their" culture, and we have certainly made some mistakes on the civil affairs and cultural analysis front. But most irksome is the type of assessment from the likes of Brannan, Esler and Strindberg.[xxxiii] The authors' premise is that extant analyses are weak or inept because, from their expert point of view, the *other* authors are working for corporations, governments or law enforcement agencies seeking to "manage the terrorist threat." The overt assumption is that writers at RAND, the Central Intelligence Agency, the Defense Intelligence Agency, various military commands and others with a stake in defeating Insanely Radical Islamist Fundamentalist Terrorists have flawed methodologies, **tainted by the mission to defeat terrorists**, and therefore have flawed conclusions. This assumption is akin to the belief that a study on the habits of computer users for example, funded by Microsoft, or funded by Apple, *necessarily* has flawed conclusions. Brannan, Esler and Strindberg's paper was completed in 2000 – pre-9/11, and before US and Coalition combat operations in Afghanistan and Iraq.

Since 2000, the volume of research on Islamic or Islamist Fundamentalists has multiplied exponentially. The better work relies on primary sources, such as interviews with detainees; captured documents, translated and declassified for scholarly use, and generally derives, still, from organizations with a stake in combating Insanely Radical Islamist Fundamentalist Terrorism. The only significant dead ends in this research have been the disposition to identify unemployment or lack of meaningful work as specific *causes* of radicalism (there *is* a relationship but it's more complex than that, and I'll discuss that), and the line of reasoning that sought to define Insanely Radical Islamist Fundamentalist Terrorists as clinically, psychiatrically insane. Really clinically insane and not insane in the pedestrian, conversational sense. The latter has been effectively dismissed by the broader community of social-psychologists, anthropologists, psychiatrists and intelligence professionals

What we have *not* seen however, are papers that evaluate the commonalities in recruiting and radicalization of "soldiers" fighting both sides of the jihad. This book offers that difference – the commonalities in social psychology in particular – and draws from the excellent work on Insanely Radical Islamist Fundamentalists over the past ten years.

The truth is…and the facts are:

Marines are jihadis, fighting a holy war, for something they hold precious: inalienable God-given freedoms.

Some jihadis *are* jihadis, fighting a holy war, for something they hold precious: and we'll explore that.

Not all jihadis (mujahidin)(mujh) are terrorists/irhabists. Many of the Muslims on the battlefields of Iraq and Afghanistan are foot soldiers with no interest in beheading prisoners, committing suicide bombings, or acts of terror with weapons of mass destruction. They just don't like foreigners hanging around their country. Like some US Marines and Soldiers, some hope to get the street creds – the parallel to medals, ribbons, minor wounds, combat experience, stories – that will boost their *wasta*, or influence, and help them pick up chicks. And some of them are not well-treated by their handlers, hate their lives, didn't get what they were expecting or "bit off more than they could chew" and seek to leave the battlefield to just go home.

Recruiting

I'm not much for numbers, but on the occasion they are simple and come in handy, they can be startling. One of the Principles of Modern Warfare is "economy of force," or the idea of sending in just enough Marines to get the job done and not tens of thousands more, as they may be needed somewhere else on the planet. Applying that principle, economy of force, and faced with the need to actively recruit qualified men and women for service in the Corps, Marines have a small cadre of officer and mostly enlisted recruiters – neither more nor less than are required to get the job done. Consider that US Marine Corps recruiters around the country are each generally required to sign up, on average, 2.5 recruits per month to meet their quotas and demonstrate proficiency as recruiters.

Some of those new recruits, typically high school seniors or recent graduates waiting to "ship" to boot camp after graduation, may even make the professional recruiter's job a bit easier by convincing their friends that the Marine Corps is better than the other options facing 17- to 25-year-olds: unemployment and hanging out at mom and dad's home; crime, gangs and drugs; entry-level jobs, including mowing lawns, construction, bagging groceries or the Army, Navy and Air Force; or college. (All of the US armed forces provide an avenue to college tuition, while on active duty and beyond.) My original dissertation dissects this process for Marines, in detail. The overall process has changed little in 20 years, or 40-50 years for that matter, but what has changed are elements of the culture on which the Corps' internal propaganda is based.

What if on the jihadi side of the radicalization and recruiting equation, we start with 10 active disciples of Salafist Islam – Osama bin Laden's version of Islam – recruiting for the jihadi cause. If in one month those 10 *each* interact with 100 fellow Muslims, have serious discussions with 10 of those fellow Muslims, and recruit just 2 wannabe jihadis, each, there could be 20 new targets in the crosshairs of our M-16-A4's. If those 20 went through the same process the next month, we would have 40 new targets. There are thousands of mosques around the globe, and thousands of madrassahs – Islamic schools. If those 40 went through the same process in the coming month, recruiting two each, we would have 80 new targets, and 160 the next month, and 320 the next. In two years, the newest crop of 83,886,080 proselytes recruiting 2 converts each for month 24 would bring in 167,772,160 new targets PLUS all of those that had shipped off to al-Qaida training camps in the previous 23 months...or a total of 335,544,300. That's more than the population of the United States!

One would think the most efficient way to rid the planet of this scourge could be nuclear weapons, but with AQ Central (al-Qaida Senior Leadership) *mostly* neutered over the past nine or ten years, and a sizable population of moderate and indifferent Muslims on the landscape, the virus has more or less aerosolized and seeped into the internet, into the underground, and hiding behind burqas and underground mosques. Osama bin Laden is a corpse; Anwar al-Aulaqi is a corpse; and Ayman Zawahiri is incapable of inspiration. Some analysts and commentators seem to think AQ has been defeated,[xxxiv] but the message and the jihadis are out there.

Getting all of those jihadis to stand still on one hillside for a group photo, with a nuclear flash, proves to be exceedingly difficult, and the current administration is loathe to nuke anything. The next best way, while we round up those who have made it onto the battlefield, has to be countering their recruiting propaganda. And Islamic Fundamentalists don't recruit like the "what if" example above anyway. Not exactly. In real terms, the little Muslim boys who were 7 in September 2001 are 19 in 2013 and old enough to pick up an AK-47. Some do; most don't. And there are nowhere near 335,544,300 jihadis, poisonous snakes or irhabists in a world of 1.5 billion Muslims.

Ultimately, both Marines and jihadis believe they are fighting for something. Superficially, it may be the US Constitution vs. the Quran. Priests and Politicians will call them; Recruiters will find them.

The Roots of Persuasion and Indoctrination

Why Capitalism – as a religion? Because America's predominantly Christian heritage is so pluralistically fragmented, albeit with roots in the Protestant Work Ethic and the freedom of faith, that the only current unifying *religion* in America is capitalism. I may find that sad, personally, but accept it as real based on decades of living in it. Even as faith in the almighty dollar is waffling, there remains a unifying belief in The American Way. Don't get me wrong…plenty of Americans, some 70 to 90 percent, according to one poll or another, express a belief in God, and the majority of Americans identify themselves as Christians.)

OK – it's not *Capitalism* per se, but there is a logic trail: First, one could say that America's warriors are Defenders of the Constitution. All American Marines and Soldiers take an oath *to defend the Constitution of the United States against all enemies, foreign and domestic*. In that sense – "Defenders of the Constitution" stand in opposition to "Defenders of the Quran" (as interpreted by Radical Salafist Muslims) in this current jihad. And, The United States of America is not a pure democracy, but a republic with democratic principles.[xxxv] Marines and Soldiers are Defenders of the Republic, therefore "republicans." But no sooner would "Republicans" roll off the presses than Democrats would cry foul. There must be at least three or four Democrats in the Marine Corps.

In the real United States of America, all students in all grades in *all* schools once upon a time would start the school day with:

I pledge allegiance to the flag of the United States of America, and to the Republic for which it stands, one nation under God, indivisible, with liberty and justice for all.

Atheists and the uber-liberals got involved and the Pledge of Allegiance became optional in some schools. But it's still out there. At the core, the Pledge is a restatement of:

I, (*NAME*), do solemnly swear (or affirm) that I will support and defend the Constitution of the United States against all enemies, foreign and domestic; that I will bear true faith and allegiance to the same; and that I will obey the orders of the President of the United States and the orders of the officers appointed over me, according to regulations and the Uniform Code of Military Justice. So help me God.

All servicemen and women enlisting in the Armed Forces of the United States take this oath, including the tiny minority who are not US citizens. This enlisted oath of office mirrors the oath administered to commissioned officers entering all branches of the US Armed Forces (all officers must be US Citizens):

I, *[name]*, do solemnly swear (or affirm) that I will support and defend the Constitution of the United States against all enemies, foreign and domestic; that I will bear true faith and allegiance to the same; that I take this obligation freely, without any mental reservation or purpose of evasion; and that I will well and faithfully discharge the duties of the office on which I am about to enter. So help me God.

Theoretically we are indoctrinating our nation's schoolchildren in *allegiance to the flag*, support and defense of our nation, and we require young men and women entering military service to swear, or *affirm* if their religion prohibits "swearing" an oath, to support and defend the Constitution of the United States (so help me God). We require the same of those from South Korea, Mexico, Canada, Jamaica or any other nation or principality who desire to enlist in the US Armed Forces – guest "workers" (lawful permanent "green card" residents) who are defending the US Constitution. But Insanely Radical Muslim Fundamentalists have waged war also on America's allies, who are *not* defending America's constitution. Now what?

What we have in common, more or less, are the *kinds* of freedoms spelled out in the US Constitution – including freedom of religion, etc., in contrast to the Quran. The majority of Americans and mainly European coalition partners – terrorism's targets – have roots in Christianity, but also the freedom to *not* proclaim Christianity. Or any other religion. Most of these allies are more or less democratic states, including constitutional monarchies with parliaments, wrapped around socialist-leaning capitalism. And finally, it is that capitalism, the nascent democracies in some historically Muslim countries, and the perceived corrupting influences of Western consumerism culture in those countries that Osama bin Laden and other fundamentalists see as diluting pure Islam.

Both Christianity and Capitalism are anathema to Insanely Radical Islamist Fundamentalist Terrorists. Toss in Democracy, *with Separation of Church and State*, and it really pisses them off. Our politicians call us to fight for those freedoms. In the end – we too are *freedom fighters*. Mujahidin "Я" Us.

Jihadis and Terrorists

Why Insanely Radical Islamist Fundamentalist Terrorists? Because not all Muslims are insanely radical; not all are "fundamentalists;" and not all call for the destruction of America and the rest of the West and Israel and everything else un-Islamic. And – some Islamic fundamentalists claim to seek to move their fellow believers in Islam "back to basics," the fundamentals of Islam of the 7th Century, without justifying terrorism. Some Muslims will explain that being a *fundamentalist* is a good thing; these are the faithful who seek to live their lives according to the principles and way of life of Mohammed and his early companions.[xxxvi] Some analysts see parallels in fundamentalist Christian evangelists who seek to move *their* faithful "back to basics." In the 16th Century, Dr. Martin Luther was a fundamentalist; the Roman Catholic Church viewed his teachings as radical. But Luther's radical concepts, 21st Century's Islamic version of radical, and, say, air travel, television and organ transplants are all vastly different versions of "radical." We need to get some windage and elevation on this target.

<u>Not all snakes are poisonous</u>

Sorting through the political, cultural and religious environment that spawns the Insanely Radical Jihadi Fundamentalist Islamists who seek to forcibly convert or kill all infidels, people who do not accept the Islamic "Allah" as the only god, from those who merely seek to impose Islam on the entire world without violent jihad, from those who "just want to get along," points to the *basic statements of belief* in Islam:

To promote accurate representation of Islam by providing correct information thereby encouraging individual responsibility for seeking and acting upon the Truth.

To increase awareness as to the extent of oppression against Muslims throughout the world and the conspiracy that exists to exterminate Muslims and the religion of Islam from the face of the Earth.

To remind Muslims of their responsibility to participate and support their brothers and sisters in Islam who are striving on a daily basis to fulfill the commandment of Allah (Most Exalted is He) in making La illaha ilallah the law of this world, (insha'Allah).[xxxvii]

La ilaha ilallah is part of the Muslim proclamation of faith, or "Shahada." The Arabic phrase translates as: "*There is no deity except God.*" (Or "there is no God except God, and there is only **one** and our Muslim version is the right one.") On the surface this is neither insidious nor threatening. Christians generally believe their understanding of God is the correct and only true understanding of God too, despite the widely divergent interpretations of how to exercise that belief...and how to convert non-believers. *Some* professed Christians may even express a belief that there are many paths to God. I dismiss this belief; and it's not relevant at this point anyway. It is not inconsistent to ask: why are there various versions of

Baptists, Methodists, Presbyterians, several versions or "synods" of Lutherans, Church of Christ, Mormons, and so on?

The contest, simplistically, would look like an inter-faith convention with Muslims, Roman Catholics, Mormons, and mainstream Christians such as Baptists, Methodists, Lutherans, Presbyterians and others sipping tea and doing their best to explain why their individual beliefs are correct. (Conservative Lutherans would not likely attend such a convention.) The probable outcome of such a conversation, of course, is that each confession believes by default *all other faiths are wrong*. All parties agree to disagree on matters of faith, then turn to topics of common concern – disaster relief, poverty or hunger.

But when instruction in faith – to children – preaches intolerance, starting with kindergarten age children and increasing in intensity through late adolescence, the concept of *La illaha ilallah* means that all infidels, people who don't accept Allah, must die. The message comes across in Hamas cartoons, directed at young children, with Disneylike characters;[xxxviii] or web sites, or classroom education. These are the foundations of radicalization and recruiting to violent jihad. The videos are still accessible on YouTube in 2013.

In 2006, a Washington Post story by Nina Shea[xxxix] added to the story of the Saudi-funded prep school in Northern Virginia. Shea observed that intolerance was the norm in Saudi "K through 12" education, but "all that was supposed to change after 9/11." Textbooks released by a Saudi dissident illustrate the scale of instruction directed at students attending Saudi-funded schools in the shadow of Washington DC:

[from the 8th grade curriculum] "As cited in Ibn Abbas: The apes are Jews, the people of the Sabbath; while the swine are the Christians, the infidels of the communion of Jesus."

[from the 6th grade curriculum] "Just as Muslims were successful in the past when they came together in a sincere endeavor to evict the Christian crusaders from Palestine, so will the Arabs and Muslims emerge victorious, God willing, against the Jews and their allies if they stand together and fight a true jihad for God, for this is within God's power."

[from the 1st grade curriculum] " Every religion other than Islam is false." "Fill in the blanks with the appropriate words (Islam, hellfire): Every religion other than _____ is false. Whoever dies outside of Islam enters _____."[xl]

The students who lived through that 8th grade curriculum, at the age of 13 to 14 in 2006, would be 20 to 21 years old in 2013. Prime *jihadi* age. Shea notes (in 2006) that the curriculum was supposed to have been "modernized" to assist Arab and Muslim students "to better prepare [our children] for the challenges of tomorrow." The changes have not been forthcoming, and if these examples highlight what is taught in Saudi-funded schools in the West, one may draw conclusions about what is taught in Saudi-funded schools, or madrassahs, around the world. As of 2011, not much has changed according to Shea's research and analysis.[xli]

In his book *Looming Tower*, Lawrence Wright asserts that, while Saudis constitute only 1 percent of the world's Muslims, they pay "90 percent of the expenses of the entire faith, overriding other traditions of Islam." Former Treasury Department General Counsel David Aufhauser and other analysts in testimony to Congress, have cited the statistic that, on an annual basis, Saudi Arabia spends three times as much in exporting Salafi ideology, also called "Wahhabism," as did the Soviets in propagating Communism during the height of the Cold War.

The phenomenon of teaching intolerance is not limited to Saudi Arabia, but is also taking shape in the "new" Egypt, post-Mubarak, for example, as well as in other Muslim-dominated countries.[xlii] Continue independent research on the topic on your own. (And don't forget when you fill up your gas tank that Saudi funding derives in large measure from petro-dollars.)

Searching for the roots of this brand of recruitment, indoctrination and radicalization, just as we will investigate the roots of recruitment and indoctrination for US Marines in the coming chapter, takes us back through Osama bin Laden's *Salafist* ideology, Wahabbi doctrine, and the nominal energy behind today's Muslim Brotherhood. But to define is to limit, and over-simplifying the lineage of America's adversaries in the war on terror will necessarily omit some of those adversaries. At the risk of over-simplifying, however, stepping back to that catalytic year of 1979 brings two Holy War adversaries into focus: apocalyptic Shi'a Islam and the Salafi house of Sunni Islam.

Shi'a

Various sources estimate the Shi'a sect of Islam comprising roughly 10 to 15 percent of the world's 1.5 billion Muslims. If there is a center for Shi'a Muslims, their historical base resides in Iran (89% Shi'a) and Iraq (60-65 % Shi'a), with Shi'a majorities in Azerbaijan and Bahrain. Geographically, this is the core of the ancient Persian Empire. As of 2013, the West is not engaged in daily kinetic combat operations against Shi'a Muslims as a bloc, although Moqtada al-Sadr's belligerents, funded and armed by Iran, raised hell for the US and British elements of "the coalition" during much of Operation Iraqi Freedom – in Baghdad, and the South and East of Iraq. Iran's 21st Century contribution to the world's cache of science and technology – "explosively formed projectiles" (EFPs – a form of improvised explosive devices – IEDs) have penetrated most current battlefields, including Iraq and Afghanistan. Iran and neighboring Syria manifest their intentions through financial, ideological and other support to proxies Hezbollah and Hamas. Hezbollah is that radical Shi'ite Islamic element that sprang up in 1982 in Lebanon to counter Israel's invasion, and is the organization responsible for the bombing of the Marine barracks in Beirut in 1983, killing 241 US Marines, soldiers and sailors. Soon after, a separate attack killed 58 French paratroopers and wounded 15 more.[xliii]

There is no love lost between the Shi'a and Sunni. Saudi Arabia and other predominantly Sunni nations see Iran as a threat, a destabilizing force in the Middle East. Some Sunnis refer to the Shi'a as *polytheists* because of the Shi'a practice of veneration of "saints" Sunnis also refer to Christianity as a polytheistic religion because their Muslim interpretation of "God the Father, God as Jesus the Son of God, and God as the Holy Spirit" necessarily means Christians worship three Gods. When Sunni and Shi'a cooperate, they cooperate as a matter of convenience, temporarily, against a common threat to Islam.

What makes the Middle East dynamic challengingly interesting, informs Shi'a culture, and impacts Shi'a propaganda and recruiting is the dogma of the apocalyptic *Twelver Shi'ites*. Libraries of source documents are available on the topic, but the basic idea is that the principal sects we know today as *Sunni* and *Shi'ite* began to grow apart in the dispute over leadership of Islam after the death of the prophet Mohammed in 632 A.D.[xliv] One faction pressed for Mohammed's closest relative – his son-in-law and cousin, Ali ibn Abu Talib, to be named as *caliph, or* commander or leader of the faithful. According to Sunni tradition, the Prophet left no succession plan; Mohammed's closest companions instead elected Abu Bakr. Abu Bakr appointed Umar, again passing up on Ali. Umar wanted his successor elected from among six leaders of the inner circle at Medina, and when Umar was assassinated, Uthman was selected. Ali was finally elected caliph following the assassination of Uthman.

Disputes between Ali's supporters and other central figures laid the groundwork for the *evolution* of a divide between what today are known as Sunni and Shi'ite, but according to Bufano, too much is made of the early rift.[xlv] Bufano's incisive research develops the thesis that "no clear line...divided Sunni and Shi'a Muslims during the formative era of Islam [610-945 A.D.], and that the concepts of Sunnism and Twelver Shi'ism took centuries to develop into the theological, legal, and spiritual characteristics that we associate with the two main sects of Islam today."

Various factions claimed the caliphate, until the 12th leader (caliph, imam):

The 12th Imam was born around 868 A.D. at a time of great persecution of Shi'ites...and in order to protect him, his father, the 11th Imam, sent him into hiding (occultation). He appeared in public briefly at the age of 6 when his father died but then went back into obscurity. Shiites believe he continues to guide Muslims, and they expect his "messianic" return to bring order from chaos and righteousness from unbelief. Muhammad al-Mahdi, also known as Hujjat ibn al-Hasan...believed by Twelvers to be in Occultation, is the individual believed by Twelver Shi'a Muslims to be the Mahdi, an ultimate savior of humankind and the final Imam of the Twelve Imams.

Twelver Shi'a believe that al-Mahdi was born in 869 and did not die but rather was hidden by God (this is referred to as the Occultation) and will later emerge with Jesus in order to fulfill their mission of bringing peace and justice to the world. He assumed the Imamate at 5 years of age. Sunnis and other Shi'a schools do not consider ibn-al-Hasan to be the Mahdi. For the apocalypticists in Shi'a, Israel must fall to allow the coming of the Mahdi.[xlvi]

Twelver Shi'a accept no caliph since then as legitimate. Again, as Bufano notes, the theology that supports this notion evolved over hundreds of years. What's important for the Global War on Terrorism (or "overseas contingency operations," or whatever the White House wants to call it this week), is that Iran's President and his fellow Twelver Shi'a apparently believe mankind can hasten the coming of the Mahdi through the incitement of cataclysmic events on Earth. War. The destruction of Israel, and by extension, the United States, and the reclamation of the Temple Mount in the Old City of Jerusalem: under Jewish sovereignty since the Six-Day war in 1967.

This fatalistic approach to world affairs inspired Iran to send tens of thousands of boy soldiers surging in human suicide waves across the minefield no-man's land at the battlefront of the war with Iraq (1980-88), and Hezbollah, based in Lebanon and sponsored by Iran, applies suicide attacks as routine strategy against Israel and other targets, and directs recruiting propaganda to children through television and video games. In this context, Iran's apparent attempt to develop nuclear weapons adds a new dimension to the Holy War.

Because there are significant doctrinal or ideological differences between Shi'a and Sunni beliefs, it occasionally seems ironic that Iran provides support to Hamas – a Sunni outgrowth of the Muslim Brotherhood.[xlvii] But both Hamas and Hezbollah provide avenues for Iran's vision of a world without Israel – Hamas from within the boundaries of what is nominally Israel (the West Bank and Gaza Strip); Hezbollah by way of rocket attacks and cross-border raids from southern Lebanon. As Arab and Persian Muslims see the US as Israel's principal benefactor, the US is directly or indirectly a target as well.

Sunni

On the Sunni side of the religious extremist equation, Osama bin Laden and al-Qaida are arguably the most recognized names in the US and Western consciousness, at least in the domain of terrorism. Yet, the execution of bin Laden in 2011 is almost irrelevant. What is important in terms of jihadi-irhabi recruitment propaganda is that the al-Qaida brand lives on, and with it bin Laden's message, the al-Qaida narrative, to both the intellectuals and the disenfranchised: the al Qaida cell leaders, the suicide bombers and the foot soldiers. Osama bin Laden's inspiration explains why all snakes are creepy. Osama bin Laden's provenance goes something like this:

(Salafist) Sunni Islam

At least a portion of bin Laden's tutelage in radical Sunni Islam was rooted in the Muslim Brotherhood, spawned in Egypt in 1928 by a teacher, Hassan al-Banna. The Muslim Brotherhood developed in the shadow of rising *Arab* Muslim political awareness – the last caliphate dissolving in Turkey as a result of the Ottoman Empire's choice to side with the losing team in World War I – and fading colonial influence in the Middle East.[xlviii]

The Muslim Brotherhood, "officially" rejecting violence, proclaims its enduring mission to apply the Quran and Sunnah[xlix] to all aspects of the Muslim individual, family, community and state[l] – in other words, political Islam. Muslim Brotherhood members see Islam as the yardstick for absolutely everything in social, cultural, religious, economic or political life. The Muslim Brotherhood "is the world's oldest, largest, and most influential Islamist organization." It is also "the most controversial, condemned by both conventional opinion in the West and radical opinion," according to the organization's website, Ikhwanweb. Outlawed in Egypt throughout the recently truncated dictatorship of Hosni Mubarak, Muslim Brotherhood members sought to enter Egyptian political relevance as "independents." Their ultimate goal is to replace secular governments, the remnants of Mubarak's in Egypt, for example, with shariah. President Morsi found continued opposition to strict shariah law, principally through the voice of the National Salvation Front, secular Egyptians and Coptic Christians. It will be interesting to see how Egypt evolves in the coming years. As of mid-2013 Morsi is *on the ropes* (held in "safe-keeping" by the Egyptian Army), a loose coalition of National Salvation Front, Coptic Christians and other anti-Islamists are holding Tahrir Square, Islamist supporters of Morsi are fighting back and the military is ostensibly poised to restore order. The Muslim Brotherhood has, over time, gone global and operates freely in the United States under various guises.[li]

Among the more influential members of the Muslim Brotherhood was Sayyid Qutb (1906-1966) in the 1950s and '60s. Following a two-year tour of the United States (1948-'50), Qutb wrote extensively, criticizing both the Muslim slackers and the decadent American lifestyle. He joined the Muslim Brotherhood early in the 1950s, eventually leading their propaganda section. Qutb's view that Western decadence, capitalism and democracy, and the Soviet Union's experiment in Marxism were all failures, all emblematic of the age of *jahiliyyah* – the time of ignorance before Muhammed – influenced his younger brother, Muhammed Qutb.

The younger Qutb edited and published Sayyid's writings. Among his own writings, however, *Islam: the Misunderstood Religion*, expands on his brother's ideas, describing the ways in which fundamentalist Islam is superior to the "perverted... inhuman... crazy...savage and backward" Western world."[lii] Considering the lack of reach of television and popular film in 1950, it is not a stretch, objectively, to understand that a religious scholar from Egypt, visiting the United States in 1950 would see stark contrasts between the ultra-conservative Muslim Egypt and the "sex-crazed" United States. According to Lawrence Wright, either or both Osama bin Laden or al-Qaida's number two, Ayman al-Zawahiri, were students of Muhammed Qutb at university in Mecca or Jeddah during the late 1970s.

As a teacher in Saudi Arabia in the mid-20th Century, Qutb would be an operator in Wahhabist Islam. Wahhabism traces its roots to Mohammad Ibn 'Abd al-Wahhab Najdi, who was a student first in southern Iraq and then Medina and Mecca while on the Hajj in the mid 18th Century. Wahhab's increasingly radical notions (destroying the grave of one of prophet Mohammed's companions to prevent the worship of saints) got him tossed out of his home town of 'Uyayna in 1740. Wahhab found sanctuary in nearby Diriyah by way of protector Muhammad ibn Saud. (Two of ibn Saud's brothers had been students of al-Wahhab.) Upon arriving in Diriyya, *a pact was made between Ibn Saud and Ibn Abd al-Wahhab, by which Ibn Saud pledged to implement and enforce Ibn Abd al-Wahhab's teachings, while Ibn Saud and his family would remain the temporal "leaders" of the movement.* From 1740 to the present, the al-Saud Family took some time to cement control of what is today known as "Saudi Arabia," but by the third decade of the 20th Century, "the Saudis" were firmly established as the political benefactors of the Wahhabist ultraconservative school of thought, which Osama bin Laden adopted as his own.[liii]

Saudi oil wealth and Wahhabist ideology have sponsored the construction of thousands of Islamic schools, or madrassahs, mosques and "Islamic centers" around the globe, and funded massive public relations and propaganda campaigns to spread the story that Islam is a religion of peace, while seeking the foothold to convert, or eventually rule – via shariah – all who live in their shadow of peace.

Salaf vs. Wahhab: al-Wahhab was, in practice, a Salafist Sunni, intently focused on ridding Islam of "innovation," the worship or veneration of saints, violating the one-ness of their god, and other practices that fall short of the practices of the purest of the Salaf – the first three generations following the prophet Muhammed. Among these are displays of wealth, Western decadence, the imposition of man-made laws (Saudi and Egyptian governments, and Hezbollah and Hamas in politics, for example; the illegitimate governments of Afghanistan and Pakistan) and various other political, social, religious, economic or banking innovations proscribed or not specifically allowed by shariah, hadith or Salafist tradition (the Sunnah). Correctly or not, *Salafist* and *Wahhabist* may be seen used interchangeably in the literature, and the history remains that the

Kingdom of Saud stands as the secular defender of the Wahhab, rooted in an accord between Saud and Wahhab more than 250 years ago.

The *therefore* of this school of thought lands squarely in bin Laden's jihad and takfir. Osama bin Laden's declaration of war against the United States and the motivation behind at least some of the independent al-Qaida *franchise* terrorist operations, rooted in al-Qaida's war against all things un-Islamic, points first to *takfir*, the practice of declaring one who was previously Muslim to be an unbeliever, or *kafir*. One who is in a state of denying Islam, or rejecting the tenets of Islam, is considered *apostate*. Most Americans have not been born into Islam (or declared their faith to be Islam) and then left the faith – the essence of *takfirism*. We're just infidels. Unbelievers. However...

The internal discord in what the uninitiated call "the world of Islam," is illustrated in an article dating to 1935, translated to English in 1996. The introduction of the English translation:

In the period of the decline of the Muslims, among the many troubles that have arisen, one serious and dangerous mischief is that of declaring one another as kafir and wrong-doer, and cursing one another. People introduced cracks within the plain and simple creed of Islam, and by means of inference and interpretation they created from them such branches and details as were mutually contradictory, and which were not explained in the Quran and Sunna, and even if these were, then God and His Prophet had not given them any importance. Then these servants of God (may God forgive them) gave so much importance to their own invented side-issues that they made them the criteria for faith, and on the basis of these they tore Islam to pieces, and made numerous sects, each sect calling every other as kafir, wrong-doer, misguided, doomed to hell, and God knows what. Whereas God in His clear Book had drawn a plain line of distinction between kufr and Islam, and had not given anyone the right to have discretion to declare anything he wants as kufr and anything he wants as

Islam. Whether the cause of this mischief is narrow-mindedness with good intentions, or selfishness, envy and self-seeking with malevolent intentions, the fact remains that probably nothing else has done the Muslims as much harm as this has done.[liv]

(It may or may not be interesting that Maudoodi's reference to *criteria for faith* applies equally to the fractures and disagreements within the Christian faith. Christians think they are *one*, but the nuances are chasms.)

In agreement on the resulting harm to Islam of the practice of calling each other *kafir* – unbeliever – Dr. David Kilcullen writes in his Preface:

Al Qaida is takfiri, and its members are universally so described by other Muslims, whom they routinely terrorize. In my view, and (compellingly for me) in the daily vocabulary of most ordinary local people, religious leaders, and tribal leaders with whom I have worked in the field, "takfirism" best describes the ideology currently threatening the Islamic world. I prefer it to the terms jihad, jihadist, jihadi, or mujahidin (literally "holy war" or "holy warrior") which cede to the enemy the sacred status they crave, and to irhabi (terrorist) or hiraba (terrorism), which address AQ's violence but not its ideology. Takfiri is also preferable to the terms salafi or salafist, which refer to the belief that true Muslims should live like the first four generations of Muslims, the "pious ancestors" (as-salaf as-salih). Most extremists are salafi, but few salafi are takfiri, and even fewer are terrorists: most, although fundamental conservatives, have no direct association with terrorism.[lv]

I have immense respect for Kilcullen's work and the manner in which he arrives at his conclusions – through boots-on-the-ground experience in conflict zones. His 2009 book, *The Accidental Guerilla*, is an outstanding source document. And while I respect his work and his conclusions (tho' I can't match his resume), I'll stick with *jihadi* until we get the rest of the West to understand the difference. With regard to "no direct association with terrorism...," I too have briefed General Petraeus directly – on the global sources of terrorist financing. The millions of "peaceful, tolerant, rational, inspiring" Muslims dropping a dime, a dollar, a shekel or a dinar in the zakat collection plate to support *JIHAD* include millions who are not dripping in oil revenues and who consider themselves fundamental conservatives and *not* terrorists. If we all agree to call al-Qaida and the knock-off AQ bubbas "takfiri," all we are doing is suggesting they are not true to the faith of Islam (that part is true as I understand Islam, as a scholar), but does not address the understanding that "The warriors on the other side of the conflict (*illegal combatants or not*) are soldiers or fighters who believe *they* are at war in the name of Allah." And then we see splits in al-Qaida factions, with one faction struggling to install shariah law in a given region and the other seeking to exploit the region as a free-trade zone for narcotics smuggling or kidnapping for ransom – while the original notional Salafist-Islamist rationale that inspired them seems to have been forgotten. It's not black and white.

Takfirism may be causing enormous internal problems for the mythical imputed "world" of Islam, and we *should* be concerned in the "non-Islamic world," but only because it spills into our streets and back yards as jihad, terrorism or war. If the tennis tournament of "You're takfir," versus: "No, you're takfir," versus "No, you're takfir," versus: "I know you're takfir, but what am I?" took place only between Morocco and Indonesia – we wouldn't give a sh*t about how al Qaida recruits for jihad.

Except for the oil. (And that concern diminishes year by year in the U.S.)

Jihad

The term *jihad* derives from the Arabic intonations *J – H – D*, and generally translates, according to many sources, as *struggle*. This struggle, or conflict, is interpreted idiomatically as "struggle in the way of Allah."

Jihad is a simple concept: On the one hand is the *greater jihad* – the internal jihad, or struggle in the way of Allah. In plain old American Presbyterian, Methodist, Baptist, Lutheran lingo – with psychology added in – this is that "**cognitive dissonance**" piece that drives all of us nuts. *Guilt.* In the Christian Bible, the Apostle Paul's letter to the Ephesians, Chapter 2, verse 10, reminds us: "For we are God's workmanship, created in Christ Jesus to do **good works**, which God prepared in advance for us to do." And in the gospel of Matthew, Jesus responds to the Pharisees, "Give to Caesar what is Caesar's and to God what is God's."

What does this mean?

In the more-Christian-than-Muslim West, salvation (eternal life in Heaven after a mortal death) is understood to be a gift of faith in the grace – unearned forgiveness of sins – offered through the atoning death of Jesus Christ. The gospels, the New Testament of the Christian Bible, remind the faithful that *good works spring from* faith (good works are not a path to salvation), and that God admonishes citizens of a nation, city, or state to follow the lawful rules and dictates of their earthly leaders – like Caesar. But it's so damn easy to buy a new car or 42-inch high-definition LED television rather than give the same money to charity (do good works)...or to drive 70 in a 55 mph zone – because everyone else is doing it and the cops aren't watching. Or because I'm not going to get caught. It's the same internal struggle. Cognitive dissonance suggests that I will relieve the mental conflict – dissonance – by justifying my actions. Especially the wrong actions. Good deeds carry built-in justification. Most relatively emotionally healthy people in any society, within any religion or with no religion at all, experience some form of this greater jihad, this internal struggle to "be good" and do right.

On the other hand is the *lesser jihad*. Contributing writer to Jihadica (www.jihadica.com) Joas Wagemakers, illustrates again why this is a Holy War – of Islam against Democracy, or against Freedom, Justice and the Capitalist American Way, in the translation and explanation of the book, *The Gift of the Unifiers on the Most Important Issues of the Basics of Islam:*

[The book starts by] focusing on one of the central terms of jihadi discourse, namely taghut *(pl.* tawaghit*). Traditionally used to refer to idols, the authors of this book describe it as something that makes you cross the proper boundary of worship and obedience. In other words, a* taghut *is anything "one appeals to* (yatahakamuna ilayhi) *besides God and his Messenger or worships besides God"….**Since God is believed to have the sole right to legislate, allowing another person to do this effectively means that one permits someone else to do part of God's job, thus treating him/her like God. This way, the authors imply, a legislator is turned into another god, an idol**. The concept of* taghut *thus gives these scholars the tools to equate political rulers and their governments with idols, making them fair game for the jihad they advocate….**A special chapter is dedicated to the concept of democracy. Because democracies are ultimately ruled by the people, the latter [people] become the source of legislation instead of God, turning the people themselves into idols**. The authors are clearly against democracy and list their grievances about that system, including freedom of conscience, the right to become an apostate, freedom of expression, equality and other things that the authors consider incompatible with Islam.*[vi] *[my emphasis]*

Translation: Insanely Radical Sunni Islamist Fundamentalist Terrorists (irhabists, takfiris) view Saudi Arabia's ruling house of al-Saud as apostate (which may be true; that's for God to judge) for not following Allah's dictates, for corruption, for allowing the Infidel Crusaders into the land of the two holy mosques, and other *serious and dangerous mischief*. Internal threats to Islam are *the near enemy of Islam*. The support provided to Saudi Arabia by the United States causes the United States to earn the title *the far enemy of Islam*. Some interpret the lesser jihad as war – to preserve Islam and to prevent the dilution of Islam by decadent Western influences. Others interpret the lesser jihad as furthering the ideals of Islam, spreading the message of Islam as a peaceful, tolerant religion.

This is the landscape. No discussion at this point about the utility of either the war in Iraq or in Afghanistan, or the strategies of either. Beliefs or attitudes about the *legality* or utility of the wars in Iraq and Afghanistan are part of the culture, both in the general public and in the armed forces. One way to evaluate the irony of young men and women trooping off to war in the 21st Century is that we Marines and Soldiers are enlisted to defend what is essentially a dissolving Westphalian state – a nation with borders, a discrete foreign policy, and a claim to global influence. The birth of independent nation-states, distinct from millennia of kingdoms and empires with perpetually expanding and contracting frontiers, found its foothold in the political debates and wars following the (radical) reformation of the Roman Catholic Church in the 16th Century. Those territorial borders and the ability of one nation, with borders, to exert influence on other nation-states are crumbling under the weight of influence by global corporate *non*-state actors, massive religious movements, drug- and non-drug-related criminal cartels, and the occasional union of convenience, generally economic convenience, of radical religious movements with trans-national criminal cartels. This dissolution of the state is accelerated by, or exacerbated by, an electronic world with instant communication.

Jason, Salim and Salam

The story isn't over, of course, for any of these warriors. Salam believed at death he would be rewarded by Allah. Westerners have come to believe that Salam had been taught:

What of the rewards in paradise? The Islamic paradise is described in great sensual detail in the Koran and the Traditions; for instance, Koran sura 56 verses 12 -40 ; sura 55 verses 54-56 ; sura 76 verses 12-22. [I shall quote the celebrated Penguin translation by NJ Dawood of sura 56 verses 12- 39:] "They shall recline on jewelled couches face to face, and there shall wait on them immortal youths with bowls and ewers and a cup of purest wine (that will neither pain their heads nor take away their reason); with fruits of their own choice and flesh of fowls that they relish. And theirs shall be the dark-eyed houris, chaste as hidden pearls: a guerdon for their deeds...We created the houris and made them virgins, loving companions for those on the right hand..."[xvii]

In this 2002 Guardian article by Ibn Warraq, the author offers a big *however*, noting that translations of the Sunnah (the traditions of Mohammad's companions) inaccurately portray the reward, which should be understood as chilled drinks and white grapes, not 72 virgins or "houri." The "houri" are apparently those "72 virgins" exploited in western texts. Hmmm.

Westerners refer to Salam as a suicide bomber, and more recently, correctly, as a homicide bomber. But as suicide is forbidden in the Quran, as in the Judeo-Christian Bible, Salam's family and friends will call him *shahid*. Martyr. Meanwhile, on Earth, Salam will have made a final testament in the form of a video – available on DVDs and through irhabist propaganda forums on the Internet. Salam's murderous legacy lives on as a digital recruiting poster.

Salam's brother, Salim: If Salim survived Fallujah II, al Fajr, and beyond, he will eventually have led a small band of fellow radicalized Sunni Muslim fighters – fewer than 20. In irregular warfare, absent the weapons and technology available to US Marines and Soldiers, Salim and his crew will engage in hit-and-run street battles, typically with improvised mortars or snipers. In time they will improve upon the improvised explosive devices (IEDs) graduating from two or three 122mm mortar shells duct-taped together with a pressure plate detonator to significantly more powerful explosives made with ammonium nitrate (fertilizer) and accelerants like sugar, diesel fuel and aluminum powder, detonated with remote control devices made from cell phones, garage door openers and remote controllers for toys...some with technical assistance from Iran.

Culturally, it is imperative that Salim marry. If he continues to survive, he may move into less-risky roles such as recruiting, finance or propaganda. Based on the ages of captured militants, the percentage of radicals still pulling triggers and placing IEDs who are over 35, just like on the US side, drops off dramatically. He will eventually father two to three future jihadis and teach them, from an early age, that martyrdom in the way of Allah is an honorable end. When Salim dies in combat, he will be buried the next day. His body will be washed and prepared for burial, wrapped in white linen; he will be buried in a grave with his head toward Mecca. Shariah forbids cremation.

As for Jason: the second battle for Fallujah delivered a 50/50 chance that Jason would be a casualty. Our Jason is wounded; many of his fellow Marines were killed. Given the advances in cybernetics and bionic prostheses in the past ten years, if Jason has lost an arm below the elbow or a leg below the knee, there is some chance he may thrive in rehabilitation and repatriate on the active duty rolls with a synthetic hand or foot. As an amputee, Jason will serve as a role model to fellow Marines and Soldiers – particularly those who might be inclined from time to time to complain about the food, the weather, the exercise.

Wounded or not, numbers suggest most enlisted Marines will exit the Marine Corps many years before their first opportunity to retire, or "go on retainer," at 20 years of service: there are *more* than 20,000 new privates each year; only a few hundred sergeants major and master gunnery sergeants at the senior ranks of the organizational pyramid. Those Marines and Soldiers who are severely wounded will be medically retired – likely at 100 percent disability, meaning they will receive a pension based on their pay grade (corporal, for example), 100 percent tax-free. Although they take leadership skills, self-confidence, courage and other qualities into the private sector, finding a second career – after serving in the infantry – will not be easy. Wounded Warrior programs, veterans' organizations and other groups offer a range of support opportunities, but Jason's future is largely up to Jason.

Chapter Three

(The Edifice Complex Chapter I: 1979-1990)

The view of 'conflict between generations of Marines,' and Marine Corps history, culture and folklore as of **1990**, as this impacted Marine Corps recruiting

Introduction

The United States Marine Corps began its history as a *band of brothers* by way of a resolution in the Continental Congress on November 10, 1775. Since that date, untold numbers of men and women have worn the Marine uniform. They have served their country at sea, in the air and ashore, at home and on foreign soil, in times of peace and war.

Little by little, like any organization over time, the Marine Corps has developed its own culture, a complex way of life that is something unto itself. Or perhaps it is better said that the organization, its people and their experiences have created a culture. In any case, the culture of the Marine Corps is unique.

Much has been written about the Corps; some is fact and some is fiction, and some is a combination. In terms of academic value, much of the nonfiction is more historical than cultural. Although research in military sociology includes the Corps, much of the research reports on the military services as a whole rather than the Corps as a separate organization. History has its purpose, but rather than discuss historical events or tactics and strategy, this study investigates findings from a study of the causes and effects of cultural changes on Marines and on the Corps. As the investigation evolves, what emerges is an understanding of how that organizational culture serves to attract, recruit and socialize generations of Marines.

This study doesn't ignore recorded histories, however, because they contribute to Marines' understanding of their culture. In combination with formal recorded histories, active and former Marines offer oral histories revealing the informal folklore of their organization and illustrate that realities for Marines differ from the realities portrayed in recorded histories.

Perspective: To the extent that a movie – a feature film – serves as a "recorded history" or ethnographic record of one, or a few, Marines' interpretation of their reality, the 2005 film "Jarhead" is offered by Hollywood as a depiction of one Marine's interpretation of "war"[lviii] in the run-up to Desert Storm just as "The Boys in Company C" was offered as historical fiction about Marines during the war in Vietnam. Each offers some fundamental historical and cultural accuracy; both introduced significant Hollywood-induced exaggeration. History, then, becomes part of the cultural narrative.

Interdisciplinary studies of the Marine Corps' culture are few in number. Little has been done to investigate the Marine Corps with the methods of anthropology, archeology, social psychology or sociology, even though the Marine Corps has a culture. Nor have in-depth studies been undertaken with the tools of educational psychology, even though the Marine Corps is, as will be seen, an educating organization. Many bits and pieces of Marine Corps culture have been recorded, but analyses have been mainly in terms of history or military tactics and the Marine Corps role in implementing the strategic doctrine of the United States.

Personal interest about "what makes the Corps tick" led to my original desire to do this research. (I was a Marine staff sergeant when I started this study, and at the conclusion of this initial research had served some 12 years in the Corps.) In addition to the stated purpose of the book, defined below, this study is my means as a researcher to make sense out of my Marine Corps experiences. Accepting a commission in the United States Navy, I continued the research with new perspectives and increasing interest. The emphasis of the research will be to present and analyze the points of view of active duty and former Marines. Research and writing resumed true to its original content and form after leaving the Marine Corps (for six years), following a year-long hiatus for Naval Aviation Officer Candidate School and a service school in Naval Intelligence.

Evidence of conflict between what may be called generations of Marines sparked my initial interest in this study. As with any culture, older members at times yearn for *the way it was*. The phrase *the old Corps* is common in sea stories, tales told by Marines about their earlier ways of life. During those first 12 years in the Corps, *old salts* often regretted that their culture was being changed. Although they may not have used the term *culture*, they indicated that their Marine Corps had changed. What seemed at first to be one of the obvious reasons for change is the constant input of new recruits day after day, generation after generation. Long before I started this study, it was apparent that older Marines viewed younger Marines as bringing decadent, civilian values – unmilitary values that more senior Marines saw as undisciplined, thus dangerous to the Corps. Yet Marines come from, maintain an identity with, and eventually return to civilian society.

Younger Marines entering the service, perhaps aspiring to be associated with the glories of past generations of Marines, or longing for a sense of identity in a peer group, answer the call of the Corps' advertising and recruiters. Perhaps they are lured by the stories, sights, sounds or colors of bravery, heroism, elitism and professionalism. Regardless of their reasons for joining, they adopt Marine Corps values, but without completely laying aside the values of civilian society.

One instinct of new initiates, it seems, is to want to belong to that elite military organization, with all of the attributes of professionalism, bravery, valor, and proper military bearing. Also, many new recruits enlist for personal but tangible reasons; for job skills training, a steady paycheck, to get away from home or to *become men*. And at least as late as my own boot camp experience in 1973, some recruits elected to enlist in the Marine Corps to avoid going to jail.

Another reason for change is that the Corps' responsibilities and expectations evolve, always within the specific missions of the organization or the less-specific final phrase of the Corps' mission: "...and such other duties as the President may direct."

These two evident causes of cultural change became the nucleus for my hypotheses. In the course of forming hypotheses, conducting research and writing conclusions, it became apparent that one axiom governs the study of change in organizations: change is inevitable. In the Marine Corps, we see this axiom active in the idea that cultural change is an ongoing, evolving process, and what older Marines think of younger Marines today is probably pretty much akin to what older Marines thought of younger Marines 50 years ago – even as this generation's Marines become the next generation's old-timers. It is the ever-present *generation gap* that was frequently a topic of discussion in American culture in the 1960s.

Conflict

In addition to finding initial evidence of two sources of cultural change, I evaluated the apparent conflict on two levels: between generations of Marines, and between the Corps and outside change agents.

The first conflict is this: As a generation of Marines ages and rises in rank, they produce, or take ownership of, identifiable changes within the culture. With new Marines coming into service, the older generation who perpetuate their culture becomes outnumbered and their Corps becomes susceptible to influence by the younger generation. War is a "young man's" game, and all of the armed forces are dominated – in numbers – by men and women aged 17 to 30. Yet while the younger soldiers, sailors, airmen and Marines *outnumber* those over 30, the lesser-populated senior ranks also represent the ranks with all of the authority, responsibility and "horsepower" in the armed forces. An interesting and delicate ballet.

Perspective: Consider a pyramid. The generals, colonels, sergeants major and master gunnery sergeants represent a small fraction of the total Marines Corps at the pinnacle of their careers. All of them have served more than 20 years, many – more than 30 years, and some approach 40 years of service. They are the policy makers and enforcers, but are outnumbered by the younger men and women who represent the majority of the Marine Corps. Some 90 percent of the Marine Corps is enlisted. Troops. And this relationship evolves gradually, daily; men and women start careers every week and other Marines exit at various stages in a career – every week. Generals and colonels make the rules (as do the civilian Secretary of Defense and US Congress). But there are also informal rules – social and cultural imperatives – and these may be influenced by Marines at any level.

One cultural break may be between the generation of combat veterans and non-combat vets. As of November 1988 there were but 24 Korean War veterans on active duty in the Corps and only three World War II veterans.

Perspective. And now – to bring this current by 20 years: The same kind of ratio holds true for the numbers of older veterans remaining on active duty. The only veterans of the first, brief, Gulf War in 1990-91 are the older Marines. The Vietnam vets have retired. However a majority of Marines on active duty in 2010 have experienced combat assignments in Iraq and Afghanistan, and those who have not have either "skillfully" avoided the assignment or "the system" hasn't caught up with them, and they are not necessarily the younger or more junior Marines. Some Marines in the past 10 years have tried and failed to get assignments in Iraq or Afghanistan.

Cultural conflict between combat veterans and non-combat veterans is expected. As suggested in the Marine saying, "For those who fight for it, freedom has a flavor the protected will never know," although the saying refers to protected civilians it seems to also be true inside the Corps, on a different level. Older Marines, especially those with combat experience, tend to see younger Marines as untested, uninitiated, often naive, soft or even undisciplined.

Because differences between generations of Marines may be shaped by wars and the breaks between wars, generations of Marines thus are also divided by changes in the civilian culture. Differences exist in preferences in music, clothes or other cultural values that seem to have nothing to do with the military but come from civilian society. For example, during early stages of research, I observed with several older, active duty Marines that the revived interest by some younger Marines in the "high 'n' tight" haircut (*white walls*, or very short hair on the sides, a bit longer on the top), during the mid-1980s was because of Punk music – some unknown numbers of younger Marines "spiked" their hair on top, after the fashion of Punk rockers, when they were on liberty. In the late 1960s and early '70s, according to older Marines and my own observations, some younger Marines wore symbols of the marijuana-smoking culture on T-shirts, belt buckles or tattoos. In the 1970s and '80s, some younger male Marines wore a single earring while out of uniform. One may see such practices as signs of rebellion or conflict – against authority, or merely as people of another generation bringing the trappings of their former civilian culture with them to the Corps. In any case, the Marine Corps eventually published official regulations to forbid wearing symbols of marijuana and the wearing of earrings by male Marines. The older generation of Marines creates and enforces the regulations, in conflict with the younger generation.

Basic training – boot camp – is designed not only to train warriors but to erase the recruits' sense of individuality so that they may fight as a team; to abolish recruits' ties with civilian culture, at least temporarily, so that recruits may be undistracted from the Corps' indoctrination.

Conflict between generations of Marines may also be rooted in the differences between strictly military cultures, rather than conflict between military and civilian. An older generation Marine, a sergeant major perhaps, might declare that back when he was a private he earned $78 a month in 1955 for example, compared to the $700 a month that privates earned in 1989. They didn't drive cars back then because they could not afford them, had to have permission to wear a moustache or get married, and didn't live in air-conditioned, hotel-style barracks with Home Box Office and MTV on color television. They went on liberty in uniform, not blue jeans, and stood inspection before and after going on liberty.

Perspective. Since 1990 – military pay has improved to keep up with the private sector. After boot camp, privates in 2010 earned base pay at $1447 per month ($1339 per month while in basic training). Keep in mind that's just over minimum wage at about $8.35 an hour – based on a business year of 2080 hours. And, the combat zones in Iraq and Afghanistan don't operate on 8-hour days, five days a week. Also, it's no longer just HBO and MTV (in the 1980s), obviously, but Wi-Fi Internet connections, social media, smart phones, etc. that contrast even more sharply with barracks life in the 1950s and '60s.

There are many more points to be made along these lines. The questions are complex and much is at stake, for as the entering generations of Marines grow in numbers and bring their own idiosyncrasies to the culture of their Corps, all the while aspiring to the legacies of their forefathers in uniform, they ultimately replace and reshape the generation before them and reshape the culture of the organization.

This evolution may or may not be good for the Corps, but I have seen it creating conflict between generations of Marines. Definitions will follow, but consider that this evolution seems to have been ongoing since the inception of the Corps, and current generations aren't necessarily as well defined as combat veteran and non-combat veteran. The term *generations* will suffice at this point to distinguish between Marines with different experiences, interests, values, ages and ranks, or other divisions that could lead to the conflicts and cultural changes discussed above.

The Edifice Complex

Changes and conflicts noted in the previous paragraphs gave rise to the title, *The Edifice Complex*, which combines two illustrative meanings. The first meaning alludes to the Oedipus Complex of Freudian psychology. As the original story goes, Oedipus' parents left him with a shepherd to be taken to die in the wilderness so that the prophetess' prediction of his fate would not come true. (The Oracle of Apollo at Delphi had prophesied that Oedipus would kill his father and marry his mother.) The shepherd instead gave Oedipus to a herdsman, who gave the boy to his master, King Polybus of Corinth. When Oedipus was grown, fighting as a warrior prince in his new environs and unaware of his true parents' identities, he killed his natural father in battle, and not long thereafter, won the hand of Jocasta, his mother, in marriage, by solving the riddle of the Sphinx at the gates of Thebes.[lix]

In the Freudian sense,[lx] the Oedipus complex is defined as "the positive libidinal feelings that a child develops toward the parent of the opposite sex and when unresolved are conceived as a source of adult personality disorder," or in rough terms, the child falling in love with the parent. The analogy in the title of this study borrows from both myth and Freud: *The Edifice Complex* is defined by younger generations of Marines *falling in love with* (even as they modify) the mystique of the Corps' military culture, and metaphorically and unknowingly *killing* the old Corps' culture, thus the older generations of Marines.[lxi] This phenomenon evolves as the younger generation becomes larger in numbers than the next older generation, and brings with it symbols, values and beliefs carried from their civilian culture. The process continues through each generation.

The second meaning of *The Edifice Complex* explains another possible cause of cultural conflict – evolution, thus change, in the belief systems and values of the Marine Corps. The *edifice* of *The Edifice Complex* represents two structures:

1. The formal structure of laws and regulations governing the Marine Corps, some of which are imposed on the Corps by Congress or presidential decree, and some of which are created internally by Marine Corps policy makers to govern the Corps, and:

2. The informal structure of belief systems and values, created by the historical evolution of the organization's folklore and imposed on Marines through formal training in the Corps' history and folklore. Considering the structure as building blocks arranged like a maze, with the blocks representing formal symbols, values, rituals, beliefs, stories and myths, even rules and regulations, one can see a maze which each Marine must negotiate through his career, however brief. That maze is the *complex* in the title, and parallels the widely accepted concept of the rites of passage. There are many rites of passage: boot camp, the rifle range, the physical fitness test, combat, officer candidate school, reenlistment, retirement, etc.

The complex becomes a *maze of meaning* (ontology) to Marines, with each Marine taking meaning, values and beliefs from the edifice, and each Marine leaving his or her own major or minor changes in either the individual building blocks of the edifice, or in the shape of the maze. And, because the Marine Corps is part of the government and shares the national culture, entities outside the Marine Corps also cause changes in the edifice.

To further define the title, the *edifice* represents all formal culture and printed or recorded history, and presents the formal concept of indoctrination for those who would be Marines and the continuing socialization of Marines who remain in the organization. The *complex*, on the other hand, is less formal and represents the map left by each Marine, or generation of Marines. The map for succeeding generations of Marines is passed on informally – transmitted in oral histories or *sea stories*. Unlike the formal edifice, the complex provides only clues to socialization, through sea stories and rituals, or through peer pressure. Every Marine takes a unique path through the organization. In other words, whereas the formal socialization laws of the edifice *proscribe* and *prescribe* behavior and performance, the informal clues of the complex *describe* or suggest behavior and performance. This does not mean that the edifice is stronger or has more influence than the complex; peer pressure at times may be greater than formal regulations.[lxii] The edifice indicates the organization's reality; the complex transmits Marines' reality, at least for the members of a generation in the same place and time in the complex. One cannot fully learn or internalize the beliefs and values of the edifice without metaphorically going through the complex, after which the individual is defined as a Marine and knows, or absorbs, both the edifice and the complex.

The edifice also serves as a facade, or the exterior face of the structure, which explains some of the Corps to outsiders with visible symbols, rituals or stories and histories. The edifice is the organization's *store front window*. For example, many civilians have seen the Marine war memorial in Arlington, Virginia, or pictures of the memorial, and recognize it as the "Marines raising the flag on Iwo Jima" during World War II. The Marines' Hymn, the Marine Corps emblem, the dress blue uniform, and dozens of other formal elements of folklore are recognizable by non-Marines.

But in addition to learning of the Corps though the edifice or the formal "exterior," some civilians also learn of the Corps from Marines directly, and some learn much of what they believe about the Corps from television, newspapers, movies, and magazines (*and the Internet*). So there are at least three primary influences or sources of information upon which civilians base their beliefs of the Corps: the formal structure of the edifice created by the organization (the way it is supposed to be), the word of mouth information from Marines who have been through the complex (the way it really is – in the individual Marine's beliefs. This may include the parents of future Marines.), and the civilian media. The presentation of folklore to civilians is important in this discussion because the recruitment of civilians to be Marines is the beginning of the indoctrination of a Marine. Those who would be Marines base their decisions to enlist or not on some combination of these influences. *Parallel influences are at work in radical Islam. The receptiveness of the actor and the credibility of the message (propaganda) are essential in the first steps toward influence..."radicalization."*

Although the three influences noted above may have the effect of propaganda, that which the Marine Corps creates – the edifice – can truly be identified as a form of propaganda, for propaganda by definition (again) is:

> a set of methods employed by an organized group that wants to bring about the active or passive participation in its actions of a mass of individuals psychologically unified.[lxiii]

Because the Corps must constantly enlist new recruits to maintain its ranks, some of the exterior of the edifice serves as propaganda in the form of advertising. The remainder of the edifice one may see as the Marine Corps actively or passively generating support for public acceptance. Discussions will follow in later chapters about *psychological unification*, and both advertising and propaganda for civilian and Congressional support. Also, there is the relatively large population of spouses and children of Marines who learn, perhaps even internalize, some of the Corps' folklore. It would take some time to determine how many children of Marines enlist, but it would be more interesting to quantify the extent to which their beliefs and decisions to enlist were influenced by their parents.

Purpose of the Study (1979-1990):

1. To describe the causes and effects of cultural changes and conflicts in the Marine Corps during an approximately 30-year period from the mid-1950s to the mid-1980s.

2. To base recommendations for conflict resolution on the study's findings.

The Edifice Complex investigates the folklore of Marine culture to reach conclusions about which change agents have the most influence on Marine culture, to explain the effects of cultural changes on Marines and on the Corps, and to find a way through the maze of meaning, or cultural definition, to resolve or explain the conflict between generations of Marines.

To the extent that such conflict and evolution may be at odds with the broader values and self-definitions of the grander whole, the Marine Corps as an entity, the conflicts may be damaging to the Corps. In one sense, the one on-going conflict between generations of Marines creates another – a conflict between people and the organization that gives them much of their identity and their military culture. In another sense however, people *are* the organization, and rather than discuss the philosophical distinction between individual men and women, and the organization that has an existence of its own but is composed of those individuals, this analysis will report the older generations of Marines as often representing or defending their judgments of what serves the best interests of the organization.

But whereas there is conflict and change, there is much continuity. Some symbols, such as the Marine Corps emblem, have survived little-changed for more than 100 years in both formal and informal folklore. Some of the favorite symbols used in informal folklore, such as tattoos, include the Marine Corps emblem, the eagle of the emblem's eagle, globe and anchor, or the bulldog mascot. Because the organization maintains an identity as long as there are people in the organization, as a corporation is an entity in the business world, the missions, histories and folklore live in the organization from generation to generation.

Although other limitations will follow, note here that the main conflict is between primarily active duty, younger, male Marines and active duty, older, male Marines. Two points surface: First, the Marine Corps either changes because of influences such as the constant influx of people or it does not, or some elements of Marine culture change while others may not. Second, as a result of cultural change and cultural conflict the Marine Corps is different now than in the past or it is not.

Perspective: I limited this <u>*original*</u> *study to a focus on the largest demographic in the Marine Corps – enlisted male Marines. In order to effectively evaluate changes in current cultural conflict, we need to investigate at least four phenomena which have evolved within Marine Corps culture during the past 20 years, as previously discussed: women Marines breaking into traditionally male occupations (the roles of women Marines in tactical aviation and in ground combat); the dissolution of the so-called Don't Ask, Don't Tell policy barring "gays" from open service in the Armed Forces; the increasing professionalization or higher academic achievement of the non-commissioned officer corps; and the gradual changes in technology impacting the world in general and Marines specifically.*

Because I accomplished this study mainly through the investigation of Marines' folklore and belief structures, I have encountered different points of view from Marines in different stages of their careers.

Hypotheses

The working hypothesis for initial research on internal conflict was:

The influx of new recruits is the major cause of cultural changes and cultural conflicts in the Marine Corps.

As I continued my research, it became apparent that the influx of new recruits equated roughly to cultural evolution, leading to the assertion that change is inevitable in the Marine Corps for a variety of reasons: New recruits are not the only influences on the Corps; civilians in local communities and Congress, the changing character of war and the resulting adaptations of the Corps' mission each may cause planned or unplanned changes in the Corps.

(Next chapter: the Marine process of indoctrinating recruits is solid. The kool-aid drinking Secretary of Defense's survey on attitudes toward homosexuals sharing shower facilities and berthing accommodations might discover the younger generation <u>entered</u> the Marine Corps with more liberal views than older Marines. The gradual creep of all things queer into American consciousness, through commercial advertising and television, radio, internet and film news and entertainment…has gradually brought "queer and gay" out of the world of shocking and into public discussion and awareness specifically during the 20- to 30-year lifespan of that the younger generation of Marines. They entered the Marine Corps (generally) with an attitude of "What's the big deal? It's been <u>in our face</u> since we were kids."[lxiv])

Still, incoming recruits appeared as a major cause of cultural change. Aside from the need to continually recruit new Marines, there are at least two related reasons why incoming recruits change the Corps' culture: First, incoming recruits bring with them the cultural values of the civilian society in which they were reared. As civilian society changes, so change the recruits the Marine Corps takes into training. Second, unless the Corps were to totally isolate itself from civilian society, it would be impossible to completely prohibit the influences of outside change agents – civilian society, for example.

As my research progressed, it became apparent that recruits are only *bearers* of cultural changes in the Marine Corps; they are only one cause of changes affecting the Marine Corps. Yet they are the targets of concern from older generation Marines in the conflict between generations. Civilian society, however, seemed to be another major cause. My guiding research questions then evolved to:

- Are there other ways civilian society causes change in the Corps' culture?
- Are there other external causes of change in Marine Corps culture?

Early conclusions indicated that cultural changes may be planned or unplanned, whether caused by internal or external change agents. Based on these questions and tentative conclusions, I started with the following hypotheses:

1. Internal planned changes affecting Marine Corps culture are caused by either dynamic, forceful, charismatic leaders individually and affect mainly the formal structure (the edifice) of Marine culture and folklore; or are caused by the Corps as an entity, in response to a perceived need to change.

2. Internal unplanned change is evolutionary; may be caused by anyone in the Corps; and affects primarily the informal structure – the complex – of Marine culture or folklore.

3. External planned changes directed at the Marine Corps are caused by change agents with the most influence on Marine Corps culture, laws, regulations, etc. Such change agents are Congress, the Secretary of Defense and the president, and also affect the edifice of formal culture. They may be forced on the Corps indirectly as a

result of changes in all the U.S. Armed Forces, or directly on the Corps because of a perceived need for change.

4. External unplanned changes affecting Marine culture may be caused by a variety of change agents: civilian society acting through recruits entering the Marine Corps, or civilian society because of its increasing proximity to Marine Corps bases and Marines' access to civilian society. External unplanned changes may also be caused by the ambiguous events going on around the Corps – wars, the technology revolution, etc. These changes may affect either the formal or informal culture of the Marine Corps.

Working with these hypotheses, I moved to the following hypotheses about the effects of change:

1. Changes affecting the formal structure of Marine culture have the most influence on older generation Marines' self-concepts, and are the primary cause of conflict between older generation Marines and the Corps, between older generation Marines and external change agents or between the Corps as an entity and external change agents.

2. Changes affecting the informal culture of the Corps have the most influence on the self-concepts of younger generation Marines, and are the primary cause of conflict between younger generation Marines and older generation Marines.

Significance of the study

The elements of folklore – symbols, rituals and myths – shape behavior and influence beliefs. These beliefs are important to members of the culture because they guide actions, provide a sense of belonging to members of the culture and exclude non-members.

In addition to explaining the Marine culture through the findings of this paper, and basing important recommendations to the

Marine Corps on the findings, it may be possible to generalize from the Marine Corps to other organizations, particularly other militaries. Perhaps the findings will be significant to the Marine Corps if for no other reason than that the findings systematically explain the organization's beliefs.

One of the organization's beliefs is expressed in the older generation's occasional claim that things "just aren't what they used to be," suggesting that things – the Corps, the culture, etc., aren't as good as they once were. The question of whether or not the Corps has deteriorated in some way over time is a central issue in this study; the study's findings will be significant if findings indicate cultural change has had a negative impact on the ability of the Marine Corps to perform its missions. Additionally, if the Marine Corps can either prevent unwanted change, or accept change with controlled conflict or conflict that is less damaging to the Corps, the organization may be able to more efficiently perform its missions.

Justification Theory

Justification Theory suggests that internal and external rewards and punishments (aversions) will justify or adequately rationalize one choice over the other. Some of these are tangible; some are intangible: Twenty years of breakfast on two sausage, egg and cheese muffins; two hash browns and super mocha latte will provide an internal, tangible punishment (aversion) in the form of clogged arteries and a heart attack. Getting stopped by a city cop for driving 70 in a 35 mph zone – in front of my office and in front of my peers – will provide both internal and external tangible and intangible punishments: a $200 (tangible) ticket and the (intangible) loss of self-esteem.

The internal, intangible reward I get when my drill instructor calls me a Marine for the first time is far superior to the external tangible rewards of a government paycheck...will last a lifetime...and (generally) will trump any misgivings I have about going into combat.

Control Theory: Perrow (cited in a later chapter) identifies "three orders of control," with first order controls being formal (abiding by written laws and formal consequences for violations); second order controls as less formal – such as standard operating procedures, with less stringent punishments. Third order controls are akin to peer pressure, and may be enforced by decision-making premises identified in cultural narratives, organizational myths or folklore.

The parallel to these concepts resides in *Conformity Theory* (see Aronson in end notes). At the first level, Marines, for example, live in a world of *Compliance* (like boot camp), where they have no choice but to submit or quit. At the next stage, *Identification*, Aronson suggests Marines will "identify" with their captors – the drill instructors...which reads a lot like the storied *Stockholm Syndrome*. Recruits will begin to adopt the dress, mannerisms, political lingo and even belief systems of their more senior Marines. In the final stage, Marines will have more or less internalized these mannerisms, lingo and beliefs as their own, and in time will have become the elder generation of Marines – who recruit and indoctrinate the next generations.

And the same process is on-going in radical Islam.

Chapter Four

Review of Research and Related Literature

Edifice Complex Chapter II

1979-1990

Perspective. Consider the pursuit of understanding "why young men are so susceptible to...'the moral and ascetic charms of war,' and therefore open to exploitation by priests and politicians who still send them off to war..." an academic pursuit. Good, clean, scholarly work should be expected to include both original data collection and analysis of other scholars' data, analysis and conclusions: primary and secondary research. Military strategy in 2010-2013, as an instrument of American National Strategy and Foreign Policy, is grounded in theory (Sun Tzu's "The Art of War," Machiavelli's "The Prince" and "The Art of War," and many other writers). These continue to influence modern political and military thought.

When diplomacy fails and armed forces are employed as an instrument of foreign policy, success in combat – until it happens – is like a **theory**. *A strategy starts with a hypothesis – a proposition that "if we do this, and the bad guys do that...we should win this battle, this campaign, this war." Military leaders test hypotheses by engaging in combat (some kinetic battles, some psychological, indirect, and non-kinetic). Failure in combat should inform the existing theory and allow military and political leaders to refine their theories. A good working strategy (theory) should, in scientific terms, have elements that are* **observable, measurable and repeatable**. *The theory should demonstrate* **internal and external validity**. *In the sense that a battle is an experiment designed to test a theory (not in the literal sense of desiring to go to war to test theories of warfare or* doctrine or the current COIN – <u>counter</u>-<u>in</u>surgency models – but in the sense that war, when it happens, is a laboratory by default), the practitioner of war draws inferences from the experiment.

Case in point: Kilcullen's "The Accidental Guerilla" discusses in detail the impact of "the surge" on combat operations in Iraq in 2007-'08, and the influences of the Anbar Awakening. While some political and military leaders were inferring in late 2007 and into 2008 and 2009 that more troops and more firepower were the primary causal factors in quelling violence in Iraq's Anbar Province, Kilcullen accurately points out that Sheikh Sattar's Anbar Awakening Council (Sahawa al-Anbar) was instrumental in turning Anbar's Sunni population away from al-Qaida. He allows and I agree that both were causes of the relatively calmer Anbar Province. Kilcullen doesn't get to Sattar until later in his book, but Kilcullen and I were in different positions in Anbar. How the general staff of Multi-National Forces – West (MNF-W) interacted with the Anbar Awakening had a significant – positive – impact on merging the effectiveness of both Sattar's irregulars and the Marines in Anbar. But to further **infer** that Anbar's Sunnis shunned al-Qaida because they wanted to join forces with the Americans (or because they finally saw the light and started to "like" the Americans) would be a grave mistake. **Internal validity** requires that the cause comes before the effect, that the two are related, and that there is no other plausible cause. The problem in war is that it becomes close to impossible to isolate a single cause-effect relationship. Sometimes it seems that the only predictable event is when you shoot someone in the right place – he dies.

External validity may also be understood as **generalizability**. This is best and briefly described in the thinking that we should be able to take the theoretical success of the Awakening Council or "Sons of Iraq" from the Sunni experiment in Iraq and apply the principles to the Pashto experiment in Afghanistan. Same religion? Kinda-sorta. Same culture? Not in a long shot. Same psychology? Only in the sense of some version of "Maslow's Hierarchy" and "people have needs..." but how they seek to *fulfill those needs varies greatly from Iraq to Afghanistan. And combat is a fluid, chaotic, continuously evolving dynamic; the external variables, like Iran, coalition support, or Pakistan, change on almost a daily basis. The collective American analysis of* **cause and effect** *in the Global War on Terror has been clumsy at best. Final chapters will dig deeper into on-going efforts to improve socio-cultural understanding.*

In this 30-year "project," my goal has been to build the art and science of this domain and add my own original research to scientific method in ethnography and military intelligence analysis; in social psychology, influence and advertising; in the analysis of history and organizational dynamics. As with the previous chapter, I will offer the original work from 1990; add perspectives that update those earlier summaries; and conclude with more recent research and supporting literature.

Introduction (as of 1987-'89)

This chapter points to prior relevant research and theory. Given that the Marine Corps is a modern (small) society with a definable culture, it is logical to investigate other cultures, or research based on other cultures, to find theories and principles that can be generalized to a study of the Marine Corps. This section is not intended to be exhaustive, but representative.

My research traced the general format:

1. The study of societies, including the controlling influences of folklore and folklore's effects on the self-images of members of a culture; organizational sagas, myths and heroes, and their influences; propaganda and its influences. Also, the study of organizational change, including technology and its effects on the Corps.

2. Social psychology and its explanation of the causes and effects of individual behavior, performance and self-concept, including the principles of propaganda, conformity and cognitive dissonance.

3. The internal susceptibility of the Corps to external influences.

4. Advertising and recruiting, including competition between the Corps and other military services, colleges and industry; the relationships from recruitment advertising to folklore, social psychology and self-concept, and conformity.

I have included illustrative terms, concepts, settings or other phenomena to explain the Marine Corps culture.

Principles of Anthropology and Sociology

Early researchers in anthropology developed their foundations in the study of primitive cultures far removed from modern America, and others more recently in the study of large, modern organizations, including colleges and private sector organizations. Generalizing scientific principles from one setting to another, from one culture to another, is the legitimate method of scientific inquiry. The first principle for discussion is ethnocentrism:

Ethnocentrism

Sumner writes that ethnocentrism is "the technical name for this view of things in which one's own group is the center of everything."[lxv] Sumner explains that folkways govern relationships within, and with people outside the society. He notes further that "each group nourishes its own pride and vanity, boasts itself superior, exalts its own divinities and looks with contempt on outsiders."[lxvi] Further explanation cites some examples of ethnocentrism, dwelling briefly on distinguishing epithets – those sayings which exalt one's own culture – sometimes at the real or imagined expense of another culture.

In militaries of the United States, non-sailors once referred to sailors as *swabbies*, from swabbing or mopping the deck in the days when ships had wooden decks. Marines also call sailors *squids*.

Likewise, American soldiers of some uncertain time ago were called *dog-faced soldiers*, hence the term *doggies* for soldiers. *Wing-wipers* and *flyboys* may be used for members of the Air Force, and Marines are sometimes called *jarheads*, from the idea that they screw their covers (hats) on their heads, or they may be called grunts, although (Army) soldiers are also sometimes called grunts.

Sumner also explains that *cultural patriotism* is a modern phenomenon. He writes: "Patriotism has become one of the first duties and one of the noblest of sentiments. It is what he (the modern man) owes to the state for what the state does for him, and the state is, for the modern man, a cluster of civic institutions from which he draws security and conditions of welfare."[lxvii] An important point in this is that even though the Corps has its own culture, Marines are part of the American culture. It isn't inconsistent to be patriotic to the United States and to the Marine Corps at the same time. Many sea stories include the tag "in front of God, Corps and Country," as in," There I was, right out in front of God, Corps and Country, when all of a sudden..."

Perspective: Consider these concepts in the analysis of radical Salafists. It may in fact be incompatible to be "patriotic" to Iraq, or Saudi Arabia or Afghanistan and to Allah – in the eyes of the Salafists, who, as discussed in earlier chapters, apparently believe that voting for humans to rule a democratic (Westphalian) state is incompatible with owing allegiance to Allah. At least as complex is the situation in kingdoms, such as Saudi Arabia, where some citizens feel disenfranchised (the 10-15 percent Shi'ite), and a sizeable percentage of the population (women) are still waiting for the right leave their own homes without a male escort and the right to drive – legally. Loyalty to the state? To the King? To Allah? To Universal Human Rights?

We can take several points from Sumner: First, American society is composed of recognizably diverse subcultures. A primary mission of Marine recruit training must be, as it indeed is, to indoctrinate recruits in beliefs unique to the Marine subculture, in spite of the many other subcultures from which recruits come. The Corps then becomes a new *melting pot* drawing from the American *melting pot. (This is al-Qaida's challenge: to indoctrinate Muslims in the propaganda of global jihad while accommodating their local grievances. It doesn't always work, or translate, smoothly.)*

Also, depending on the political climate of the day, American society may or may not be completely supportive of the military. It may not be a popular thing to be in the military, as during the Vietnam War. Yet, Sumner writes, "The masses are always patriotic."[lxviii] One senses here that since the draft resistors of the 1960s felt that the war was wrong, the right thing for the nation to do to maintain its self respect was to withdraw from the war, as it did eventually. But this discussion borders on debating the merits of the war, and the point is that the cultural norms of the Corps must at times compete with the cultural undercurrent of the larger society or other masses.

Perspective. American war protestors have been part of the social and political landscape in the US since our colonial days and the Revolution. Interestingly – the wars in Iraq and Afghanistan may be at least as illegitimate or ill-conceived experiments as Vietnam in some respects yet support for the American G.I. has never been stronger in the years since September 11, 2001. We need to counter Insanely Radical Islamist Fundamentalist Terrorism just like we needed to counter Communism – but **how** *we go about it truly does matter.*

Sumner also asserts that ethnocentric displays of "jealousy, vanity, truculency and ambition are... easily awakened in a crowd and...[are] sure to be popular."[lxix] The idea is that people tend to believe their in-group is good, wise, powerful, etc., and that other groups are less so. Within a subculture this may be cohesive; between societies, truculence can be destructive, even lead to war. That collective cultural self-images of goodness, rightness and wisdom can be cohesive leads to a deeper investigation of purposes for cultural self-images. Ethnocentrism may be displayed through stories, which in my view, are long epithets.

It's obvious that evaluation of the phenomenon of ethnocentrism invades this manuscript. Initial discussions of religious, ethnic, cultural and political ethnocentric points of view were presented in the first two chapters. We will dissect this phenomenon more. The year (2009-'10) I spent working in psychological operations – American propaganda – provided ample opportunity for casual reading during off-hours on the subject of American exceptionalism. Those who write national strategy and policy carefully consider domains such as "air, land and sea superiority and supremacy," building, maintaining and fielding the world's finest air, land and naval forces, as well as space, nuclear and cyber (including information) warfare. While we have a new cyberwarfare command and speak of information and influence dominance, we don't necessarily understand the cultures we seek to influence as well as we are able to dominate other nations militarily. When Americans express "God Bless America," do they mean "to the exclusion of...or at the expense of... all people of all other nations? This gets to the core of ethnocentrism.

Myths, legends and sagas

Wilkins writes: "Though anthropologists have found the myths and legends of primitive tribes critical to the understanding of...social groupings, students of contemporary work organizations have with few exceptions neglected phenomena such as stories and legends..."[lxx] Wilkins makes his point after a prologue of stories and research based in educational and industrial organizations. One thing *The Edifice Complex* emphasizes is that the study of the roles of stories and sagas in modern work organizations **has** largely been ignored, but when studies of work organizations have been conducted, to borrow from Wilkins' lament, students of stories and sagas have almost completely neglected researching militaries.

My final chapters will address the changes in socio-cultural, ethnographic and anthropological research since the start of the wars in Afghanistan and Iraq. Some of the recommendations I made in this book – in 1990 – have finally come to see light in the creation of the **Human Terrain System (HTS)** and **Female Engagement Teams (FETs)**, both off to a rocky start, and neither certain of continued funding. The general idea of the programs is a focus on assisting Army and Marine infantry commanders at the brigade (Army) and regimental (Marine) level, with an improved understanding of local cultures and social structures. Human Terrain Team members typically include professionals with academic degrees in anthropology, sociology, or regional cultural and language studies relevant to Iraq and Afghanistan. The question of funding and longevity for these programs lies in the cultural predisposition of the military and the ability of those who organize, train and equip HTTs and FETs to professionalize their cadre.

Little boys and girls who grow up to become battalion commanders or even commanders of brigades, regiments, divisions and corps likely grew up playing "army," "cops and robbers," or "cowboys and Indians." (Or cowboys and Pakistanis.) They played with guns and didn't likely express a desire between the ages of, say, 5 and 12 to become high risk ethnographers, civil-military operations officers, sociologists or combat anthropologists. They wanted to be soldiers and Marines. They wanted to carry guns and go into combat. I don't even feel a need to defend this assertion. It should be obvious that the armed forces (emphasis on "armed") is heavily weighted to a culture of kinetic warfare. Combat.

A significant deficit still remains in researching and understanding our own military culture.

Control functions

By way of elaboration and definition, Wilkins notes that "stories appear to perform control functions in organizations, which Perrow[lxxi] labeled 'third order controls,' and Simon (cited in Wilkins) called 'control over decision premises'." Ouchi (also cited in Wilkins) discussed similar phenomena, that is "organizational control through shared traditions."[lxxii] That the Marine Corps is replete with shared traditions is yet to be documented and analyzed, but accept for the moment that shared traditions, including stories, are not unique as control agents in primitive tribes or modern educational or industrial organizations. Stories and shared traditions exist in the Marine Corps as well.

Geertz defined stories as symbols: "any object, act, event, quality or relation which serves as a vehicle for conception...(the conception [is] the symbol's meaning),...tangible formulations of notions, abstractions from experience fixed in perceptible forms, concrete embodiments of ideas, attitudes, judgments, longings or beliefs."[lxxiii] The gist is that symbols are tangible or intangible vehicles which communicate shared cultural values.

Stories, or myths as other researchers have called them, communicate shared values and symbolism.[lxxiv] Wilkins notes that they communicate values and unify members of the culture; they can tell of the founding of the organization, of charismatic leaders, military heroes, or other significant events in the organization. Such events in the Marine Corps could include battles and wars, but may also include events not directly related to the defense mission of the Corps, such as the worst inspection, the best night on the town in Olongapo in the Philippines, or "how tough my drill instructor was."

Before moving to other definitions of controlling stories and myths, note above that Wilkins describes stories as performing a control function akin to Perrow's *third-order* controls. Wilkins interprets *first-order controls* as being those formal controls based on direct supervision, *second-order controls* as a bit less formal standard operating procedures, and *third-order controls* as cultural givens.[lxxv] As with other organizations, all three forms of control may be found in the Marine Corps. But because the Corps is a military organization, it may be expected that first-order controls would be more common or more necessary because of the need to maintain order and discipline. This study has uncovered which forms of controls are used in what situations and why.

Wilkins also noted that other elements of a culture, such as language, ritual and magic, may perform similar controlling functions. He also described stories as the window to the tacit knowledge of an organization, a *map* by which to read an organization's culture. This parallels the concept of *The Edifice Complex's* "maze of meaning."

Legitimization

Similarly, Kamens describes the myths of an organization as legitimizing for both the organization and the individuals of the organization.[lxxvi] Although his research is based on educational organizations, it is a small cognitive step to either see the Marine Corps as an educational organization, or generalize the concept of legitimization to the Corps. Kamens' research points to the understanding that society uses schools to create "categories of membership in society to which important job and other rights and social meanings are attached."[lxxvii] Kamens also notes that schools *legitimize* these rights by "institutionalizing ideas about the qualities and abilities of graduates versus non-graduates." Society expects certain things of graduates of certain schools; images or ideas about Harvard graduates differ from images or ideas of graduates from small colleges with unfamiliar names, in part because of these institutionalized societal myths. In other words – over time, organizations develop a set of expectations: we expect a particular level of quality from Cadillac or BMW, from MacDonald's or Ruth's Chris Steakhouse, from Harvard or the University of Phoenix, or from the Marine Corps and Marines.

Likewise, although civilian images and ideas about Marines

differ from their images of airmen, sailors or soldiers, differences in cross-societal images seem to be more distinct between the cultures of the four military services. Just as there is an "edifice complex" behind which the Marine Corps remains relatively anonymous from the civilian world, there is a collective edifice complex of similar understanding surrounding the militaries as a whole. As a generalization (now based on more than 30 years of observation), militaries understand each other better than they understand civilian organizations, or better than civilian organizations understand the militaries. Members of the military have certain images and expectations of the other services which differ from the images and expectations held by civilians.

Kamens explains that schools are "the agencies that ritually certify graduates as members of social status groups to whose privileges they are entitled. All of these processes operate independently of any direct socialization effects schools have on students."[lxxviii] He explains further that schools symbolically redefine graduates as possessing skills or qualities which separate them from non-graduates.

Schools may "redefine graduates as possessing skills...," but the notion in practice seems slightly flawed in its application to the Marine Corps or other military services. *Symbolic* redefinition only works to a point. Not all Harvard graduates are created equal. Not all freshly minted privates or 2nd lieutenants are equal. The concept only works in the military when graduates demonstrate the skills embedded in society's cultural myths. The Corps promises a basically trained Marine private out of boot camp, but cannot guarantee combat performance. Courage is less quantifiable than the intellectual skills taught in boot camp, and the Marine Corps doesn't promise "courage." With boot camp and a follow-on school, the basic Marine can "shoot, move and communicate."

Perspective. This is not an update in cultural changes but in my own theory base. As a college professor and as a management consultant teaching leadership skills in the private sector, I've come to define the Marine, the Harvard MBA and the industrial engineer also with the **theory metaphor.** *Each is a hypothesis – waiting to be tested in his or her own unique work environment. We want to see that their efforts (causes) lead to certain effects, are co-related, and that there are no plausible alternative causes. We want to see that their efforts are observable, measurable and repeatable. The individual as a theory parallels doctrine, or the organization, as a theory as described earlier.[lxxix]*

Non-performers are weeded out of the system by more formal evaluation in the military than in civilian work organizations, many of which do not have structured processes of written annual or semi-annual evaluation, as in the military. Yet, when there is a civilian image of soldiers, sailors, airmen or Marines having courage in combat, that image is based on stories of the services' performance in battle. Combat both legitimizes heroes and exposes felons. But because of the broader social myth, the single Marine can become a small town "hero" just by association with the Corps and its myths.

To parallel Kamens' argument, Marine recruits are symbolically redefined with a recognizable Marine haircut, Marine uniforms, Marine language and other tangible and intangible attributes of a Marine Corps identity. Fluctuating social norms and values over time impact the status of Marines as a collective whole, and when it is admirable to be a Marine, Marines are admired, but individuals and the experiences of the corporate whole have defined the individual as a Marine.

A Marine or solider walking through an airport – in uniform – stands out. A Marine or soldier – in civilian attire – still stands out, but most civilians would probably guess "military." Fellow Marines, active duty or retired, would likely be able to distinguish between a Marine and a soldier in civilian clothes. And the difference between a Marine and a sailor or airman, in civilian attire, would generally be more apparent. It's the haircut, the build, how they dress, how they carry themselves, maybe tattoos (but not necessarily)…but mostly an indefinable "bearing."

Demographics and social control

One of Kamens' key points is in the description of organizational structures used to legitimize graduates. Demographic structure and geographical location, he wrote, are used to "isolate initiates from potential sources of disruption and corruption."[lxxx] Isolation, Kamens noted, is from cities and the corruption of urban society; demographic structure may include the separation of the sexes.

The urbanization of areas surrounding Marine bases over the past several decades has been one external source of unplanned change affecting Marine Corps culture. An inter-related influence on the Corps' culture is rooted in the increased mobility of individual Marines. With higher pay and better standards of living, for especially lower ranking enlisted military people, owning cars and having mobility is far more common in the 1980s than 50, 25 or even 15 years earlier. Other than institutionalized isolation during boot camp, the built-in isolation from civilian life caused by geography or income in years past has all-but faded. *(Now in 2013 one might rightly observe that this isolation has diminished even more. There are exceptions. Some military bases are still relatively isolated, by design, and the diversions and entertainment "outside the gate" at locations like Marine Corps Base Camp Lejeune, NC; MCB 29 Palms, CA; or Fort Bragg, NC, are extremely limited. Air Force missile sites in North Dakota and tiny Naval outposts (like Diego Garcia in the Indian Ocean) have similar challenges.)*

As for demographic separation of the sexes, men and women still undergo a segregated training regimen in enlisted Marine boot camp. But, whereas until the 1970s and before, women typically reported to a Women Marines' company after basic training and lived in a barracks guarded by an armed sentry, today women are integrated into mixed platoons, companies and battalions and the armed sentries around their barracks are gone.

Perspective. As noted above, women Marines have been serving in Iraq and Afghanistan, with distinction, since 2003 and 2001, respectively. And women have been graduating from US service academies (West Point, Air Force Academy and the Naval Academy) – but not without consequence.[lxxxi]

The act of separating men from women in training is a form of social control. Alone it may not seem significant or symbolic. But consider the power of the organization; in dictating who goes where and how they train, the organization is exercising control. This is especially true in the services' policies on fraternization. Legislating who can date whom based on rank, or governing who should or should not fall in love is a form of denying some of the **civil liberties** civilian Americans take for granted. Military people give up certain liberties when they enlist, and the military has historically been given the power to control such things. Similar examples have been found over the years with regard to homosexuality and regulations governing hair length, off-duty employment, etc. (I recall the story of an attractive woman Marine who made the newspapers when the Corps discharged her for posing unclothed in a men's magazine. Her choice of off-duty employment was not in keeping with the image the Corps wished to project.[lxxxii])

Control is symbolic. It sets the organization apart from the individual. The organization is more powerful collectively than any one individual, even though the organization is composed of the individuals. The ubiquitous *they*, as in: "They screwed up my pay," "They won't let me go on leave," "They made me get a haircut," is the organization. Speaking for the organization are those in positions of responsibility, generally, and who by virtue of rank are obligated to praise or punish in the name of the organization. That is why at the start of *The Edifice Complex* I saw the older generation as representing the organization. The older generation, like the organization, is generally more conservative than the younger generation. Fraternization and homosexuality did not seem to be problems in past decades. These were either quietly hushed or did not surface. Perhaps civilian norms and the attention of the media have caused more attention to be paid to homosexuality and fraternization, and perhaps these were indeed not problems in the past.

Perspective: Fraternization issues, at least in the Marine Corps, have not made the news lately as much as the broader Department of Defense discussions surrounding the topic of gays in the military – leading up to the dissolution of Don't Ask, Don't Tell. In my observation, media choices tend toward conflict stories, and gays in the military as a topic is more controversial, offers more conflict and "sells more papers." On the other hand, reports of sexual assault in the armed forces have multiplied exponentially in 2013, leading to Congressional investigations with service chiefs (Commandant of the Marine Corps, Chiefs of Staff of the Army and Air Force, Chief of Naval Operations) testifying on Capitol Hill. Despite some of the blame being laid on "stress on the military due to 12 years of war," and the concept that some men in uniform (may) tend to view women as something like "second-class soldiers" because they have been prohibited from direct combat assignments, it is not clear if sexual assaults have increased or if reporting has increased – to reflect that phrase "Actual numbers are likely much higher." What is interesting is that men as victims of sexual assault in the military outnumber women as victims.[lxxxiii]

While deployed to Iraq, I was tangentially involved in a fraternization issue. I advised a junior officer on bringing charges of fraternization against a senior officer accused of attempted fraternization and sexual harassment in the case of a junior enlisted Marine. The case was not "swept under the rug," but dealt with expeditiously and professionally. With regard to "representing the organization," I started this manuscript while I was a staff sergeant and tended to see those senior to me as representatives of the Corps. With 20 years of headlines and hindsight, allow me to amend that perception. Even junior Marines charged (and convicted or acquitted) in incidents of rape, for example, or violations of the laws of armed combat make the news and instantly represent the Marine Corps to outside observers as well.[lxxxiv][lxxxv]

What we get in a new generation of men and women serving side-by-side in a combat zone are some challenging phenomena: Husbands and wives serving in the same unit. Do we enforce a no-conjugal visits forward operating base (FOB)? It varied from commander to commander in Iraq. And then there are phrases like "Baghdad Beautiful" and "Fallujah Cute." Both men and women who would not have earned a second glance in the States – based on physical attractiveness – are found to be temporarily "good looking enough" while deployed. But for the adventurous – how are they supposed to "date" (they're not.) when the only places to go were work, the chow hall, and the gym. Sleeping quarters: 12-foot X 42-foot trailers with three 12X14 rooms, with two sets of bunk beds, cordoned off by rows of 8-foot high "Texas T"concrete blast walls and Hesco Barriers – were designed as much to keep the men away from the women as they were to protect the occupants from rockets and mortars. And the Marine Corps didn't send them off to Iraq and Afghanistan to "hook up with" boyfriends and girlfriends anyway.

In any case, it seems civilian society has set the standard which has allowed Marines to challenge policies on such issues. Those who do challenge the system challenge the organization and the older generation.

In exercising social control the Marine Corps manifests itself as an entity. The Corps legitimizes itself. Social control, however, is but one symbolic manifestation of the organization. As noted above, other elements of the culture also define the society. Manning suggests four assumptions in the analysis of symbolic social control:

1. Social object and process take on meaning and significance from the frame of reference within which they are placed.

2. By focusing on and extracting meaning from some feature of a behavioral display, people attempt to constrain and control each other. They not only are aware of the ritualization of social order, they are able to call on its principles to create and maintain interpersonal control.

3. Social order and the social hierarchies on which it is based are represented symbolically in the selective display of symbols that large segments of the population are predisposed or prepared to accept.

4. The process of symbol selection, the capacity to select and disseminate symbols and to limit the range of meanings attributed to social action are all fundamentally based on power.[lxxxvi]

The first point describes the creation of symbols and rituals. Manning based his research on social control of the sort practiced by police departments. It's clearly possible to apply these assumptions to the creation of symbols and rituals by the Marine Corps; the precept is generalizable from both archeological and anthropological perspectives. Organizations and units within organizations create symbols, rituals and stories (badges, patches, songs and "ditties," tales and other folklore). Those who are affected by them ascribe meaning to them. Or, as Manning writes, "The objects and processes take on meaning." *(See notes below on al-Qaida.)*

Manning's second assumption tells of both organizational control and peer pressure. The sound of a siren and the appearance of flashing lights should cause most drivers to react a certain way, to move to the shoulder of a highway for example. Not to do so is deviant behavior. As enforcers of social controls, policemen can also rely on other symbols to cause people to exert peer pressure as a social control in their absence. Stop lights usually cause people to stop and go on signal at intersections (but likely more effectively when other people are watching).

The same type of social control is evident in Marine boot camp. Once recruits learn the actual and symbolic power of the drill instructor, they will respond to his commands. The *Smokey the Bear* hat (known in the Marine Corps as a *campaign cover*) worn by drill instructors is a powerful symbol to recruits and other Marines.

The *mutually accepted symbols* that cause peer pressure to take over as social control take a bit longer to understand and internalize. This concept can be seen in the ceremony of the parade: Recruits in the rear of a platoon cannot be visually supervised by the single drill instructor in command of the platoon. Yet, if properly disciplined (self-disciplined), they will not speak or move.

One purpose of recruit training is to instill a feeling for teamwork; recruits soon learn to chastise, sometimes violently perhaps, other recruits who get the whole platoon in trouble through deviant behavior. Where discipline instilled by the drill instructor stops, indoctrinated self-discipline and peer pressure take over.

(This concept was more or less accurately depicted in the 1992 film "A Few Good Men," with the Navy trial lawyer portrayed by Tom Cruise taking on the Marine Colonel played by Jack Nicholson. Cruise is defending two enlisted Marines charged with the murder of a fellow Marine at the Marine Barracks in Guantanamo, Cuba, but ends up getting Nicholson to launch a tirade (You can't handle the truth!) on the challenges of defending the "walls" of America and admitting that he ordered "the code red," – the extrajudicial punishment of the Marine who died.) A colleague still on active duty reminds me that the Marine Corps jealously guards its image, a mindset that informs the Corps' decisions on whether or not to lend advisory support to Hollywood films, for example. My colleague indicates that the Corps provided advisory support to "True Lies," with Arnold Schwarzenegger, and not "A Few Good Men," based on the scripts.)

The third assumption, that hierarchies are displayed by the selective use of symbols, tells of that process in the Corps whereby

Marines are reminded of their place in their society. That is, it is common to see Marines display their rank even while not in uniform, by placing rank stickers in their car windows for example, or the renewed popularity of tattoos – on both men and women. Rank stickers in a car window subtly enforce the cultural taboo against mingling ranks. Officers and enlisted Marines usually live in separate housing areas; they go to separate on-base clubs. There are many such examples of the selective use of symbols in the Marine Corps.

Perspective. Although the armed forces continue to maintain separate on-post housing areas for officers and enlisted service members, the "cultural taboos against the mingling of ranks" continue to fade. In my estimation, combat operations in Iraq and Afghanistan put particularly junior officers and enlisted Marines in closer quarters, and those enlisted Marines have earned respect.

Another primary factor, which I will evaluate in more detail in coming chapters, is the continuing professionalization and higher education of the enlisted cadre of the Marine Corps. When I enlisted in 1973, perhaps 50 percent of my recruit training platoon entered the service with a high school diploma. Some could barely read. Many enlisted Marines served entire careers of 20 to 30 years without attending college. In 2013 it is not uncommon to find staff sergeants and gunnery sergeants with bachelor's and master's degrees; and the occasional master sergeant or master gunnery sergeant finishing a PhD (although it has taken 15 to 20 years to complete eight years of college – between deployments and combat assignments).

But officers and enlisted Marines can go to the same off-base clubs, a situation which has led to many fraternization cases. This is a situation over which the Marine Corps seems to have no formal control, and the Corps relies on the sense and good judgment of especially the senior fraternizer to stop illicit relationships once discovered. Access to clubs off base is another example of the result of higher pay and increasing urbanization around military bases.

Predisposition

The idea that a population is "predisposed or prepared to accept as legitimate" relates to two kindred ideas in the Corps. Predisposition is that inclination of new recruits to accept national symbols as legitimate. The Stars and Stripes and National Anthem are tangible symbols; the primacy of the United States as a superpower and the war on terror are symbolic in concept.

Preparation in advance of predisposition is another matter. Recruits are not at first prepared to accept the authority of rank; it is probably alien to most young civilian men and women. Preparation comes through indoctrination. Recruits don't come *tabula rasa* in every sense, but drill instructors exploit their relative youth and willingness to accept Marine Corps values during the initial indoctrination of Marine Corps basic training. Recruits' attitudes are not so much changed as added to and molded to fit the Corps' culture.

Perspective. Two points: To bring this paper forward 20 years, the reader might consider the concept of predisposition with regard to current thinking regarding Muslims and their impact on the United States. Are Americans predisposed to "hate" Muslims (all snakes are creepy)? Or are Americans transferring the understandable feelings from 9/11 to "all" Muslims in the US? Just Arabs? Or – is it just human…ethnocentric…to mistrust "people who are not like us?" Second: it's important to note that while it is possible to enlist in the US Army up to age 42, the age limit for Marines with no prior service is 28, and recruiters observe that their primary target audience is the 17- to 24-year-old recruit. In plain English, and intuitively, older recruits are less "predisposed" to accept a drill instructor's legitimacy than are the younger recruits. A 28-year-old recruit might be older than his drill instructors. Still trainable – but with a different point of view than his younger peers.

Manning's final assumption about power suggests two kinds

of power: organizational and individual. The first, organizational power, is inherent in the laws which establish the Marine Corps. That same organizational power is likewise inherent in the creation, manipulation and application of symbols. Mass media America disseminates symbols through television, radio, movies, newspapers, and magazines *(and now the Internet, video games and cell phones)*, but also by way of T-shirts, hats with logos, belt buckles, tattoos, rings, tie pins, watches, golf balls and many more curios and souvenirs. The Corps creates and officially sanctions some of these; official and unofficial organizations and agencies like the Marine Corps Association and Marine Corps League create and distribute others. All have a potential impact on creating that predisposition to accept or not accept the Marine Corps; many therefore also impact recruiting. *(The Marine Corps has a trademark / licensing office based in the Headquarters Marine Corps offices in the Pentagon.)*

The Corps' symbols have come into existence over time: the Marine Corps emblem, the bulldog mascot, the scarlet and gold colors, etc. The artifacts which carry the symbols evolve over time. Flags change; T-shirts carry different slogans; souvenir coins have become more common as collectibles while embroidered patches have become less so.

Unplanned Internal Change

In relatively modern times, Marines are commonly observed expressing the Latin motto of the Corps, *Semper Fidelis* (always faithful) informally as *Semper Fi*. But the phrase *Semper Fi* never appeared on a bumper sticker until the 1980s. It was usually the complete *Semper Fidelis*. In the aftermath of the bomb blast that killed 220 Marines in Beirut, Lebanon, in October 1983, the Indianapolis Star delivered the following story:

While the Commandant [of the Marine Corps, General Paul X. Kelley] was visiting an intensive care ward at Frankfurt, Germany, on Oct.

25, he observed [Lance Corporal] Nashton [who was wounded in the Beirut bombing] 'with more tubes going in and out of his body than [he] had ever seen.' [The Commandant said,] 'When he heard me say who I was, he grabbed my camouflaged coat, went up to the collar and counted the stars. He squeezed my hand, and then he wrote…'Semper Fi.'"[lxxxvii]

The rest of the story explains how the Commandant was understandably moved by the experience. He later presented the Marine with a plaque bearing the four stars of his rank, the Marine Corps emblem and a personal message. That scribbling of *Semper Fi* led to the launch of a bumper sticker with the abbreviated motto in the short form.[lxxxviii] A junior Marine with no real power had a hand in re-creating a symbol. The lance corporal and his junior-ranking peers, members of the most numerous segment of their culture, help popularize informal symbols and influence the folklore of their culture.

An interesting sidelight to this story is the information provided by a colleague who noted that during World War II and for some time thereafter, Marines used the term *Semper Fi* in the expression "*Semper Fi Mac!*" – which literally meant, "Screw you. I got mine; get your own!"

Through his investigation of policemen, Manning explains the necessity of expressing symbols, in one sense to test the acceptance of the symbols by others. His example is of "an 'old time' policeman" demonstrating the dexterous use of a night stick in the presence of potentially troublesome boys on a city street. There is symbolism in the ritual; there is a message in the symbol to be accepted or not accepted by the observer. In the Corps such posturing could be in the sporting of tattoos, wearing T-shirts emblazoned with any of several Marine symbols, or some other patriotic or ethnocentric act. There are differences, however; how one displays such behavior is situational, depending on the audience and the purpose. Some kinds of expression of self are appropriate in front of peers, other kinds of behavior are appropriate in front of non-peer Marines, and still others in the company of civilians.

A verbal expression of self in the Corps is the guttural utterance of "*arrugah*," or "*oo-ragh*," a war whoop of sorts. It is a sound of satisfaction, pride, acceptance and the like. It has been likened to the primal scream. Marines make this sound and variations of it almost anywhere in a peer setting, but not as commonly in a civilian environment. Another example is the act of going home on leave in uniform; it is in fact encouraged by the Marine Corps. In both acts there is the expression of self through ritual and symbolism.

Perspective. This "ar-RUGH-ah" utterance has been emasculated in the past 20 years – likely since the day after I retired the first time and is now a spoken "oo. rah." This is one of those signs of the artificial gentrification of the Marine Corps in the past generation.

Manning noted that various "props and settings, fronts and appearances, expressive control, mystification and misrepresentation" can be used to "convince the audience of the ideal nature of the actor's motives and intentions, one's belief in the part being played, and the truth of the message."[lxxxix] Perhaps the purest form of this expression is in the act of going into combat, which is legitimizing for the individual and symbolic for the individual and the organization; it is symbolic of patriotism and legitimizes completely the title *combat Marine* or warrior.

Perspective. Expressing or displaying the "legitimization" of combat comes in various forms. On all but the camouflage utility uniform (which Marines wear to work at most stateside duty assignments), Marines wear ribbons – personal and unit awards and decorations – above the left breast pocket. (Or medals on the distinctive dress blue uniform.) Marines and other service members can quickly "size up" a fellow warrior – read a "rack of ribbons" like a short biography, and determine if he or she has had duty in Iraq, Afghanistan, Bosnia or Desert Storm, for example. Awards for bravery in combat, the Bronze Star, Silver Star, Navy Cross or Medal of Honor, are additional symbols. But because Marines wear that camouflage utility uniform to work at stateside duty stations (and there are no readily visible, telling signs of "combat veteran" status), Marines might then resort to stories from their assignments in Iraq or Afghanistan, or bumper stickers or T-shirts signaling the same kind of information.

As for misrepresentation, Marines know better than anyone when another Marine exaggerates. My drill instructor in boot camp often chided recruits not to exaggerate when writing home because he claimed he once had a recruit who wrote, "Dear Mom, I'm writing from a burning tank." (There are no tanks at boot camp.) *Do an independent Internet search on the concept of "stolen valor." In the Internet age – it's more than difficult to pass off lies about heroism and military service.*

Of the many expressions of symbol and ritual described above, we've investigated several in this text, but ritual and symbol are only two elements of folklore. Ritual and symbol lead up to and presage combat experiences, the practice for war many Marines never fight. Through the experiences of those who do go into combat, ritual and symbol emerge in a continuing cycle.

And now, after ten-plus years in Afghanistan and eight years in Iraq, most Marines have seen combat; they all have their war stories. There's a pecking order of sorts for those who go "downrange," or travel to "the sandbox" for a combat tour of duty. In Iraq, for example, many Marines and other servicemen and women have been based on forward operating bases, <u>including</u> the rifle companies and brigade or regimental combat team headquarters. But it was the supply convoys, infantry rifle platoons and companies who went outside the wire and engaged in combat, or faced the dangers of improvised explosive devices (IEDs). Marines who spent most or all of their time "on the FOB," such as support elements like intelligence, legal, administrative headquarters, motor transport mechanics, logistics, in relatively safer conditions were referred to as "fobbits."

Different levels of sacrifice earn different levels of respect: Marines revere and memorialize their comrades killed in action; wounded survivors of combat earn a higher measure of respect, as do those awarded medals for valor. Combat veterans with multiple tours rate more than those with one tour, and combat veterans with any time "in the box" rate more than those who have apparently evaded a combat tour – even if beyond their control.

Myth, saga and story

Myth too leads into and comes from combat training and combat. Myths and other elements of folklore shape beliefs and actions, and emerge through each evolution either reinforced or somehow changed.

Myth has been a powerful bond for *tribes* of people for at least all of recorded history. Joseph Campbell, interviewed by journalist Bill Moyers, said:

[Campbell:] Greek and Latin and biblical literature used to be part of everyone's education. Now, when these were dropped, a whole tradition of Occidental mythological information was lost. It used to be that these stories were in the minds of the people. When the story is in your mind, then you see its relevance to something happening in your own life. It gives you perspective on what's happening to you.

[Moyers:] So we tell stories to try to come to terms with the world, to harmonize our lives with reality?

[Campbell:] Yes.[xc]

Marines tell stories about themselves and about each other. Sometimes they're true, sometimes they're embellished truths, sometimes they're outright lies. But the story is not the myth; the *feeling*, *sense*, or *meaning* of the story is the myth.

Ellul lists some of the myths of modern man as "hero, nation, work, youth and happiness."[xci] We can understand myths as ideals or goals for members of a tribe, group or organization. Stories with embedded myths can be used to instruct, to point the way to an ideal. Modern man is often disappointed in his affected sophistication when reality doesn't match the ideal: when heroes fall, when the nation errs, when youth is lost. Moyers also asked Campbell:

What happens when a society no longer embraces a powerful mythology?

[Campbell:] What we've got on our hands. If you want to see what it means to have a society without any rituals, read the New York Times.[xcii]

Perspective. Here I will comment more as a (young) senior citizen (I'm over 55) than as a scholar: And again – I am divided. By the time I started this research, in my 20's, I was already a father. I could see the decay in the United States…dilution of the American culture I grew up in in the 1950's and '60s. I wondered, as many fathers and mothers have, "What kind of world have I brought my children into?" Yet, when I returned from Iraq in 2007, and made a short trip back to Houston, Texas, on consulting business, I joined a friend and his wife at their son's little league baseball game. I witnessed two-parent families cheering their sons and daughters in America's pastime. They grilled hot dogs on the sidelines. They drove Chevrolets. The only thing missing that afternoon was apple pie. America's myths aren't dead, but they are certainly competing for influence in a pluralistic culture layered over with other influences, other cultural narratives, amplified by mass media and commercial entertainment.

Clark uses the term *sagas* to define stories which express the myth of a corporate self. In his investigation of organizational saga he presents research from Antioch, Reed and Swarthmore colleges. Clark explains:

An organizational saga is a collective understanding of a unique accomplishment based on historical exploits of a formal organization,

offering strong normative bonds within and outside the organization.
Believers give loyalty to the organization and take pride and identity from
it.[xciii]

Clark explains that a saga is more than a history; belief is crucial. His retelling of sagas from these three colleges serves to illustrate the power sagas have in moving people to action.

With Antioch College, for example, in the early years of the 20th Century the school was at the end of a 60-year period of "little money, weak staff, few students and obscurity. In 1919 a charismatic utopian reformer, Arthur E. Morgan…" led the school to become characterized "by a sense of exciting history, unique practice and exceptional performance."[xciv]

This setting is one of three Clark said may be exploited in the heroic saga; it is the organization in crisis seeking a charismatic leader. The other two settings Clark described are the autonomous new organization with no rigid structure, and the established organization that is neither new nor in a crisis, but "ready for evolutionary change." Clark's findings appear empirically sound, given the simplicity of the hypothesis that belief and emotion enveloped by a charismatic leader can control or influence the organization when embraced by most members of the organization.

Planned internal change

The Marine Corps went through the new organization phase many years ago and, according to its histories, shared in the glories of winning the Revolutionary War. Yet the young Corps had its troubles. Millett writes that during his time as Commandant of the Marine Corps from 1820 to 1859, Archibald Henderson had repeated chronic problems with officers and enlisted men. There were problems with keeping officers in service, widespread practice of political patronage and use of social connections. The Navy paid better at sea and officers commonly "skirted Henderson's orders on recruiting, discipline, accounting and drill." By law and Navy Department policy, the Corps was to enlist only native-born Americans between 21 and 40, but officers also enlisted aliens, minors and indentured servants characterized by "illiteracy, social and emotional immaturity and...lack of useful skills."[xcv]

Henderson shaped the Corps during what is still the longest tenure for a Marine commandant. Millett writes that Henderson argued with the Navy and Army over control of Marines and the Corps, and battled presidents and Congress for better pay, food, and clothing. He is revered by Marines as "the Grand Old Man of the Corps." Yet, Millett observes, even though he "increased clothing allowances, cut liquor rations, improved training, granted discharges, improved ration and fuel allowances and persuaded Congress to build better barracks, Henderson made little progress in making the Corps attractive."

Commandant Henderson was one of the early charismatic leaders of the type Clark described at *academic* organizations. We'll take a look at other Marines later to draw conclusions and further support the application of Clark's findings.

Note Clark's description of the organizational saga:

With a general emphasis on normative bonds, organizational saga refers to a unified set of publicly expressed beliefs about a formal group that (a) is rooted in history, (b) claims unique accomplishment, and (c) is held with sentiment by the group.[xcvi]

Clark explains the utility of sagas as: 1. a tool with which the worker rationalizes his existence in the organization, claiming identity of self, 2. a means of allowing the worker to see the organization as valuable to himself, and 3. a means of allowing or causing the worker to disassociate himself from the outside world, seeing his organization as "the only reality."

Perspective. Consider this third concept in relation to irhabists and takfiri who define absolutely everyone who doesn't believe what they believe as either kaffir (apostate) or infidel – and worthy of death. Consider also that Islam has existed for 1400 years; Islam and its various sects have created artifacts, symbols, rituals and sagas which correspond with each of Clark's descriptions and under-pin the message that sustains (or propaganda that radicalizes) the faithful, the irhabist, the takfir.

In this context, consider the assessment of al-Qaida as of mid-2013, from US Special Operations Command Intelligence Directorate:

Ideology – The Tie That Binds

The ideology is the common link binding the core, affiliates, and adherents into a transnational brotherhood of believers. The ideology retains its pull because it incorporates a potent mix of anti-Western/anti-Zionist propaganda, utopianism, and socio-political and cultural grievances. Moreover, it provides religious justification for violence and integrates members into a struggle of global significance. The ideology offers an asymmetric strategy to defeat the U.S. through a prolonged battle of attrition, which is intended to exhaust the political will and financial resources of the U.S. The combination of Islamism (prescribed Islamic beliefs, laws and customs) and Salafism (a literal interpretation of Islamic doctrine) ensures the ideology will endure even if al-Qaida core leaders are eliminated.

The Hadith recites the Prophet Muhammad saying, "If you see the black banners coming from Khorasan, join that army….they will reach Jerusalem and plant their flag." Khorasan is the term for a historical region spanning Northeastern and Eastern Iran and parts of Turkmenistan, Uzbekistan, Tajikistan, Afghanistan, and Northwestern Pakistan. The region has critical importance in Islamic theology, law and philosophy and was the seat of two major Islamic empires (Umayyad and Abbasid).

Bin Laden's 1996 declaration of war against the United States, a main text for al-Qaida members, ends with the dateline "Friday, August 23, 1996, in the Hindu Kush, Khorasan, Afghanistan." It's not a coincidence that Bin Laden made al-Qaida's flag black; he also regularly cited the hadith and referenced Khorasan when recruiting, motivating and fundraising. Detained al-Qaida operatives have repeatedly stated they were convinced that by joining al-Qaida, they were fulfilling words of the Prophet and contributing to Islam's expansion that will instigate a final battle between good and evil. (Ali Soufan, The Black Banners).

Endurance of the Ideology

There is a saying in the Corps that "a lifer is a Marine who can't do without the Corps and a career Marine is one the Corps can't do without." One could surmise that the *lifer* sees his organization as the only true reality. This is not a central issue, but one can see there may be varying degrees, levels or styles of loyalty, or perhaps obsession, in affiliation with the Marine Corps. Some Marines opine that the *career Marine* is aware of "life after the Corps" and makes adequate plans for that life; the *lifer* tends to be the guy who "can't let it go…"

After the new organization phase, the Corps went through many crisis periods. Millett told of at least 10 attempts initiated by the Navy, Army, Congress or a president to disband the Corps, merge it into the Navy or Army, or sharply reduce its size. The Civil War and technology brought identity problems for the Corps, a bastard child with missions on land and sea. But two more recent examples would better serve to illustrate crisis:

On April 8, 1956, six male recruits drowned in the swamps behind the rifle range at Marine Corps Recruit Depot, Parris Island, South Carolina. The tragedy came to be known as the Ribbon Creek Incident. The six men were members of a platoon under supervision of an assistant drill instructor, Staff Sergeant Matthew C. McKeon. Findings in McKeon's court martial showed that he had taken the recruits into the swamps where tidal inlets from nearby rivers swelled during high tides. The six had trouble fording the creek and drowned. McKeon was found responsible, court-martialed, reduced in rank and eventually left the Marine Corps a corporal "in oblivion" in 1959.[xcvii]

Perspective. When I wrote the final draft of this original text in 1989-1990, McKeon was retired from a second career and living in Massachusetts. He died on Veterans Day, 2003. In the long hindsight since 1990, and still longer since the 1950's, some view the incident as the event that not only led to an overhaul of recruit training but signaled "the demise of the Old Corps."[xcviii] The Ribbon Creek incident led the Marine Corps to issue the iconic "Smokey the Bear" hat to drill instructors, a matter of respecting or acknowledging the DI's long hours in the sun, training recruits. But the Corps also added more drill instructors per platoon, more officer supervision in the lower ranks (lieutenants and captains), and recruit training commands led by (then) brigadier generals, at the Marine Corps Recruit Depots of San Diego, CA, and Parris Island, SC.

That loss of the "the old Corps" lamented in some of the contemporary blogs and commentary in modern times is an acknowledgement that the Marine Corps could no longer carry on its demanding training "behind closed doors." That point of view speaks directly to the core of this part of the analysis – the conflict between generations of Marines, a conflict in which older generation Marines observe, to younger Marines, "You didn't have it as tough as we had it." The reality is that there were abuses "behind closed doors." In 1973, my drill instructors had our platoon perform "close order drill" with footlockers, leading to bruised heads and bloodied knuckles.[xcix] Even in 1973, extra "motivational" physical training – designed to get recruits' attention and "square them away" – had some limits. On another occasion, our drill instructors marched our platoon of 70 recruits to a closed handball court…out of sight of the company's senior staff NCOs and officers…for some of that extra motivation (jumping jacks, squat-thrusts, push-ups and other exercises – in close quarters).

By the 1990s, most of the excesses had been eliminated. Drill instructors are even more carefully screened and the Marine Corps sends an officer to tell recruits early in training that they play a role in reporting if their civil rights are violated. Yet DI schools and veteran drill instructors teach new DIs how to stress recruits without hitting them or pushing them beyond "reasonable limits." The Marine Corps and the armed forces in general, as public servants, are ever more susceptible to public scrutiny, in part because of greater willingness of insiders to question excesses and in part because the Internet provides countless venues for publication. Training must remain demanding and stressful because combat is even more demanding and stressful. Excesses and accidents in recruit training have caused the Corps to fine tune the arts and sciences of training and stressing recruits, instilling self-discipline, so that those recruits can reasonably be expected to perform in the demanding environments of combat.

The Corps executed some of its own changes, and endured other externally imposed changes in the 20 years following the Ribbon Creek Incident, in recruit training especially, some influenced by Congress and anxious parents who had contacted their Congressional representatives. Although the Corps attempted to manage its own challenges internally through the 1960s and '70s, Marine Corps commandants have regularly been called to testify before Congressional hearings concerning problems (as well as successes) in the Marine Corps.

Excerpts will be presented later from the Congressional testimonies presented in 1976 by Rear Admiral D. Earl Brown, Jr., who went undercover as a Marine drill instructor while he was a Navy psychiatrist at the neuro-psychiatric unit at Parris Island, and by Brigadier General Richard C. Schulze, then Director of Marine Corps Manpower, Plans and Policies Division. Their testimonies were in response to at least a decade of perceived problems in recruit training, including possible abuses of recruits by drill instructors and stress levels on recruits and drill instructors.

Perspective. Here we go again? As the wars in Iraq and Afghanistan wind down, the Corps has again served as America's second Army. The Marine Corps has been plussed-up from the previous cuts in "end strength," or total numbers of Marines on active duty. Now in the face of enormous federal deficits, eyes are on the Department of Defense broadly, and the Marine Corps is again responding to questions about its relevance, its historical role as an amphibious assault force in the 21st century. Plans to shift focus to the Pacific will undoubtedly preserve a Marine Corps mission – but for a significantly smaller Corps.

Planned and unplanned external change

The Corps is corporately a public servant with a public identity. Understanding that identity and appreciating the culture comes in degrees. Although it is impossible to completely understand what it means to be a Marine without going through the training and living the life, some uninitiated *get it* more than others: a Marine's family, or soldiers, sailors and airmen who serve with Marines. During this generation, satellite television and newspapers have enabled reporters to bring news, and speculation, to the public more rapidly than ever. The public consumer of news, and speculation, can now form opinions about events in progress rather than about old news. There is a contrast between the period of World War II or before and the time from Vietnam to the present, notably with the Marines in Beirut and Grenada, or the Marines involved in the spy scandals in the American Embassy in Moscow, or Lieutenant Colonel Oliver North and the *Contragate* hearings on Capitol Hill.

...An even sharper contrast from the 1990s to 2013. This phenomenon has only accelerated in the past 20 years, of course, with more satellites, more television news channels and the Internet. We will dig deeper into the Internet, its application in jihadi/takfiri Muslim recruiting, and the impact of negative propaganda gone viral (abu Ghraib prison interrogation photos, for example – an Army (not Marine Corps) debacle).

"The Corps' elitist combat reputation and functional role in the U.S. armed forces" was endangered in the years following Vietnam.[c] Millett's essay of the Corps' adaptation to post-Vietnam years began with: "Everyone knows that the Marines are a breed apart." Millett also quoted a Russian book on naval infantry about U.S. Marines:

We know what kind they are by their examples in South Vietnam, Cambodia, Laos and Lebanon. Wherever American Marines have appeared, they have sowed death and destruction....They emerge as oppressors of national liberation movements...such is the savage make-up of the American Marine, the supreme guardian of the U.S. imperialists.[d]

Millett made this observation following the Russian comment:

One can imagine the ghosts of the legendary Dan Daly and 'Chesty' Puller laughing as they jam more bullets into their Springfield rifles. It is no wonder that Americans probably think of the Marine Corps as a primitive warrior tribe led by John Wayne and 'the Great Santini' rather than a large, highly complex, military organization."

Marines would take the Soviets' observations as words of praise.

And yet another identity crisis plagued the Marine Corps. Millett noted in his prologue the difference between public opinion during World War II and Korea, and the mood of the times during Vietnam. In Southeast Asia the Corps fought a war for which it was neither prepared nor designed. The Marine Corps fought a ground war for the duration but has historically been an amphibious force designed to "seize and defend advance naval bases." There were more Marine casualties (both killed and wounded) in Vietnam than World War II. Shorter enlistments and combat tours led to erosion of depth of professional career noncommissioned officers and officers. World War II and Korea were more popular at home than Vietnam, although even veterans of the Korean War felt some of the American apathy that Vietnam veterans experienced in the 1960s and early 70s. Examples of the differences, according to Millett, can be found by comparing Robert Leckie's book *Helmet for My Pillow* with Philip Caputo's *A Rumor of War*, and the movies *The Sands of Iwo Jima* with *The Boys of Company C.*[cii]

The differences in these books and films are that during and after World War II the Marines were glorified, and during Vietnam the Corps was satirized. The struggle on the eve of the 1980s was to combat "a critical dilution of experience and skill in virtually every rank and occupational category [that] all eroded Marine morale and efficiency."[ciii]

Perspective. Lots of water under the bridge since then, and the attitudes of Americans toward Marines and soldiers serving in Iraq and Afghanistan have changed palpably in contrast to Vietnam. When I returned from Iraq in March 2007, I flew to Dallas, in uniform, to spend a long weekend reconnecting with my daughter. I had been able to call her from Iraq once a week to read to her on the phone at her bed time. She was 10. On that quick trip home, flight attendants offered me a first-class seat, and I accepted many "thank-you's" from strangers on the flight. A sharp contrast from my flight home from boot camp in 1973 as the US was winding down and exiting from Vietnam.

One of the many charismatic leaders between 1956 and 1980 was General Louis H. Wilson who mandated, as Commandant of the Marine Corps in 1976, that the Corps would enlist more high school graduates. Already underway in the early 1970s was the purging of "Vietnam-era *in-effectives* (largely drug users and Black protestors)."[civ]

Commandants during the Vietnam era struggled with *indiscipline indices*: "men in the brig, drug use, "primary group indisciplines of petty crimes and insubordination, and unauthorized absences," according to Millett. Under General Wilson (and then

Gen. Robert H. Barrow), the Corps' goal was to enlist more than 75 percent high school graduates and lower its indicators of indiscipline closer to other services. One problem was that the Corps was (still is) the *youngest* service. That is, of all the services' enlisted ranks, more Marines are in lower ranks, and of all enlisted, Marines are proportionately younger. As of the mid 1980s, enlisted Marines 25 and younger represented about 77 percent of the Corps' enlisted population. The Army had about 62 percent; the Navy, approximately 63 percent and the Air Force about 55 percent.[cv] The point is that younger, first-term enlisted men are statistically more prone to get involved in discipline problems than older men.

(Although the numbers fluctuate on a daily basis with men and women entering and leaving each of the armed services, the overall trend remains the same 20 years later. As a percentage, more Marines are younger and serve at more junior ranks. The most populous pay grade – rank – in the Marine Corps' enlisted ranks is E3 (lance corporal). The most densely populated pay grade in the Army is E-4 (corporal), and E-5 in the Navy and Air Force (2nd class petty officer and staff sergeant, respectively).[cvi]

Millett also observed that the Corps' standards of discipline maintained "the most rigid, traditional definitions of 'unmilitary' behavior."[cvii] In Millett's view, a particular violation would be seen as more serious in the Marine Corps than in another service, or that it is easier to get in trouble in the Corps than in the other services.

The result of Wilson's goals was that the Marine Corps had enlisted 102 percent of its quantity objectives in 1982, and 85 percent high school graduates – then short of the Army by one percent and the Air Force by nine percent.[cviii]

Millett's analysis was that drug and alcohol problems had been effectively addressed, that doubling the percentage of Black enlisted and officer Marines did not hurt the Corps, and that keeping the percentage of women low (4.5 percent of all enlisted in 1982, compared to 9.7 percent in the Army, 7.9 percent in the Navy and 11.4 percent in the Air Force) has been beneficial to unit identity and group cohesion because of "the limitations of women Marines in terms of field service and marriage-pregnancy problems."[cix])

This detailing of Marine Corps adaptation to post-Vietnam years does not parallel exactly Clark's definition of a "unique accomplishment," because the Corps' sister services have had similar successes with post-Vietnam recruiting (at least until 1987). A story of courage, bravery or honor might be better suited to this analogy, but the idea is that the Corps takes great corporate pride in maintaining its eliteness.

During a visit of civic leaders, educators and school counselors from Baltimore in 1981, Major General Robert E. Haebel, then commanding general of the recruit depot at Parris Island, remarked, "We show you what we do here because we are proud of it; we have nothing to hide."

As community relations chief at Parris Island during General Haebel's tenure as commanding general, I witnessed many similar expressions from the general, including his stories about having been in commercial airports during his travels, where people told him how proud they were of his Marines. One of General Haebel's favorite sayings was: "Baseball, hot dogs, apple pie and the Marine Corps."

The general was expressing a public image of the Corps, telling the organizational saga of success in the 1970s and 80s. The saga is part of a facade, but is not necessarily a false front; it is **one** front – the exterior facade of the edifice. The telling of the saga to outsiders is telling them part of the little they can know without experiencing the culture as Marines do by going through training.

To return to Clark's analysis of saga, he also wrote that the saga becomes fixed "in the minds of outside believers devoted to the organization, usually the alumni."[cx] The Corps' "alumni" surpasses in size even the few hundred thousand alumni from large universities. Tens of thousands of men and women leave the Marine Corps each year through normal first-term and mid-career attrition, and retirement. No known poll has been taken, but it can be assumed that a certain share, perhaps a large share, remain devoted to the organization to some degree. The number of Marine Corps associations and other veterans' organizations which active and former Marines may join attests to the lingering sense of brotherhood begun in uniform: The American Legion, AMVETS, Veterans of Foreign Wars, the Marine Corps Association, the Marine Corps League, associations of the 1st, 2nd, 3rd, 4th, 5th and 6th divisions, Marine Raider Battalion organizations, etc.

Clark's observation, below, is valid and generalizable to the Corps:

"The alumni are best located to hold certain beliefs enduringly pure, since they can be as strongly identified with a special organizational history as the older faculty and administrators and yet do not have to face directly the new problems generated by a changing environment or students."[cxi]

Substitute *young Marines* for students and *senior noncommissioned officers and officers* for faculty and administrators and the logic in Clark's findings holds true for the Corps as well. Former Marines seem to hit a stasis when they leave the Marine Corps; the images they have of the Corps solidify when they leave or retire. They may be well aware that changes are taking place in the Corps, but they are not experiencing the changes. The phenomenon is similar to an adult returning to a childhood place and discovering that the mental image is based on the last recollections of the place. Such recollections are "enduringly pure," as Clark put it.

In addition to former Marines, there is another, often

forgotten body of believers kindred to the Corps: the families of Marines. Again, it is difficult to determine how many or what percentage of parents, spouses or other kin feel devoted in any measure to the Corps. Indeed there may be many who harbor animosity over the death of a relative during a war, or because of the separation of families during duty-related deployments at sea or to other countries.

(In my current assignment, I cross paths with several Marines on a daily basis – mainly with the majors, lieutenant colonels and colonels. Most of them (like me) were "base brats." Their dads or moms were in the Marine Corps, as was my oldest son – a 3rd generation Marine.)

At the recruit training depots at Parris Island and San Diego, recruit graduations are held two to five times weekly, depending on the time of year. There is an influx of recruits in summer months following high school graduation, and a corresponding surge in graduations as recruits finish training. During graduation ceremonies at Parris Island, the commanding officer of the battalion graduating the recruits greets parents and other relatives, gives a speech about the rigors of training and asks visitors to "go home and tell the Parris Island story." The speech is the same from graduation to graduation; it is memorized but is delivered with emotion obvious to the visitors.

In addition, many parents take a bus tour of the training complex and see how recruits train; they get a picture of what their sons and daughters went through. They may also visit the museum on base, talk with other Marines, and have the opportunity to buy Marine souvenirs: T-shirts, ash trays, flags, books, belt buckles, cigarette lighters, posters, bumper stickers, key chains, etc. The fast food restaurant on base once had "Recruit Burgers," and "DI Burgers."

Sagas and the Corps as a cult

The saga becomes fixed not only in the minds of new

Marines, but to a lesser degree also in the minds of significant others. The importance or duration of the saga's message depends on whether the saga is held or believed by a Marine who has experienced the event, or by a civilian who has only observed it. Clark noted:

> With deep emotional commitments, believers define themselves by their organizational affiliation, and in their bond to other believers they share an intense sense of the unique. In an organization defined by a strong saga, there is the feeling that there is the small world of the lucky few and the large, routine one of the rest of the world. Such an emotional bond turns the membership into a community, even a cult."[cxii]

A Marine Corps of about 200,000 may be too large to describe as a cult, but the idea may not be far off the mark. Yet there is evidence of cults or tribes in the reconnaissance battalions, the clique of drill instructors, bands, rifle and pistol teams, etc., where there are even more specialized language, more exclusive membership rites or more demanding duties. (*And now the Marine Corps has a Special Operations force, building toward par with Navy SEALS, Army and Air Force special forces.*)

While I was a member of the Second Marine Division Band at Camp Lejeune in 1974, the men in the band had a chant (*we had Rap before Rap was Rap)* that started with: "We are the men of the Second Mar civvy-divvy, left-hand, sh*t-can, jump down, turn around, chicken eatin' wishbone band." Other Marines in the same battalion never understood the proclamation. Band members got it, however; it complained about the long tours on the road, loading and unloading instruments and the many "free" dinners of Kentucky Fried Chicken at just about every public gig we played.

The same kinds of self-proclaimed uniqueness are evident in the competition between Marine artillery and infantry units, or between Marines assigned to ground elements and those assigned to aviation units. There is a strong emotional bond between Marines, as spoken in the slogan, "We few, we proud, we band of brothers," but there are subcultures within the culture.

The image of brotherhoods can conjure images of monks in a monastery, living lives apart from the rest of a world not involved in their mission, tonsures, chanting, religious uniformity. In fact it is common at the recruit depots to see recruits waiting for classes, sitting in rows (squads) chanting by rote the maximum effective range of the M-16 rifle, the life saving steps of first aid, the chain of command, the Code of Conduct and hundreds of other essential facts for graduating Marines. The **bible** is the Red Book, which recruits call the **Red Monster**. *(In 2013, it is the Green Monster.)*

The appointed recruit leader, the platoon guide, stands in front of his fellow recruits and reads from the book, almost like a chant: "The first life saving step is: Check for breathing." The 40 to 70 recruits repeat in unison. The guide reads the second life saving step, the third and so on, followed by other facts until the platoon is called into a classroom or off to some other duty. When drill instructors approach a recruit and ask questions from the Red (or Green) Monster, the recruit is expected to know the answers. Recruits are tested at inspections verbally, and on written examinations. The air of mysticism one may feel in the observation of this minor ritual supports a comparison of education to the Christian church. Whereas a minister consecrates wine and bread (in, with and under) as the body and blood of Jesus Christ in the sacrament of Holy Communion, information becomes knowledge through the guidance – consecration – of the educator. In the experience of Marine Corps basic training, all the parallel trappings of a religious order make the analogy even stronger. The drill instructor becomes father-confessor to novice, shave-headed **monk** recruits. The rest of the chain of command parallels the church hierarchy.

There is another parallel to religion, in that in many

Christian religions, faith is more important than observation of the law. The law, the 10 Commandments, for example, must be followed, but in the belief of the Christian church, man is by nature sinful and cannot uphold the law. He therefore is saved from his sins by faith. The most remarkable heroes of the Corps' history have been those who lived better by the **spirit** of the word rather than the law: the much storied "Pappy" Boyington of World War II aviation in the Pacific, "Chesty" Puller, who is said to have abhorred paperwork, and World War II mortarman Lou Diamond, who was infamous for his drinking and womanizing, but who could "put a mortar down the stack of a Japanese destroyer from a mile away." It was as if they knew they could not live with all the regulations imposed on them, or did not want to, and fought their wars the most efficient way they knew how – in the spirit of the Corps' values. Even Oliver North, a comparative renegade, seems to have acted in the spirit of Marine traditions with less regard for larger consequences.

Rites of passage

Even though the monastic, tribal rites of passage of basic training include training in the knowledge and skills every basic infantry Marine must have, many Marines will never directly apply but a small share of the (infantry) combat skills they learn. Many Marines will work in jobs other than infantry, artillery or tactical aviation. With the passing of time between combat experiences, save for the forays such as operations in Lebanon and Grenada, generations of Marines will have gone through four years or more of the Marine Corps experience with no combat. What they should learn subconsciously, and begin to apply subconsciously at first, are internal qualities: self discipline, confidence, respect for authority, instant, willing obedience to orders, and a variety of other values and actions based on beliefs indoctrinated during basic training.

Obviously much has changed since I was a staff sergeant writing the paragraphs above. Most Marines have rotated into and out of either Iraq or

Afghanistan or both battlefields, many with multiple combat tours. More Marines on active duty in 2013 have combat experience than at any time since World War II. And yet, Marines in support roles such as personnel and administration, finance, supply and logistics, intelligence, etc., still will not engage in tactical combat. Meanwhile, internalization of those qualities noted above still holds true.

A statement of the purpose of recruit training is written on a plaque behind the commanding officer's desk at the Recruit Training Regiment headquarters at Parris Island: "To indoctrinate the recruit in the fundamentals of service life and to develop discipline, proficiency in marksmanship and love of Corps and Country."

That young men and women will willingly undergo this indoctrination may be astonishing to some people considering the physical and mental demands of the 10 to 11 weeks, not to mention the possibility of death or disability in combat and the other challenges of military life. But others view enlistment as common or natural for young men. Dyer called basic training a necessity for large, modern armies and a fulfilling experience for young men:

The cultural norms that encourage aggression and gang behavior amongst teenage males are probably several million years old. They are designed to produce warriors, which is what was needed for the old inter-tribal warfare. But the same basic institutions have survived and flourished in our far more complicated societies, and now provide the raw material for a very different product: soldiers. These archaic male rituals would probably have survived anyway, for they have become deeply imbedded in most cultures' definitions of masculinity....As anybody knows who has been through it, basic training is a primitive form of brain washing, intended to produce a new and highly artificial set of 'military instincts.'[xviii]

Dyer's observations were made in the proposal for a documentary film series titled *WAR*. (The series was shown on Canadian and U.S. public television, and was later published in written form as the book *WAR*.[cxiv]) One of the six films was shot at Parris Island, and was intended to portray the *archaic* male rituals, as training, in the midst of a series of films dealing with the history of war, guerilla war, conventional war, and so on. Dyer's conclusions, perhaps less scientifically qualified but no less accurate it seems, echo the findings of researchers writing in Margaret Mead-like themes and theories. Military training provides an outlet for the needs of male youths to belong to a peer group and hold steady jobs. It seems no less unusual to step from high school athletic teams and other primary male social groups into basic training, than to go from adolescence to adulthood through some tribal ritual of New Guinea in the 1930s or some other backward culture. Going to boot camp is metaphorically killing a lion (one of the rites of passage before deploying into combat (the battle) – another rite of passage in itself).

As for the archaic male rituals and contrasts between the modern military and backward cultures, Millett too observed:

Throughout its history the Marine Corps has impressed non-Marines (and a considerable number of Marines themselves) as a marvelous anachronism, a bastion of military traditionalism given to the excessive worship of its heroic past....The Corps has purposefully dramatized its traditional characteristics for public consumption, but Marines actually glory in their commitment to warrior values within their own society. The socio-psychological uniqueness of the Corps, found only in elite portions of other services, masks an institutional capacity for functional innovation that is an underappreciated asset within the U.S. armed forces.[cxv]

This observation brings up two points, one about the *functional innovation* of the Marine Corps, and the other about the socio-psychological uniqueness of which Millett wrote. (It should be noted that Millett's perspectives parallel mine to an extent.[cxvi] That is, I was indoctrinated as a Marine as well, served as an enlisted Marine and as a Marine officer and write with an insider's point of view. Millett's findings are based on fact, and although colorfully written, are no less valid when compared to findings from other researchers who are not, and have not been Marines.)

The first of these points, functional innovation, is a topic that has gained a great deal of attention, most notably through the work of the Inter-University Seminar on Armed Forces and Society. In the past two or three generations, the interrelationships of militaries and their host societies have changed the character of *professional soldiers*, as these researchers call them, partly because of advances in technology.[cxvii] [cxviii] Some of what Janowitz, Millett and their colleagues are saying is that civilian images of the military include the view that modern militaries still abide by strict disciplinarian codes of conduct, are anachronistic in their ritual practices of parades and other mystical ceremonies like basic training, and shun liberal civilian management philosophies.

This is so far from the truth. In actuality, the Corps and other armed forces have adopted a wide range of civilian management philosophies, and do take an active role in the research and development of sophisticated computer systems and weaponry. And although discipline is required, the implied emphasis during this century has increasingly been on self-discipline rather than discipline imposed by martinet officers and noncommissioned officers.

During these years of the All-Volunteer Force, a title which leaders at the Pentagon reportedly no longer like, Janowitz observed:

Men must be motivated to make the organization work, but not all of them have to be so motivated, nor must they all agree on details of social philosophy or be bound by ties of friendship in order for a functioning organization to exist....The best single predictor of combat behavior is the simple fact of institutionalized role: knowing that a man is a soldier rather than a civilian. The soldier role is a vehicle for getting a man into the position in which he has to fight or take the institutionalized consequences.[cxix]

According to these writers, the purpose of the military is to redefine the civilian as a soldier. The soldier is still a citizen, but goes through some internal and external conflict between civilian values and military values, the strongest conflict until combat being during boot camp. The longer a Marine stays on active duty, the greater strength the Corps' values have in relation to civilian values.

Perspectives: Keep in mind that this process is going on in the mosques and madrassahs within the ummah – the world of Islam.

But there is evidence that the level to which Marine training overrides civilian values has diminished during the past 30 years or so (*as of 1990*). Janowitz wrote that there are signs of change as a result of several important forces:

1. The growing dollar amount of national income devoted to defense spending (somewhat curtailed by the Graham-Rudman legislation which in 1987 led to restricted military spending to help balance the economy);

2. The socialization of war (the notion that war affects everyone because of the nuclear threat, rather than threatening only soldiers on the battlefield);

3. The national trend away from rapid expansion and demobilization, and toward gradual changes in the size of militaries; and, perhaps most important;

4. The increasing use of technology in the military for both weapons and management.

The main idea here is that as technology seeps into the Marine Corps, there is necessarily closer cooperation between the Corps and defense contractors. A parallel note comes from my observations in 1988 as a Navy officer: Several civilians from various research, aviation and computer corporations lived and worked aboard the aircraft carrier USS Nimitz. The same phenomenon is found in the Marine Corps, notably in aviation, but also with non-aviation units working with advanced technological equipment.

Perspective: This too has changed. After a three-year stint back in uniform, I re-entered the "other workforce" as a defense contractor. The division I work in – as one of the greybeards – is heavily populated with retired senior enlisted and officers, mostly retired colonels and lieutenant colonels or commanders (US Navy). Both US Central Command and SOCOM rely heavily on the decades of expertise from retired military officers and senior non-commissioned officers. The US Department of Defense is more open to "commercial off-the-shelf technology" (COTS) than it was a generation ago, meaning less inclined to contract for military-specific hardware and greater use of commercial innovation. The partnerships with industry and the academic community improve upon the relationships of the 1970's and '80's. Industry, the academic community and the Department of Defense all benefit immensely, but at a price. In the informal lingo of half a generation ago, lifting your tent flaps allows alternate influences into the culture. Some is positive; some is not.

The so-called technological invasion, as well as the education of officers and enlisted Marines who work on advanced weapons systems and computers has allowed the gradual acceptance of some civilian management styles. The conflict evident in this acceptance of *management* is that it is not wholly accepted; some old salts swear by old-fashioned leadership, something they say has no room for "management." *(That truly was a debate in the 1980s, but some…not all…in the Marine Corps and the other services have come to accept that Management and Leadership are distinctly separate skill sets – and that it's OK for Marines to learn both.)*

Some lines between what is military and what is civilian have blurred over the decades following World War II, according to Janowitz and others.[cxx] Yet the distinction between *military* and *civilian* has not been eliminated because there is still a need for people and an organization prepared to fight, especially ground wars.[cxxi]

To come full circle on the theoretical framework established in this review of what other experts have found in their research, note that Janowitz stressed a need for authority and discipline based on domination, to the effective use of manipulation, influence and internal justification.[cxxii] This notion closely parallels Perrow's third order controls discussed earlier. In plain language it means that there is a need for, or there should be a move toward, the greater use of the positive mechanics of social and behavioral psychology to instill self-discipline in a well-trained force, rather than the application of force by officers and NCOs. The "old salts" recognize that a Corps of volunteers who fight because they are internally motivated is a far better body of men than those who are coerced.

Perspective: Rather than the term "coerced," Marine drill instructors and the officers responsible for training recruits speak in terms of "stress." Retired and former Marines in the audience who remember boot camp prior to the mid-1970's may recall instances of drill instructors punching or slapping recruits, to get their attention or to "discipline" or punish them, or otherwise physically "abusing" recruits with excessive physical demands (exercise, running, stress positions, or requiring them to perform rifle drills with footlockers) and excessively foul language and name calling. It's certain drill instructors exceeded their limits; I experienced it and witnessed it. It's impossible to suggest how common these practices were as some instances were not witnessed or were never reported, as with sexual harassment or rape. After Vietnam, beginning in the mid-1970s, the Marine Corps applied new internal regulations limiting contact between DI's and recruits, restricting stress: what kind and how much physical activity a DI can administer to a recruit – based in part on how long the recruit had been in training, and on the conditions (hot summer days limit activity) – and better training for DIs.

Janowitz wrote that "manipulation involves positive incentives rather than physical threats; and retains the threat of exclusion from the group as a control...[it] is designed to take into account the individual soldier's predispositions."[cxxiii] [cxxiv]

Those psychological predispositions are what I found to be

the underpinnings of *propaganda* in the Marine Corps.[cxxv] A prospective Marine predisposed to accept a particular message is fertile for recruitment advertising. Studies in propaganda have found that people (psychologically predisposed) tend to identify with the speaker of the propaganda message, much as prisoners of war sometimes identify with their captors. The phenomenon is most powerful when the speaker has some characteristic with which the audience identifies. An obvious example in this study is in basic training, during which recruits see that the drill instructor has rank, pay, decorations (ribbons and medals), prestige, status, and freedom. Personal observation suggests that increasing status may subdue the desire for freedom, that is – graduation from boot camp for recruits, as a most important aspiration the longer one is exposed to the socializing propaganda of basic training. It only takes a few weeks.

Propaganda

Ellul explains that the myths of society are the bases for a successful propaganda.[cxxvi] As noted, some of the American myths are the work ethic, the *American dream*, manhood, independence, youth, success, etc. These are the American *narrative*. What Ellul described as society's myths are conceptually equivalent to cultural themes in the ethnographic research method. By whatever name, these values are the predispositions upon which propaganda plays.

My conclusions of the investigation of propaganda in the Marine Corps, based on Ellul's discussion of propagandas as social phenomena are that recruitment advertising, boot camp education and indoctrination, and the socialization of the career Marine can be defined as propagandas. There are certain socio-psychological machinations at work in the successful propaganda campaign. Included are: three levels of conformity (compliance, identification and internalization); internal and external justification of cognitive dissonance; and rationalization.

To return to the second point expressed above, based on Millett's study, the Marine Corps does have a unique set of socio-psychological variables. As a military force, it shares traditions with other services. But although there are strong rivalries between the Corps and other services, Marines should admit they would want a strong Army, Air Force or Navy alongside in the event of war. Beyond that, Marines tend to say that they have better uniforms and wear them with more military precision, that the Corps has more disciplined troops, better training and stronger values. It doesn't matter if such concepts are true or even quantifiable; what matters is that Marines believe it.[cxxvii]

This ethnocentrism underscores Millett's point about the uniqueness of the Marine Corps: Marine recruits go through basic training almost completely isolated from civilian influences; newspapers on Sunday and mail are about the only distractors during training. Boot camp lasts from two to four weeks longer than the other services' basic training. Marine recruits are supervised 24 hours a day by a drill instructor for the duration of training, whereas other services' recruits are not supervised by other than another recruit in a leadership position after the end of the work day almost from the beginning. The invisible boundaries between ranks is more strongly enforced – a private first class (E1) does not call a staff sergeant (E6) by his first name in the Marine Corps, but that level of informality may be observed in the Navy or Air Force. Marines learn during basic training, and are tested on, the date and circumstances of the foundation of the Marine Corps, historic battles, Medal of Honor recipients and other heroes and their exploits.

The main idea is that from recruitment through retirement, Marines take great pains to "worship their heroic past," and this is nowhere more tangible than when Marines gather, in ballrooms with their dates or in combat zones with fellow Marines, to celebrate the Marine Corps birthday. Thus Marines are, to use the words of

Geertz, Wilkins, and Ellul, above, "psychologically unified." They are different; they know it, they are proud of it and they express it.

Again, the groundwork for this unification resides in the symbols, rituals and myths of national and Marine folklore. All Marines learn most of the organization's mainstream folklore over time. The ritualized indoctrination of Marines in their folklore seems to be broader and more intense than in other U.S. armed forces.

Why unification works is a function of the socio-psychological uniqueness of which Millett wrote. By combining the theoretical assertions of Ellul, and Aronson,[cxxviii] I described in my master's thesis parallel interactions among types of propaganda, phases in a Marine's career and level of conformity. Aronson described the increasing levels of conformity as "compliance, identification and internalization."

Conformity Theory

Compliance

Propaganda or direct communication between two people can generate compliance, but in the Marine Corps, compliance can be best illustrated with a mass of individuals. (Peer pressure may incite compliance.) Compliance, the parallel to Perrow's first-order control, is a result of coercion. Compliance comes about in a civilian to some degree in the young man interested in the Marine Corps, even though he is not physically coerced to enlist. Or, the predisposition described above may prepare the civilian to accept the values or beliefs that lead to the first stages of identification and the decision to enlist. The animated drill instructor yelling apparently unintelligible commands can also generate compliance.

Identification

Identification becomes evident in the recruit as he goes through basic training, begins to learn the folklore of the Marine

Corps, and eventually identifies with role models, initially in the form of drill instructors. Recruits in either Marine Corps boot camp or al-Qaida training camps are certain to identify with their trainers.

Internalization

Internalization begins later in basic training and continues through the life of the Marine. As the folklore of the Corps becomes deeply imbedded in the individual, the values of the organization, thus the organization itself, become more important to the individual.

In my master's thesis, I described various views of the compliance-identification-internalization phenomenon. One may see all three levels of conformity taking place in each phase of a Marine's career – showing the Marine increasing in levels of conformity dependent in the current situation. Or, one may see levels of compliance build through the entire career, viewing the career as a single setting.

Echoing Janowitz' observations, Pinch suggested that "a voluntary manpower system renders the military extraordinarily sensitive to trends and perturbations within other societal institutions, for example, the educational system and the civilian labor force."[cxxix] Two observations surface here. The mid- and late-career Marines must either accept the responsibility of training and socializing new recruits, who may have different values than the veteran Marines did when they were recruits, or the veteran Marines can refuse to adapt, complain and make no progress, or leave the service.

The second point is based on Pinch's observation that "the United States [and] other All-Volunteer Force militaries are...fighting a losing battle to attract high school graduates."[cxxx] Such battles fluctuate with the size of the labor force, *baby booms* and so on. Pinch's argument was that there should be better "articulation" and less competition between militaries, education and industry. But his losing battle statistics were from 1979 and his article appeared in 1982. Take into account Fiscal Year 1983 recruiting statistics for the Marine Corps:

FY (fiscal year) 1983 was a banner year for Marine recruiting. Recruiters surpassed all previous numerical and quality goals for new Marines. Ninety-two percent were high school graduates with 63 percent ranking in the upper half of the nationally normed range of test scores. At this pace, the Marine Corps is confident of achieving one of its major goals: to have a sufficient number of high school graduates in the AFQT (Armed Forces Qualification Test) ranges qualified to operate today's high technology systems, and qualified to become noncommissioned officers as well.[cxxxi]

(Now on the eve of the 1990s the military services are again dealing with the shrinking pool of available recruits. Concurrently however, there is increasing Congressional pressure to decrease the size of the militaries in order to reduce the federal budget, helped in no small way by Soviet propaganda in the form of Glasnost and Perestroika that purports to diminish the threat from America's perceived enemy.)

Perspective: I've purposely left the paragraphs above as originally written for the most part. As we view a national debt surpassing $16 trillion in 2013, eyes are again on the US armed forces' budget as congressional leaders of both parties seek to rein in the fiscal headaches. Recruiting, however, is bolstered by unemployment, and since 2009 the Marine Corps has consistently exceeded its needs.[cxxxii]

One side of the argument in the conflict between generations, expressed many times on behalf of the newer generation, is that better educated Marines are more trainable. In addition, higher educational levels accompany higher levels of self-esteem.[cxxxiii] Regarding the Congressional testimony noted earlier: during the mid-1970s, the Corps specifically sought high school graduates, with graduation being a primary intellectual indicator of trainability and a statistical indicator of a recruit's tenacity. That is, if one has the "stick-to-it-iveness" to complete high school, one probably has a better chance of completing training than would a **quitter** (a high school quitter). As has been the case in the Marine Corps over time, the emphasis in recruiting is on quality not quantity.

Brigadier General Richard C. Schulze, Director of Marine Corps Manpower, Plans and Policies Division in the mid-1970s, spoke of other qualities the Corps desires in a prospective Marine. In response to a question from Representative Nedzi: "Have you looked to developing a profile for a good candidate for the Marine Corps as opposed to just the high school graduate?" General Schulze responded:

Yes, sir. A high school graduate. He's better if he's around 17, or 18, or 19, than if he's older than that; if he comes from a home that is not broken; if he has participated in local activities; if he doesn't have a juvenile record. We do have a profile in that regard...and...criteria that specify his weight and height. [cxxxiv]

The other side of the argument is that Marines of earlier generations were more patriotic, or fought for real values, not money. A private in 1989 earned more than 10 times what a private earned during World War II. Marines in some job skills earned as much as $16,000 in reenlistment bonus for a six-year reenlistment (in 1989), and some qualified for more than one bonus at different stages in their careers. What this study has questioned is whether the values of the Corps, as told in the Corps' folklore, have changed in such a way as to make contemporary Marines little more than mercenaries. The answer is a qualified "no," but this will be elaborated upon in the final chapter.

Perspective: The wars in Iraq and Afghanistan, and the general public support for the armed forces, have likely influenced upward pressure *on military pay scales. Yet military pay – base pay – really just keeps pace with civilian sector pay. Base pay was discussed in Chapter 3 and will be touched on again in the final chapters. Re-enlistment bonuses now exceed $64,000. On the other end of the scale, a two-star general (major general) earns approximately $157,000 a year in base pay (and current legislation allows retiring service members to add multiples toward their pension so that a general or sergeant major (for example) retiring with 40 years of service will receive 100% of his or her base pay as a retainer.)*

In comparison with corporate presidents and CEOs in the private sector, senior officers with enormous responsibilities in manpower, budgets and strategic results are not over-compensated by any means. And yes – privates today earn ten times what privates earned in the previous generation. But – if a new car in that generation was priced at $1900 and a similar level car today is priced at $19,000…if gas was 35 cents a gallon and is now $3.50 a gallon…just add a zero. Military pay just keeps pace with the private sector.

Gene Alvarez, a colleague who has studied the Marine Corps as a historian, noted that the alleged increase in quality in the past decade, with the concurrent ability to recruit the required numbers of recruits is not an anomaly.[cxxxv]

Alvarez explained that, in his view, the phenomenon parallels the 1930s when there was a depression and the Marine Corps recruited a very high percentage of high school graduates – who had all their teeth. (Major General Haebel often said something to the effect that new Marines left Parris Island with big smiles because 60 percent of them came with dental problems and left with the problems corrected. Alvarez found that amusing.) Alvarez felt the economic problems of the early 1980s, the recession and high unemployment, helped recruiters of all services.

An additional question arises on the subject of recruiting, and this mitigates Pinch's argument somewhat: Will the Marine Corps continue to enlist 90 percent high school graduates in the numbers it needs? Time and competition between the militaries, higher education and industry will tell, but two factors are at work. As the pool of potential enlistees shrinks with the aging of the baby boom generation and the military services compete more heavily with education and industry, the military must make life in the service appear more attractive than the other alternatives. This becomes especially true when the national economy is healthy. The problem is compounded as more and more Marines and other servicemen and women are trained in ever-increasing levels of advanced technology, and civilian jobs with higher pay lure them out of uniform.

(Information technology specialists, trained in computer skills in the military and earning $40,000 to $50,000 at the 4- to 6-year point in an initial enlistment may be able to double or triple their salary leaving the service. Significant reenlistment bonuses are offered to entice them to stay. SEALS and Rangers, with similar pay scales and ample training in special warfare skills, were lured into contractor security jobs – making $200,000 or more annually in Iraq and Afghanistan.)

The second factor, outside of natural competition between military services and colleges or trade schools and industry, is the distance in time and memory between civilian images of Vietnam and current recruiting years. Negative civilian images of the military may be cyclical, but it is intuitively evident that entering the military in 2013 is a more acceptable option for a high school graduate than it was between 1965 and 1975.

Advertising

Competition for recruits leads to a discussion of the creation and manipulation of image. The need to advertise for recruits, particularly with the advent of the All Volunteer Force in 1973, caused the services to employ advertisers or step up on-going advertising efforts.

The advertising company retained by the Marine Corps is J. Walter Thompson (JWT), one of the largest advertising companies in the United States. The relationship between the two organizations "began in 1948 when Sam Meekes, a top JWT executive, came to Washington and offered JWT's services free of charge to the Marine Corps."[cxxxvi]

Young explained the development of the advertising program:

Meekes, a World War I Marine Corps veteran, thought the Marine Corps and its outstanding accomplishments in World War II would be forgotten. The Marine Corps accepted Meekes' offer and JWT and the USMC joined forces and began a long and successful campaign. The first campaign introduced was "The Marine Corps Builds Men." Throughout the 1950s and 1960s, years of the draft, JWT served in a public relations capacity handling the creation of poster and collateral artwork and all exposure in the media. In 1971, amid rumor that the draft would be eliminated, JWT decided to produce a marketing and advertising plan for the Corps. JWT approached Commandant Cushman, in 1971, with a proposal which was built on the tagline "The Marines are Looking for a Few Good Men."[cxxxvii]

With the advent of the All Volunteer Force in 1973 came the push by the Army to allow the use of paid military advertising, which debuted in the mid 1970s. Young noted that military advertising first appeared on television in 1976, the same year as the tagline "The Few – The Proud – The Marines," was introduced. In 1984, "We're Looking for a Few Good Men" returned. Young, a public affairs specialist assigned to Headquarters Marine Corps in 1984, closed his letter by writing: "The 36-year JWT-USMC association has...evolved from a charitable service provided to the USMC into J. Walter Thompson's fourteenth largest client. Simultaneously, the Marine Corps has grown into the military service most revered by the American public."

In fulfilling the recruitment advertising needs for the Marine Corps, JWT conducts market surveys in the civilian sector, measuring demographics, opinions about the military (especially the Marine Corps) and market characteristics of interest to the Corps. The Marine Corps expresses its needs in terms of, among other things, quality and quantity. J. Walter Thompson's advertising plans interpret the Corps' needs in a national picture, looking for "men who are high school graduates between the ages of 17 and 24 who are in good physical condition. Within the parameters of this national target are approximately 16 million men."[cxxxviii]

The advertising plan further explained that "the target population is expected to decrease by one to two percent per year, that there is a national trend of 18-year-olds to finish high school, and a declining trend of those graduates going on to four-year colleges."[cxxxix]

Other findings indicate that fathers tend to lean toward their sons going into the service; mothers are mostly neutral but lean toward being negative; wives and girlfriends are strongly negative; and the most positive influencer group is made up of friends who have some military experience. Considering these findings, the advertising plan noted that the most important single influencer may be the recruiter. Forty percent of the young men interviewed indicated they had a more positive feeling toward the service after talking with a recruiter. Eight percent indicated they had a less positive feeling. [cxl cxli]

J. Walter Thompson reported that before enlistment:

Prospects tend to see Air Force as offering a challenging job, the Navy in terms of opportunity to travel and the Army as having good benefits. Prospects tend to see the Marine Corps as the most combat ready or most reliable of the services. Prospects tend to look at the other services in terms of material benefits. They look at the Marine Corps in terms of personal benefits. They tend to see the other services as being somewhat the same and the Marines as being somewhat unique.[cxlii]

<u>Recruiting</u>

In the recruiting sales pitch, recruiters exploit prospects' views and expressed needs, predispositions and values with **incentive tags** (key fob-like devices). I observed the process: After some introductory conversation, focused on the prospect's interests, needs, and goals, the recruiter would lay tags with the following inscriptions on a table:

PRIDE OF BELONGING TO THE TOP SERVICE; SELF

RELIANCE; SELF DIRECTION; DISCIPLINE; LEADERSHIP

SKILLS & ATTITUDES, SECURITY; ADVANCEMENT &

BENEFITS; COURAGE; POISE; SELF CONFIDENCE;

TRAVEL AND ADVENTURE; EDUCATIONAL

OPPORTUNITY; TECHNICAL SKILLS

The recruiter would then tell the prospect to "Pick one," or ask, "Which one appeals to you?" The recruiter's job then is to pick up on the needs and describe how the Marine Corps can fulfill the needs. (**Of course**, the Marine Corps can fulfill all these needs, according to the recruiter, and he will be well-schooled in artfully explaining how.) This first meeting usually is when the civilian's image of the Corps confronts the real Marine Corps. Recall however that there are seemingly unlimited variations in the prospects' backgrounds, with some prospects having had relatives in the Corps, thus having probably more exposure to and understanding of the Corps and its culture.

<u>Peer pressure and *Poolees*</u>

Recruiters have discovered the power of the peer group, and have developed a cadre of *assistant recruiters* in the form of those young men and women who have enlisted but have not yet left for training. They are called **poolees**, because they are in the *pool* of those waiting to go to boot camp. They attend meetings with their recruiters, conduct physical training (PT) sessions, and learn much of the rote memory work that will be required in boot camp, such as information about the M-16 service rifle, the chain of command and orders for sentries. Most importantly, they tell their friends about the Marine Corps.

In any case, this is the stage at which the first level of conformity – compliance – should be expected to influence the prospect to enlist as a result of influences from advertising, psychological peer reinforcement, the recruiter, and from interaction with folklore in movies, video games, news stories, books, and television programs (History Channel, the Military Channel, etc).[cxliii]

Later in training, identification should replace compliance as the dominant form of conformity, as a result of influences from the drill instructors, education, constant association with symbols, rituals and myths, and from the pressures of the peer group.

I found that internalization was the dominant form of conformity during the career phases, and is a complex interaction of Marine, media, peers, seniors and subordinates, and (untested) external, dependent variables. The influencers which add to or detract from complete internalization, the level which might help influence a Marine to stay 20 years or more in the Corps, were seen as tangibles and intangibles, or extrinsic and intrinsic values.[cxliv] Tangibles are, for example, pay raises and promotions. Intangibles are realized in personal satisfaction, goals accomplished or other forms of personal reward.

Dissonance Theory

The purpose of recalling the levels and causes of conformity is to introduce the concept of cognitive dissonance and justification theory. Based on Aronson's studies, it can be seen that the individual Marine's internal decision-making conflicts follow precisely what is expected based on the theoretical framework established in the discipline of social psychology. Aronson described cognitive dissonance as:

Tension that occurs whenever an individual holds two cognitions (attitudes, beliefs, opinions etc.) that are psychologically inconsistent. Two cognitions are dissonant if, considering these two cognitions alone, the opposite of one follows from the other.[cxlv]

In other words, as prospects, recruits and Marines move through the phases of a career, come in contact with the influences of propaganda in folklore, and move from one level of conformity to the next, decision-making stress should cause cognitive dissonance.

The resolution of stress, conflict or dissonance, is accomplished through what are called internal and external justification. Aronson described these forms of justification in terms of rewards and punishments. The essence of the theory is that a reward for accepting one decision over another, when the two are dissonant, will help one justify his decision. Likewise, a punishment or threat of punishment can help justify not accepting one in place of another. This precept holds true even in choosing between the lesser of two evils, when one punishment is not as bad as another.

Rewards and punishments provide external justification. But, in the absence of sufficient reward or punishment, a person should tend to look to his internal values to guide decision-making. In other words, when a person avoids doing something wrong when there is no evident threat of punishment, or does something good or right for no tangible reward, there is internal justification for the decision.

An example would be stopping at a stop sign in the middle of the night a block or two from home when there is no traffic and there are no policemen present. If questioned by a friend, the driver might say the action was habit, or it is the law. The original reason for placing the stop sign on a particular corner is not a factor on a deserted street in the middle of the night. The driver acts subconsciously based on indoctrination in the rules of driving, habit, or perhaps values. The values of a driver who would drive through the stop sign in the absence of traffic may include a belief that some traffic laws are silly and can be ignored in given circumstances. (In other words, good judgment based on sound logic – in the absence of clear rules – is justifiable.)

Aronson found that external rewards and punishments are more active in the compliance and identification levels of conformity. Internal justification is more active in identification and internalization. The continuum shows tangible rewards or punishments paralleling compliance, and intangible rewards paralleling internalization. Intangible rewards can come in the form of positive self esteem; intangible punishments can come in the form of negative responses from peers.

The longer an individual remains in the internalization stage of conformity, Aronson explained, the stronger the belief or value systems guiding one's actions become. The role of symbols, rituals and myths in this conformity-dissonance-justification experience will be discussed in the analytical section of this study. What I discovered in the early stage of research suggests that without the unifying focus and intangible rewards of the Corps' folklore, motivation for joining the service and staying would have to become more extrinsic or tangible (financial).

This point returns to a central question of the study: If the values of the Marine Corps are imbedded in the folklore of the Corps, and Marine Corps folklore is changing, it is possible that diminishing the value of folklore's symbols, rituals and myths could lead to a greater need for external rewards (higher pay, for example) to keep Marines serving. An allied concern is the effect such a change would have on the Corps' ability to perform its mission.

Organizational Change Theory

Studies in organizational change offer yet another perspective of cultural change in the Corps. Two excellent texts hit the book shelves in the 1980s. *In Search of Excellence*, (Peters & Waterman, 1982) presented, as indicated in its subtitle, *Lessons from the Best-run Corporations in America*. Lessons in theory from this book include an affirmation that organizations driven by "the explicit attention they pay to values, and by the way in which their leaders have created exciting environments through personal attention, persistence and direct intervention..." are those organizations which fit the description of excellence.[cxlvi]

Peters and Waterman also wrote: "As we did this research, we were struck by the wealth of non-monetary incentives."[cxlvii] They reinforced the point that people not only worked for a paycheck providing necessary external justification, but excellent organizations seemed to have more non-monetary incentives providing internal justification.

Recalling Maslow's widely understood hierarchy of needs from basic textbook sociology, this phenomenon can be interpreted as excellent companies' workers having met their psychological, safety and affective needs and moving through esteem toward self-actualization.

My conclusions parallel Aronson's findings: internal justification based on intangible rewards is stronger and of more importance to the individual and the organization than punishments, tangible rewards or negative reinforcement. Peters and Waterman agreed that monetary rewards are important, but the symbolic, intangible rewards are stronger and deeper in their support for organizational commitment.

Dozens of other quotes could be presented from Peters and Waterman, but the essence of their findings is that the several companies they defined as excellent were fairly uniformly identified by characteristics like family feelings, small units, simplicity rather than complexity, acceptance of failure but with rewards for success, flexibility in the face of change, simultaneous centralized and decentralized authority, evidence of genuine leadership skills in managers, lean staff and productivity through people.[cxlviii]

One notable failing in *In Search of Excellence* is the common reference to the *military model*, referring to an apparent belief that militaries are unfamiliar with improvisation, innovation or excellence. Just as civilian researchers may expect some military people to be naive of civilian research and management methods, Peters and Waterman have an uninitiated, perhaps naive view of the military.

The second text mentioned above is *Corporate Cultures* (Deal & Kennedy, 1982), whose acknowledgements recognize Peters as the "intellectual and spiritual godfather" of research in the sociology of (business) organizations.[cxlix]

Rather than first presenting a discussion of their findings, note the questions which guided the initial research for *Corporate Cultures*:

Does company X have one or more visible beliefs?

If so, what are they?

Do people in the organization know these beliefs?

If so, who? How many?

How do these beliefs affect day-to-day business?

How are these beliefs communicated to the organization?

Are the beliefs reinforced by formal personnel processes, recognition, rewards?

How would you characterize the performance of the company?[cl]

The purpose of their study was to find beliefs, determine how these beliefs got into the company and how the beliefs were transmitted. Their findings included these elements: Each of the successful companies studied performed some activity "very well" in a business environment, and were characterized by values, heroes and rites and rituals. Throughout the text, Deal and Kennedy voiced again what was presented earlier in this chapter, that values or beliefs, heroes or heroic stories, and rites and rituals serve as cultural maps that spell out how people are supposed to behave, and unify adherents of the culture toward the effective accomplishment of the organization's mission. *(A parallel set of identical factors serve to radicalize, then recruit, adherents to radical Islam.)*

That this exactly parallels the study at hand does not need repeating. What *is* important is Deal's confirmation that this study can easily follow the same theoretical framework as *Corporate Cultures.*[di] Deal's response, by telephone, to the question: "Would it be possible to duplicate this study in the Marine Corps?" was, "Absolutely, this is what the Marine Corps, the military, is all about."

In addition to the theoretical support found in *Corporate Cultures* and *In Search of Excellence*, further guidance on how to organize a study such *as The Edifice Complex* can be found in other works by Deal and others. Deal and Derr undertook a study of the mechanics of change in educational organizations. Among other things, they reported that schools are "controlled by institutional values and myths,"[cli] very similar to the postulates applied to the studies of industrial organizations noted above.

The purpose of their study was to recommend a **contingency**

theory for guiding change and reform, or a theory to be applied by an organization *desiring* change. It is important to note, however, that the purposeful change to be described below and evolutionary change in the Marine Corps must follow similar rules or patterns. That is, Deal and Derr recommend incorporating structures, processes and symbols in the planned change of an organization.

Understanding unplanned evolutionary change in an organization must take into account the same elements – structure, process and symbol. The apparent differences, as discovered in *The Edifice Complex*, lie in the organization's ability to control, absorb or counter unplanned change, and the effects of unplanned versus planned changes. Deal and Derr's description of each dimension was:

Structure consists of lateral and vertical role differentiation….Processes can be characterized as the ways of interacting and accomplishing work. The symbolic dimension is a constellation of non-rational, non-verifiable, self-reinforcing meanings and understandings often overlooked or ignored.[ciii]

Deal and Derr reached the same conclusions I had, that the three dimensions are interlocking:

Symbolism overlaps with the other two dimensions. Policies can be mythical; meetings are often ceremonial; and evaluation (performance appraisals in the Marine Corps are called "fitness reports" or "proficiency and conduct scores" for junior enlisted Marines – either way, a process) serves as an important ritual.[civ]

One of the conclusions Deal and Derr reached was that symbolism is the most difficult dimension of the three to change; it is easier to effect planned changes in processes or structures. On the other hand, the most lasting change, if effected successfully, can be in symbolism, as long as the other two dimensions are taken into account. That is, if symbolism is changed, parallel changes in structures and processes may follow to reflect those changes.

The Edifice Complex discusses changes in all three dimensions of the Marine Corps' culture – symbolism, structures and processes. I have generalized the principles of planned change in symbolism, structures and processes to both planned and unplanned change. The important factor in this generalization is Deal and Derr's description of the strength of symbolism compared to structures and processes. Their definition of **symbolism** closely parallels the concept of **folklore** in this study. Symbolism is equivalent to the **spirit** or **faith** noted above, in that this concept or construct is the most difficult to change, but is also the most powerful influence over those who take part in the culture. Processes and structures, especially those artificially imposed, are the laws, or first and second order controls discussed by Perrow and others, above.

Perspective: Working through 2009 and 2010 as a consultant in the military domain of **influence operations** *I was reminded that PSYOP may be applied to either changing behavior or changing attitudes – or both.*[clv] *Psychological operations (PSYOP) morphed in 2010 by way of Secretary of Defense edict, to the euphemistic term* **military information support operations MISO**, *as if we change the name the bad guys will think we've stopped using psychology. The change is really for the squeamish on Capitol Hill.*

Summary

This chapter provides the theoretical foundation for a discussion of planned and unplanned changes affecting the Marine Corps. I have presented findings from research in anthropology, social psychology, social control in industry and educational institutions, folklore, advertising and military sociology.

The working relationships among theoretical subsets in each discipline and their imputed relationship to phases in a Marine's

Types and levels of control

	Career Phase		
	Pre-Induction	**Basic Training**	Career
Propaganda types	Information	Influence	Conformity
Conformity levels	Compliance	Identification	Internalization
	Compliance	Compliance Identification	Compliance Identification Internalization
Perrow's Orders of Control	Third	First and Second	First Second Third
Justification and Rewards	External Tangible and Intangible	External tangible to Internal Intangible	Variable and Situation Dependent

Table I

career are presented in Table I. I noted that the three conformity levels are observed in small cycles in each phase but the three levels may also define the total career.[clvi]

The effects of Conformity may be applied to any rite of passage of some period longer than a few weeks. Note also that Perrow's orders of control increase or progress in the career phase, with more reliance on self-discipline, peer pressure and maturity paralleling control through internal adherence to the values of the organization.

Chapter Five

Review of Research and Related Literature

as of 2011

Overview of Research and Related Literature Pertaining to Internal Conflicts within Islam, and the Propaganda, Recruitment, Themes, Messages and Symbols of al-Qaida, Hamas, Hezbollah, etc.

Research and Analysis

As one of the four main cultural changes impacting the Marine Corps over the past 20 years is the infusion of technology, broadly, it certainly makes sense to make good use of technology to fill in the gaps of the past two decades. For perspective: I started my master's thesis on this topic of organizational propaganda in 1979 on a legal pad with a box of pens, with endless hours in libraries with real books and "in the field" collecting anthropological field data. Interviewing people never ends. I continued on an Olivetti electric typewriter, and finished on a Tandy Color Computer that originally came with 16K of core memory and a cassette recorder for external storage. I eventually upgraded that computer to 64K, then bought an Apple IIe with a dual floppy disk drive. My first IBM clone operated at 4MHz, with a 10 MHz button for "turbo."

That was more than 30 years ago. My new HP has a 6-gig motherboard with a terabyte hard drive for internal storage, 3-gig processing speed and wireless access to my home server serving four other computers for family members in my home. I have instant access to the Internet and an additional terabyte of external memory. Like Marines and Insanely Radical Islamists, we access our Facebook pages from home and smart phones, we text, we Skype, we send e-mail, and we use the Internet to collect information about our competitors and plot the overthrow of small, dysfunctional countries.

I have bookmarked < http://www.ctc.usma.edu/sentinel/> on the Internet for ready reference to incisive studies on a wide range of counter-terrorism topics, many based on primary sources: first-hand accounts of recruiting, propaganda and indoctrination from Islamist combatants captured in Iraq, Afghanistan and other locations, captured and translated documents and other material.

For an idea of the range of topics evaluated by the Countering Terrorism Center (CTC) at the US Military Academy at West Point, consider the CTC topics reviewed and reported on by other outlets listed at the Appendices.

As of this writing, the CTC Sentinel's web site identifies its Editorial Board as two colonels, a lieutenant colonel and an FBI fellow. Recall previous observation regarding Brannan, Esler and Strindberg's premise that authors working for corporations, governments or law enforcement agencies deliver weak analyses because they seek to "manage the terrorist threat."[clvii] The suggestion is that academicians as theorists are the better qualified (more objective?) analysts of terrorists and their ideology. The US Military Academy is an accredited academic institution, as are the Navy, Air Force and Army War Colleges, the Naval Postgraduate School, Marine Corps Command and Staff College, National Defense University, and so on. Military students, including a substantial number of allied nation military students, at these institutions routinely write master's theses on specific topics of interest to countering terrorism, conflicts in Islam, Insanely Radical Islamist Fundamentalism and related issues.

Emblematic of the range of output from Western analysts: consider the perspectives of Clarke and Knake, writing in the

February 2008 issue of the CTC Sentinel, *Counter-Terrorism Issues for the Next President* at the end of the Bush administration):

> *"The next president will inherit from the current administration a dysfunctional counter-terrorism apparatus. The U.S. military has been stretched thin by the wars in Iraq and Afghanistan, the intelligence community has been discredited by the lack of weapons of mass destruction in Iraq and the ongoing failed hunt for Osama bin Laden, and the Department of Homeland Security has so many missions and so many disparate agencies that it is ineffective. An even more challenging task will be to restore United States credibility in the world and to reduce the number of people who bear us ill will.... America is not fighting a "Global War on Terrorism" anymore than it fought a "war on Drugs in the 1990s....[the] war metaphor [is] counterproductive. Since this problem has been framed as the GWOT, the Pentagon has been the driving force behind U.S. counter-terrorism policy. Yet, the military is a sometimes ineffective tool. As General David Petraeus has noted, sometimes the best weapons don't shoot. To defeat the al-Qa`ida movement, it must be recognized as a cancer infecting only a small percentage of the greater body of peace-loving Muslims worldwide.*[cviii] [my emphasis]*

They are entitled to their opinion – and this is an opinion piece. A couple of issues are relevant. Acknowledging that military efforts to fight terrorism have had some failures suggests that what Clarke and Knake are trying to say is that *kinetic* military operations have pissed off a lot of Muslims. They would be correct. Drone strikes in Yemen and Pakistan and unexploded ordnance in Afghanistan – that kills non-combatants, including especially children – go a long way toward radicalizing otherwise moderate citizens. When one says WAR to the armed forces, in general, most of the armed forces think "bombs, bullets, foot soldiers, tanks, fighter jets and aircraft carriers." Fighting ideology with bombs and bullets – instead of fighting ideology with ideology – provides the mythical "Muslim World" (the "ummah") with fodder for expanding their own kinetic war and fuels their recruiting propaganda. The blitzkrieg, "shock and awe" operation in Iraq was clumsy at times but was not a complete failure. Yes – Iraq still operates as a dysfunctional country sitting on potentially the second largest oil reserves in the world; and now that we've left Iraq, the country still has issues (the Kurds, the Sunni-Shi'a divide, Iran's influence) and the war is just beginning. Our record on winning hearts and minds is mixed at best.

Likewise Afghanistan. Osama bin Laden's execution in May 2011 dealt a blow to al Qaida, but during the ten years of working the intelligence networks to find him, al Qaida aerosolized, seeped into the Internet, and morphed into franchise operations in North Africa and the Middle East. "Someone" let the Taliban re-arm, re-congregate, and bring the war against the US, International Security Assistance Forces (NATO) and Afghanistan's puppet government back to 1980's Soviet proportions. And when we leave Afghanistan and Iraq both, we will still have a global war on terror in some form.

The second issue is: While Clarke and Knake are suggesting a revamped Intelligence Community, what they have not adequately articulated is that if we should be fighting ideology with ideology instead of with weapons, and some measure of this ideology may be cast as influence by way of development aid, how-to in business and international trade, governance, agriculture, mining and minerals, health and education, and so on – then shouldn't some of that burden be borne by other agencies of the US Government? State Department? Commerce? Justice? And others?

Well...these agencies *are* in fact present in Iraq and Afghanistan and most countries around the world. But their budgets are tiny compared to Defense budgets, volunteers are few, and security training (hostile environment survival skills) for those willing to go into hostile areas is minimal.

The point, for this text, is that it has taken pundits,

Washington policy-makers and Pentagon leaders ten years of evolutionary thinking to migrate the Marine Corps and Army toward a war of influence.[clix] National policy shapes strategy; strategy impacts operations; reflections on operations tell us what our doctrine is (a gradually evolving concept); and all of these impact training, education, socialization and enculturation of our Marines. We have to be able to tell Marines what kind of war they're fighting. We can't insert development programs (wells, generators, schools and clinics) into fragile nation states unless we have security. And security is guaranteed with guns, bombs, foot soldiers – and Marines. In the background, typically quietly, the non-kinetic *war* is being waged by Special Operations Forces (SOF), in "small footprint" relationship-building operations designed to assist other nations' militaries to provide for their own defense.

The most important point in Clarke and Knake's three-page diatribe against the US Intelligence Community, however, is the reference to *the greater body of peace-loving Muslims worldwide*. Considering their credentials, one might assume Clarke and Knake have some statistics on that assertion. Convincing combat veteran Marines that there is a *greater body of peace-loving Muslims worldwide* may need some salesmanship. That greater body has not been terribly vocal, and organizations that purport to speak for "that greater body" – CAIR and the Muslim Brotherhood – come with questionable credentials.

Contrast this to Dr. Tom O'Connor. O'Connor's website indicates he is Program Manager of CJ and Homeland Security, and Director, Institute for Global Security Studies, at Austin Peay State University, Clarksville, TN.[clx]

O'Connor writes:

Too often, the study of Islamic extremism (or Islamist extremism if one prefers to reference only political Islam) is suppressed out of charitable deference to multicultural sensitivities or a desire to leave well enough alone. Stereotyping is, of course, always to be avoided, as is any ethnic profiling or the falsehood that every Muslim is a degree or two separation from a terrorist. Not every Muslim is an extremist. However, there are various shades of extremism that we urgently need to become familiar with. In fact, there is even [Islamic] anti-Islamist extremism. So, the phrase "Islamic extremism" is used here to encompass the broader phenomenon. What do we really know about extremism?[clxi]

And:

Many levels of Islamic belief are hard to separate from different forms of Islamic extremism. More or less "mainstream" forms of extremism may co-exist with more or less dangerous "brands" of militancy. Clearly, only certain forms of extremism and militancy border on terrorism, but it's also been argued there's no such thing as a "moderate" Muslim since even "mainstream" Islam teaches to disgrace, humiliate, and belittle non-Muslims (Ye'or 1996). For Western infidels to keep quiet about this is called dhimmitude, the humiliating, subservient status of non-Muslims commanded by the Koran or Qur'an (Sura 9:29). Dhimmitude is exactly what Islamic extremists depend on and strive for (Ye'or 2002; 2005). Any student of Islam would quickly note that, far from being a religion of peace, much of the language and narrative of Islamic discourse is draped in the context of enemies - enemies of God or enemies of Islam. Islamic extremism has no problem recruiting large numbers of (holy) warriors (mujahideen) because of this built-in vilification of the enemy. [my underline emphasis][clxii]

O'Connor's essay reads like a fairly level-headed analysis of the broader questions posed by the un-read and uninitiated. He identifies the various divisions within Islam, the debate over Islam being inherently violent,[clxiii] socio-cultural differences between Arab Islam and the West, the thesis that Islamists have hijacked Islam, and so on. For the scholar, O'Connor's brief but on-target descriptions on the following are worth visiting his web site:

Islamism

Islamofascism

Jihad

Jihadism

Qutbism

Salafism

Sufism

Wahhabism

As for application, O'Connor arrives at the question: "Can Islamic extremism be prevented?" Following brief discourse, including a quote from the Ayatollah Khomeini (*"there are no jokes in Islam."*), O'Connor suggests ridicule might be one of our most potent weapons:

> *Speaking of humor, one of the best weapons against Islamic extremism is ridicule since terrorists fear that more than death. They fear losing at psychological warfare, at having their leaders appear as bumbling idiots. Even dictators cannot survive a climate of free speech characterized by satire and ridicule. One of the first things Fidel Castro did, for example, after taking power was to put up signs saying "No counterrevolutionary jokes here." In the Muslim world, **pride, honor and shame** are profoundly important, so ridicule as a weapon might have some effect, although backlash can be expected. Mike Waller's Fourth World Blog has long advocated the weapon of ridicule.[clxiv]*

For the scholar seeking to revalidate (or refute) my findings and analysis, O'Connor provides a lengthy bibliography of his primary references and an additional list of Internet resources.

Two other Internet-based resources I have come to rely on

are Jihadica (http://www.jihadica.com) and Jihad Watch (http://www.jihadwatch.org). Jihadica's "About" blurb tells us:

Jihadica

Jihadica is a clearinghouse for materials related to militant, transnational Sunni Islamism, commonly known as Jihadism. At the moment, much of this material is diffuse, known only to a few specialists, and inaccessible to the public and policymakers unless they pay a fee. Jihadica provides this material for free and keeps a daily record of its dissemination that can be easily searched and studied. These records are accompanied by the expert commentary of people who have the requisite language training to understand the primary source material and advanced degrees in relevant fields.[clxv]

Both Jihadica and Jihad Watch have done an exemplary job of presenting a wide range of articles and other posts, with critical analysis. Jihadica's archives cover a wide swath (see Appendix I).

One of the more interesting running blogs was the debate between Jordanian Abu Muhammad al-Maqdisi and Maqdisi's criticism of former student Abu Mus`ab al-Zarqawi (the Jordanian butcher who ran rampant at the head of al-Qaida in Iraq / Islamic State of Iraq during 2004 through June 2006 when the US Air Force dropped a few bombs on the lad). For those who don't remember the headlines from Iraq during those bloodiest days, Zarqawi was the evil mastermind behind many of the suicide bombers and the beheadings, in addition to blowing up several hotels in Amman, Jordan.[clxvi] Jihadica posts:

In the past, Will, Brynjar and Thomas [guest bloggers] have written excellent posts on Jihadica about the Jordanian ideologue Abu Muhammad al-Maqdisi's credibility problems. Just to refresh everyone's memory: as a result of al-Maqdisi's criticism of his former pupil Abu Mus`ab al-Zarqawi's extreme use of violence in Iraq in 2004 and 2005, *some fellow jihadis accused him of reneging on his earlier, supposedly more radical beliefs and of betraying the* mujahidin. *This criticism was expressed particularly fiercely on the Midad al-Suyuf forum by contributors such as al-Mihdar, Layth Makka and especially al-Zarqawi's brother-in-law, Abu Qudama Salih al-Hami.*[clxvii]

The blog continues, and further discussion of divisions within Islam are searchable with keywords (Maqdisi, Zarqawi, conflict, debate, etc.) Refer back to O'Connor's observations on humor, sarcasm and ridicule. Islamist leaders apparently don't take criticism well.

Hegghammer also refers to West Point's CTC, with advice on "What to read over the holidays:"

...advice for those of you wondering what to read over the Christmas break:...the Combating Terrorism Center at West Point has released its long-awaited report on ideological divisions in the jihadi movement. I had the great pleasure of reading it in advance as an external reviewer, and all I need to say is that it is destined to become a classic in the field of jihadism studies.

As with Americans expressing their points of view (that free speech thing), debates between real or self-appointed leaders in the Islamic community find their way into public forums. At issue, commonly, is who claims to have the purest interpretation of the Quran, and how many fatwas he can line up to discredit the other mouthpiece. It may be that internal strife will eventually lead to the demise of the most radical of the Insanely Radical Islamist Fundamentalist Terrorists. On the American side of the equation, when one leader blasts another, we generally know who is going to lose because we have a real chain of command and the Islamists don't.[clxviii]

Emblematic of that lack of a clear chain of command in al-Qaida is the internal struggle between AQ's imputed leader, Ayman al-Zawahiri and one of his regional commanders, Abu Bakr al-Baghdadi, over who commands AQ forces in Iraq and Syria in 2013. The discord is highlighted by Stratfor:[clxix]

In a June 15 audio message, a man identified as Abu Bakr al-Baghdadi, leader of the Islamic State of Iraq, did something no leader of an al Qaeda franchise had ever done: He publicly defied a directive from Ayman al-Zawahiri, the leader of the al Qaeda core organization. As we have noted for many years, the al Qaeda core has struggled to remain relevant on the physical and ideological battlefields. We've also discussed since 2005 the internal frictions between the core and some of the more independent franchise commanders, such as Abu Musab al-Zarqawi, the leader of al Qaeda in Iraq until his death in June 2006. If al-Baghdadi's revolt goes unchecked, it very well might spell the end of the concept of a global, centrally directed jihad, and it could be the next step in the devolution of the jihadist movement as it becomes even more regionally focused.

The debates are not just between Jordanians, Egyptians and Iraqis. An October 2009 post reflects apparent tension between al-Qaida and the Taliban:

Mullah Omar's Afghan Taliban and al-Qa'ida's senior leaders have been issuing some very mixed messages of late, and the online jihadi community is in an uproar, with some calling these developments "the beginning of the end of relations" between the two movements.[clxx]

And finally, from Jihadica, Hegghammer notes:

Nelly Lahoud's much-awaited new book, the Jihadis' Path to Self-Destruction, is out. Lahoud, who recently joined West Point's Combating Terrorism Center as an associate professor, is one of the finest scholars of jihadi ideology around. Her book is a brilliant dissection of contemporary jihadi discourse with an original twist, namely an in-depth comparison of modern jihadism with early Kharijism. She argues convincingly that the takfiri reflexes of contemporary militants will lead to their internal fragmentation and political marginalization, just as it did with the Kharijites. A very impressive work.[clxxi]

Jihad Watch

In contrast to Jihadica.com, *Jihad Watch* offers a bit more invective, pejorative and sarcasm. Jihad Watch is the progeny of Robert Spencer. The web site does not have an apparent "About" page, but more than adequate biographical and bibliographic information. "About Robert Spencer" tells us:

> *ROBERT SPENCER is the director of Jihad Watch, a program of the David Horowitz Freedom Center, and the author of ten books, including the New York Times bestsellers The Truth About Muhammad and The Politically Incorrect Guide to Islam (and the Crusades) (both Regnery). He is coauthor, with Pamela Geller, of The Post-American Presidency: The Obama Administration's War On America (Threshold Editions/Simon & Schuster).*
>
> *Spencer is a weekly columnist for Human Events and FrontPage Magazine, and has led seminars on Islam and jihad for the United States Central Command, United States Army Command and General Staff College, the U.S. Army's Asymmetric Warfare Group, the FBI, the Joint Terrorism Task Force, and the U.S. intelligence community.[dcxii]*

Spencer's bio and bibliography include the notes that "Spencer (MA, Religious Studies, University of North Carolina at Chapel Hill) has been studying Islamic theology, law, and history in depth since 1980. As an Adjunct Fellow with the Free Congress Foundation in 2002 and 2003, he wrote a series of monographs on Islam: *An Introduction to the Qur'an*; *Women and Islam*; *An Islamic Primer*; *Islam and the West*; *The Islamic Disinformation Lobby*; *Islam vs. Christianity*; and *Jihad in Context*. More recently he has also written monographs for the David Horowitz Freedom Center: *What Americans Need to Know About Jihad*; *The Violent Oppression of Women In Islam* (with Phyllis Chesler); *Islamic Leaders' Plan for Genocide*; and *Muslim Persecution of Christians*."

...and some frequently asked questions (FAQs) , the first of which is:

> Q: *Why should I believe what you say about Islam?*
>
> RS: *Pick up any of my books, and you will see that they are made up largely of quotations from Islamic jihadists and the traditional Islamic sources to which they appeal to justify violence and terrorism. My work sheds light on what these sources say. The evidence stands by itself; readers can evaluate it for themselves. I would, of course, be happy to debate any scholar about Islam and jihad; this is a standing invitation.*

Spencer fancies himself an authority. His analyses are often biting, insightful (and inciteful), but always on point. In December 2010's archives is the article *The New Conquistadors.* With regard to "All snakes are creepy, but not all snakes are poisonous," and the issues of radicalization and reclaiming the caliphate, Spencer writes:

> *I used to think that this was the whole story: Europeans didn't want to clean their own toilets or have their own children, so they outsourced both tasks to hungry immigrants from impoverished Muslim countries--often their own former colonies. What enabled this staggering act of civic vandalism was a complex of factors: lingering guilt over colonial abuses, cultural indifferentism, a disdain for religion, and a lazy confidence in the power of aging, decadent societies to dissolve ancient traditions. And all of these factors are real. What I didn't know is that <u>Islamic theology</u> has since its beginnings <u>considered mass migration a tool of conquest</u>. That's the insight offered by Sam Solomon & Elias Al Maqdisi in their new book* Modern Day Trojan Horse: The Islamic Doctrine of Immigration, *which Henrik R. Clausen of Europe News reviews at length. [my underline emphasis]*

Spencer's site is worth a scholar's time. Even more biting than Jihad Watch is *Islam: The Religion of Peace (and a big stack of dead bodies)*, at http://www.thereligionofpeace.com/.

<u>US Military Analysts</u>

From an academic point of view, one of the best sources I've returned to on numerous occasions is the 2005 master's thesis of (then) Major Stephen P. Lambert, US Air Force Research Fellow: *Y: The Sources of Islamic Revolutionary Conduct.*[clxxiii] (as of 2010, Lambert was a lieutenant colonel.) For a sense of what Lambert is getting at, refer to two notes in the Commentaries:

> *The title of this book naturally brings to mind the renowned diplomatic telegram from 1946, composed by "X" to explain "The Sources of Soviet Conduct." The anonymous George Kennan grasped the essence of the Soviet challenge, and the subsequent Containment Strategy became the foundation for strategic thought and action by the U.S. and its allies. The relatively brief "Cold War" of the late 20th century, we can now see, ironically carried the very name given in 13th century Spain to the ancient and ongoing conflict between Christians and Moors (Maghreb Moslems), a point underscored by Adda Bozeman. In the present work, Stephen Lambert convincingly argues that an effective, strategic appreciation of our present, worldwide contest, especially as it reflects the historic conflict between religious ideologies, cannot be achieved without public discussion of the religious foundations of individual and collective belief and action, whatever label we chose to apply to the struggle. He captures the metaphysical foundation of a struggle that is at the same time entirely physical and real for those in the arena. Ideas are in conflict, and ideas rule the world.*

> *Dr. Russell G. Swenson, Center for Strategic Intelligence Research, Washington, DC.*[clxxiv]

Dr. Mark Dever, PhD in Theological History at Cambridge University, offers this (segment) from the Commentary following Swenson:

> *Part 2 is in many ways the heart of Lambert's argument. I say this not because I am a theologian, but because Lambert's thesis is that our enemy is deeply theological. Part of our problem, he argues, is that though our language about religion is neutral, Western ideas about it are not – we naively and probably unwittingly assume that other religions are like Christianity, when, in some very important ways, they are not....It's not*

psychologically abnormal people, but rather committed Muslims, who refuse to separate the political from the religious....Lambert disturbingly concludes that we are already engaged in a religious war, whether we recognize it or not, and that success in it is compromised by our not recognizing it.[clxxv]

Dever writes: "...refuse to separate the religious from the political." Think on this. The "holy roman empire" was church and state for centuries. Martin Luther's radical approach to failures[clxxvi] in the (universal) Roman Catholic Church were *not* directed at the inviolability of the church + state in the 16th Century, but against doctrinal issues from the papacy (sola scriptorium). Yet his challenge led to on-again / off-again war for 130 years – which resulted in a Western European model which recognized that a state cannot dictate what its citizens believe in or worship. This did *not* spell the end of the Christian faith (and in fact the faith continued to multiply – even as it fragmented internally over the next centuries on doctrinal nuances). But what this suggests to a planet that is contemplating reaching for the stars is that Islam is 500 years behind the rest of the world and someone (some leader in Islam) needs to start thinking in terms of working *with* the rest of the world instead of against it.

Just in case that's not clear: that was an *opinion*.

Think about it like this: military leaders, political leaders, the moms and dads of fallen soldiers...all want "the terrorists" to change their behavior (stop fighting, stop blowing themselves up in order to kill bystanders), but as discussed in earlier chapters, changing behavior is not the same as changing attitudes (beliefs). **We're not just asking them to change their behavior; we're asking them to change what they believe.**

As discussed earlier – and we'll return to this in final analysis – some scholars deny this war on terror as a *holy war* specifically because terrorists are not practicing true Islam. And they can prove it by citing the Quran. The bad guys aren't jihadis – they're takfir.

They aren't mujahidin – they're irhabists. But if consistent, even predictable, behavior is a window to attitudes or beliefs, then the bad guys – some of the bad guys – must truly believe that Allah condones killing in the name of their religion. Beliefs and attitudes shape behaviors.

Inasmuch as Lambert's Part II (On Islam and Christendom: Comparisons and Imperatives) may be seen as the core of his thesis, Part III offers explanation to the questions of the Why and How of radicalization, recruiting, indoctrination and justification.

Part III of *Y: The Sources of Islamic Revolutionary Conduct* is "In the mind of the faithful: Identity, Trauma, Ressentiment and Transnational Islamic Revival," and it is this concept of "Ressentiment" that fuels the global jihad and provides the justification to move "passive, peace-loving Muslims" to moderates, moderates to militants, and militants to terrorists.[clxxvii] Lambert writes:

> *As outlined in Part II of this work, the Islamic world has inherited an undeniable political and historical imperative. The combined and powerful legacies of the Qur'an and the prophet bequeathed to the identity and faithful of Islam a decidedly deterministic theological perspective. The all-encompassing unity of Allah, the righteous truth in the Qur'an, the model life of the prophet, and the rightly guided way of Islamic law historically inspired an unprecedented political and military expansion of Islam's sacred geography.* **This sacred space was expected to bring justice, equality, and peace to all of mankind.** *[read: shariah justice, equality under Islam alone, and Mohammed's version of peace] For the first millennium of Islam, the growing and expanding kingdom of Allah seemed to be fulfilling its original mandate. However, modernity* **and Western secularism brought that historical advance to a grinding halt.** *In 1924, the political manifestation of that sacred geography, the Islamic Caliphate, was officially dissolved. Simultaneously, Western influences brought heretofore-unparalleled pressures to bear on the Islamic ummah.*

*The effects of Western incursion, inability to defeat European colonialism, the succession of military defeats at the hands of Western powers, and perception of technological and scientific backwardness, combine to form **a prevailing undercurrent of helplessness and impotency.** The extent to which Islam is, in the minds of the faithful, the irreducibly, final, and ultimate truth, makes this Western incursion even more injurious....**The inability to effectively respond to these challenges has resulted in a collective phenomenon of ressentiment in the minds of the faithful, and its powerful tonic is sustained by ongoing frustration and perceived hopelessness.**[clxxviii] (my emphasis, in bold)*

Lambert's assessment is no opinion. Compare Lambert's view to elements of Osama bin Laden's 1996 *fatwa* – declaring war on the United States:

It should not be hidden from you that the people of Islam had suffered from aggression, iniquity and injustice imposed on them by the Zionist-Crusaders alliance and their collaborators; to the extent that the Muslims blood became the cheapest and their wealth as loot in the hands of the enemies....The people of Islam awakened and realised that they are the main target for the aggression of the Zionist-Crusaders alliance. All false claims and propaganda about "Human Rights" were hammered down and exposed by the massacres that took place against the Muslims in every part of the world....The latest and the greatest of these aggressions, incurred by the Muslims since the death of the Prophet (ALLAH'S BLESSING AND SALUTATIONS ON HIM) is the occupation of the land of the two Holy Places -the foundation of the house of Islam, the place of the revelation, the source of the message and the place of the noble Ka'ba, the Qiblah of all Muslims- by the armies of the American Crusaders and their allies....The explosion at Riyadh and Al-Khobar is a warning of this volcanic eruption emerging as a result of the severe oppression, suffering, excessive iniquity, humiliation and poverty....People are fully concerned about their every day livings; everybody talks about the deterioration of the economy, inflation, ever increasing debts and jails full of prisoners. Government employees with limited income talk about debts of ten thousands and hundred thousands of Saudi Riyals. They complain that the value of the Riyal is greatly and continuously deteriorating among most of the main currencies. Great merchants and contractors speak about hundreds and thousands of million Riyals owed to them by the government. More than three hundred forty billions of Riyal owed by the government to the people in addition to the daily accumulated interest, let alone the foreign debt. People wonder whether we are the largest oil exporting country?! They even believe that this situation is a curse put on them by Allah for not objecting to the oppressive and illegitimate behaviour and measures of the ruling regime: Ignoring the divine Shari'ah law; depriving people of their legitimate rights; allowing the American to occupy the land of the two Holy Places; imprisonment, unjustly, of the sincere scholars.[clxxix]

...and so on and so on. Bin Laden's fatwa, single-spaced, runs some 30 pages. In truth – bin Laden had a *lot* of good points. No wonder he was pissed off. Most of his – their – grievances are represented in the brief passage above. Common questions for intelligence analysts, policy makers, strategists and others, in the US and many other countries, are:

- How deeply does bin Laden's message resonate in the *ummah* (the broader community (of 1.5 billion) of "the faithful?"
- In 2013 – is a dead bin Laden still relevant?
- Can his message be neutered? And if so – how?
- Do the assassinations of Anwar al–Aulaqi and Samir Khan in Yemen, in late September 2011, cut the propaganda machine off at the knees?
- To what extent are the *next* generation of jihadi/takfiri/irhabi speakers resonating with the *ummah?* (recipients of Anwar al-Aulaqi's message – the Las Cruces, New Mexico-born American who once talked trash from Yemen, for example.)

The point is: some percentage of Muslims are pissed off that, in their view:

- They forgot to develop *modern* technology (even though they invented the zero, and made significant contributions to optics, medicine, aeronautics and other sciences – centuries ago).
  - As a result, they have to import (or steal) Western weapons to fight Western armies – and each other.
- They live with corrupt despots in many countries (Egypt, Saudi Arabia, Bahrain, Syria, Tunisia, Kuwait, etc.) who are fueled by American imperialists, who preach about human rights but don't really do anything about it. (The "Arab Spring" revolutions, beginning with the overthrow of despots in Tunisia and Egypt – Zine al-Abidine Ben Ali and Hosni Mubarak – may eventually provide the counter-narrative we've been searching for.) The arrest of Egypt's President Mohammed Morsi on July 3rd 2013 signals not a coup but a revolution of the secular and moderate against the Muslim Brotherhood and Shariah, supported by the nation's military.
- Many of their people are unemployed and therefore destitute (despite historical, sociological and anthropological evidence that tells us that wealthier countries have lower birthrates and Arab Muslim multiplication rates make HP calculators blush) and lead to "youth bulges" that portend endless poverty and unrest.
  - They might not be unemployed if their despotic rulers put some cash, from oil proceeds, into industrial development – into something useful, like turning sand into silicon, or engineering sciences to convert sea water to potable water and converting the desert into farm land.
- That Israel occupies "Palestine" even though a wide swath of Arab countries had the opportunity to participate in the partitioning of Balfour's Palestine in 1947, and then lost every war fought against Israel after that.

- That Western armies, centered on US Forces, arrived in the land of the two mosques: Mecca and Medina, in Saudi Arabia in 2000 – 2001 to fend off Saddam Hussein's attack on Kuwait and threats to Saudi Arabia's oil fields.
- That the United States has Hooters, Victoria's Secret, Home Depot, bourbon, Rock 'n' Roll and "R" rated movies.
- And so on…

- And so on.

By way of opinion, one of the most important of bin Laden's assertions – and the general sense of Wahhabist / Salafist doctrine – is the declaration of *takfir*, *declaring or* proclaiming "wayward" Islamic practices (Shi`ite and non-Salafist Sunni) to be apostate or unbelievers. Kilcullen and Guirard, above, agree. Placing them on the same plane as American "infidels" (those without faith) offers a least the suggestion of a promise of future fractures within Islam. Bin Laden's branch of Islam shares some wishful thinking with the Taliban in Afghanistan, despite doctrinal differences, in seeking a revival, a renaissance, reform or a return to the "purer" ways of Mohammed and his followers in the 7th Century.

In comparison, Lambert's analysis delves into the relatively modern Reformation of the 16th Century, instigated in large measure by Dr. Martin Luther, John Calvin and others. The American culture from which young men and women grow into Marines is interestingly, or ironically, a blend of that Protestant Reformation and an eventual Protestant work ethic supporting America's religion of capitalism and individualism, of the Age of Reason and the Enlightenment, and the conflict that tore through Europe following the Reformation. To this, Lambert responds: "If man were perfectible, and man's capacity for reason and science was infinite, then there was no need for God, church, or religion."[clxxx]

Doctrines of the Enlightenment: The battle between religion and the secular elements of society was not a new phenomenon in late-eighteenth century Europe. In 1517, Martin Luther's epoch-making 95 theses had initiated a period of religious tension that evolved into 130 years of on-and-off again warfare and bloodshed, ultimately culminating in the pivotal 1648 Peace of Westphalia.[clxxxi]

As noted earlier, that Westphalian state construct provides our United States Republic a portion of its legitimacy – a legitimacy that should serve as the gold standard upon which America's message *to* or influence *in* the world is measured. But the United States finds itself competing for influence with forces beyond its control: technology and international media; the rise of 2nd World nations such as China, India, Russia, Iran, Brazil; the prevailing influence of global corporations that have become stateless transnational entities; and stateless actors – drug lords and other criminal cabals intersecting with radical religious elements. Of the latter – the crime/drug/religious extremist elements don't care about "legitimate borders, air supremacy, naval superiority" or constitutions.

Meanwhile, Lambert's conclusions provide the observation:

*The enemy is a revolutionary – not a terrorist. The war he is engaged in is an epochal struggle between his ideas about the affairs of mankind and our ideas about the affairs of mankind....He has not hijacked his religion and he is not its nominal follower – rather, he is an Islamic purist, and passionately follows the example of his Prophet Mohammad....He wields a diverse arsenal and is skilled not only in killing and destruction, but also in political propaganda and religious manipulation. He is driven by historical imperatives, a millennial tradition of Islamic doctrine, and the supererogatory promises of his eschatological foundation...**He will not yield, he will not negotiate, and he will not compromise**. This is the enemy – the revolutionary Islamic vanguard.*[clxxxii] [my bold emphasis]

Think about that.

Psychology, Radicalization and Recruitment

Among the more prolific producers of professional analysis in the domains of counter-terrorism, radicalization and a *lot* of other topics is the RAND Corporation, which bills itself as *a nonprofit research organization providing objective analysis and effective solutions that address the challenges facing the public and private sectors around the world.* RAND eschews the use of adjectives and adverbs, and provides an enormously useful array of usually rock-solid, unclassified intelligence analysis. Consider the prologues of the foregoing chapters. RAND's analysis of the processes of recruiting the next generation of takfiri/jihadi/irhabi fighters reads antiseptically (my adverb):

At one time, al Qaeda dispatched recruiters, but the jihadists never created a central recruiting organization. Instead, they relied upon a loose network of like-minded extremists who constantly proselytized on behalf of jihad. Recruiting was always diffused, localized, and informal. Self-radicalization was often the norm, even before the worldwide crackdown on al Qaeda and its jihadist allies forced them to decentralize and disperse. Those who arrived at jihadist training camps <u>were already radicalized</u>. At the camps, they bonded through shared beliefs and hardships, underwent advanced training, gained combat experience, and were selected by al Qaeda's planners for specific terrorist operations. There is a distinction between radicalization and recruitment.

Radicalization comprises <u>internalizing</u> a set of beliefs, a militant mindset that embraces violent jihad as the paramount test of one's conviction. It is the mental prerequisite to recruitment. Recruitment is turning others or transforming oneself into a weapon of jihad. It means joining a terrorist organization or bonding with like-minded individuals to form an autonomous terrorist cell. It means going operational, seeking out the means and preparing for an actual terrorist operation – the ultimate step in jihad.[clxxxiii] *[my emphasis].*

The concept of *shared adversity* will re-appear in my analysis in the final chapters. This concept drives directly to the image of "does this burqa make me look fat?" The mostly young, mostly men who self-radicalize and find others of like mind (shared adversity and shared beliefs), and undergo training and combat experience with those of like mind are going through exactly the same experiences, in terms of social psychology, as the young, male, American G.I. The cultures are vastly different; the psychology is basically the same.

The primary difference lies in the <u>social</u> side of social psychology in that Arab Islam is mainly a collective culture and American GI's grow up in an individualistic society. That phrase *"At the camps, they bonded through shared beliefs and hardships, underwent advanced training, gained combat experience, and were selected by al Qaeda's planners for specific terrorist operations"* could easily transform into a description of Marine Corps or Special Forces experiences. Change "al Qaeda" and the words "terrorist operations…"

The bigger picture is that every culture delivers its population unique *social* settings in which to play out <u>predictable human psychology</u>, which contrast or conflict with other cultures and social settings, as proposed in Dyer's script for the film *Anybody's Son Will Do*, discussed above. Can't present this idea any simpler than this.

To work within any other construct would be to suggest that there is an Arab psychology and an Aryan psychology, and necessarily an Anglo American psychology but also a Japanese psychology, Argentinian psychology and Inuit psychology. This then necessitates a White Anglo Saxon, over-50, 6-foot tall, marathon-running, Protestant, college educated, Heinekin beer-drinking, cigar-smoking, Maserati-driving…male psychology. And my point is: generals, policy makers, Homeland Security analysts, intelligence experts and others use *culture* and *psychology* interchangeably (and incorrectly), and, as with Kilcullen's and Guirard's admonitions to "use the right word," we did <u>not</u> have a good body of knowledge about al Qaida's culture,

Salafist or Wahhabist Islam, or Arab Muslim *culture* at the start of this war, but we had all we needed to know about their psychology. I posed this issue 30 years ago.

How American Marines and soldiers fulfill these needs varies a little or a lot from their adversaries – but human needs are human needs. Self-actualization in the mind of a suicide bomber may be manifest in those 72 doe-eyed virgins he expects to greet him in paradise. And I don't want to make too big a deal out of *Maslow's Hierarchy* in particular; there are endless theories or schools devoted to understanding human motivation. Challenges to the Maslow school of thought charge that *Maslow's Hierarchy* itself is ethnocentric and does not account for observable, quantifiable differences between collective cultures and individualistic cultures.[clxxxiv]

Maslow's Hierarchy

American warriors' needs	*Takfiri / Irhabi/Jihadi needs*
Self-actualization: Vitality, creativity, self-sufficiency, authenticity, meaningfulness	Self-actualization: Vitality, creativity, self-sufficiency, authenticity, meaningfulness
Self-esteem	Self-esteem
Love & belongingness	Love & belongingness
Safety & Security	Safety & Security
Physiological needs: Air, water, food, shelter, sleep, sex	Physiological needs: Air, water, food, shelter, sleep, sex

Table II [clxxxv]

The HOW of Radicalization and Recruitment

The next section will explore a number of changes which have, or will, impact Marine Corps culture, among them the infusion of technology. But this is a double-edged sword and we don't call it the **World Wide** web for fun. Insanely Radical Islamist Fundamentalists blog, have e-mail accounts, browse the Internet and use Google Maps. And they share their irhabist invective using the latest gadgets.

Jihadica's guest blogger Nico Prucha offers a look at trends in terrorist recruiting:

In October 2009 the Arabic "al-Ansar al-Mujahideen Forum" offered a special data-package designed for mobile phones. Published by a newly created "Mobile Detachment" the contents are aimed at sympathizers and adherents of jihadist principles. Provided with a special software the mobile users can access the documents or watch videos on their portable device while being able to send out these highly indoctrinating and radicalizing sources via Bluetooth to other, unwary, Bluetooth enabled devices. The data offered in these conveniently administrated packages provides nearly everything of the grand-genre of jihadist materials.[clxxxvi]

Prucha's post discusses the technology and encryption software, and texts, videos, still images and audio files available for download and sharing with other Bluetooth-enable devices: "The content of all data-packages is well chosen and partially comprises of new, up-to-date materials, but also capitalizes on older fundamental documents that are of ultimate importance in the jihadists' mindset." The general aim is described in a "mission statement" that includes an invitation to join the endeavor of spreading jihadist materials and to "develop the jihadist media." Content includes audio ("There is nothing like Falluja"), pictures (the 9/11 attacks), video (such as al-Sahab videos showing the martyrdom operation against the Danish embassy in Pakistan) and so on.

Symbols, Rituals and Myths

The US Military Academy's CTC web site (http://www.ctc. usma.edu/imagery/imagery_introduction.asp) includes a section reserved for the *Islamic Imagery Project*. As discussed in the previous chapter, the core of a society's culture – symbols, images, colors, symbolic rituals and stories – combine as *folklore* and evoke passion, passionate response and collective action. These are the foundation of *shared* in shared adversity and collective psychological predisposition...to accept, as legitimate, the rallying cry – to "jihad" for example. Every organization needs a logo or flag to rally 'round.

CTC's *Islamic Imagery Project* offers analysis of a range of images and symbols, which serve as reference points to rituals (i.e. martyrdom) and myths (the storied "heroism" of the 19 suicide hijackers of 9/11). Subsections are: Geography and Political (images and symbols), Nature, People, Warfare and Afterlife, and Other. At the CTC, this information resides in the public domain.

Examples include:[clxxxvii]

Sun	In jihadi images, the sun is generally used to evoke notions of regional identity and the divine, and it may be used literally or figuratively...When the sun is invoked, the symbols, items, or individuals with which it is associated are also associated with the divine. In this manner, the sun is used to associate things with God, and thus, to legitimize them spiritually and religiously.
Moon	The moon is a very important and complex symbol in Islamic culture. It is imbued with astrological significance as well as wider religious and spiritual meanings. Its use in jihadi visual propaganda, however, is usually less complex and almost always indicates aspects of religious identity and notions of the afterlife and the divine.

Green crescent	The green crescent, like the white crescent, carries the meaning of Islamic identity, purity, and religious piety as the white crescent; however, it is a more politicized reference to Islam. The green crescent evokes strong notions of the Prophet Muhammad, and thus further emphasizes the Islamic nature of the symbol.
Water drop	Jihadi visual propagandists generally employ water in order to evoke notions of purity, the divine, heavenly paradise, and religious piety.
White rose	A white rose often appears as a symbol of purity and martyrdom in Islamic culture. In jihadi propaganda, the white rose is most often utilized to evoke the act (and goal) of martyrdom, and may be used with the image of an individual martyr.
Palm tree	In jihadi imagery, palm trees are often employed in order to evoke a sense of Arab or Islamic pride and concern....Because of their importance in Islamic history, they can also conjure up Salafi notions of the Prophet, his companions, and early Islamic history in general.
Sandy desert	Although sandy desert landscapes are not actually that common in the Middle East, landscapes similar to those shown in the film "Lawrence of Arabia" are important markers of Islam, with particular relevance to Arab traditions and cultures. In this manner, depictions of sandy deserts are generally used to evoke a sense of Arab-Islamic identity and the early history of Islam. Sandy deserts are thus commonly used by Salafi groups as an evocation of the first generation of Muslims, and can serve as a reference to both their success in jihad and the purity of their faith.
Lion (with Jihadi leaders)	An example shows a large lion's head surrounded by the photographs of major jihadi leaders. At the center of the image, superimposed on the lion's face, and thus symbolically becoming the head of

	the lion (or, in this case, the head "lion"), is a picture of Osama bin Laden. Flanking both sides of the lion's head are two emblems of Arabic calligraphy, each reading "God is Great" (*allahuakbar*).
Globe (literal)	Jihadi visual propaganda uses the globe, or Earth, to globalize specific issues and conflicts, as well as to articulate the global aims of particular groups. In the primary image selected... we see the globe as a background with Saudi Arabia at its center. Specific jihadi leaders and martyrs are superimposed on the globe, with Osama bin Laden firing a rifle in the center. This image uses the globe to highlight the global aims and success of al-Qaeda, as well as to suggest the importance of the jihadist struggle in Saudi Arabia as part of the greater (i.e. global) jihadi struggle.
American flag	The American flag is used liberally in jihadi propaganda, always evoking the unpopular sentiment surrounding U.S. foreign policy and military campaigns.
Stars and Stripes	In the first image selected, the Stars and Stripes are used to "color" a cross. The image itself is a comment on the Abu Ghraib abuses, and the Arabic text at the top of the image states: "a story of a captive of the Crusaders." In this manner, the propagandists explicitly link—both textually and symbolically—the U.S. occupation of Iraq and the Abu Ghraib abuses with Christianity and the Crusades. This conjures up the historical memory of the Crusades, and frames the U.S. occupation of Iraq as a form of neo-Crusading: i.e. a renewed war instigated by the Christian West against the Muslim East.
Star of David	The Star of David is always used explicitly in reference to the Israeli occupation of Palestine. By extension, it also evokes fears of a greater Jewish conspiracy and a general anti-Semitism.

Foreign currency	All Jihadi propaganda plays on popular sentiments in the Muslim world, one of which is the belief that the U.S. and other Western powers are only concerned with the Middle East because of its oil deposits. Many Muslims believe that Western society is greedy and materialistic, and that Westerners are slaves to money. Jihadi propagandists use the motif of foreign currency as a means of capitalizing on these sentiments.
Important defeats	Jihadi propaganda frequently reminds its audience of important political and violent events. These images draw attention to events that have helped to shape the current jihadi movement, and they allow the propagandists to reinterpret these events through their own ideological and cultural frameworks.
Important victories	Jihadi propaganda often marks important violent events in order to establish these events as key milestones that shape the current jihadi movement. These events are then reinterpreted to match the jihadists' assertion that these events were successful. These "successes," which can range from suicide bombings to large-scale terrorist attacks, are presented to the audience as examples of jihadi victory against much stronger and more powerful Western forces. Propagandists often exaggerate and inflate these events, and portray them as evidence of the imminent victory of jihadist Islam over Western imperialism and secularism. These events are used to promote faith and confidence in the jihadi enterprise, as well as to inspire others to join in the growing success of the jihadi movement.
Kaaba	The Kaaba in Mecca is the symbolic and literal center of the Islamic faith for all Muslims, and it is a common motif in jihadi imagery. It is the single most important, and holiest, site in Islam and evokes the strongest sense of Islamic identity and

	tradition across all Muslim sects and groups. Although it is inherently pan-Islamic, the Kaaba can also be employed to draw attention to issues concerning Saudi Arabia. Use of the Kaaba motif may also internationalize, or pan-Islamize, specific Saudi-centered jihadi concerns, such as the "occupation" of the Saudi holy sites by American forces during the first Gulf War. [The U.S. did not "occupy" Mecca or Medina.]
Jihadi Leader – Osama bin Laden (or Usama bin Laden – UBL)	The motif of "Osama bin Laden" is used by jihadi propagandists to symbolize resistance to unjust authority and dedication to jihad. Images of OBL (UBL) are ubiquitous in jihadi propaganda, closely followed by Ayman al-Zawahiri, Abu Musab al-Zarqawi, Mullah Omar, and Ibn al-Khattab.
Martyr with weapons and Koran	The "before shot" or "last will and testament" image is common in jihadi propaganda. These photographs, generally taken before a suicide mission to mark that event, almost always include weapons, the Koran, and other religious symbols. They combine these disparate items into a single overall message: the religious importance of martyrdom and its violent nature.
Women	Women hold powerful symbolic value in Islamic culture. Women symbolize masculine honor and purity, and are central to nearly every Muslim man's sense of pride. To this effect, women are a common motif in jihadi visual propaganda, and are usually depicted as either symbols of purity and honor, or as innocent victims of anti-Muslim oppression.
Paradise – the heavenly garden	There is perhaps no greater inspiration for jihadi activists than the belief that they will be rewarded for their sacrifice by being granted entrance into the garden (*janna*) of heavenly paradise. Symbols and images may allude to paradise indirectly or directly. The word used to indicate heaven, janna,

	also means "garden" and indicates the garden of paradise that awaits those Muslims who have lived particularly just, obedient, and pious lives.
Weapons, pre-modern	Weapons are symbolically important in Islamic culture and are commonly used as motifs in jihadi visual propaganda. Depictions of weapons can be broadly categorized as either modern or pre-modern. Pre-modern weaponry includes swords or spears, and is used to suggest the violent reality of the jihadi struggle. These images also link jihadi struggle to early Islamic history and the first generation of Muslims. Swords are seen as noble weapons that embody the purity, nobility, and overall righteousness that is associated with early Islamic heroes and their jihadi campaigns.
Weapons, modern	Modern weapons, such as rifles and RPGs, illustrate the violent nature of jihadi warfare and also exaggerate the power of the jihadists' military technology. Modern weapons evoke modern jihadi victories (or perceived victories) such as the expulsion of the Soviets from Afghanistan. In this manner, modern weapons embody the inherent capacity of the jihadi movement to overcome and defeat the West, using the latter's own military technology.
Blood on desert	In this image, blood is shown spilled on a shield and the ground. It suggests the sacrifice that jihad entails and alludes to the goal of martyrdom for jihadi fighters. That the blood is shown on the desert ground is significant for two reasons: 1) It speaks to the active jihad in Iraq, while also making this movement broader and thus more inclusive to a non-Iraqi, sympathetic Muslim audience. 2) It evokes the deep historical traditions related to Muslim jihad campaigns in early Islamic history. The sword and the shield, which are both symbols of pre-modern Islam, have Salafi connotations and remind Muslims that

	jihad requires sacrifice.
Black	The color black is a very significant color in the Islamic tradition. It is linked to both the battle flag of Muhammad (al-rawa) and to the medieval Abbasid Caliphate. In this sense, it most often represents jihad and the caliphate, evoking a historical sense of both concepts. Black is also used to show religious adherence and strict piety in both the Sunni and Shiite traditions.
Hand of God	References to divine assistance and intervention speak of the jihadists' sincere belief that they are agents of God's will, doing God's work.

Table III

In ethnographic terms, symbols, rituals and myths (or stories) have meaning. The RAND testimony noted above, *Building an Army of Believers*, discusses the presentation of these symbolic cultural imperatives to the needs of the target populations – typically parallel in age and needs to the target population sought by Marine recruiters: young men and women who need a job, who seek kinship bonds with like-minded people, who are beginning to feel some ideological spirit (political, patriotic, religious), who seek adventure, and whose hormones are peaking:

In the core Arab countries, where potential jihadists may share the basic beliefs of the dominant national culture or a fundamentalist subculture, they confront hostility and oppression from the central political authorities and therefore must go abroad or operate underground. [Consider the political tension in Tunisia, Egypt, Jordan, Syria and Yemen in 2011 through 2013.] The situation in the West is still different, and there are further differences between recruiting in Europe, where there are large and largely unassimilated Muslim immigrant populations, and recruiting in the United States, a nation with a long tradition of assimilating immigrants. Potential jihadist recruits in Western countries are part of a marginalized immigrant subculture or are themselves cut off even from family and friends within that community.

The more vulnerable are those who are at a stage of life where they are seeking an identity, while looking for approval and validations. They are searching for causes that can be religiously and culturally justified, that provide them a way to identify who they are, and that provide a clear call for action. The jihadist agenda is action-oriented, claims to be religiously justified, and appeals to this relatively young, action-oriented populations. Self-radicalization begins the day that an individual seeks out jihadist websites. In the real world, they seek support among local jihadist mentors and like-minded fanatics. This is the group that currently poses the biggest danger to the West. Jihadists recruit one person at a time. The message from the global jihad is aimed directly at the individual.[clxxxviii]

As Jenkins notes in this depiction of recruitment: "There is a distinction between radicalization and recruitment. Radicalization comprises internalizing a set of beliefs, a militant mindset that embraces violent jihad as the paramount test of one's conviction. It is the mental prerequisite to recruitment."

The Propaganda Process

As discussed in previous chapters, propaganda responds to individual needs. The future jihadi, irhabist, (willing) suicide bomber or terrorist is at the same point in his development and maturation as the future Marine. He's 15 or 16 years old…up to perhaps his mid- to late 20s or early 30s, and his testosterone is surging and he may be attracted to those "ascetic charms of war." Even some moderate narratives in Islam paint the US as a target – as an occupying force in Muslim nations, or as a defender of Israel. Every verified and countless wrongly attributed *collateral damage* death fuels the propaganda that American Marines kill Muslims, while Muslim clerics debate their own rationale for killing innocents – including Muslims or Christians or Americans of any confession.

The wannabe jihadi seeks a cause or purpose. He may have

role models in other males, including family members who have "fought jihad." He seeks validation or justification through a peer group. Decades of theoretical foundations clearly explain that the meaning embedded in the symbols, rituals and myths, the cultural narratives discussed above, provide internal, intangible *justification* and relieves that *cognitive dissonance* that comes with difficult decisions – like waging war. When peers are caught up in the same narratives, radicalization is one possible outcome. Those peers may be small groups who play soccer together; they may be virtual peers in chat rooms and blogs. In small groups they become mutually reinforcing.

Four Examples of Recruitment

1. The consensus in this community is that poverty, per se, is not a causal factor in radicalization. I agree. But consider the following steps: During the deadliest year in Iraq, from early 2006 through early 2007, when al-Qaida in Iraq (AQI) was stacking up dead bodies by the hundreds on an almost daily basis, an AQI operative might approach an *unemployed* 16- to 19-year-old with an offer of $250 per month to fight the occupying American forces. AQI might offer $500 or $1000 to emplace roadside bombs (IEDs), or $1000 a month for snipers. If the teenager had hoped to someday attend university, had not yet determined if Sadam Hussein's demise in December 2006 was a good thing or a bad thing, or if the Americans or AQI were the lesser of two evils – $250 a month was a *lot* of money. He does not need to have been religiously "radical" to begin with; American soldiers could be seen merely as invaders to his country, province or village. If he resists, the AQI operative could threaten to kill other members of his family, which they did. In the language of social psychology – this is *Compliance*.

If the teen hangs around and is feeling some "cognitive dissonance," but sees that the AQI "regulars" have AK-47s, and cars, and money (from robbing banks, kidnapping, smuggling oil, counterfeiting, etc.), and those regulars are justifying their side of the war in religious ideology, the teen may begin to identify with his more senior fellow "jihadis." This is *Identification*.

The longer he hangs around – and survives – the more likely he is to *Internalize* the justification for his jihad, especially if one or more of his family members is killed in the war and that death is more or less reasonably attributable to the Crusaders. He may become one of the "captains" of his unit, and take part in planning attacks. He may take part in recruiting the next converts. Most AQ cells have leaders, or emirs, for military action, for spiritual guidance, for administrative functions, for finances, and for propaganda. This model repeats itself over and over, from North Africa to Indonesia. These foot soldiers are not radicalized by unemployment, hunger or poverty; they are radicalized by other radicals – networks of peers who share a radical ideology. The fact that they are unemployed makes them *susceptible*, but university students are likewise as susceptible, as are young doctors and computer technicians.

2. Isolated diasporas: For a variety of historical reasons, rooted mostly in old colonial relationships, immigrants from majority Muslim countries have found their way to countries in Europe. Tens of thousands of Turks have built communities in Germany, seeking work. Pakistanis have migrated to the United Kingdom; Moroccans, Tunisians and Algerians to France and Spain; Libyans and Tunisians to Italy. These are not exclusive relationships, of course, as there are Pakistanis in Germany, Algerians in the UK, and so on, as well as enclaves of Muslim immigrants in the BENELUX and Scandinavian states as well.

In many of these communities, particularly smaller diasporic enclaves, the local Muslim community, isolated from their homeland and native Sunni or Shi'a norms, may have only one mosque. That mosque's message, the imam's message, may be Shi'a or Salafist Sunni. Or the Salafists hang around the mosque and have "study groups" for small groups of 16- to 20-year-olds. Second- and even third-generation immigrants are targets for one side of a larger Muslim story.

These diaspora communities have roots in the United States as well, with growing populations of migrants from virtually all Muslim-majority countries. The Somali community in Minneapolis is a case in point. During the past 5 years, some 15 to 20 Somali men, "called to jihad," left Minneapolis, found their way to Somalia, and hooked up with AQ offshoot al Shabaab. At least 10 of them have been killed in fighting against Transitional Government forces.[clxxxix]

But this group of Somalis doesn't fit the expectations of FBI and other researchers trying to come to grips:

For many of the men, the path to Somalia offered something personal as well — a sense of adventure, purpose and even renewal. In the first wave of Somalis who left were men whose uprooted lives resembled those of immigrants in Europe who have joined the jihad. They faced barriers of race and class, religion and language. Mr. Ahmed, the 26-year-old suicide bomber, struggled at community colleges before dropping out. His friend Zakaria Maruf, 30, fell in with a violent street gang and later stocked shelves at a Wal-Mart.

If failure had shadowed this first group of men, the young Minnesotans who followed them to Somalia were succeeding in America. Mr. Hassan, the engineering student, was a rising star in his college community. Another of the men was a pre-med student who had once set his sights on an internship at the Mayo Clinic. They did not leave the United States for a lack of opportunity, their friends said; if anything, they seemed driven by unfulfilled ambition.[cxc]

Again – these foot soldiers in jihad were not radicalized by either poverty *or* bourgeois coffee shop theorists; they were radicalized, then recruited, in small groups (psychologically unified) responding to a propaganda message. Their parents had brought them from war-torn Somalia in search of a better life. Many Somalis found those opportunities, but some attended to the call to defend their native homeland (at least that's the message) with a peer group. Two layers deeper, the al-Qaida-inspired Salafist roots of al-Shabaab run counter to the Shi'a and Sufi beliefs of large swaths of the Somali tribes, and al-Shabaab's success in Somalia is far from certain.

3. Converts. There are several elements to this: In addition to peer groups, parents play a significant role, or *fail* to play a role, in the critical stages of their children's development. Killed with Anwar al-Aulaqi by an apparent drone strike on September 30, 2011, Samir Khan, who was raised in the US, appealed to an English speaking audience with his rap and smart-ass invective.[cxci]

"I always felt like I was going to get this call," said Jibril Hough, a spokesman for the Islamic Center of Charlotte, North Carolina, who said he had tried to steer Khan away from extremism.

"I set up two interventions in my home," Hough told ABC affiliate WSOC in Charlotte, "and we tried to take him by the hand [and say], "Look you're going down the wrong path.'" Hough said Khan's parents had distanced themselves from their son's radical views. Khan was born in Saudi Arabia and raised from the age of seven in Queens, New York. He was a normal city teenager who listened to hip hop and wore baggy clothing.

Even before his family relocated to Charlotte, North Carolina in 2004, however, Khan had begun to take an interest in Islam. He ditched his baggy pants for jalabiyas, the long white robes traditionally favored by Saudis. He joined two Islamic groups, but neither espoused violence.

But with the move south, Khan took a turn towards radicalism. In 2004, after watching online videos of suicide bombers blowing themselves up at American military checkpoints in Iraq, Khan began to openly support Osama bin Laden and Al Qaeda and to express that support on-line."

Whether from Khan, or Aulaqi, or other English-speaking recruiters and propagandists, as through AQ in the Arab Peninsula (AQAP) magazine *INSPIRE*, some small numbers of Americans and other English-speaking converts have shown up on various battlefields. Among these, and rising to prominence as a traitor, is Adam Gadahn:

Adam Yahiye Gadahn; born Adam Pearlman, (September 1, 1978) is an American who is a senior operative, cultural interpreter, spokesman and media advisor for the Sunni Islamist group Al-Qaeda. Since 2004, he appeared in a number of videos produced by Al-Qaeda as "Azzam the American" ('Azzam al-Amriki, sometimes transcribed as Ezzam Al-Amerikee). Gadahn converted to Sunni Islam in 1995, at the age of 17, at a California mosque and is described as a "homegrown," meaning that he has converted to an ideology so firmly that he is now willing to harm his country of origin.[cxii]

Gadahn leads the pack of radicalized converts, now that Aulaqi is making out with 72 virgins, and there are others. Gadahn was 17. Where were his parents? Where were Samir Khan's parents? The parents of the Somali boys are still wringing their hands, wondering how these tragic events could happen.

4. Kilcullen's "legit" jihadis: *The Accidental Guerilla* discusses eloquently the phenomenon of "resistance forces." What may start as an insurgency, in East Timor, Thailand, Afghanistan or Indonesia...offers the potential to blossom into regional or global threats. An example of this is the Nigerian group known as Boko Haram (literally: Western education is a sin), also known as "The Nigerian Taliban." Boko Haram's original grievances included the claim that the Nigerian state was pulling in a lot of cash from the sale of oil, that there was a marked divide in prosperity between the wealthier Christian majority south, the Niger Delta region, and the Muslim majority north, and that the group was asking the country's leaders for a share of jobs in the government and the military. Those

grievances have apparently gone unmet to the extent that Boko Haram leaders have taken to larger and more sophisticated attacks:

Boko Haram opposes not only Western education, but Western culture and modern science as well. The group also forbids the wearing of shirts and pants and the act of voting in elections. In its view, the Nigerian state is run by non-believers. In a 2009 BBC interview, Mohammed Yusuf, then the group's leader, stated that he rejects the fact that the earth is a sphere and views it as contrary to Islam, along with Darwinism and the fact that rain comes from water evaporated by the sun.

On August 26 [2011], the UN headquarters in Abuja was blown up by a suicide car bomber, leaving at least 21 dead and dozens more injured. A Boko Haram spokesman later claimed responsibility. Four men appeared in an Abuja magistrates' court charged with organising the bombing, and were remanded in custody to a federal high court hearing.[cxciii]

The suicide car bomb is indicative of al-Qaida-inspired tactics, and suggests the possibility of links to AQIM – al-Qaida in the Lands of the Islamic Maghreb – operating in nearby Mali, or to al-Shabaab, based in Somalia. A brute force response to "eradicate these terrorists" has every possibility of playing to Boko Haram's hand, further radicalizing "disenfranchised Muslim youth," and encouraging their recruiting efforts in the northern tier of the country.

Increasingly, al-Qaida seeks "clean" travelers: potential terrorists who are not recognized as terrorists and are not on *No Fly* lists, and who may be able to obtain student or work visas to visit the US, UK or other target country.

What once was an insurgency or resistance force – like the French Resistance against the German Nazis of World War II – are potentially radicalized or further radicalized by violence and suppression.

Additional references

Research, analysis and commentary are available from a wide range of additional sources, including proprietary publications from think tanks like RAND, professional journals, print and electronic newspaper, magazine and broadcast television sources. Refer to additional source material in the Appendices.

Chapter Six

<u>Review of Research and Related Literature</u>

as of 2011

Overview of Research and Related Literature Pertaining to Conflicts Between Generations of Marines, and the Propaganda, Recruitment, Themes, Messages and Symbols of the Marine Corps

As discussed, planned and unplanned changes have impacted or presently have the potential to impact Marine Corps culture. Part of this book's mission is to bring the appreciation of this phenomenon current by about 20 to 25 years – from 1988-1990 to approximately 2012-13. Some of these changes have been imposed by external forces; some internal. My own set of experiences offers a unique perspective on changes in the Marine Corps.

While in Iraq in 2006-07, I was reminded of the story of Rip van Winkle (I was Rip van Winkle): Others may have a different take on this, but consider the experience of leaving your family, moving to another state or another country and not seeing your loved ones for 10 years. When you leave, your married kid brother or sister has small children; your parents are of a certain age. When you return 10 years later, you notice the dramatic contrasts between then and now: Your niece and nephew are 13 and 17 instead of 3 and 7. Your parents are no longer "in their 50's" but "in their 60's", and those who have lived with the gradual changes have absorbed the impact minute by minute, hour by hour, day by day – for 10 years. For you – it's a dramatic change. That's my view of the Marine Corps from 1995 to 2005.

My goal in this section is not to provide an exhaustive assessment of all of the changes infiltrating the Marine Corps since 1990, but rather to offer a window to the kinds of changes one might take notice of after a 10-year hiatus.

As previewed, the changes I've observed, and continue to watch as a result of my relative proximity to the armed forces, are:

- Influences of technology (use of computers, the internet, social networks, impact on uniforms, weapons systems, etc.)
- Increasing professionalization and academic achievement levels of enlisted Marines
- The implementation of repealing "Don't Ask, Don't Tell
- The inclusion of women into previously all-male domains, including aviation and combat support roles, and the proposal to open combat assignments to women.

Technology

Computers, cell phones, satellite telecommunications, LCD flat-panel televisions and computer monitors, social networking and virtual worlds (and more) are ubiquitous for personal use, as are these and related overlapping, integrated technologies in advanced weapons systems and training venues, not just for the US Marine Corps and the rest of the US Department of Defense (Army, Navy, Air Force) but for the bad guys too.

Marines, soldiers, sailors and airmen are invited to log on to http://www.togetherweserved.com/. The concept is along the lines of a virtual "American Legion" or "Veterans of Foreign Wars." (My father, an infantry Marine with service in the Korean War, was a member and local branch leader in the American Legion and VFW.) Rather than driving to the local VFW lodge to share a beer and some war stories with fellow GI's, which people still do, Together We Served works along the lines of a military *Facebook*, with log-ins for each of the armed services. Adequate internal policing allows members to call out imposters and posers.

Together We Served (TWS) basic registration is free, with additional features and applications available for a fee. Basic features include the shadow box, where Marines display their personal and unit awards (ribbons, with devices), shooting badges (marksman, sharpshooter or expert) and specialties (parachute or dive qualifications, for example).

TWS has added a link to *Facebook*, and provides guest registration at Army, Navy, Air Force and Coast Guard TWS. Most Marines will eventually serve with or interact with servicemen and women from other branches.

Additional applications include: Reflections (free-form reminiscences from Marines on their Marine careers), invitations for other Marines to join TWS; an e-mail drop box; photos; a TWS education and career center; unit, association and college pages; a jobs board; special profiles for fallen Marines (and a Roll of Honor for those killed in Vietnam, Afghanistan and Iraq). Interest group pages include: computers and internet, health and fitness, food and beverage, travel, music, motorcycles, cars, benefits and claims, hunting and fishing, Christianity, babies and toddlers – and more. The splash page for TWS notes that registered users on the Marine side number 308,000 (as of 2011). Registered Navy users number 520,000; Army – 300,000; Air Force – 138,000; Coast Guard – 6000; and a recently added section for Police (a common second career for military veterans) – 1,800.[cxciv]

Another social networking site is www.leatherneck.com, whose *about us* page explains:

Marines are simply a cut above the rest. Their honor, loyalty and pride separate them from the other Armed Forces. It is only fitting that Marines have their very own presence on the Internet. Now they do.

Leatherneck.com is the #1 Marine Corps online community. Launched on November 10, 2001 to coincide with the Marine Corps Birthday, we are dedicated to providing service, support and the most information pertaining to the Marine Corps as possible. Designed for Marines, by Marines, Leatherneck.com is a virtual home for all Marines...Past, Present and Future! Though not endorsed by the United States Marine Corps or the Department of Defense, Leatherneck.com prides itself on following the same dedication, traditions and high standards of the United States Marine Corps.[cxcv]

This site, supported more by advertisements and commercial enterprises than subscriptions, includes a range of popular social networking links, including a locator (for finding lost buddies); the "drifter's place" (*a place for old salts...to deploy some wisdom for the up and comers*); Inspirational Stories; Uniforms; the Slop Chute (*belly up to the bar and share stories*); Women Marines; Devil Doc's [sic] (for Hospital Corpsmen – who keep Marines alive on the battlefield and other places); Marine Corps League (*the* Former Marines' association); Royal Marines Commando (for our British Royal Marine brothers); and several others.

What leatherneck.com, and other sites like it, offers that Together We Served does not is an "amazon.com-like" access to T-shirts, belt buckles, books, jackets, ball caps, cigarette lighters and thousands of other "college bookstore" kinds of things on which Marine Corps emblems and slogans might be emblazoned.

A tour through google.com/images for *Marine tattoos*, or *Marine tribal tattoos* reinforces themes apparent in the original 1990 version of this manuscript: Marines still get tattoos, perhaps more than ever; common themes are the Marine Corps emblem, the Marine *colors* (*flag*) and US colors; the motto *Semper Fi* (Semper Fidelis – always faithful); the mascot bulldog; and religious themes.

As the body art industry has continually improved over the

past two decades, and as women, in and out of the military, have increasingly joined the ranks of decorated bodies, additional themes with near-photograph quality art work include images of fallen comrades and combat operations. As a result of the popularity of body art, the Marine Corps has drawn the line, literally, restricting the size, placement and content of tattoos. According to Major Karl Tinson, Commanding Officer of Marine Corps Recruiting District, Dallas, Texas, prospects for enlistment in the Corps may not have tattoos visible on the head, neck or wrists. In 2007, Marines with *sleeve tattoos* were required to have their art photographed and recorded – and were grandfathered out of the new policy. Additional limits address content: "Tattoos or brands that are prejudicial to good order, discipline and morale, or are of a nature to bring discredit upon the Marine Corps. These may include, but are not limited to, any tattoo that is sexist, racist, vulgar, anti-American, anti-social, gang related, or extremist group or organization related."[cxcvi]

Additional Internet sites include:

http://www.marines.mil/ - is the official USMC web site, with news and information, plus links to *Marines Magazine*, Marine Corps orders and directives, blogs, career counseling, suicide prevention and other sites.

http://www.marines.com/ - leads to the (enlisted) Marine recruiting site, and is designed to attract the 16-24 year old prospect, in or out of high school. One banner invites: "This is the ultimate proving ground for those who are driven by purpose, guided by values, and aspire to earn the title Marine. Explore each week of the training required to defend our nation as one of the few."

http://officer.marines.com/ - is a more subdued site, directed to college age professionals (those who will complete undergraduate degrees) who seek roles as commissioned officers in uniform.

http://www.usmilitary.com/ and http://www.military.com/ -

both commercial sites with information of interest to all military services.

Leatherneck.com lists "the" Marine Corps Top Ten web sites, which are emblematic of the seemingly endless range of cyber networking options available to Marines and veterans: Delta Company, 1st Battalion, 27th Marines, Vietnam 1968; Provisional Rifle Company, Vietnam 1969-1970; 3rd Bridge Company (Combat Engineers); Eric Navatie's Web Page (India Company, 3rd Battalion, 7th Marines); Parris Island 1952; Iwo Jima – A look back (the battle for Iwo Jima (WWII) as recorded in the official accounts); 2nd and Weapons Platoons; Golf Company, 2nd Battalion, 26th Marines; Royal Netherlands Marines (all about the Royal Dutch Marines, unit links, and links to Marines all over the world); the Fighting Fourth (4th Marine Division in WWII Central Pacific); Women Marines memoirs; and Embassy Marine – dedicated to Marine Security Guards, from 1949 forward).

This foregoing list continues for pages and pages, with scores of web sites and chronicles of individuals; specific occupations – mainly infantry – campaigns; and units.[cxcvii]

The other nation

In contrast to web sites for Marines, web sites for takfiris and irhabists may be more difficult for Westerners to find. When Marines go looking for information on their adversaries, a key word search of terms leads to http://www.ummah.com for example. The *ummah* is, variously, the community of believers in Islam, or the global, pan-Arab Islamic "nation." Ummah.com is a typical special-interest site, with links and forums relating to: ummahradio.com; Ramadhan (Ramadan) forum; hajj forum (with tips on travel agents, trips, visas); ummah lounge (open forum); campaigns and action alerts (the author will abdicate responsibility for investigating this link to someone else); Islamic lifestyle and social issues; poetry corner; marriage in Islam; and Islamic parenting. In a multimedia section, subscribers with passwords may post links to listen or download lectures in audio format.

Some web sites appealing to the *ummah* feature links where one might locate sermons from the late American-born Anwar Nasser Abdulla Aulaqi, who wrote jihad from Yemen, was designated as a terrorist by the US Treasury Department, was implicated in providing operational guidance and training to ersatz US Army Major Nidal Hassan (accused as the Fort Hood assassin), and the "Christmas Day bomber" Umar Farouk Abdulmutallab, and is now a non-pork sacrifice. Aulaqi's message was also easily reachable through *Inspire magazine*. Key word searches lead to an exhausting array of information: Muslim information, the sunnah, hadith, Council on American-Islamic Relations (CAIR), the Muslim Brotherhood, al Jazeera, and so on.

The site www.youtube.com offers another look at both sides of the conflict between Marines and Islamist extremists. The key word *jihad*, for example, in youtube.com, provides a sample of the complex exchange in this war of ideas – with a range of topics from both Western and Islamist videographers, as well as from the jokers on the sidelines, who have nothing to do with anybody's jihad, who seek to make good use of the familiarity of the word *jihad* in the common vernacular.

Books

Keeping up with print and digital books dealing with Marines, Islamist extremists, the war on terror and combat operations in Iraq, Afghanistan and other combat zones could be an endless occupation. As of August 2011, amazon.com lists, under the search term *Marines* (for example):

Marine at War, by M. Michael (a novel), 2010.

Shadow of the Sword: A Marine's Journey of War, Heroism, and Redemption, by Jeremiah Workman and John Bruning, 2009.

Victory Point: Operations Red Wings and Whalers - the Marine Corps' Battle for Freedom in Afghanistan, by Ed Darack, 2010.

Sniper: American Single-Shot Warriors in Iraq and Afghanistan, by Matt Larsen, Gina Cavallaro and Richard A. Cody (Ret.), 2010.

Silver Star: Navy and Marine Corps Gallantry in Iraq, Afghanistan and Other Conflicts (Blue Jacket Bks), by James E. Wise Jr. and Scott Baron, 2008

A Nightmare's Prayer: A Marine Harrier Pilot's War in Afghanistan, by Michael Franzak, 2011.

One Bullet Away: The Making of a Marine Officer, by Nathaniel Fick, 2006.

Hogs in the Shadows: Combat Stories from Marine Snipers in Iraq, by Milo S. Afong, 2008.

The Wrong War: Grit, Strategy, and the Way Out of Afghanistan, by Francis J. West, 2011.

There are scores more, and the next genres in Amazon run into overarching themes, such as terrorist financing, foreign policy, counter-insurgency (COIN) doctrine and COIN wins and losses, biographies, more memoires, weapons and tactics, and many more.

Movies

As with books by and about Marines, films depicting Marines serve as another ethnographic record of Marine Corps culture, with symbols, rituals and myths: culturally specific language, combat and conflict, hierarchies and relationships, artifacts (weapons, flags, uniforms, emblems, etc.), taboos and belief systems. Movies released since the 1989 completion of *The Edifice Complex* include:[cxcviii]

A Few Good Men (Rob Reiner, Dir., 1992), with Tom Cruise, Jack Nicholson, Demi Moore and Kevin Bacon. (Four Oscars)

Battle for Haditha (Nick Broomfield, Dir., 2008)

Born on the Fourth of July (Oliver Stone, Dir. 1989), with Tom Cruise.

Flags of Our Fathers (Clint Eastwood, Dir., 2006), with Ryan Phillippe, Jesse Bradford, and Adam Beach. This film depicts the Marines who raised the flag on Iwo Jima during the island-hopping campaign of World War II. *Letters from Iwo Jima* tells the complementary story from the Japanese point of view.)

Generation Kill (Susanna White and Simon Cellan-Jones, Dir., 2008), with Alexander Skarsgard and Lee Tergesen – an HBO miniseries based on the book by Evan Wright, tells the story of 1st Reconnaissance Battalion during the invasion of Iraq in 2003.

Jarhead (Sam Mendes, Dir., 2005), with Jake Gyllenhaal and Jamie Foxx – depicts the memoire of a Marine scout sniper during the First Gulf War.

Rules of Engagement (William Friedkin, Dir. 2000), with Tommy Lee Jones and Samuel L. Jackson.

Taking Chance (Ross Katz, Dir., 2009), with Kevin Bacon.

The Pacific – the miniseries, in parallel with *Band of Brothers*, which follows a US Army unit in the European theater of World War II, depicts Marines in the Pacific Theater.

Windtalkers (John Woo, Dir., 2002), with Nicolas Cage, Adam Beach and Christian Slater. *Windtalkers* refers to the Navajo *code talkers* enlisted by the Corps to confound Japanese crypto-linguists during World War II.

The more historically accurate a film, the more appreciative Marines and the Marine Corps are. Not listed at Wikipedia.com's site, based on the search for "films depicting Marines," is the 1994 movie *True Lies* (James Cameron, Dir.), featuring Arnold Schwarzenegger, Jamie Lee Curtis and Tom Arnold. Based on personal experience in…and personal communication with officers in Marine Corps Public Affairs, the Corps will lend official behind-the-scenes advice and assistance to a film – if it serves the Marine Corps. In other words, if the film *accurately and fairly* depicts the Marine Corps, generally in a positive light and especially if the film is a potential recruiting tool. Flight time for the AV-8B Harrier jet is expensive, and the $25 million to $30 million Harriers flown by Marine pilots in making the film are not engaged in combat operations, so such support is arranged as a *training mission*. The director gets "B-roll" footage, Marine pilots get a training flight and the Corps gets some positive action-adventure propaganda with an A-list box office draw.

(As Arnold Schwarzenegger and Jamie Lee Curtis dance the final tango at the end of the film, the Marine colonels in the film are actual Marine Corps Public Affairs Officers. And the "Harrier" flown by Arnold Schwarzenegger as he is rescuing his daughter – was a plywood movie set model.)

Chapter Seven

Findings and Analysis: 1990

Introduction

A story is told in the Marine Corps about the first Marine recruit. It goes something like this: Captain Samuel Nicholas, the first commissioned officer of the Continental Marines, was about his business recruiting tall, rugged, intelligent (probably handsome), physically fit young men for the new Marine Corps. The date was November 10, 1775, as every Marine knows, and the place was Tun Tavern, in Philadelphia, as every Marine knows. The first young man signed on the dotted line, raised his hand to swear in, and was sent to the pier to one of John Paul Jones' ships.

The new Marine marched smartly up the gangplank, faced aft and saluted the ship's ensign (flag), then faced the officer of the deck smartly and properly, and requested "permission to come aboard." Permission was granted, whereupon the chief bo's'un's mate approached and asked the Marine who, or what, he was.

"I'm the first Marine, chief," the recruit answered.

"What the hell is a Marine?" the chief demanded.

The recruit replied that he wasn't quite sure, but he knew that he was a lover, a fighter and a hell-raiser enlisted to beat the Red Coats. So, the chief sent him below until something could be found for the young man to do. The Marine set about preparing for inspection, cleaning his musket and polishing everything in sight.

On the very next day, another recruit enlisted at the Tavern and was sent to the same ship where he was also sent below, and where he found the first Marine, squared away, standing at parade rest and ready for anything, with coiled ropes, blackened cannon balls, polished brass, and neatly pressed uniforms. The second Marine was duly impressed and remarked, "Life sure looks tough around here!"

The first Marine replied, "You should have seen what it was like in the old Corps."

Many points can be made from this one story, and more stories will be used to illustrate the findings of this study. One point is about myth. What every Marine believes may not necessarily be true. One of the first things a Marine learns is that his Corps' birthday is November 10, 1775. He may even recall a few words of the resolution from the Continental Congress, reiterated at the annual Marine Birthday Ball: "Resolved, that two battalions of Marines be raised...." Although it is officially recognized that the two battalions were not immediately raised,[cxcix] most Marines are probably unconcerned with when their cultural ancestors actually got official permission to begin fighting as a team; the date of the original resolution is enough.

What the birthday provides is a sense of identity and legitimacy, a common source of *creation* found in most cultures' religions. That the *United States* Marine Corps did not get formally organized until July 11, 1798, by an act of Congress is unimportant to the myth; Continental Marines did fight in the Revolutionary War. Among other conflicts, some 230 officers and men of the Continental Marines sailed for the Bahamas in February 1776 with the small Navy to fight the British. [cc]

Another point from the story is that Marines have probably been telling sea stories to each other and to the civilian public since the beginnings of the Marine Corps. The Marine Corps story serves as a starting point for the analytical section of this study because, since all Marines were at one time civilians (although some Marines may claim otherwise, as in: "I've been a Marine since Christ was a corporal.") – all must hear of the Marine Corps somewhere.

For want of a more logical sequence, the rest of this chapter will loosely follow the chronology of entering the Marine Corps and going through the rites of passage, changing from civilian to Marine. As noted above, the influences of the Marine Corps story, whether in advertising or elsewhere, provide a starting point.

Early Publicity

It was not until the times of World War I that any sort of public relations or advertising was organized in the Marine Corps. Lindsay records the following tribute to a pioneer in Marine Corps public relations:

> In all probability, no man has done more to apprise the American public of the Marine Corps and its achievements as MTSgt. [master technical sergeant] Percy Webb, Ret'd. Known as the 'walking encyclopedia of the Marine Corps,' Sgt. Webb became nationally known to newspaper and magazine publishers and radio chains....Among other duties, he released at intervals mimeograph stories of the Corps to newspapers. These were, in all instances, the result of painstaking research plus his own experiences, and were singularly free from bombastic braggadocio.[cci]

Webb served the Corps some 35 years, spending nearly 30 years in public relations during the 1910's, '20s and '30s. Other names from Marine Corps public relations surfaced in the years between the world wars, notably post-World War I Secretary of the Navy Edwin Denby, a former Marine who put the Corps to the task of guarding the U.S. mail in 1921 and '22. Lindsay observed that guarding the mail helped keep the Marine Corps from sliding back into relative oblivion. Regarding that period Millett observed:

Headquarters made sure the media knew the Marines were more than a match for mail robbers. Marine recruiters began to cultivate local businessmen, and Headquarters ordered post commanders as well to put public relations high on their list of duties. Convinced that the Corps' good health depended upon public acceptance – expressed in influence upon Congress – Lejeune systematically organized and developed a public relations program envied by the other services and noted for big achievements and a small staff.[ccii]

Public relations, or publicity, as it was called those decades ago, has always been closely tied to recruiting efforts, but it was in the 1920s that recruiting, publicity and internal morale began to be tied together in athletics. Major General Commandant John A. Lejeune and a recruiting-publicity officer, Major Joseph C. Fegan, saw the opportunity to show the Corps to the American public as a positive influence on the young men of the country who might decide to enlist. Varsity football and baseball teams, notably the teams of Quantico, Virginia, compiled impressive records against semi-professional teams, colleges and the other services.

The December 1, 1925, issue of Headquarters Bulletin, originally a bi-monthly newsletter of sorts, originated by Lejeune, included the following declaration:

The effect of the new athletic policy as originated and promulgated by the Major General Commandant has been far reaching in proving to the public that the Marine Corps is abreast of the times in a matter which is of common interest as well as to the interest of the future of the Corps from an advertising viewpoint. We have pledged ourselves to Congress to make better men out of young Americans who enlist in the Marine Corps. This pledge has been accomplished principally through athletics.[cciii]

It was the Marine Corps' intention at the time (between World War I and World War II) to endear itself to the American public by offering a haven to young men who could not afford to go to college. The Corps earned this endearment by playing and winning football games, thus showing America that young men who enlisted in the Corps would turn out to be physically fit and possessed of a winning attitude.

A motion picture section was added to Marine public relations in 1926, as part of the recruiting bureau at Philadelphia. Earlier that year, former Marine Gene Tunney was featured in the commercial film *The Fighting Marine*, and Lon Chaney (Sr.) appeared in *Tell It to the Marines* in 1927.

By World War II, the combat correspondent was conceived. Journalists, cameramen, engineers and other people with press experience were commissioned and enlisted to cover the war in the Pacific. The hometown touch was added with personalized bylines from the front and stories tailored to fit the needs and interests of hometown readers and newspaper editors. By the end of the war it seemed the Corps had adequately attached itself to the hearts and minds of an admiring American public.

It is clear at this point that the purpose of Marine public relations was twofold, to get new recruits and to ensure its own survival as an institution. Even as late as 1932, the Marine Corps felt it was in danger of extinction. Another story from Lindsay serves to illustrate:

The year (1932) was...the low tide in Marine Corps annals. Major General Commandant Ben H. Fuller...was concerned with preserving the Marine Corps intact in the face of a concerted effort to abolish it and merge it with the Army. Documentation of the Marine Corps' 1932 difficulties is virtually nonexistent except in the public press. An interesting, if possibly biased, version of what may have happened is contained in a Memorandum for the Record concerning the affair in the files of the Historical Archives at Headquarters, Marine Corps... dated April 2, 1932. The memorandum relates that during the height of the Congressional appropriation-cutting activities in the summer of 1932, Rep. Melvin J. Maas, a Minnesota Democrat, was in Quantico for a brief training tour as a Marine Corps Reserve major.

Learning the Army was attempting to persuade President Hoover to transfer the Corps to the Army, Maas hurried back to Washington, where he attempted to get an appointment with the President. According to the memorandum, after twice failing to be granted an audience with Hoover, Maas obtained time on a radio network, and then told the White House that 'unless the President saw him at once he was prepared to inform a nationwide radio audience of the real reasons for the move to transfer the Corps to the Army.' Hoover then agreed to see Maas, who, in company with Fiorello H. LaGuardia, told the President of his impending radio time. 'The President,' the memorandum states, 'then promised to drop the idea.'[xciv]

Finally, with the National Security Act of 1947 and the Douglas-Mansfield Act of 1952 (*now part of Title 10, United States Code*), the Corps' identity was formalized and its legitimacy written into public law. Millett notes that the "definition of roles and missions" of the 1947 legislation "was largely drafted by a group of Marine officers."[ccv]

This brief historical account is important in understanding the development of today's Marine Corps public affairs mentality, for it is in response to the threats of dissolution – the feeling that the Corps is the underdog – that much of Marine Corps public relations was built. But now with a Corps firmly and legally rooted in the institutional fabric of American society, the mentality seems to linger.

Although a bit simplified, it appears to work something like this: The Marine Corps advertises an exciting, challenging, rewarding, discipline-instilling initiation to a job, career or lifestyle. For a variety of personal reasons people enlist or get commissioned into the Corps, and individually or collectively, accomplish something, usually in combat, worthy of public or Congressional note. The Marine Corps public relations division exploits the successes which best suit the Corps' needs. Civilian newspapers also write about the exploits, but present more balance with some left-leaning and some right wing journalists telling all sides of the story (*theoretically*).

Some examples are: the good parts of the invasion of Grenada (accomplishing the mission of deterring Communism); stories about the Marines in Beirut and of those who were among the 50-some Americans held hostage for 444 days in Iran during the last year and a half of President Carter's administration; the higher percentages of high school graduates enlisting; fewer incidences of drug or alcohol abuse and higher retention rates among career Marines.

As expected from any public relations enterprise, stories of success are written in terms that benefit the institution. Then, the Corps can point to success and impress Congress and the American public. Recruitment advertising, playing on the successes, word of mouth advertising from Marines fresh out of boot camp, and the skills of the recruiter start the cycle over again, drawing new recruits to the enlistment office.

Obviously it is not that simple. Neither Congress nor the American public are so easily fooled. Or are they? *Newsweek* magazine, among other news magazines and newspapers, carried the stories of the 1987 **Contragate** hearings. By the end of Lieutenant Colonel Oliver North's testimony, he was being painted as a folk hero. The July 20, 1987 cover of *Newsweek* depicts North in uniform at the witness stand, gesturing. The cover headline reads: *Lt. Col. Oliver North, The Making of a Folk Hero*. Attempting to cash in on the hero, merchants of all kinds produced bumper stickers, T-shirts, Ollie Burger sandwiches and **The Ollie Cut** haircut for men who wanted to look more like North.

He was popular because he represented the little guy, the

underdog telling Congress where to go. He was a modern Robin Hood. Perhaps one would expect Marines to readily accept North as a hero, but what civilians learned of North was superficial compared to what Marines know about other Marines. Somewhat isolated from more than a few dozen Marines while serving in Korea during the Contragate hearings, I also expected Marines to see North as a type of hero. According to an informal poll by *Navy Times* however, this was not the case. A summary of reactions shows that Marines and sailors of all ranks felt North's adventures were not a Marine Corps matter, that he was involved in a political mess that should have no reflection on the Corps. Burlage, *Navy Times* staff writer, writes:

What most Marines were watching for was how North presented himself as he testified in uniform. Reaction to the uniform ranged from a lance corporal's notion 'he's bringing back a good name for the Marines,' to an officer's opinion that 'a lot of folks wish he had appeared in a civilian suit instead of uniform, because what he was on the Hill about occurred while he was wearing a civilian suit.' [North had been assigned as a Marine officer in the offices of the National Security Staff – a "coat and tie" day job in Washington.][ccvi]

One explanation for the contrast in reactions from civilians and Marines may be that civilian media sometimes need (or make) heroes – perhaps to sell newspapers and magazines. There is no question that if North is or was a folk hero, the media helped make him one. Marines on the other hand, want heroes made in combat. And truthfully, Marines in combat don't so much want heroes as much as they strive to keep their brothers alive. Some of those interviewed by *Navy Times* expressed feelings similar to some of the civilian feelings, that North was a folk hero; some did not.

Yet, North's military bearing seemed to help present the Marine Corps in a good light, aside from the different impressions his testimony may have made. The lance corporal's statement that North was "bringing back a good name for the Marines" alludes to the negative press from the spy scandal involving Sergeant Clayton Lonetree, convicted of fraternizing with a Soviet woman and illegal association with KGB agents while assigned as a guard at the U.S. Embassy in Moscow. Lonetree's trial for espionage and 12 related charges began July 22, 1987, at Quantico. North undoubtedly received more press and provided a comparatively positive distraction despite the negative aspects impacts of the Contragate affair.[ccvii]

Burlage writes: "Marine Corps officials...tried to distance the Corps from what North did in the White House. Headquarters directed commands worldwide to stay out of the fracas."[ccviii]

In essence, if a story is good for the Marine Corps, the Marine Corps will exploit it. If a story is negative, the Corps will be at least as open as law requires. And if it is an internal problem, the Corps will defend the right to handle the problem internally as much as possible. When internal problems such as the Ribbon Creek incident plague the Corps, or when other recruit deaths make the news, the Marine Corps is generally very quick to tell its own story to the public and Congress. Somewhere in all this public relations, and from other influences mentioned earlier, young men and women get their first impressions of the Corps.

Marine Corps Public Affairs

As indicated in previous chapters, Marine Corps public affairs is divided into three specific functions: internal information, external information and community relations. External information is a means of informing civilians about what goes on in the Corps, and may be informally divided into three categories for evaluation.

Marine journalists write news and feature stories and prepare broadcast releases, usually for internal release first, and then through mechanics established by the Division of Public Affairs at Headquarters, Marine Corps, send these releases to civilian media.

The next two categories of external information do not really belong to the Marine Corps. One is the body of news, feature and documentary print and broadcast releases prepared by civilians who have never been Marines. Another category comprises an unknown number of journalists, broadcasters and film makers who have been Marines. It seems that an old fascination for the Corps lives in some of these former Marines who have access to the tools of print and broadcast media. They each contact some segment of the American public.

Columnist Art Buchwald, a former Marine, occasionally reflected on his experiences in the Marine Corps during World War II, usually with some humor.[ccix] In a series of articles about former Marines in *The Boot*, Parris Island's base newspaper, public affairs officer Major Gary Weaver related that Buchwald visited Parris Island with his former drill instructor, Corporal Peter Bonardi, in 1965 for *Life* magazine. Weaver contacted Buchwald in 1983 for more background on that visit, noting:

In a snappy 'Old Corps-New Corps' personal glimpse he told Life readers that from what he observed DIs were still 'saber-toothed, man-eating Marine Corps drill instructors, whose main nourishment was chewing on the nerves of raw recruits.' The Island was then known as 'Alcatraz East,' and no one who had spent more than 24 hours in boot camp ever hoped to leave it alive.[ccx]

Of course this story is colorfully written, and the reader should recognize it was written in humor, but what is an impressionable high school boy to think when a humorist agrees with the other stories about the *dangers* of boot camp? In preparation for his story, Weaver wrote to Buchwald, and noted the response:

The most important part of my entire Marine Corps experience was Parris Island. The people there changed my life, hopefully for the better. They made a man out of me. At least they showed me how important it was to be a man. When I went back for Life I told one of the master sergeants that the Marine Corps had been the first father figure I had ever had. He said that 50% of the kids who went through there had the same experience.[cxi]

At least Buchwald admitted the Marine Corps made a man out of him, rather than leave readers wondering how he really felt. It may be difficult to sift truth from humor and Marines might be more adept than civilians at recognizing the humor in stories about Parris Island. There truly are, for example, alligators and sharks in the waters around the island, as recruits learn from their DI's, or from *sea stories* soon after they arrive at Parris Island, whether they've heard these cautions before or not.

A personal experience with another writer will illustrate a different type of interaction between a former Marine and the Corps.

In 1981, Richard L. Stack, who identified himself as Director of Photography, Group PAM/U.S.A., requested permission to go to Parris Island to do a photographic essay. I was assigned to escort Stack and his two colleagues, with a verbal caution from the public affairs officer to "keep an eye on them." Stack spent three days at Parris Island. He followed the rules and kept his team of photographers together so that one escort could monitor their whereabouts.

Stack and his fellows visited the more visually attractive scenes often photographed by other journalists: pugil stick fighting, rappelling, the confidence course and the infiltration course. During the brief visit, he gave me a copy of a book, *Warriors*, which he had photographed at Parris Island in 1971. The contents of the book were intriguing, given the nature of the Corps in 1981 – soft on recruit training in some Marines' opinions. The following letters led up to and followed publication of Stack's 1971 book:

(From Richard Stack)
July 8, 1971

General Leonard Chapman
Headquarters Marine Corps
Washington, D.C.

Dear General Chapman:

I am a 25 year old photojournalist working in New York City for Black Star Publishing company which is the largest and most reputable agency in the world. I was honorably discharged from the U.S. Marine Corps on August 7, 1967 as a Sergeant E5 Serial #205XXXX. I served in the Marine Corps for four years, two of which were in Vietnam.

I have been thinking and working out ideas for two years and I believe this is the proper time to put my plans into action. I would like to do a photographic story on Parris Island, the Recruit Training and most important the Drill Instructors showing the dedication of these men towards their job, the Corps and Country.

The story I would like to do would be made into a photographic book. Since my first conception of such a book some two years ago the draft has ended and the blitz of Army, Navy and Air Force campaigns for the soft life of the service has started. All quite distasteful in my own opinion I might add. My story will show the special kind of person it takes to gain the honor to be called a Marine. The project would take 3-3 1/2 months to shoot and would be paid for by my personal funds in the event I do not receive outside assistance. I have not discussed this with my publishers or editors, including those at Black Star. It is my intention to have the go-ahead from you before I started to ask publishers of their interest.

signed/

Stack was afforded a month-long stay later in 1971 and the public affairs officer and other concerned officers at Parris Island were instructed by Headquarters, Marine Corps, to accommodate him. The result of his visit, *Warriors*, was published by Harper & Row in 1975. It will be described below. Next was a letter from Nahum Waxman, an editor at Harper & Row, following publication of the book:

November 21, 1975

General Louis H. Wilson,
Marine Corps Commandant
Room 2004
Arlington Annex
Columbia Pike and Arlington Ridge Road

Dear General Wilson:

Recently, we sent you for your interest a copy of a new photographic book WARRIORS by Richard Stack, a book dealing with recruit training at the Parris Island Depot.

I have already received some reaction from within the Marine Corps, which, I think, requires that I make our position clear at the outset. There seems to be some feeling that this book was done to embarrass the USMC and that somehow its publication does the Corps discredit. May we please make the very strong point that that was not our intention, nor do we believe that the book should be seen as damaging to the Marine Corps. Richard Stack, who served himself, has genuine respect for the Service. He promised when he undertook the book that he would do an honest job of it. We think he has indeed done that and that anyone who has in fact been through boot camp knows that this is a fair representation of what is, and has to be a very rigorous process. All of the pictures in the book are of things that took place; all of the text was actually recorded or gathered at Parris Island from recruits and Drill Instructors there. Not a word has been changed and the selection of what has taken place was not done to mislead or distort.

I do not want to make too large an issue of this, since I have not heard your own reaction, in any case, but it has already been suggested to me from within the Marine Corps that WARRIORS was being perceived as a hostile book. We'd like it to be a book regarded in the spirit in which it was prepared. Because it used frank pictures and the real language of the training camp does not mean the book was not done with honesty and respect. By this letter I simply wanted you to know this directly and to have our reassurance in this regard.

Yours sincerely,
signed/

Following is the response from General Louis H. Wilson, commandant of the Marine Corps:

29 Dec 1975

Mr. Nahum Waxman, Editor
Harper and Row, Publishers, Inc.
10 East 53rd Street
New York, New York 10022

Mr. Waxman:

Your concern that the Marine Corps is not completely pleased with Warriors by Richard Stack, is not without foundation.

While the book has many good points, several parts represent the exception rather than the norm in recruit training. Moreover, the other favorable aspects about recruit training are ignored altogether. Taken collectively, the exceptions with the omissions give a false picture of the recruit training experience.

Addressing the exceptions: Foul language and demanding speech are not condoned in recruit training and have no place in the making of a Marine. While profanity and degrading language might exist, I believe such instances to be isolated exceptions. It would be unfortunate for any reader to judge the recruit training experiences portrayed in Warriors as being typical. Indeed it is not.

As to positive features not covered, I believe that a better-balanced presentation would have given coverage to the admirable results achieved in recruit training. Specifically, omitted from the book is a fully developed theme showing the transition from boy to man, civilian to Marine. Another neglected aspect is the failure to show the evolution of discipline and spirit in the Marine-building process – a trait which we feel is distinct to Marine Corps training.

It is my understanding that Mr. Stack's last visit to Parris Island took place in 1971, when the photographs were taken and the interviews were conducted. I think you will find in the intervening years a number of changes have taken place which would tend to mitigate the image portrayed in the book.

To give a new – and valid – perspective I suggest Mr. Stack return to Parris Island for a fresh look at our recruit training procedures.

Your position as stated in your letter of November 21, 1975 is appreciated and I'm sure you can appreciate ours.

Sincerely,
signed/

Several points are immediately open for analysis. First, upon Stack's second visit to Parris Island, we discussed his time in the Corps and especially in Vietnam. He gave me the impression, as had hundreds of Marines and former Marines passing through Parris Island before and after his visit, that his Marine experiences were good ones. He spoke highly of his drill instructors, fellow enlisted Marines and officers. It seems his editor's protestations and his own declarations of sincerity in the first two letters are indeed sincere.

What General Wilson said Stack left out is what Marines leave out when they tell sea stories. If they don't exaggerate, Marines at least tend to emphasize experiences that make them feel tough, macho, or masculine. Marines rarely give more than passing reference to history class, first aid class, uniform fitting, tests and evaluation, etc. These are not exciting times in boot camp, but the rifle range is, obstacle courses are, inspections can be memorable, and physical training and close order drill must be discussed to be compared in severity.

<u>Stasis</u>

The first major finding of *The Edifice Complex* is that a former Marine's image of his or her Corps virtually freezes or crystallizes when he or she leaves the service. There are varying degrees of this phenomenon, depending on the closeness of the association with the Corps after separation from the service. Credit for suggesting this idea goes to one of the historical writers at the Marine Historical Center, Keith Fleming.[ccxii]

The fact that Stack's book was published in 1975 was in a sense a bit unfortunate for Stack as 1975 and 1976 have been noted in all the data collected as the hallmark years for recent change in Marine boot camp (*as of the late 1980s*). General Wilson's response is a legitimate observation that what Stack recorded at Parris Island in 1971 did not represent the boot camp of 1975.

General Wilson wrote that the book lacks themes such as turning civilians into Marines, boys to men, or discipline building. Interviews with drill instructors of the 1970s and mid 1980s indicate they mark the changes of 1975-76 as the time when it was evident that recruits were no longer fully disciplined during training. The finishing process began taking place in the Fleet Marine Forces – the combat Marine Corps – especially for those Marines who went on to join infantry units.

What Stack suggested in *Warriors*, in pictures, is that the boy who endures becomes a man, that discipline had been instilled. In fact, *Warriors* presents a historical picture of recruit training pretty much like I remember it; with vulgar language, sweat, hard work, mud, and victory. The graduation and meritorious promotion scenes depict the emerging young man who is no longer a civilian or a boy but a Marine. Generals and other powerful people in the Marine Corps sincerely want the parents of recruits to know the Marine Corps is instilling pride, discipline and other positive qualities in the future Marine; they do not want parents or Congress to get the idea that recruits are being abused, physically or verbally.

From personal experience, *thumping* (hitting recruits) did happen in training in the early 1970s; the use of vulgar language by drill instructors was the rule rather than the exception. Drill instructors did not commonly use vulgar language in the presence of officers however, and recruits did not tell officers when they heard vulgar language. They usually did not tell when they were "thumped" because they expected it and drill instructors suggested to recruits that it would be disloyal to their leaders (DIs) or unit to tell of such minor things outside the unit – to officer, in other words.

This introduces another point, which enlisted Marines who experienced the boot camp of the early 1970s or before would almost certainly say that they were disciplined with tough training. If the theories of cognitive dissonance hold true, they would have to admit that the rigors of training had made them men. This is the essence of telling about the Old Corps.

My findings indicate that enlisted Marines tend to believe that officers who have not been enlisted somehow do not understand that boot camp is tough. And recruits somehow get the impression in enlisted folklore that officer candidate school is far easier than enlisted training [not true]. Older Marines, especially those who are or have been drill instructors, further tend to believe that officers do not need to know what goes on behind the scenes.

The confusion stems from two points of view. On the one hand, some drill instructors believe the Recruit Training SOP is too restrictive, that DIs cannot train or properly discipline recruits within the limits of the SOP. This group of drill instructors tends to want to follow the letter of the SOP and tend not to thump recruits, but tend to see the restrictions as being imposed on them by authority figures in their chain of command. The commanding general of the recruit depot has overall local responsibility for enforcing the SOP, but his responsibilities are delegated through the recruit training regiment chain of command. The regiment commander is a colonel; lieutenant colonels command each of the training battalions; captains command recruit training companies, and so on.

Restrictions in the SOP have changed over time, usually becoming more exact and more strictly enforced. The kinds of limits referred to include restrictions against hitting or touching recruits, calling them derogatory names, singling them out for punishment, or at other times in the past, applying mass punishment, the amount of uninterrupted sleep recruits get, amount and type of incentive physical training (PT), and in general pushing recruits beyond their limits.

A clearer perspective of this conflict was told by Rear Admiral Brown, the medical officer who went undercover as a DI in 1960-61 and served incognito as a gunnery sergeant intermittently for a year and a half. At that time he would have been a lieutenant or lieutenant commander – equivalent to a Marine captain or major, and roughly the right age to be a gunnery sergeant. Before the Subcommittee on Military Personnel, House Armed Services Committee, Brown stated:

I did feel that [although] the SOP was certainly compatible with what the DI's had in mind…the main problem was the interpretation of the

SOP to the drill instructors, as it went down the chain of command [it] became too restrictive. I did feel that they need more latitude, that the drill instructors did have ability that was not being utilized.[ccxiii]

Brown added that he made recommendations to the commanding general based on his observations, some of which were acted upon. For example, singling out a recruit for discipline, or having one march behind the platoon until he marched better was allowed based on Brown's research and recommendations. The current SOP notes that mass punishment is not allowed.

The point of this discussion is that Brown felt DIs could train recruits within the guidelines of the SOP without abusing them. Brown also stated that he observed no instances of physical abuse, although he heard of some. It was his impression that any group of individuals given latitude will have some who break the rules. Additional evidence from drill instructors I interviewed indicates that whereas most felt the SOP is too restrictive, some revealed that the restrictions come from company, battalion, regimental and depot orders published to amplify the SOP or interpret the SOP according to a commander's view. *(In other words – the Marine Corps writes a "standard" operating procedure, and every commander in the chain has the potential opportunity to add interpretation or clarification. Some commanders do; some don't.)*

The second point relates to the probably small number of DIs who also tend to see the SOP as too restrictive, but who tend to *thump* or hit recruits. Based on personal experience in recruit training at San Diego in 1973, Brown's testimony in 1976 and interviews with drill instructors from 1980 through 1984, it is clear that those who tend to physically abuse recruits have one or both of two characteristics: Their drill instructors likely hit them and they believed the tactic would make a better Marine, or they were immature – usually younger, lower ranking, or both.

The Marine Corps attempts to stress a distinction between sensible and unnecessary demands on recruits. The Corps officially proscribes thumping or hitting because it's not unnecessary in recruit training. Making recruits work harder than they think they can is apparently possible within the limits of the training SOP, according to most drill instructors I interviewed, as long as the SOP is not interpreted by additional restrictive limits on the initiative of the DI by intermediate levels of command.[ccxiv]

Changes in boot camp also include an increase in the number of drill instructors supervising recruits, the amount of time spent with recruits and the number of officers and staff non-commissioned officers appointed to supervise drill instructors. From one or two drill instructors normally supervising a platoon of 40 to 50 recruits in the 1950s, there are now three or four drill instructors for 60 to 70 recruits. There are also two lieutenants supervising the training of four platoons (a series commander and an assistant series commander) instead of one officer in the past.

Thumping was more common in past decades partly because supervisors were less aware it was happening, and partly, perhaps, because some supervisors believed, as some drill instructors evidently did, if it was not severe, thumping served the purpose of toughening the prospective Marine and prepared him for the much more demanding abuses of combat. Supervisors would then tend to ignore minor instances of thumping. By 1973, speaking from personal experience, thumping was still common, but it was a private matter. If a DI felt it necessary to *tighten up* a recruit, he did it in private and made sure the recruit knew it would be disloyal to speak about it. My concern when I was hit as a recruit was that the assistant drill instructor not tell my senior DI. He assured me it was our little secret. I had been prepared for thumping by stories from other Marines.

One DI, again, in personal experience, made the mistake of

thumping another recruit publicly, unknowingly in the presence of the battalion commander, a lieutenant colonel. The battalion commander applied non-judicial punishment[ccxv] within minutes, in the drill instructor's office, reduced the DI from sergeant (E-5) to corporal (E-4) and dismissed from drill instructor duties. (I had been walking a step behind the commander from another wing of the barracks; the drill instructor – unaware the lieutenant colonel was in the building – was screaming at the recruit, and happened to punch the recruit in the chest as the battalion commander (and I) rounded the corner into the squad bay. In addition to the commander witnessing the event, others had seen it too. Swift, fair, appropriate discipline.)

Officers who discussed boot camp of the 1950s and 60s tended to be divided; some said that before the changes of 1975-76, officers looked the other way because they too believed that minor instances of thumping would do more good than bad in preparing a recruit for combat. Other officers quoted in news stories or observed in my public affairs experience tended to say that vulgar language and thumping have no place in creating a tough training environment, that training is tough enough already. More substantial support for these observations will follow in the chapter, and the points on cognitive dissonance will be more fully developed in later analysis.

Perspective: What all of this gets to, of course, is that Marines – combat veterans in particular – are intimately aware of the dangers and stresses of combat, and will point out that enemy soldiers are unlikely to say "please and thank you." Boot Camp is a transition from the relatively easy life of high school or college, in rural, urban or suburban America to a life that includes physical and mental demands far beyond what most civilians can possibly imagine.

As for the book *Warriors*, segments of the book that could be found offensive in any situation other than Marine boot camp of 1971 include offensive language by drill instructors and recruits, as

243

well as photographs of scenes that would be unthinkable at Parris Island or San Diego today.

For example, one photograph shows two DIs facing a recruit. One DI is smiling; the other, menacingly close, is evidently barking some command. The caption reads: "Boy, I don't like you. You better move, you Communist mutherf***er. I know the Kremlin sent you to f*** up my Marine Corps."

Another caption accompanying a similar picture of one drill instructor and one recruit reads:

You, Private!

Yes, Sir!

Louder!

Yes SIR!

LOUDER! [Drill instructors join in unison]

YES SIR!

I'll bet you're a pussy. Are you a pussy?

NO SIR!

Then you better sound off!

Responses from recruits to a questionnaire: "What do you think about pugil stick practice?"

I like getting out there and try to knock someone's head off.

Scared of getting sh*t-kicked.

Beat the f*** out of that pigf***er.

I got the sh*t beat out of me.[ccxvi]

Nine photographs depict the now defunct motivation course. Before it was abolished in the mid-1970s, a one-day visit to the course was referred to at San Diego boot camp as *one day moto*; at Parris Island it was the *mote ditch*, or *one day mote*. Recruits who had motivation problems were sent to the one-day course. A return visit was usually for seven days and usually preceded a drop from recruit training – a discharge.[ccxvii]

One photograph from *Warriors* shows recruits in the motivation course standing in line with rifles, the barrels filed with lead, which weighed about 10 pounds. The recruits are covered with mud. Another picture shows recruits crawling through the mud on their bellies, rifles cradled in their arms, doing the low crawl. Yet another picture shows a recruit trudging through the mud and water-filled ditch with rifle held in front of him a port arms. A sardonic quote from the Red Book serves as a caption: (1) Flowers are not worn while in uniform. (2) Umbrellas are not carried while in uniform.

Veterans of any generation would find the satire amusing, after the fact. They've been through it.

The range of vulgar language runs the gamut. It would serve no purpose to present more, but there is a lot of it. There are scenes from the rifle range, the infiltration course and meal time (chow call). Photographs early in the book show sloppy boys in civilian clothes who, it must be said, look stupid and afraid. The book covers in-processing to graduation. Included in the graduation pictures is the ritual of **pinning on stripes**, during which anyone senior to the Marine getting promoted punches the honored one on the arm where the stripes have been sewn on. In this case it is the drill instructors pinning stripes on a new Marine being meritoriously promoted to private first class.

Allow Stack's pictorial record of Parris Island to make two

points: Stack recorded what was real to him, and indeed was real to a great many Marines of his generation. His book, when read by prospective recruits, probably added to the mystique of Parris Island. It also probably did not lure anyone looking for an easy job. Those excesses of the 1960s and early '70s are largely gone, and have been replaced with carefully measured stress and the Crucible – an exhausting three- to four-day rite of passage event that marks the evolution from civilian to Marine.

Exaggeration

A second major finding in *The Edifice Complex* is that Marines exaggerate; it is the nature of sea stories. Although exaggeration and stories are not unique to the Marine Corps, most of the content of the stories is. The mystique surrounding recruit training grows when graduates tell stories about boot camp or combat, often with some exaggeration. Those who do enlist are certain they will experience the worst time of their lives, but certainly expect some reward for the experience.

External information and non-Marines

The second form of external information is that told by those who have never been Marines. Another personal experience will illustrate this category of media influence on civilian images of the Marine Corps:

In February 1981, the National Film Board of Canada sent a four-man team to film a documentary of recruit training at Parris Island. The documentary was originally to become half of a one-hour film on training in a six-part series titled *WAR*, as discussed above. The second half of the film, to depict officer training, was to be done at the British Royal Military Academy, Sandhurst, England. The officer training half was never done because the film crew could not get permission to stay at Sandhurst more than a week to 10 days, and required a month.

The film, eventually titled *Anybody's Son Will Do* was first aired on Canadian and U.S. public television in 1984. Gwynne Dyer, who wrote the proposal for the series, has been introduced in *The Edifice Complex*. He holds a doctorate from the University of London, and according to Dyer, is a former reserve naval officer of the United States, Canadian and British navies. Dyer spoke as host and narrator on the films, but was at Parris Island only a few days.

The film crew included Paul Cowan, an admitted perpetual civilian, and a cameraman, a soundman and a business manager. Correspondence with Cowan, which continues today for personal interests and originally to discuss the film's reception in Canada and the United States, supports the following findings:

During the 30-day filming at Parris Island, it was my responsibility, along with a fellow staff sergeant, to set shooting schedules, accompany the crew everywhere on Parris Island and get or help the crew get whatever they needed. It also happened that a strong mutual trust developed during conversations with the crew. Never was there an indication of insidious motives on their part, nor a hint that the Marine Corps was presenting some made-up *nice* representation of boot camp just for filming.[ccxviii]

Like *Warriors*, *Anybody's Son Will Do* depicts recruit training. But gone is the foul language, evidence of physical abuse or extreme measures to discipline a recruit or get his attention.

Some of the philosophies or assumptions guiding the film are taken from Dyer's proposal for the film:

The basic principles of military training have changed hardly at all in thousands of years. It takes ritual aggression of young males infected with the warrior ethic and converts (perverts?) it into the disciplined killing reflex of the soldier. Aggression happens between individuals, and is often turned aside by gestures of submission; military killing is an impersonal skill that has to be taught....The cultural norms that encourage aggression and gang behavior amongst teenage males are probably several million years old. They are designed to produce warriors, which is what was needed for the old inter-tribal warfare...As anybody knows who has been through it, basic training is a primitive form of brainwashing, intended to produce a new and highly artificial set of 'military instincts'.[ccxix]

The latter quote was included in Dyer's narration in the film. Much of the narration interprets what is going on in the film – Marine boot camp – in terms of tribal warfare, gang behavior, old warrior ethics and rituals, group violence and small unit bonds.

Anybody's Son Will Do presents a universal cultural theme that belongs to armies everywhere. That is, according to Dyer, it takes no one special to become a Marine, a member of the elite Soviet Spetznaz, the U.S. Navy SEALS, Marine Special Forces, Army Airborne or Ranger units, or any other elite or regular military organization. Dyer suggests that average young men are *redefined* in the process of training; they come to see themselves as special or elite because they attach themselves to the elite history of the unit.

Some of the more visually striking or colorful scenes of the film include non-judicial punishment proceedings against a recruit, and an academic class on military leadership, the central figure of which in each case is the company commander of the recruits shown throughout most of the film. The company commander, a **mustang captain**, wore his dress blue uniform during the classroom presentation.[ccxx] Several rows of decorations, including the Purple Heart, are conspicuous.

The captain, already possessed of an imposing stature at 6-feet and some 200 pounds, brought the wayward recruit to tears during the non-judicial punishment proceedings with a firm voice and strong, but not vulgar, language.

The film also depicts drill instructors in the field, away from garrison areas, in *the boonies* where recruits learn how to assemble tents and conduct squad combat tactics, during drill and at several of the courses recruits must master. In the field, one drill instructor is demonstrating to his recruits how to get the *grunt* into "arrugah."

Woven through the film are segments of Vietnam veterans discussing combat experiences, boot camp experiences of their generation and *the old Corps* in general. The in-processing of recruits, from the incoming bus and first haircuts, through discussions between a receiving barracks DI and a recruit who is determined to go home, and virtually all aspects of recruit training, are all vividly shown in the film.

As the military advisor on this film, I was present during three-fourths or more of the filming. The point is that nothing was manipulated to suit the filmmakers. The series – four platoons – of recruits and the drill instructors serving in that series were selected at random from several series approaching graduation. The crew also filmed scenes from the first 6-8 weeks of training with other randomly selected platoons or series involved in different activities.

Marine officers who viewed the film were broadly negative. Some felt the comparison with the Soviet Army was inappropriate; others – that the film did not represent drill instructors well. Indeed some of the recruits and drill instructors were not terribly articulate, but these were not "Harvard grads" and it was a documentary. The only person in the film with a script was Dyer, the narrator. In 2013 – it has been nearly 30 years since the series WAR first aired on public broadcasting in Canada and the US. Generally speaking, enlisted Marines are better-educated…and based on personal observation – more articulate than 30 years ago."[ccxxi]

Internal and external information by Marines

In the recruiter's office prospects can find Marine Corps base newspapers and several issues of *Leatherneck* or *Marines* magazines lying on a table or placed in a magazine rack with *Sports Afield, Jet, People, Gung Ho, Ebony or Soldier of Fortune.*

Perspective: According to Major Tinson, cited previously, recruiters in his Dallas Recruiting District offices are emblematic of all recruiters' offices – which no longer feature non-military publications such as Jet, Ebony, People magazine or sports magazines.

MARINES is published by the Division of Public Affairs, primarily for informational purposes for junior enlisted Marines. In the recruiter's office it can give the prospect or poolee a view of the entire Marine Corps (in several issues) because *MARINES* magazine uses stories from all Marine commands.

Staff Sergeant Fred Carr, editor of *MARINES* during my 18-day trip to East Coast Marine bases in 1984, discussed the value and purposes of the magazine:

We leave discussion of strategy to the Marine Corps Gazette and other higher echelon publications. The [MARINES] magazine is published mostly for privates through sergeants, and although it's historically been theme oriented, we've gotten away from that lately. Our stock is stories about all MOSs [military occupational specialties]; the inside tells Marines stuff they need to know. We emphasize leadership on the fire team and squad [small unit] level. What really 'sells' the magazine is the posters. Go by the career planner's office to see how Marines love posters.

We romanticize things the administrative clerk or computer operator doesn't get to see or do very often after boot camp. We all have an appetite for things 'oorah-ish' or romantic. The posters, on the back cover and inside the front, provide something we can all identify with. It goes clear back to boot camp, when we joined. There was something there to make you feel good about joining the Corps – Chesty Puller, some familiar saying, Dan Daly. It's oorah. And the more oorah-ish it is the better the Commandant likes it.[ccxxii]

Advertising

Another realm of influence on those who consider enlisting in the services is advertising. As noted, the civilian advertising company J. Walter Thompson has handled Marine Corps advertising since 1948. I've already presented the definition of the target population for recruitment advertising.

Additional demographic factors which influence recruiting and advertising strategies include:

96% of 18-year-olds are single; 34% of 24-year-olds are single.

A white who is in the 18-24 age group is more apt to be single than his non-white counterpart.

The percentage of single males in the 18- to 24-year-old category is increasing.

The closer a male gets to the age of 24 the more apt he is to be employed.

The majority of 18 to 24-year-olds who are employed are blue collar workers.

There is a growing tendency for educators to push students who are in lower mental groups through high school; the high school diploma is not always the only criterion for judging a qualified prospect. If this trend continues, recruiters will have to screen prospects more thoroughly to determine their true potential.

The 18- to 24-year-old male [is] more experimental compared to males who are older (i.e., more open-minded).

Unemployment, although it appears to be a golden opportunity, can be a pitfall to USMC recruiting.

Quality standards for recruits have risen sharply. The percent of required high school graduates will remain at 75% for the foreseeable future. Unemployment and lack of education tend to parallel each other. It follows that the most desirable recruit is the one who is more capable of securing employment in today's tight teenage job market.[ccxxiii]

Because market demographics change with the economy and other social factors, it is noteworthy that unemployment dropped after 1981 and the trend to push lower-ability students through high school may have seen a reversing trend. Although the high school diploma is not the only indicator of quality in a prospect, the Corps has continued to use it as an important *measure of tenacity*. As noted, the Marine Corps enlisted more than 85 percent high school graduates in 1982, and surpassed 85 percent in every year up to 1990.

Recruiters learn to screen prospects for many factors of adaptability to service life. The Corps wants young recruits, not only because of the physical demands of service life, but because the older a man gets the more likely he is to move from the probable blue collar job to a settled job he is reluctant to leave. The older man is more likely to have a wife, who is negative about his enlisting. Older recruits are also less likely to see the drill instructor, or the Marine Corps, as a *father figure*.

The 18- to 24-year-old man is seen as being impressionable, perhaps looking for intangibles such as *meaning in his life* or peer group recognition. Perhaps he is looking for tangibles like a steady job or tuition money offered by the services. The attitude survey identified the following supporting information:[ccxxiv]

Good things about being in the Armed Forces for you (Non-college men):

	Total	White	Black
Job training/ learn a job	40%	40%	39%
Travel	29%	29%	28%
Educational opportunities	16%	16%	13%
Money/income	13%	12%	13%
Benefits	12%	12%	8%
Meet people	7%	7%	8%

Table IV[ccxxv]

Marketing and advertising strategies are complex. As one might expect, advertising campaigns are based on what JWT learns about the market. Advertising takes many forms: Direct mail can be targeted to specific audiences, and is not limited by the time and space constraints of radio or television. Direct mail packages include a letter to the prospect, a brochure about opportunities in the Marine Corps and a return post card.

Spot advertising on television telling only of the Marine Corps is used for specific market areas – major metropolitan areas generally. Network advertising, reaching nationwide markets, comes in the form of joint advertising about all the services, so the Marine Corps must share segments with the other services.

One spot commercial (from 1983-1985) shows the silent drill team described in the sunset parade above; another, directed at Marine officer prospects, shows the forming of raw steel into a Marine officer's sword. The analogy is the tempering of the young man in the attitudes of the Marine way of life. (The chief drill instructor at Naval Aviation Officer Candidate School frequently said to candidates: "Adversity tempers steel," particularly to those who came to his *personal attention* because of problems adjusting to military life. The analogy is a common theme in the Marine psyche.)

The 6th Marine Corps Recruiting District's recruiting plan for 1980 notes that national radio advertising, recognized as more cost effective than television, is purchased through network radio. If a local station is "not affiliated with a national network, it will not air the paid message unless purchased individually by the National or District level (recruiting public affairs office)."[ccxxvi]

Finally, when the prospect decides to visit the recruiter's office, or visits at the invitation of a recruiter or friend, there are more symbols, rituals and myths seen and heard through word of mouth advertising by the recruiter and peers. There is folklore –

propaganda as advertising – in the forms of posters, hats, jackets and other souvenirs bearing Marine Corps messages and symbols.

In addition to measuring demographics, JWT periodically surveys the market to determine the awareness level of its advertising, the effect of slogans used and the prevailing attitude of young men in the market. One survey sampled "507 unmarried males between the ages of 17 and 24 who had neither served nor been accepted for service in any branch of the U.S. military." They were telephoned at random in 18 major markets in the United States. Of the total number called, 337 responded (with and without assistance of the interviewer) that they were aware of particular messages in Marine Corps advertising.[ccxxvii]

Findings of interest to *The Edifice Complex* include: "Recognition and status" and slogans continue to be the predominant messages recalled from Marine Corps advertising. Seeking *maturity* is another major reason for enlisting recalled by young men. Offers and promises continue to be felt generally believable by three out of five young men. Further:

Overall, the unique image of the Marine Corps, built up over many years, continues unchanged. In terms of the four...services, the Marine Corps continues to be most often perceived as...providing the most challenging training; the most elite and exclusive branch; able to shape an individual into a mature, self-disciplined, physically fit individual; able to instill a sense of self-confidence, a new self-esteem commanding the respect of others; and providing the greatest feeling of pride.[ccxxviii] (1983, pp. 7-8)

Benefit or advantage	Percent who mentioned
Education	22.0
Job training	16.0
Maturity	13.9

Recognition and status	11.3
Travel/see the world	8.9
Good pay/good salary	8.6
Career opportunities	6.5
Physical fitness	6.2
Excitement and adventure	5.6
Patriotic/serve country	3.6

Table V

Currently (1983) about 51% (of young men surveyed) say they have seen, heard or read 'a moderate amount' or 'a great deal' of advertising for the Marine Corps. Of the 337 young men who had recall of advertising, 64 percent recalled one or more of the following as reasons for joining the Marine Corps:[ccxxix]

With the foregoing in mind, note the categories of enlistees Millett described:

Although motivated to join the Corps for job training and patriotic sentiment, the new recruit of the early 80s fell into one of four [equally]...distributed personality motivation categories. The first group of youths seeks an ordered, disciplined environment in which to develop job skills under the direction of firm, inspirational leaders. The second group is attracted by the prospect of joining a physically fit, combat-ready, masculine warrior cult; these recruits tend to be athletes and outdoorsmen, but not...scholars. A third group of enlistees are [sic] motivated almost entirely by perceived self-interest, relating to job training and immediate economic security; the least 'gung ho' group, they are also disproportionately black. The fourth group of enlistees are the 'losers,' youths with a record of failure and low self-esteem. They view the Marine Corps as an organization that can give them experiences and training that will improve their self-respect and confidence. For all but the economic self-interest group, the Marine

Corps appears to offer discipline, leadership, physical challenges, organizational esprit, and the potential thrill of combat – or at least the thrill of combat readiness.[cxxx]

Recruiting

If the reader will imagine a young man or woman between 18 and 24 having seen one or more movies or newspaper stories, read a book or magazine article about the Marine Corps, seen or heard the Marine Corps advertised in any media, met a recruiter or had a friend or relative mention the Corps, in passing or by way of suggesting an occupation, then the reader can imagine a potential recruit facing the decision to enlist as one option after high school.

There are some young men or women who may never see or hear of the Marine Corps. Considering that such movies as *Heartbreak Ridge* with Clint Eastwood, *Full Metal Jacket* (with the now more-famous R. Lee Ermey) and *Aliens* (*Alien 2*), which depict Marines in *blood and guts* roles, or *Officer and a Gentleman*, which depicts the tough-talking Marine drill instructor embodied in Lou Gossett, Jr., have been box office successes; and considering the Marine Corps is frequently in television and print news, it is unlikely that there are very large numbers of young Americans who know nothing of the Corps.

But even if a young man has never heard of the Marine Corps by the time he gets to high school, there is still the probability that a Marine recruiter will visit his school, and the recruiter may approach him directly or telephone him. One way or another, either on their own initiative or through the direct or indirect actions of a recruiter, many thousands of young men and women come to the decision to visit or talk to a Marine recruiter.

(Although initially inclined to delete the following sections on The Recruiter and Boot Camp for this edition, the sections remain – as a historical view, both for what has changed and what has not.)

The Recruiter

Interviewing recruiters in the Indianapolis area over a three-month period from April to July 1984, I conducted nine interviews, lasting two to three hours each. Over time, five different men worked in the same office, although I had established rapport with one staff sergeant in particular who provided the bulk of the data.

Staff Sergeant Bryan

"I was born in Terre Haute, Indiana, in 1955. I was raised in Indiana, but lived a while in Illinois.

"As a kid I played cowboys and Indians, you know – army stuff. As I grew up, people – neighbors – talked about the Marine Corps. I never remember people talking about the Army. I was married when I was 19.

"When I got older I had a good job as a heavy equipment operator; I made good money, but I wasn't going anywhere. I was doing the same thing every day, and making no progress. One day I walked into the recruiter's office and said, 'Take me.'

"I wanted to have the decisions on the outcomes of my own goals. I wanted to be able to move up based not on who I knew, but on what I knew and how I applied myself. I wanted rewards based on initiative and I saw this from friends who talked about the Marine Corps. I guess my image of the Marine Corps at 17 to 19 years old was the same as any kid at the same age today: The Corps is a kick-ass outfit. It's different than any other service. My friends would say time in the Army was a waste. I never heard a Marine or former Marine badmouth the Corps.

"I like recruiting, overall, though I don't like the hours or the pressures. Someone is always on your ass, wanting to know where the next one's coming from. They have these *phaselines*. It's a quota system designed to make sure a recruiter gets to a certain point by a certain time of the month. I need to average two and a half bodies a month."

Bryan offered more biographical information, including the fact that he was divorced a year and a half after he first enlisted. He noted that he was then free to move. He had no relatives in the Marine Corps. He went to boot camp at San Diego, and his primary MOS was 2531, field radio operator, which he described as being something like a police radio dispatcher. In his job as a radio operator, in combat or in routine work in the Fleet Marine Forces, he would transmit and receive radio or field telephone messages.

During the next few meetings Bryan guided me on a "grand tour" of his office. At the front of the office area was a testing area. Bryan explained: "This is where we do our sifting. We administer a screening test because one of the first things we need to determine is whether they're mentally qualified to join the Corps.

"When they first walk in we establish rapport, try to get buddy-buddy. Most of them are nervous, hesitant. We try to set 'em at ease, get 'em relaxed."

Bryan showed me the reception area. On one wall there was a bulletin board with pictures of boot camp graduates who enlisted out of his office. They were pictured in the dress blue uniform in a head-and-shoulders pose. The faces were stern, unsmiling and suntanned. While we were discussing boot camp honor graduates, also pictured on the bulletin board, a young man walked in. I discovered that he was a private who had recently graduated from boot camp in San Diego and was home on leave in Indianapolis. They spoke:

"How ya doin' sir?" the private said.

Staff Sergeant Bryan smiled and kidded the private about saying "sir," "You can't keep saying that, you know. I'm not your drill instructor. You're not in boot camp anymore. I'm a staff sergeant.

You do that in the fleet and some NCO is gonna jump in your sh*t."

"Yes sir," the private replied, covering himself with an, "Oh well, I'll get over it." The private saw we were talking, so he sat on a couch and picked up a magazine.

On the same wall as the bulletin board with pictures of boot camp graduates there was another bulletin board with private first class chevrons (one stripe) stapled to it. There were also a cloth poolee shoulder patch to be worn on a jacket, a post card that read: "The Few, The Proud, The Marines," and a round bumper sticker with the Marine Corps seal – the eagle, globe and anchor of the Marine Corps emblem in gold on a scarlet background with UNITED STATES MARINE CORPS in white on a black background circling the emblem.

Staff Sergeant Jack

Bryan introduced me to Staff Sergeant "Jack" on my return visit to ask questions designed to gather more detail on the making of a recruiter. Jack was a bit shorter than Bryan, but stocky, perhaps five feet, nine inches tall, and 180 pounds. He looked like he lifted weights for PT. Jack later confirmed this. He too told his own story:

"I'm a 5811. That's criminal investigations in military police. I've been a recruiter 10 months, and I'm from Brownsburg, Indiana. It's real common in recruiting to get close to home. The Corps likes to get the team close to a place where they can relate to people.

"I'm married and have two kids, and I've been in the Corps nine years. Do I like recruiting? Yeah, I like it now. I like putting someone in the Corps, givin' 'em a chance, for school especially. I didn't come in 'til I was 25. I was pounding doors, and I spent time as a bricklayer. There's nothing about it I don't like now.

"We've got a new boss. With him if you bust butt, you get

rewarded, you get time off. Before, it was 16 to 18 hours a day, no matter what you did. Now recruiting is fun. The most rewarding part is seeing someone have a chance to succeed.

"Before – before the new boss – I didn't like the hours and the pressures. I didn't know what the f*** was going on. We have to depend on these pukes on the streets. You need a boss who knows what the f*** is going on. In the Fleet it's different. There you can depend on yourself and your buddies."

The pressures described by these recruiters often refer to quotas. Recruiting is more than anything a sales job. It's generally rather easy to "sell" the Marine Corps – especially for those who believe in the Marine Corps and its message. It's quite another challenge to get qualified prospects to "buy."

"The school: well, we learn how to sell. There's one school, at San Diego. It's seven weeks long. They teach salesmanship. We get a salesmanship certificate from XEROX; they send their civilians to teach the salesmanship part of the course. It's called "Professional Selling Skills." The rest is learning to be forward, outgoing."

Perspective: The commanding officer at Marine Corps District, Dallas, Texas, indicates that interviewing, prospecting and salesmanship training is now provided commercially by Achieve Global. Recruiters still rely on the "incentive tags" discussed in a previous chapter (Pride in Belonging to the Top Service; Self-Reliance; Self-Direction; Discipline, etc.), and as discussed earlier – at the entry level, it's not the Marine Corps most new recruits are looking for (it's not the beer or the pickup truck), but what the Marine Corps can provide that responds to the recruits' needs. It is the recruiter's job to discover what those needs are.

Staff Sergeant Jack explained that much of the application of these professional selling skills is spent on the road: "The office is authorized two cars: two pieces of junk. One is a 1982 Ford Fairmont with over 70,000 miles on it and the other is a '79 Horizon. They're badly in need of repair. We tell the gunny we need more or better cars. We're over TO (table of organization). That means we have four recruiters in this office and we only rate three for the area. So the shop only rates two vehicles and everybody drives them.

"So we sometimes use our own cars and we gotta pay for the gas. We get 'ROPES': reimbursement for out-of-pocket expenses like parking fees, dinner, lunches, official phone calls out of the office, stuff like that. But we don't get ROPES for gas in the personal vehicles.

"Also, being over TO means each recruiter has less 'QMA' than there should be. QMA is 'qualified male applicants.' It's a number derived from the total number of male high school seniors in local high schools assigned to an area of responsibility, plus the last two graduating classes, plus the next senior class. That number equals the total QMA. We have 15 high schools to cover.

Meeting prospects

By way of putting their job in perspective and covering recruiting from start to finish, Jack and Bryan collaborated on an unforgettable story about one prospect:

"It was March or April '83. We were working on one guy for six or eight months. He was a senior at one of the high schools. He was a wimp, a mama's boy. I finally got sick of him, so I ripped his card and sh*t-canned him.

"The gunny pulled his card from the sh*tcan and told me the kid had a poor family life. His dad wasn't quite as bad as the old lady, but they mistreated the kid pretty bad. The man took everything the kid owned, put it in a pile in the garage and burned it. His kid sister was on drugs. The kid couldn't make a decision on his own because of his parents. Gunny said the kid needed the Corps. So he took the card and said he'd work on him.

"The gunny worked on him two or three more months, and almost had him. At the last second the kid backed out. We'd call his home, the normal routine of supposedly good recruiters. Arrugh Arrugh. We fixed bayonets and charged up the hill. We knew we could help the kid.

"So the kid finally realized he couldn't let his parents dictate his every move. He decided to enlist but not tell his parents. He was 18 and a senior in high school, so it was legal. He had passed the written test but had to pass the physical. He stayed at the gunny's office overnight for a while until he took the test. His parents thought he had disappeared. It was unique because I had quit working the kid but his mother came to my office. She chewed me like I was a dog; she wore me out. One time she came in with a boyfriend and another time she came in with her husband.

"They thought they were bad-asses. They came in four times and I was the only one around. One time the father had on a coat, and I didn't know it at the time but he was recording our conversation. They told me they were going to go to the FBI. They felt we were hiding the kid, that we had kidnapped him. I could honestly say that I hadn't seen him. I knew the Corps was better for him than this.

"Well, they contacted Senator Lugar's office. Then Senator Lugar called me. Then the whole command got involved. The truth came out and none of us got in trouble from the brass 'cause the kid was 18 and legal. But while the kid was waiting his parents had a change of heart.

"The kid finally enlisted in the Corps. When he had graduated and was home on leave, his mother came into the office to tell me she was as proud of him as she could be.

"To fully appreciate the whole affair you'd've had to been here. They really had the Corps stereotyped as bloodthirsty baby-eaters. Why? Ignorance of the Corps. She finally saw he was basically the same kid but now able to make his own decisions. She probably felt good in the end about what we had done for him."

Phone calls

In addition to meeting with prospects who walk into the office, recruiters contact many prospects by telephone. Sometimes a prospect calls in when no recruiter is around and leaves his own number on the answering machine. Recruiters get other telephone numbers from a national clearinghouse that distributes prospect cards which applicants have mailed in for information.

Staff Sergeants Jack and Bryan explained that there are cold calls and regular calls. A cold call is to a prospect that recruiters have not talked to; regular calls are follow-ups, or calls to people they have met or talked to before. People they have met may have been through an area canvas, walking through a shopping mall, down the street or at a high school. Jack and Bryan both said they open with easy questions that require an answer, like, "Have you ever thought about the Marine Corps?"

No matter how they get the telephone numbers, the numbers are valuable, because the telephone is a tool that allows the recruiter to put a prospect in the position to think of nothing else but the Marine Corps, even if only for a few seconds. Some calls are productive; many more are frustrating or dead ends. Eventually, the recruits who do sign up will "ship" or head off to basic training: boot camp.

Boot Camp

Receiving and first phase

Most recruits arrive at San Diego or Parris Island in groups.

On the way to Parris Island, most congregate at the airport at Charleston, where there is a Marine liaison unit, and take a Greyhound bus that is scheduled to arrive at Parris Island in the predawn hours. The timing adds to the effect of shaking the civilian out of the boy. Each group of recruits from a recruiting station has a leader who carries the orders for all the recruits in the group. (Marines never move from station to station without official written orders – travel documents.)

As the bus arrives at the depot, a drill instructor "encourages" recruits to get off the bus with forceful language: **"Get outside! Move! Get off the damn bus! Move it! Move it! Move it!"** Receiving DIs do not wear campaign covers now, and vulgar language is no longer permitted – notable changes from 1973. According to a receiving barracks DI, they now wear the **garrison cover** or **piss cutter** because it's less threatening to recruits.

In my experience, there were also Marines stationed at the airport: Lindbergh Field, San Diego's international airport. The corporal who drove the bus from the airport to the recruit depot was not a drill instructor but swore superlatively and had recruits take seats on the bus from front to rear, then on the middle deck. No talking was allowed. The DIs met the bus on the depot at San Diego, somewhere behind the barber shop. Recruits then and now, and as far back as this author can find records, stood on footprints painted on the street, heels together, toes at a 45-degree angle.

At San Diego, while waiting for our first haircut, someone ordered our **mob** to memorize five articles of the Uniform Code of Military Justice painted on a sign on the side of the building. These were the five articles recruits most often violated (as I recall):

Disobedience of a lawful order

Disrespect (to non-commissioned officers)

Missing a movement

Absent without leave (AWOL)

Desertion

The first haircut is quick and easy. It takes less than a minute and recruits pay for this one as they will for each of the weekly haircuts throughout training. They don't reach in their pockets for the 50 or 75 cents ($2 to $2.50 in the 1980s); it's taken in credit from their pay when they are issued *chit books*. During training, money is credited to the recruits in a booklet of chits, or pieces of paper coupons, that have monetary values printed on them. Chit books help prevent theft, and are used at the PX, barbershop and in the collection plate at chapel, if a recruit desires.

The haircut's main purpose is sanitation. The SOP notes that another purpose is to equalize recruits.

During the next few days, while recruits are generally immobilized with fear, frustration and the inability to do anything that pleases the receiving barracks DIs, they undergo a battery of academic aptitude tests, physical examinations and inoculations, and an inventory physical fitness test.

Recruits are issued all the clothing, equipment and personal toilet articles they will be allowed to use during boot camp. Their personal civilian articles are packaged and stored or shipped home. In years past, much of the smaller toilet articles came in a steel bucket which recruits sometimes wore over their heads as symbols of shame during training at the discretion of their drill instructors. The buckets were also useful during washday and for other utilitarian duties. The **chrome dome** was kept highly shined at all times.

Another letter to the Editor from the May, 1984, *Leatherneck* Magazine better describes some of the uses for the bucket:

Dear Sir:

I just finished reading R.R. Warner's story 'Bucket, Steel, Galvanized,' in the March 1984 issue. That brought back memories....Late in the afternoon of June 21, 1959, I was introduced to my bucket and bucket issue in the Receiving Barracks at San Diego. I remember the first thing we did upon receiving our bucket was to inventory its contents. Of course, this was done 'by the numbers.' The DI called out each item and we'd hold the item high in the air. Immediately following this, we paid for the contents of our bucket issue by coupons (also contained in the bucket issue). This amounted to something in the order of $17. Note: all our expenses in boot camp such as haircuts, laundry, PX supplies, etc., were paid for by chits from our coupon book. I do not recall that we ever used money in boot camp. Also note that a private received $78 a month at that time. Another item in the bucket...was the little red pocket edition of the 'Guidebook for Marines.' Whenever we had a few moments, we were to break out our little book and study its contents.

Boot camp at San Diego provided the background for one of my most remembered nightly rituals. Every night we would fall out with our buckets to water and cut the grass. Basically, we would fill our buckets with water, which we then sprinkled on the sand around our Quonset huts. Once the water dried and formed a crust on the sand, we would rake and make nice, parallel lines in the sand. We would stretch a string across the end of the platoon street, cut the residue sand with the back of the rake and sweep the excess sand away.

You could take pity on the poor lowly recruit that stepped on the 'grass!'

Richard A. Bishop

The steel bucket and its rituals are now gone.

The purpose for holding recruits in a receiving barracks is to allow enough numbers to accumulate to form a series, or four platoons of between 60 and 80 recruits. Once the series reaches that number, the platoons are *picked up* by their teams of DIs, after they are *welcomed* to recruit training. The following account is from two Marines who served as DIs during the late 1970s and 1980s. They are brothers-in-law, Staff Sergeant "Bo" and Gunny "Keith:"

"Recruits were brought in and sat down, then talked to by the battalion commander, the company commander, the series commander. Now it's just the series commander. All these officers come up telling 'em things about Parris Island in a conversational tone, almost like it was an indoc for their senior year at school from their homeroom teacher.

"Then they bring out the drill instructors. The senior starts his speech. It's about a four-minute speech. It's in a bit sterner voice now; he's trying to implant in their minds that he's running the show. He goes through his little speech and shows 'em how to stand at the position of attention. Then he says to the different platoons, "You're going here and you're going there." Then he says, "*MOVE!*"

"As soon as he says, 'Move!' these three maniacs appear – the junior drill instructors. The recruits say that was the biggest shock they've ever had, seeing such a changeover from the conversational tone of the officers and the senior. We call it 'sh*t hits the fan'. The drill instructors have a chance to assert themselves. It's effective, but it only last four hours."

The drill instructors know what to do. They want to act like that all the time, but there are so many restrictions. It only lasts two to four days now.

During pickup at San Diego in 1973, my platoon was **marched** (straggled) to the barracks we would use during first phase. "'H' hotel" barracks they were called: three stories, H-shaped from an overhead view, with wash racks in the courtyards on either end of the buildings. On our receiving day in the new H-hotel barracks, the platoon was instructed to busy itself preparing for an inspection; we were to meet our drill instructors, who were then in *the house*, or duty hut. At about the time we thought our uniforms were neatly squared away in the footlockers at the end of our racks, and had our chosen racks neatly made with the corners we learned in receiving barracks, the four maniacs appeared, screaming obscenities.

The next several hours were miserable. The maniacs threw mattresses, boots and shoes, and footlockers and their contents were spread over the squadbay. One recruit had a Bible in his personal gear. A drill instructor screamed at him, "What the hell is this for sweet pea? I'm your god. You don't need no god but me. I am your god, your father, your mother. Everything! You got that?" The recruit was reduced to tears. He was one of the few high school grads in the platoon, did rather well and had been meritoriously promoted to corporal the last time I saw him on Okinawa two years later.

Our platoon was herded out of the squad bay to stand in formation with empty footlocker boxes several times during this melee. Not once did the platoon of some 74 recruits make it through the one double hatch in acceptable time. So the drill was repeated, many times. When the introduction to the DIs ended, remarkably, it seems, no one was hurt.

In addition to learning how to march from the first days of training, recruits go through an established regimen of academic and physical training divided into three phases. During first phase, recruits learn and are evaluated on:

- discipline
- military skills
- the rifle
- history, customs and courtesies
- first aid
- interior guard

- drill
- close combat
- military bearing
- physical fitness
- esprit

During first phase, training with the rifle is in the care, cleaning, disassembly and assembly of the weapon. Late in first phase recruits begin to learn some of the basics of marksmanship, but actual marksmanship training takes place during second phase.

History classes include the history and traditions of the Marine Corps, and recruits are tested on such names and dates as: the date of the founding of the Corps; the first Marine recruiter, Captain Samuel Nichols; and the place he recruited from, Tun Tavern, Philadelphia; the Grand Old Man of the Corps, Colonel Archibald Henderson; the origins of the NCO's and officer's swords; Medal of Honor recipients and other heroes from a number of wars and the dates of the wars.

Customs and courtesies classes include training in the rituals of saluting and boarding ships, lessons about the Marine birthday and other customs of the Marine Corps. First aid and field sanitation classes include the basic life saving skills, application of combat field dressings, and the basics of personal and small unit field sanitation. Practical application testing comes at the end of first phase and late in second phase.

Interior guard training begins in the classroom, but includes practical application and evaluation. Drill instructors organize recruits into an interior guard unit, with a sergeant of the guard, corporal of the guard and several sentries. Recruits memorize the 11 general orders for sentries, below, long before interior guard practical application. In fact, if recruiters have done their job, poolees will have memorized the 11 general orders before going to boot camp.

General Orders for Sentries
(A Marine on guard has no friends)

- To take charge of this post and all government property in view.

- To walk my post in a military manner, keeping always on the alert and observing everything that takes place within sight and hearing.

- To report all violations of orders I am instructed to enforce.

- To repeat all calls more distant from the guardhouse than my own.

- To quit my post only when properly relieved.

- To receive, obey and pass on to the sentry who relieves me all orders from the commanding officer, officer of the day and officers and noncommissioned officers of the guard only.

- To talk to no one except in the line of duty.

- To give the alarm in case of fire or disorder.

- To give the alarm in any case not covered by instructions.

- To salute all officers and all colors and standards not cased.

- To be especially watchful at night, and during the time for challenging, to challenge all persons on or near my post, allowing no one to pass without proper authority.

Close combat training includes offensive and defensive training with the rifle armed with a bayonet. Recruits also have their first run at some of the obstacle courses, including the confidence course.

The SOP for male recruit training (October, 1981) lists the following purposes for close combat and physical training:

Close combat training: develops individual confidence and the spirit of the offensive through instruction, demonstration and controlled application of bayonet fighting.

The Daily Seven: is designed to develop strength, endurance and coordination...and to serve as a light workout and warm-up before more strenuous events. This set of exercises consists of side straddle hops [jumping jacks], bends and reaches, toe-touchers, trunk twisters, squat benders, two-count pushups and boot slappers.

Running exercises: develop the involuntary muscles, and thereby increase circulo-respiration, or 'wind.' Secondly, running exercises develop strength, endurance and stamina throughout the body. No other drill instructor nor other recruits will physically push, shove or drag a recruit in order to enable him to keep up with or finish a run.[ccxxxi]

Close order drill (marching) is a daily occupation for recruits. Standing in line waiting to go to chow, classes, testing or inoculations, a single DI can teach recruits many of the basics of marching. The intricacies of drill are too long and varied to detail in this book. There are two purposes for close order drill: to get a unit from one location to another in an orderly manner, and from the SOP: "The principle by which a recruit develops a high state of discipline, respect for authority, teamwork, unit esprit, and an instant, willing response to orders."

There is no question, in this analysis, that close order drill is one of the most important tools a drill instructor has to develop small unit identity and cohesion. Drill bonds recruits to each other, to their drill instructor and to the identity of the Marine Corps. At San Diego in particular, where the noise of the commercial airliners at the adjacent Lindberg Field makes hearing normal conversation difficult, sorting out the unique sound of one DI from 20 others while a jet is taking off seems impossible. *(There may easily be 20 platoons engaged in close order drill on the parade deck at any given time – as the parade deck at MCRD San Diego is a half-mile long and quarter mile wide.)* Analysis of journalistic and ethnographic interviews with former Marines from every decade back to the 1920s reveals that drill is the most remembered part of training. What seems to be unintelligible to the untrained ear is: "Left, right, left, right; column left, march; column right, march;" and "to the rear, march," etc.

Drill competition between platoons at the end of first phase, "Initial Drill Comp," yields a *Drill Comp* winner. By that time in training, about five weeks, recruits have learned how to read their DIs. Winning drill competition usually gets a very positive reaction from the drill instructors, which serves to unify the men in the platoon. The senior DI may decide to punish a platoon that does poorly in drill competition by banding its guidon (the banner, or flag, with the platoon number on it) by wrapping or covering it with the green elastic blousing garters recruits use to blouse the bottoms of their utility trousers. This sign of disgrace should cause a measure of depression in the platoon, but can motivate the recruits to try harder. Whether they win or lose, recruits do so as a team.

During first phase, recruits should be moving through externally imposed discipline into self-discipline. The drill instructors of each platoon are around the platoon from breakfast through supper, and one DI, the duty **Hat**, sleeps at the barracks through the night. Staff Sergeant "Bo" and Gunny "Keith" explained that the duty drill instructor gets about four hours of sleep on a duty night.

But discipline does not come only through training in close order drill. Recruits must be trained to pay attention to details and strive for perfection in personal hygiene, military bearing, uniforms and appearance, physical fitness, academic proficiency and teamwork. In order to instill discipline in these areas, the DI must correct recruits when they make mistakes.

In the terms of behavioral psychology, a recruit should be punished for a mistake and rewarded for a correct response or success.

Most of the nine drill instructors and three former drill

instructors interviewed for this study agreed that changes to the SOP from the mid-70s to mid-1980s made it increasingly difficult to discipline recruits with rewards and punishments. Incentive PT is one of the legal punishments.

In Staff Sergeant "Bo's" words, "Of course we're role playing. Acting like animals ain't normal. It's in the DIs' minds that they have to do certain things to get recruits trained for what they're going to be facing in the FMF. The constant hell-raising only lasts three or four days. After that it's only sporadic. You got your recruits that are totally unsat and you go off on them. After two or three days it starts mellowing out because the important thing now is to get them to appointments. What it comes down to is you don't have time to use that stress like you want to. If you've got shots, you can't PT 'em for 12 hours after shots. This is in forming (the first week or so). A recruit can do just about anything and you can't PT 'em.

"Restrictions? You've got a half-hour before chow and an hour after (when recruits cannot get PT'd). If you get back from morning chow and have scheduled PT later, you can't PT a recruit a half-hour before that or after that. There are mornings when you can't bend and thrust a private until just before noon chow because of the schedule."

(Question:) "Isn't immediate punishment seen as more effective than delayed?"

"Yes, but what you see now is drill instructors walking around with little books taking down names and saying, 'We'll catch up with you.' They have to remind a recruit why he's on the quarterdeck. He could've completely forgotten why; maybe he didn't move fast enough or he was scratching his face.

"Our biggest problem is the *casuals* and the *sea lawyers*. We've got a little recruit training card that lists our restrictions. Recruits don't know that. But I've found from experience that if you get a recruit who does know he'll push it to the limit. They find out in the chow hall from the casuals [those on the way out of training, not graduated]. Say a first phase recruit thinks he's made a big mistake and all he wants to do is get out of here [Parris Island] the quickest way he can. Casual recruits or sea lawyers in the chow hall tell 'em, 'You want to get out of here, tell 'em you wanna see a psychiatrist. He'll get you out. Simple as that. Or refuse to train.' It's when they get to mingle with the bad seeds, the ones going off Parris Island, the ones that seem to know the ropes. The sea lawyers."

The conclusion of all but one of these present and former drill instructors was that there are now too many restrictions on the drill instructor, imposed by changes in the SOP, and too much supervision by officers whose main purpose is to enforce the SOP.

Staff Sergeant "Bo" said, "There are DIs who are what you'd call gun shy. They want to train recruits to their utmost, but they're so afraid of making a mistake that they're not fulfilling their potential as drill instructors. They're afraid for their rank, afraid for their money. I think they ought to go back to the old system, with one series officer instead of two (lieutenants).

"We don't need this micromanagement. It's not because the officers want to do it, they're told to do it. They have to go to every class, every function, for some un-God-known reason. There's been series commanders and assistant series commanders come up to me and said, 'If I were to die today, they wouldn't even know I left.' He's a figurehead. A body. Someone so you can look around and see there's someone here. There's some bars (a lieutenant)."

One of the former drill instructors offered similar observations about the restrictions on drill instructors and the resulting impact on recruits:

"Recruit training doesn't have to have logic. It should be hard enough to remember. The purpose is to instill instant, willing obedience to orders so the Marine and his unit can survive in combat.

"Today the Marine Corps is a business. The Army and Navy are too. It's like Disneyworld East, and it's all press. Big press. All this public stuff is superficial in making a Marine."

The former Marine observed what I had seen at Parris Island during the early 1980s. What he referred to were the public relations gimmicks, such as the visitors' PX and the bus tour around the base for relatives and friends of graduating recruits. Before the tour, the tourists assembled in the visitors' center, adjacent to the public affairs office, then walked across the street to the base theater for a brief recruiting film, *Such as Regiments Hand Down Forever*. That film alone was enough to cause some visitors to jokingly ask where they could sign up. The base motor pool supplied a bus for the tour, which made stops or pauses in areas where recruits trained, including the high visibility areas: the obstacle courses and confidence course, the rifle range, Page Field (a closed World War II-era airfield) and the infantry field training areas, and some of the historical landmarks.

Sections of Parris Island are preserved as National Historic Sites, and are listed in the National Register of Historic Places. One area includes the commanding general's quarters (a large 19th century home) and the wooden dry dock once used to service the *Great White Fleet*. There are also monuments on the southeastern side of the island, erected in recognition of 16th century European explorers who first landed and attempted to settle Parris Island: Frenchman Jean Ribault, and a band of Spanish settlers who maintained a presence from about 1562 to 1580.

Following the tour, which was designed in part to give visitors something to do while waiting for their soon-to-graduate recruits, a guide escorted visitors back to the visitors' center. As recruits were released from their duties, parents and friends met them at the visitors' center. Some of the family and friends waited in the visitors' gift shop, buying T-shirts, books, coffee cups or other souvenirs of Parris Island. Since most of the visitors are neither active duty nor retired from the military, thus do not rate a government ID card and cannot use the post exchange, the gift shop was established to allow them to take home souvenirs of Parris Island.

They could then visit with graduates at the visitors' center or go to the base snack bar for a light lunch. On the menu of the fast food restaurant were *DI burgers* and *Recruit burgers*.

The essence of the former Marine's observations is that the treatment of visitors may be good public relations, but it has nothing to do with training Marines. He also mentioned the superlatives, "Every year they say, 'These are the best recruits or best Marines we've ever had.' How good can they get? Today's drill instructors get nowhere near the respect they did in the '50s. And NCOs are not what they used to be. They're too young. A corporal used to be a god.

"Discipline and esprit de corps go hand in hand. If recruits can't make it in boot camp, how can they be expected to take it in combat? The changes come from mothers and Congress. Some of the problems started with the Ribbon Creek incident in the '50s, but today's problems started with the McClure incident in 1975 (when a Private McClure died while in recruit training at San Diego as the result of an injury to the head during a pugil stick bout.)"

Another drill instructor on the field during 1984, Gunny "Everette," noted, "The stress has gone down a lot in the past 10 years. One big thing we lost is the mote ditch. It did away with a lot of motivation recycles. Instead of recycling a private for lack of motivation, [we would] just send him to the mote' ditch. They came back with a new sense of motivation."

Note: I recall that in 1973, the stories told by veterans of one-day moto provided their own form of motivation to other recruits. The ditch at San Diego was filled with slimy green water. Recruits went to moto with utility trousers held up by a string (so as not to destroy a belt or buckle), boots and socks, skivvy drawers and shirt, and no **cover** (hat).

When they returned at the end of the day, exhausted, they were covered with caked greenish mud and were given 10 minutes to appear showered, shaved and in a clean uniform. My platoon never lost a private who had completed one-day moto.

Gunny Everette added, "You can get discipline without esprit, but if you've got esprit, you've got discipline. Everybody's so worried about the damn private. He's got to get his eight hours' sleep a day. Ain't nobody worried about the DI gettin' his sleep. The work week is 100 hours, more or less, depending on the phase.

"Instilling discipline...the DI's got tools. Peer pressure and small unit esprit de corps. Privates use the buddy system making their racks; they use the buddy system making a **hump** (hike).

(Question:) What about positive rewards?

"Motivation. There's the motivation table. We put awards the recruits won on the table, and some DIs put their awards on the table, especially if they got combat awards like a Silver Star or Bronze Star. There's also the motivation board or hog board. We gotta keep the porn shots off, but there's motivation in waitin' to see your girl.

"Most recruits take pride in a nickname. I had one boy who went four years to Bob Jones University. We called him 'preacher.' He took pride in that. There was another kid we called 'snaggletooth.' He loved it."

Gunny Everette said the younger DIs know the SOP better,

but don't know the ins and outs, how to get around the restrictions. He observed that if a DI operates within the spirit of the SOP, he can train recruits well enough without thumping or cursing.

"We sit down with privates near the end of training and they know we work hard; they know they've worked hard. [We get closer to recruits then and] slip [curse] sometimes. We ain't supposed to curse, but, [the SOP treats it as if] they could get killed if someone says, 'F***.' We're gonna be in a hurt locker next time we go to war. All they got to do is put a big damn loudspeaker on with a bunch of cusswords. People will freak out; they won't know what to do.

"But some people went overboard with verbal abuse; just like incentive PT. Five minutes' incentive PT to a third phase recruit ain't trash. PT 'em five minutes and they just laugh. Incentive PT is the best thing we got, and there's too many restrictions on that."

To balance the observations of those above, one DI said that he thinks today's (1984) drill instructors are lazy, they don't learn the SOP. Gunny "D" said, "Today's DI believes he can't train recruits as well as they were trained before, because they think the SOP prohibits him from doing certain things." He added, for example, that on rainy days, recruits can do PT indoors, "If DIs had to set up an indoor circuit course, they wouldn't be able to state the purpose. It's because they didn't take the time to learn the lesson plans. And, they don't learn the SOP until they get in trouble. Then they look in the SOP to see if they're right or wrong. Why? Laziness or procrastination.

"In my opinion you can train a recruit hard with the SOP and lesson plans. The SOP says don't exhaust a recruit. How do you measure exhaustion? DIs were standing around under trees until I got here. I put a stop to that. They've got to get out there and put the privates' dicks in the dirt. They can do that without touching a recruit; they can do it without hazing or maltreating a recruit.

"What DIs are confusing is the hard work and physical exertion of training and the misperception that they have to punish recruits to train them."

To add more of a sense of clarity to the foregoing, it has been noted by all of those interviewed that most drill instructors identify with their own DIs. When they learn **command voice** in DI School, they often emulate the voice of one of their own DIs, even though it may have been five to ten years or more since boot camp. When they get **on the street**, working as a DI, they want to be the DI their DI was. The justification in this is: "If I'm a good Marine (and I must be), it's because my DI made me this way. If I act like he did, I'll produce good Marines." The logic in this begins to fail if a Marine's DI was a thumper and the newer generation DI thumps too.

The introduction and welcome by the series commander includes the caution to recruits to tell someone in authority if they are ever thumped or subjected to any form of hazing, verbal abuse or other maltreatment. According to the DIs of the mid-1980s, there is almost no way a DI can get away with thumping recruits.

In 1973, DIs spoke of loyalty. If a DI saw fit to tighten up a recruit, he did it in private. In addition to the DI from my platoon who was busted for striking a recruit, my platoon lost another DI while at the rifle range, for "maltreatment." During an inspection, the company commander asked a private why the shoes under his rack were not shined. The recruit replied that he had been shining the house mouse's shoes. The captain called for the house mouse, and asked to see his shoes, which were shined. The captain asked why the other private had shined his shoes, and the house mouse replied that he had shined the king rat's shoes. The captain called over king rat, who, as the saying goes, in front of God, Corps and Country, said he had been shining the drill instructor's shoes. Personal servitude was not and is not allowed. That sergeant was gone in a day. (Two house mouses cleaned the DIs' office, the duty hut, and were supervised by the king rat, who helped clean the office.)

In the 1960s and 70s, as the saying goes, a DI would ask a private to jump and the private would only ask, "How high?" Ask a private to sh*t and he would ask, "What color?" Ask a private to steal, and he would ask, "How much?" (as long as he could reasonably ascertain that the theft was for the unit, not the DI.) Now, either recruits are too smart for this mentality, or the bonding between the DI and the recruit has disintegrated to the relationship between teacher and student, rather than the relationship between two men who would rely on each other for survival in combat, or a combination of both, in the views of the DIs of the mid-1980s.

Going over the hill

There are recruits who, for whatever personal reasons, feel they cannot take the training or feel they made a mistake so grave as to want to leave Parris Island or San Diego. Some of them may let a drill instructor know their feelings, see a Navy doctor at the neuropsychiatric unit or a unit chaplain. Others just walk off base or go over the fence. There are many stories about recruits who decide to leave training or go AWOL (absent without leave). At San Diego in 1973, the first story my platoon heard from a drill instructor was about the private who climbed over the fence into Lindbergh Field – San Diego International Airport – and climbed into the wheel wells of a commercial jet. The jet would fly at over 30,000 feet, well above the freezing altitude. When the plane landed in Chicago, they said, the private fell out when the landing gear was extended, and bounced, frozen, on the runway.

From the bus returning to begin 3rd phase at San Diego after three weeks of rifle range and infantry training at Camp Pendleton, we spotted a wayfaring recruit was about to walk in the gate. He had a recruit haircut and wore the sateen green utilities and boots of a Marine recruit. There was no telling how long he had been off base.

At Parris Island, as a journalist, I wrote a story for the base newspaper about the manager of the local Greyhound bus station who returned a number of recruits each year to Parris Island, according to his account. There is a $25 reward offered to civilians who return deserters and AWOL servicemen to the government. He related that recruits are not hard to spot. They sometimes steal uniforms on base, but the rank on the uniform doesn't fit the age of the person trying to buy a bus ticket. Other recruits steal clothes off clothes lines on the walk from Parris Island to the bus station in Beaufort.

And, there are some recruits who don't think they can make it out Parris Island's gate, which is at the end of a narrow, mile-long causeway with a two-lane road. Some of these recruits attempt to swim the Beaufort River or Broad River. While at Parris Island, a fellow staff sergeant and I pulled one private from the Beaufort River and called the military police. On another occasion, in the mudflats on the southern end of the island a fisherman found the remains of a man, determined through a later autopsy to be in his late teens or early 20s. The only remains of clothing were combat boots, but it was never determined if the person was once a recruit. Nevertheless, the incident made for a good story.

Second Phase

Through a combination of education and various motivational techniques, including close order drill, incentive PT and positive motivational rewards, recruits pass from first phase into second phase with some measure of self-discipline. There is general disagreement as to how the recruits of the 1980s compare with those of decades past, but those who train them tend to feel restricted. DI's feel that the openness of the training area to civilians is too disturbing, and telling recruits of their rights and the awareness of civil rights by recruits today makes them too concerned with whether or not they get hit or cussed at. Those who recruit new prospects tend to feel recruits are more trainable.

There is a general feeling that intervention by Congress and "letters from moms" have had the most restricting impact on the DI's ability to train recruits, by way of the SOP and further restrictions put in place by intermediate commanders. Congressional inquiries are evidently as feared by officers as allegations of abuse from recruits are by DIs. Most DIs feel recruit training is the business of non-commissioned officers and staff NCOs; that officers should rarely be seen in the training areas.

However, most drill instructors agreed that recruits are recognizably disciplined as they enter second phase, which is primarily rifle marksmanship and field training. Drill instructors tend to back off a little; stress is reduced a bit so recruits can concentrate on marksmanship.

There is actually little drill instruction during the two weeks of rifle range and the week of infantry training following. Primary marksmanship instructors conduct most of the training during rifle marksmanship. They too wear the Smokey the Bear hats, by custom, as do members of the Marine rifle and pistol team.

Recruits spend the first week of marksmanship training in outdoor classrooms learning the arts of marksmanship: getting "sight picture and sight alignment," and learning BRASS (breathe, relax, aim, slack, squeeze). Recruits learn a new kind of physical discipline during **snapping in** in the four firing positions: standing or offhand, sitting, kneeling and prone.

During snapping in, recruits form a large circle around target barrels and dry fire – aim their unloaded rifles at barrels painted white with miniature black targets. They are required to stay in each of the four positions for many hours during the first week so they can use the positions comfortably during firing the next week. Recruits who do not work hard at snapping in don't stretch their muscles adequately and may experience trouble shooting. Marksmanship instructors sometimes expel the monotony of training with tales of the exploits of Marine sharpshooters in past wars.

Firing for practice usually begins on a Monday, with two *strings* of fire of 50 rounds each for each recruit. Recruits and Marines in the FMF fire for initial qualification and requalification on the KD, or *known distance*, course with the following requirements:

200-yard line:

five rounds each, slow fire (five rounds in five

minutes); standing, sitting and kneeling

ten rounds, rapid fire (in one minute); sitting

300-yard line:

five rounds, slow fire; sitting

ten rounds, rapid fire; prone

500-yard line:

ten rounds slow fire; prone

Rapid fire targets are bullseye-shaped; shooters earn five, four, three or two points decreasing as the impact of the bullet is farther from the center of the target. A miss is called a *maggie's drawers*, because the recruit in the *butts* marking targets signals a miss by waving a disc on a pole past the front of the target like a pair of drawers. Slow fire targets are human silhouette-shaped. A similar scoring method is used for the silhouette targets. Recruits shoot for qualification on a Friday, although if firing is rained out, Thursday's score can count *for record*.

Marking targets has its own subculture. A Marine in a

concrete shed in the butts talks to the tower NCO at the firing line. With a loudspeaker, the butts NCO instructs *the butt crew* to raise and lower targets on command. When a string of fire is complete, the butts NCO in charge commands, "Stand by for the stand by! Bring your 'Able' targets to half-mast! On the sound of the whistle we gonna bring those 'Able' targets high in the sky...3--2--1, Phweet!" (The butts NCO blows a whistle and the butts crew responds.) The targets are paper on canvas, mounted on wooden frames inserted into large metal carriages with chains and pulleys that allow one target to be in the air while another is in the butts.

Recruits may spend hours in the butts without a drill instructor's supervision. Some drill instructors acknowledge that the time at the range is too slack for their liking, but if it helps the recruits score well on the range, it is worth the extra work to re-instill some discipline after the range. The platoon with the highest averages – usually with the highest number of expert marksmen, or highest aggregate score – wins the range. Such a win is comparable to winning drill competition.

The week following marksmanship training is spent in field training. At Parris Island, recruits go to Page Field, (an old airstrip overgrown with weeds, surrounded by pine trees) and Elliot's Beach for combat field training. At San Diego, recruits board buses and travel to Camp Pendleton, some 30-40 miles north of San Diego for marksmanship training, rifle qualification and field training.

During this week, recruits learn about mines and booby traps, pyrotechnics; nuclear, biological and chemical warfare (NBC) training (which includes going through a gas chamber with a gas mask), and apply some of the practical applications of squad level tactics and map and compass reading. Drill instructors are less in the public eye during the week and use the time to reinforce discipline as required, while allowing recruits to feel their accomplishments. When the recruits return to their mainside barracks they will be in third phase and will be expected to set an example for first phase recruits. Third phase is about three weeks long. If a recruit has not displayed self-discipline, teamwork, esprit de corps or some measure of initiative by the start of third phase, if he's sliding, skating or gold bricking in other words, his senior drill instructor may take the liberty of recommending the recruit for a motivation recycle (although a motivation recycle can happen at any time, including the day before graduation).

Third Phase

During third phase recruits get final fitting and tailoring on their uniforms. Many recruits change shape during the 10-11 weeks; some lose weight, some add muscle, some grow an inch or more. Different levels of command inspect the platoon until the final week when the battalion commander inspects each recruit, ensuring among other things that all uniforms fit properly. Recruits are also expected to know by rote such things as the maximum range or maximum rate of fire of an M-16 rifle, or any of the general orders for sentries, or certain first aid steps, and all of the chain of command. Some may be asked leadership questions.

Even though most recruits are learning the proper values and developing self-confidence, self-discipline and esprit de corps, there are times when they feel they can get away with more, or they get careless. Individual incentive PT is still conducted, but as noted by other drill instructors above, third phase recruits laugh inside at five minutes of strenuous PT. If the platoon as a whole is slipping, the platoon guidon can still be banded, but in years gone by, the platoon would get incentive PT en masse. My DIs called the PT area **the pit**. The pit call (as in chow call, mail call, etc., originally from bugle calls), could be held anywhere, but was often held with 70 recruits *asshole-to-belly button* in a dirt rectangle large enough to accommodate 40 (about the size of a sandy volleyball court).

Sometimes a pit call had to be held out of sight of authority figures, so a handball court was used, or recruits were marched to out-of-the-way areas behind little-used buildings. There were stories in the 70s about platoons of 35 to 40 recruits being ordered into dumpster trash bins to do PT or the manual of arms with rifles.

Mail call also provided opportunities for PT, but with a far different purpose. Until the mid-1970s, recruits who received food in the mail were given the food – sometimes whole cakes – to eat alone. Or, they could share the food (as the drill instructor ensured that everyone but the receiver got something to eat.) Mail call rituals allowed recruits time to genuinely relax, depending on their progress during the day and the mood of the DI. Rituals varied from DI to DI. Mail call today is supposed to be restricted to the drill instructor calling out the name on the letter, the recruit answering, "Here," and going to the DI to retrieve the letter.

Recruits make transportation arrangements and plan 10-day boot leave en route their first duty stations. Drill instruction continues through third phase and some platoons learn intricate drill maneuvers, depending on the skills or inclinations of the drill instructor and the time available. There is a final drill comp, which seems to carry as much weight for the DIs of the winning platoon as for the recruits; such a win is a symbol of the DIs' skills. Hand-to-hand combat and close combat training and competition continue, as do practice and evaluation on the obstacle courses.

Drill instructors hold parade practice, like much of drill instruction, on the parade deck, or **grinder**. Now recruits know they are preparing to graduate. They are **short** or **short timers**. Each platoon will have an honor graduate, selected by the platoon's drill instructor, but designated by the battalion commander, according to the SOP. Each of the four honor graduates will be awarded the dress blue uniform from the Leatherneck Association and meritoriously promoted to private first class upon graduation. The series staff – DIs and officers – interview and evaluate the four platoon honor graduates, and select one as the series honor graduate.

In addition, battalion commanders may promote up to 20 percent of the graduating recruits meritoriously to private first class upon graduation. Selection is based on leadership, personal appearance, high personal standards, personal integrity, maturity and motivation. Recruits who score the maximum 300 points on the physical fitness test also earn individual awards, as do the highest scoring shooters in each platoon.

The graduation ceremony lasts about an hour. Many parents and other friends and relatives attend the ceremonies, sometimes traveling thousands of miles to spend a day or two at San Diego or Parris Island. It is not unusual to hear many middle-aged men or women note that they are former Marines.

Most new privates will go to schools of varying duration after a 10-day leave. Some privates will spend an extra 30 days or more at home, participating in the hometown recruiter program, helping convince other young men or women to enlist. Having recently experienced the rites of passage and being the same age as the buddies they left behind about 10 weeks earlier makes them potentially very credible spokesmen.

In addition to getting a little extra time off at home before reporting to school, getting people to enlist can earn a new Marine a meritorious promotion and special remarks in his record book.

Any Marine will recognize this is a very brief overview of recruit training, and leaves out many details. There are many books which detail the experience of Marine boot camp through the eyes of those who have experienced it, as well as through the interpretation of non-Marines.

Following recruit training, Marines enter schools and earn a primary military occupational specialty (MOS) upon graduation. Some Marines will go to one of the three infantry divisions (at Camp Lejeune, North Carolina; Camp Pendleton, California; and Okinawa, Japan) or the First Marine Brigade (in Hawaii) as infantry Marines, or **grunts**. Some of these will specialize as mortarmen or machine gunners; some will go to the elite reconnaissance (recon) units (which are only quasi-elite, because the Marine Corps feels the Corps is elite in itself and does not need any internally elite units like the Army's Airborne or Ranger units.) Some Marines go to artillery, some to aviation school. There are hundreds of MOSs, including individual MOSs for scores of linguists in various languages, musicians, specialists in aircraft, computers and communications equipment, etc.

Perspective: Organizationally, the Department of Defense restructured the armed forces as a whole after I retired in 1995. These changes are beyond the scope of this analysis, but one change in the Marine Corps – the creation of Marine Corps Special Operations Command (MARSOC), primarily out of the 1ˢᵗ and 2ⁿᵈ Reconnaissance Battalions, in stages between 2006 and 2008 – has led some Marines in the blogosphere to comment on the newly "elite" unit. Although MARSOC laid plans to re-name the units after the storied World War II raider battalions (Edson's Raiders, Carlson's Raiders), Marine Commandant, General Amos, declined the opportunity – not wanting to single out any Marine Unit.[ccxxxii]

The point is that after basic training, the language and culture of Marines begins to specialize somewhat. In addition to the large body of culture shared by *all* Marines, each job has its unique stories and language, artifacts and rituals (patches, coins, signs, colors, T-shirts, etc.). This is evident in analyzing the jobs of the drill instructors and recruiters. But these drill instructors and recruiters come from other jobs; they have been and will again be grunts, military policemen, musicians, avionics technicians, cooks, computer specialists, clerks, artillerymen, air traffic controllers and so on.

Later Socialization

Socialization and continual indoctrination in the ways of the Marine Corps continue at least as long as one stays in the Corps. There are internal rites of passage at schools and at other entry points, such as DI school or infantry training school. Most of the later indoctrination is over-laid on the boot camp experience rather than replacing it, so little is lost as a result of further indoctrination.

One thing that *is* lost is the self-image of recruit, which is synonymous with *boot*. The junior man in any unit, or junior man in a rank at a unit is still the *boot* (boot corporal, for example), but that boot knows he outranks all Marines in the ranks below him. So whereas a new Marine may be called a "boot," he recognizes he is not a recruit. Shedding the recruit self-image requires not acting like one, including not calling NCOs and Staff NCOs "Sir." In contrast to the little ritual of saying, "Don't call me sir; I work for a living," some senior staff NCOs – the sergeant major – appreciate being called "sir" by junior enlisted Marines. How much else the new Marine sheds is a factor of the men in his unit. If the NCOs in his first unit enforce respect to NCOs and others more senior, much of the respect for seniors learned in boot camp will stay.

Likewise, if the unit has esprit de corps, the new arrival should fall in line and become part of the cohesive unit, although he will bear the burden of being the boot, "the new guy," until the next boot arrives. If Marines in his unit display respect for the values of the Corps and use Marine lingo, the new Marine will be socialized in continuing Marine ways.

(My assessment from 1989) What has continued to develop through the 1970s and '80s is a trend away from small unit cohesion and the use of uniquely Marine language. During the 1970s and '80s, there were changes in the ways Marines lived on base. In addition to allowing single Marines to live in off-base housing in greater numbers, new on-base quarters built since the start of the 1970s have been large buildings with many rooms for two, three or four Marines each – akin to college dormitories. Until this change, 20 to 40 Marines in a unit lived in a single squad bay or Quonset hut. Older generation Marines have expressed the observation that increases in theft were related to the impersonality created by living apart; Marines were no longer responsible for each other. Marines used to stop strangers in their building; now the other Marines who live in the hotel-style buildings *are* strangers.

Another apparent impact on changing how Marines live after boot camp has been caused by encroaching civilian communities. One concern of the military services is the loss of ability to conduct training without endangering or bothering surrounding civilians. The sociological impact has evidently been that service members, including Marines, have a short drive to get to off-base activities. Again, there is less cohesion because Marines are no longer forced by geography and economics to associate with other Marines or use on-base activities.

Summary

The foregoing chapter combines the findings of years of research and reading with analysis and personal observation as a member of the culture. What follows in Chapter VIII is the display of additional data gained through ethnographic research. As academic literature on ethnography clearly warns, reduction and display of ethnographic data is extensively time consuming. This chapter presented mainly narrative findings from ethnographic research conducted with public relations, recruiting and basic training. Time and location prevented interviews with recruits, even if the Marine Corps would have allowed such interviews. Some of the reality of mid-1980s recruits has been presented through the interpretation of the drill instructors interviewed from 1980 through 1984. This reality has also been compared and contrasted with the experiences of the researcher and others who undertook Marine boot camp during other years past.

The foregoing chapter also presented the different types and purposes of Marine public relations. And, the format of the preceding chapter allows one to follow a civilian through the recruiting process and a recruit through the indoctrination process of basic training. Taken together, one can see that the person who accepts the challenge of becoming a Marine faces Marine propaganda in a number of forms: advertising, indoctrination and education. To relate the complete process to the theoretical foundations presented in earlier chapters, the individual may be seen as going through the three phases of compliance over a career, which includes the three phases of civilian, recruit and Marine, or through smaller cycles of each form of compliance in each phase.

The civilian sees the symbols, rituals and myths of the Corps in many forms, and at some time in his late teens or early 20s, sees a Marine recruiter. Peer pressure from poolees may cause coercion to get the prospect to talk seriously with a recruiter. Predisposition to accept the Corps' values, which are based on national symbols, may lead the prospect to identify with the Corps at first. And if he signs up and becomes a poolee, he may begin to internalize, on a basic level, the values of the Corps.

The socio-psychological manipulations at work begin with external justification – rationalizing the decision to visit a recruiter with a friend, or rationalizing the decision to enlist with the projected financial or educational benefits, or seeing the enlistment as the lesser of two evils even if the greater evil is being stuck in a small town with no excitement or opportunity for college. Internal justification takes over as the prospect begins to identify with the Corps. That's why recruiters offer jackets, hats, belt buckles and bumper stickers to poolees; they must also internally rationalize why they are wearing Marine Corps symbols before they even leave high school. One answer may be simply, "I helped the recruiter get someone else to enlist." Those thoughts may shift to, "I believe in the Corps." The poolee may even be found attending movies like *Heartbreak Ridge* or other Marine Corps films that he wouldn't have before.

A similar cycle begins in boot camp. There is no question the recruit is coerced during early phases of training, but soon he too begins to identify with the Corps. As part of a unit, he identifies with the platoon's number. If his platoon wins an award in drill competition or marksmanship, there is internal justification. The threats of the drill instructor and other negative influences are eventually replaced as motivators as the recruit moves from external justification to internal rewards and justification. All the while, the values of the Corps, carried in the symbols, rituals and myths of the Corps, take on greater and greater *meaning* to the recruit, as each recruit builds his or her own *narrative*. Peers become increasingly important and the recruit views his patriotism in vertical progression from platoon and DI to series and series commanders, to recruit training, the total Marine Corps and the United States.

In the end, propaganda has succeeded; a mass of individuals, predisposed to psychological unification, are moved to action through the shared values inherent in the organization's folklore. Control of recruits has progressed from first-order rules and regulations to third-order control relying on the self-discipline of the graduating Marine.

After training, a Marine may be seen as going through all three levels of compliance and progressing from external to internal justification again. Junior Marines are more under the control of first-order controls than senior Marines who have greater relative independence. And, relative to senior Marines, junior Marines are more manipulated by coercion and identification. Senior Marines, especially those who have re-enlisted several times and have decided to make the Corps a career, have internalized the values of the Corps.

In terms taken from dissonance theory, the behavior of senior Marines is guided by the internal justification of cognitive dissonance; they are guided (rather than coerced) with Perrow's third-order controls. In layman's terms, senior Marines are expectedly more mature, but have spent 15 to 20 years, or more, absorbing the values of the Corps. One might say these non-commissioned and staff non-commissioned officers are on "autopilot;" they just know what to do and how to do it. Ethnology defines this acquired but often unwritten knowledge as *tacit* knowledge, with the folklore of the Corps guiding rather than proscribing actions.

Going over the hill – jihadi style

The final two chapters of this text review parallels in the radicalization, indoctrination and recruitment of *soldiers* in any country, for any cause. In all cases, the 17- to 25-year-old male is already pre-disposed to accept the organizational patriotism of his nation or global religion; they have been exposed to the symbols, rituals and myths for two decades.

When hopeful *jihadis* signed on to wage war in the 1990s, and overlapping 9/11, some of them ended up facing far more than they had bargained for – just as some Marine recruits arriving at Parris Island and San Diego discover, year after year, that they had signed on to more than they had expected. (My recruiter lied to me.)

One of many excellent analyses of this phenomenon, looking at the Islamist Extremist side of the equation, emanates from Cheryl Benard with the Rand Initiative on Middle Eastern Youth (1995). Key points from Benard's interviews with some 50 detainees at the detention center at Guantanamo include:[ccxxxiii]

In the accounts of many young men who went to participate in jihad in Afghanistan, one striking theme is the extent to which they found themselves confronted with situations and outcomes they had not anticipated and did not feel prepared for. Many detainees related what we can refer to as "they never told me" events and experiences. They were left to deal with difficulties they had not been prepared for, ultimately including the utterly unimagined situation of imprisonment.

Reasons for Joining jihad

Many of the young men had been motivated by Imams and recruiters in their local mosques to leave their countries of origin for Afghanistan, or Chechnya, or Palestine. Visual displays of persecuted Muslims were well-used by the recruiters, and recruits were routinely exposed to films that featured suffering women and children in refugee camps in Chechnya, Palestine or Afghanistan. Multiple persuasions were employed to motivate the young to go to Afghanistan: to perform "zakat," i.e. to distribute charitable donations to widows, orphans and refugees; to teach the Koran; to visit a country governed by Shariah (strict Islamic rule); to perform one's duty as a Muslim male and learn to use weapons to protect one's family; to help Muslim brothers fight off oppressors; to fight against the West, and to stop the corruption threatening Islam everywhere. Besides one-on-one recruitment practices with visual aids, it is interesting to note that detainees also mention radio ads as a method of recruitment.

Equally compelling were the other reasons a young Muslim male might want to leave home: unemployment, a failed business, a criminal conviction with impending jail time or a drug or alcohol problem. Unemployment motivated a number of Gulf States detainees, particularly young unskilled and semi-skilled laborers. For them, going on jihad was "alternative employment."

In contrast, educated young Saudis departing for jihad were more likely to be motivated by a sense of self-discovery and challenge. They felt inspired to go and observe a "pure" Islamic state, as Afghanistan was touted to be. This proved to be a great hook for the more idealistic and wealthier youth. A number of young Saudis with college level education left on jihad, *not because they had economic or academic difficulties, but to see how the Taliban had put the rule of Islam (Shariah) into motion in Afghanistan in contrast to the Western-tainted Saudi monarchy they despised. For the religious and the political alike, jihad offered a chance to put their spiritual and physical lives in order.*

*Many young detainees mentioned being recruited via the hajj experience. The hajj is a pilgrimage to Mecca with religious activities that last a week. The **intensely emotional** setting of this event was used by more than one clever Al Qaeda recruiter to connect a young man to his next great religious experience: jihad. This was made easier by the fact that, embedded in jihad, are elements **seductive** to young adults: the **rite of passage into manhood** and the clear demonstration of one's commitment to Islam, the religion of one's fathers. [my emphasis]*

Conditions in the Afghan Training Camps

Training facilities in Afghanistan were language specific. Since a shared language speeded up learning, training camps were largely organized by language group. Al Qaeda trained Arabs; Libyans trained North Africans; Uzbeks trained other Uzbeks and Tajiks. Leaving Western Europe or Saudi Arabia behind and going to Afghanistan also meant doing without the medical system and level of care one was accustomed to. Many detainees reported that they became ill at camp within the first month. It was apparently common for a recruit to come down with malaria and dysentery while in training; these and other illnesses could incapacitate the person for months. Central Asians, Europeans and Africans mention sickness experienced at the training camps less often. Gulf State and Saudi recruits talk about extended, debilitating illnesses that prevented them from finishing their training and even left them useless for combat. It is striking that the recruiters in Saudi Arabia or Yemen allowed young men to leave for a destination without vaccinations for common regional illnesses (malaria, or yellow fever or tetanus). Al Qaeda knew what recruits would be exposed to in Afghanistan, yet neglected to educate them about the most common health risks and did not vaccinate them. Money for jihad was spent on plane tickets, hotel reservations, and transportation to safe houses and training camps, yet Al Qaeda put at risk, and lost, a significant amount of man power and man hours as its recruits fell ill in Afghanistan.

This study is complex, and adds more to this book from a variety of angles. It's worth an analyst's read. (More within the article explains the concept of "I didn't realize I was signing up for this; "I just want to go home," and "The only way I'm going to fight jihad again in the future is if my homeland is threatened." The same thing happens at MCRD Parris Island and MCRD San Diego on a fairly regular basis.)

Benard's complete text is fascinating and gets to the parallels of young men trooping off to "the glories of war" only to find that war is not so glory-ful. More than a few Marines, soldiers, sailor and airmen over the decades have experienced the same.

Some wannabe jihadis did indeed "go over the hill," seeking a border with Pakistan or some other nearby country. Part of this gets to the notion of "How do we make 'fighting jihad' less appealing?"

Chapter Eight

<u>Findings and Analysis – 2013</u>

Filling in important gaps and bringing this ethnographic record current by roughly 20 years, the following update to the original Findings and Analysis chapter is presented in two broad sections. The first portion: information regarding Marine Corps public affairs; advertising, market demographics and recruiting, and basic training or boot camp. The second: interviews with 15 active duty Marine officers and senior staff NCOs – with careers of 18 to 23 years regarding their assessments of the cultural impact of four phenomena introduced previously. These Marines started their careers about the time I completed the original study and have lived through the changes of the past 20 years or so.

<u>Public Affairs</u>

The mission for Marine Corps Division of Public Affairs (DIVPA) has not significantly changed in 20 years.[ccxxxiv] The advent and widespread use of computers and the Internet, however, *have* changed the way Marines in this field conduct business in countless ways. To put 20 to 30 years in perspective – when I taught *Print Journalism* at the (Department of) Defense Information School from 1982 to early 1985, my Army, Navy, Air Force and Marine enlisted public affairs students used manual typewriters. Final class projects were mimeograph newspapers and four-page folio newspapers printed by the school's "Repro" section.

Headquarters Marine Corps' Division of Public Affairs continues to maintain missions in community relations, and internal and external information. The Public Affairs Division website (http://www.marines.mil/unit/divpa/) provides links to Marine Public Affairs offices in New York and Los Angeles, to a Trademark and Licensing branch; Plans; Media; the Marine Band and Community Relations.

With advances in technology, the *MARINES* magazine discussed earlier is presented on line, as are both "print" and "Marines TV" stories produced by Marines about Marines and the Corps. As print and broadcast public affairs continue to support units in both combat and stateside assignments, the stories in these media range from training Afghan soldiers to Labor Day safety programs for Marines in the US.

As in the past, print and broadcast public affairs Marines release stories to the civilian media through DIVPA – and civilian journalists cover Marines and other services in the normal course of their print or broadcast assignments. Some media are broad interest publications, like the Wall Street Journal (print and on-line), with stories like "On the Marines' Wish List: A Pricey Jet Fighter," from July 30, 2011. Other media include the weekly service-centric publications from Gannett, based in Springfield, VA: *Marine Corps Times* (and *Navy, Air Force and Army Times*).

Headlines from the various *Times* publications during 2010-2011 include stories on the Corps' new commandant, General Jim Amos, and his views on a range of topics, including combat operations, the repeal of "Don't ask, Don't tell," Marine Special Operations Command, and others; stories on uniforms and equipment (new helmets), mixed martial arts, pay and bonus topics; stories about heroes in combat, drug testing, housing and barracks, sports, health and family issues.

Many of these are <u>not</u> different from the ummah.com web site noted in a previous chapter – and the point is: It doesn't matter if you're a Marine at Camp Pendleton or a wannabe jihadist in Minneapolis, Abu Dhabi,

Lahore or Tikrit. If you're 19 or 20 years old and you have a wife and a kid (or a husband and a kid), you need food, shelter, furniture, a place to go to the bathroom, clothes, an M-16A4 or AK-47 (and lots of bullets), a sense of belonging and someone to provide leadership, a lot of other stuff....but most importantly: a peer group and a sense of relevance.

Interestingly, the March 3, 2010 issue of *Air Force Times* carried a cover story on combat fitness. The headline reads: *Train like Marines*. Because the wars in Afghanistan and Iraq have taken on a counterinsurgency/counter-terrorist character over the past 10 years, the Navy and Air Force have played *smaller* roles, in comparison with Army and Marine sister services, and in contrast to Navy and Air Force missions in "grand battles" like World War II. Both services have seen manpower reductions while the Marine Corps and Army were both beefed up for surges in Iraq and Afghanistan.

As a result, the Navy and Air Force have both deployed thousands of officers and enlisted professionals in the combat areas of operations – often in "individual augmentee" assignments at larger headquarters, in critical intelligence, logistics, planning or other support roles. In this context, what both services have discovered is that training to deploy on a ship, or to a tactical air base, both differ significantly from training to operate in the comparatively spartan environments that soldiers and Marines experience in combat.

With the "Sequester" and enormous fiscal constraints facing the United States in 2013, and the gradual "pivot" to focus on Asia and the Pacific rim, the Marine Corps and Army may see significant reductions in troop levels in the near term while Navy and Air Force capabilities are more protected as part of a shifting global strategy.

Public Affairs and Publicity

The early days of Marine Corps public relations grew out of the Madison Avenue-like concept of commercial *publicity*. DIVPA continues to serve the American public as the conduit to the Marine

Band – the President's Own. Little has changed in the process of scheduling the Band for hundreds of public performances each year; and those requests that cannot be filled by the elite President's Own are passed to the Director of Marine Corps Field Music. As of 2011, the Marine Corps maintained 12 field bands, with 11 in the continental US and one serving Marine Units in the Pacific rim.[ccxxxv]

J. Walter Thompson has since become simply JWT, and continues a close relationship with Marine Corps Public Affairs. JWT's Atlanta office is the headquarters for JWT's contract with the Marine Corps. JWT goes well beyond creating bumper stickers, billboards and recruiting commercials for television:

To help America reconnect with her Marine Corps, we made a television production into more than a shoot. Beyond developing a complex multiplatform America's Marines branding campaign, we created an event featuring hundreds of Marines in 15 locations across the country and invited thousands of parents, supporters and veterans to attend the filming.[ccxxxvi]

Visit http://www.jwt.com/#!/content/424910/united-states-marine-corps. Perhaps even the radical Islamist takfiri jihadis would be motivated to enlist.

Each of the six Recruiting District headquarters provides an enlisted Marine public affairs representative to coordinate with JWT on "publicity" and recruitment advertising. Observations in the original Chapters II and IV remain more or less accurate: wives, girlfriends, parents and peers continue to be key influencers; prospects differentiate between the Marine Corps and other services – seeing the Corps more for intangible benefits (leadership, team work, character-building) and the other services more for tangible benefits (pay, bonuses, tuition assistance, specific job skill assignments and training (computer skills and high-tech jobs)).

Intangibles are more powerful internal motivators than tangibles such as financial rewards. But this applies to jihadis as well as Marines. False jihadis – the takfiri and irhabi – on the other hand, have taken to robbing banks, kidnapping for ransom, smuggling and other nefarious activities to fund their operations. In the earlier days of the wars in Iraq and Afghanistan, analysts speculated that much of al-Qaida's funding came from Osama bin Laden's own treasury, combined with donations from wealthy Middle East benefactors and slush funds squeezed out of various charities. Painstakingly over time, many of those donations have been eliminated, with charities shut down, donors exposed and money transfer companies (hawalas) closed. As a result, terrorists are left to fund their operations with proceeds from drug trafficking, human trafficking, extortion and illicit trade in timber, gems, animals, counterfeit goods. Some profit, enormously, as a result.

What is changing and directly impacts recruitment advertising and JWT's messaging about the Marine Corps are the size of the total pool of available age recruits (16- to 24-year-olds), the shifting ethnic composition of the United States, and contrasts in attitudes toward the military between Millennials (recruiting age population) and their parents (Baby Boomers and Gen Xers). JWT's June 2011 study illustrates each of these phenomena.[ccxxxvii]

Highlights from this study include: The Millennial boom is over. In total numbers, the peak for the 16-20 year-old population occurred in 2010 (22.1 million. This level will not be seen again for another 14 years.)

The racial composition of the Marine Corps is moving farther away from the face of the nation. White and Black populations [will] contract in the next 14 years while Hispanics, Asians and Mixed/Other Races will continue to grow. On the JWT question: "Please indicate your favorability toward the Marine Corps," in a race/gender breakdown:

	Parents	Millennials
White Male	69% (favorable)	51%
White Female	61%	42%
Black Male	50%	27%
Black Female	35%	30%
Hispanic Male	60%	40%
Hispanic Female	51%	40%

Table VI

On average, Millennial views toward the military are 50% less favorable than the views of their parents' generation – and this appears to be quickly becoming a highly politicized issue.

	Democrat	Independent	Republican
Military	50%	61	81
USMC	49	59	73
Army	46	58	74
Air Force	56	65	81
Navy	52	62	78

Table VII

JWT reports that "Among Parents, political party affiliation is not as powerful as race as a way of explaining (favorability) views of the military / branches." JWT notes that "...understanding the "political culture" of Millennials is critical. Giving back, staying connected with friends, family and those with shared interests are integral elements of the Millennial generation that transcend race and politics."

My analysis at this point, based on where the US is on current global missions and the evolving Marine Corps: As the US seeks to fill the current Administration's campaign promises to withdraw from both Iraq and Afghanistan, the residual forces in both countries will be Special Operations Forces – SOF. Marine Corps Special Operations Command (MARSOC) stood up as a functional unit in 2006.[ccxxxviii] Increasingly in the coming decade(s), US armed forces, with a range of other government and non-government partners – State Department, USAID, non-profit aid agencies, academia, law enforcement, and others – will be engaged in "Phase Zero" operations designed to *prevent* conflict – often in the form of disrupting transnational religious extremists and organized criminal elements from gaining a foothold. Marine and other *special operators* (SEALS, Rangers) will be involved in humanitarian assistance, disaster relief, foreign internal defense training and other "non-kinetic" missions designed to prevent conflict in less-than-stable countries. The Millennials don't know it yet – but these missions fit within their preferences for "Helping people in need, wherever they may live."

Millennials are also the "Facebook" generation (although their parents are quickly catching up). These features and interests will necessarily fold into evolving Marine Corps missions – which remain imbedded in the natural "medium-weight, expeditionary force in readiness" missions of the Corps.

JWT's findings illustrate that the concept of "Helping people in need, wherever they may live" ranks highly with Millennials, but is detached from "Serving in the military." Serving in the armed forces is not all kinetic, not all combat. Getting this message to a generation, split amongst seven identified demographics, will be a challenge to JWT and the Corps. *Part* of the truth in the Marine

Corps meeting or exceeding its recruiting goals for the past four to five years is that the Marine Corps is the coolest, sexiest place to fight jihad for the United States. *Another* part of the truth is that the recession that started impacting the US and global economies, starting in 2007, started to shrink the job market for unemployed and comparatively uneducated young people. The Armed Forces have always been a refuge for the unemployed, and that includes the Marine Corps.

Of the recruiting population, JWT identifies seven clusters for the broader 22 million 16- to 24-year-olds through Segmentation Analysis:

Southern Conservatives	20%
Multi-Cultural Moderates	16%
Minority Liberals	14%
Anti-Military Establishment	14%
Middle Americans	13%
Disengaged	13%
Cynics	10%

In (population) Segmentation Analysis, JWT writes:

Southern Conservatives

...are a distinctly defined cluster of youth in both their demographics and values. More often White, male and Southern, with half "Born Again" Christians, they have the highest propensity [toward both the military generally and Marine Corps specifically] of all youth segments. Eight in ten have had a close family member serve in the military. Politically, they are most likely to believe the country is on the wrong track, [are] intensely supportive of the US Military and

Afghanistan war, and the strongest believers in forceful response to attacks from another country or terrorists. They are more propensed to the Marine Corps than other youth segments. [ccxxxix]

The Multi-Cultural Moderates

...are one of the youngest of the seven segments, less than half White and one-third Hispanic (mostly Mexican). Predominantly Roman Catholic, they believe very strongly that good citizenship means giving back both locally and globally. Importantly, they are the most likely of any segment to equate military service to good citizenship and hold the most favorable view of the Marines of any segment. Not a part of the 2008 Obama movement, a majority of this segment is independent – with some leanings to the right when it comes to domestic social issues.

Minority Liberals

...are disproportionately Southern and Western, and two-thirds are either Hispanic or Black. They are likely to be enrolled in junior or 4-year colleges (58%), and are somewhat higher on the military propensity likelihood than most other groups, especially if it would afford them better education and job opportunities. Minority liberals are more propensed toward the Air Force than other segments examined. [Meaning: among these seven segments of the recruitable generation, minority liberals (one of the seven segments) would be more inclined toward enlisting in the US Air Force than in the Marine Corps, Army or Navy.]

Politically, these youth are quite liberal, almost all Obama supporters, and moderately favorable toward the military. Over half have had a close relative serve in the military. They have a strong sense of obligation to the community and feel that good citizenship means both helping those in need and serving their country. They place high importance on voting in all elections and keeping up with what's going on in the world. They are *three time more likely* than the overall sample to want to be famous. [my italics]

Anti-Military Establishment

…is a strongly Democratic, racially heterogeneous, highly educated youth demographic, characterized by being disproportionately female and older. This group was a significant part of Obama's 2008 base, but has become less enthusiastic to date. Less than one in five believe our country is on the right track. The group expresses high negative propensity to military service, which may be partly gender driven, but no doubt a function of their quite liberal politics and very unfavorable stances toward war and the Military in general. Only 3% of this group supports US troops in Afghanistan. This group feels a heightened sense of global responsibility; however, it manifests in humanitarian interventions like natural disasters more than militaristic ones.

Middle American

…youth represent largely what their label implies: a somewhat whiter segment of youth, equally split by gender, and very close to the mean on most demographic traits. If Hispanic, they tend not to be Spanish proficient. They are disproportionately Midwesterners.

This group's likelihood to enlist in the service is lower than both Minority Liberal and Southern Conservative youth, but higher than all other segments. Ideologically, these youth are moderate, but remain strong Obama supporters nonetheless. They have a mixed opinion of the Military, as often positive as not. They are liberal on most social issues, motivated by humanitarian needs, but also supportive of military intervention to help allies under attack and help in genocide situations.

The Disengaged

…is the larger of the two less active groups and is notably the most socially and politically alienated of the segments under examination.

It is disproportionately White and male, and not clearly distinctive by region of the country. A significant proportion is still in high school, but they have a higher dropout rate than any other segment (9%). Among those of voting age, over half did not vote in 2008. This group gave neutral responses to most opinion items, suggesting a disinterest or unfamiliarity with the issues – especially those focused on military missions.

Cynics

…[are] a disengaged segment that represents a small cluster of youth. Cynics show low support for the military and the war, and are unsupportive of the current administration. They place little importance on keeping up with national and world news and have low voting rates. This group is more often male and not inclined to join the Military under any circumstances. They also have the highest rate of refusal to [respond to] many survey questions.

That's the market. It doesn't matter what one is selling; recruiters are in sales and they need to know the market. But 16- to 24-year-olds don't walk into Marine recruiter's offices with name tags identifying them as "Cynic" or "Anti-Military Establishment Bitch." In fact – recruiters don't meet most of their prospects as walk-ins off the street; they meet many of them by phone from telephone, post card or e-mail queries, at high schools in their districts, at shopping malls, as referrals from high school seniors or graduates who have already enlisted but not "shipped," and other venues.

A complex set of circumstances, socialization factors, history, geography, family relationships, teachers and other influences over 16 to 24 years deposits these young men and women into these fairly well-defined demographic clusters. Some would never join any military under any circumstances (and might flee the country to avoid a draft) – and the military wouldn't want most of them in their ranks anyway. Some of them grow up knowing their destiny is in the

Marine Corps. In this group, many have had fathers and other relatives in military service. Between these two extremes, recruiters, JWT marketing, television shows and movies, YouTube and other social media, family and friends, the Marine Band and a variety of other influences conspire to *inspire* the middle ranks to join those who grew up knowing they would grow into a Marine uniform.[ccxl]

Occasionally available on YouTube are homegrown videos depicting Marines teaching their 3- to 5-year-old children how to dress, walk, talk and act like little Marines. In balance, one may also find takfiri, irhabi or jihadi videos depicting the same sort of process. (Key word searches: little Marine; little jihadi, littlest drill instructor.)

Cultural Influences and Shifts

The first motivation for dusting off a 20-year-old dissertation that described the Marine Corps in ethnographic terms – completed less than a year before Desert Storm – with a likely readership of five in 1990, was to assess certain cultural changes in those 20 years. Having retired in 1995, but having the opportunity to serve again from mid-2005 to mid-2008, I lived in that culture only eight years since 1990. Relying on active duty Marines to fill in the details, I built my updated evaluation around four phenomena that have evolved noticeably since 1990. As noted previously:

- Increasing academic achievement levels of enlisted Marines
- Influences of technology
- The repeal of "Don't Ask, Don't Tell"
- The inclusion of women into previously all-male domains

Over the course of 18 months in 2010 and 2011, I had the opportunity to interview more than a dozen Marines, male and female, officer and enlisted. All have served 18 to 23 years on active duty, and as of this writing are master sergeants and master gunnery sergeants, majors and lieutenant colonels. (Some of the officers are prior enlisted Marines. All identities are muted to protect their privacy and opinions on some contentious issues. In their words (all are direct quotes)):

Enlisted Marine Academic Standards

(A master sergeant) Higher academic standards for younger Marines is a good thing. It enhances them careerwise and post-career. It's important we allow them to pursue college when they can. When I enlisted, you had to have at least a GED; now they're all high school grads. It's important for the Marine, but it's also good organizationally. It makes a better Marine Corps – a smarter Corps. I've assisted at least a dozen Marines applying to NDIC [National Defense Intelligence College] to get into degree programs.[ccxli]

Are they easier to lead and manage? There are pros and cons. Better educated [junior] enlisted Marines should bring a higher level of maturity, but some of them may feel smarter than the "crusty old Staff NCOs." We don't need a battalion of PhDs in the infantry.

That's off-duty education and incoming standards. As far as on-duty, I attended a pilot [course] for a new E-8/E-9 (master sergeant and 1st sergeant; sergeant major and master gunnery sergeant) course. It was a week of "death by PowerPoint." But the course does go further in providing senior enlisted advanced PME [professional military education]. We had critical thinking skills, writing courses, guest speakers and discussion groups. The senior enlisted asked for more PME and we got it – but it needs to get better.

(A lieutenant colonel) This professionalization thing has ebbed and flowed. We had the [President] Clinton drawdown...and we had enlisted Marines with two jobs and going to college. The Corps was seen as a vehicle for opportunity. We recruited fewer people but we got good folks in who really wanted to make a difference. We didn't have the pay raises and at that time the military didn't make as much [as their counterparts in the civilian sector], but we had people making money in the stock market – and we had a time of relative peace.

Then we had 9/11. Since then we've had this schism – we still have these brilliant people [in the enlisted ranks], but to "make the numbers," we've had to bring in the "bottom feeders." There are heroes who love the Corps, and they've deployed to Iraq and Afghanistan three and four and five times; and we have the bottom five percent – some of the non-rates (privates, privates first class and lance corporals)[ccxlii] who have no desire to do anything but exist. They "fall out" of PT and have no motivation. There was no middle.

With the wars, we've had this "plus-up" and we get a generation from "the Nintendo Society." We are a reflection of our society and they're better prepared with technology, but they're an entitled generation. They feel like they're entitled to everything.

(A master gunnery sergeant) When I enlisted most Staff NCOs were Viet Nam vets, some had served in Beirut. They didn't have college degrees. Now – it's pushed more [by the Corps] – not like the Army, where it counts more toward promotions – and people find ways around obstacles, with on-line courses for example. I see more and more peers, especially in Intelligence, with college degrees, but if you don't have a degree – it's not frowned on, especially if someone has deployed four or five times.

Most talk about the difference between financial benefits versus personal growth. I'm interested in the personal growth. Do we get better quality Marines? Sure – and it counts in the "tech" fields – computers and communications systems, but we're talking about Nintendo generation Marines and we're not making analysts [in the intelligence field], we're making computer users.

There is a difference between generations. There is less talk about the Corps as a calling these days, but we do get an attitude of "service." I think technology [social media and video games] distracts the younger generation. They're not going out for team sports like the old days. I think we pay lip service to the concept that "Every Marine is a Rifleman." When it comes to fighting, however – there's really no difference through the generations. In boot camp, you get this thing in the back of your head about "all those Marines who have gone before." Yes, today you gotta be smarter, but I don't think the younger generation spends as much time on PT. I'm 47 and can max the run [3 miles in 18 minutes] and still score a 280 on the PFT.[ccxliii]

(A "mustang" Major – prior enlisted, then commissioned) The Marine Corps hit the nail on the head – giving Marines the opportunity to go to college. I'm a product of that thinking. I had high SAT and ACT scores but enlisted [rather than go to college]. I had fun in EOD [explosive ordnance disposal] but wasn't meeting my potential. It took me years of night school to get a BS in Finance. (*The major earned his commission, the hard way. In addition to having significantly more responsibility as a commissioned officer, the financial difference in where he stands today compared to where he would have been had he remained enlisted (likely an E9, or master gunnery sergeant) – with 23 years of service, is worth more than $30,000 annually in just base pay. That difference will continue into retirement.*)

Repeal of "Don't Ask, Don't Tell"[ccxliv]

The law enacted under the previous (Clinton) Democratic administration in 1993 emerged as a campaign promise under the Obama administration. Following months of legal wrangling, legal rulings and Congressional voting, U.S. Senators Joe Lieberman and Susan Collins introduced bill S.4022 on December 9, 2010, as a stand-alone bill in reaction to the failure to open discussion on the Defense Authorization Act. Following an additional year of study by the Defense Department and reports from service chiefs to the Secretary of Defense on potential impact to military morale and readiness, the Repeal Law took effect on September 20, 2011.

Military Times writers William H. McMichael and Brendan McGarry reported in early 2010 *"How troops really feel about gays serving openly."*[ccxlv] Their Army Times story carries a sidebar explaining their survey methodology. McMichael and McGarry reported that opposition to Repeal dropped steadily from 2003 to 2009 from 63 percent to 51 percent. In the same period, those in favor increased from 24 percent of respondents to 30 percent. Those neutral or declining to answer increased also, from 11 percent to 20 percent. The article notes that "Women were about three times more likely to report being gay than men (5.4 percent to 1.7 percent), and that the general US population of those who report their homosexuality was estimated at 1.6 percent, according to a Congressional Research Service Report. What the Army Times article does not address is differences by generation (Baby Boomers versus Millennials and Gen-Xers), or differences by service.

As the Times writers acknowledge: "Perhaps no issue is quite as divisive as whether the law should be changed." It is in this context I sought perspectives from the career Marines I interviewed.

(The major) I'm a fiscal conservative but on social issues – more liberal. But on this repeal, I don't think it's a fit for the military. I think most [straight] male Marines view homosexual males as submissive and disgusting, not compatible with our perceived warrior ethos – and that's hard to reconcile. Have I run into females I thought were gay? Yes. But males, males in the Marine Corps – no. Never. I don't think the military needs this distraction. Those who will be openly serving will be viewed with contempt. And it's about their personal "rights," not about the organization. (*Which runs contrary to Marine Corps recruiting advertising, focused on "being part of something bigger than yourself.*) But - we'll deal with it.

(Master Gunnery Sergeant) From within the Corps and from

policy makers in Washington what we get is: 'You're just the old guys.' We don't agree with this [policy], but first – we're going to follow orders. Certification? That people have been "trained?" (Required "sensitivity" training focused on adapting to the new law, leading to a "sensitivity training certificate." What does that mean? People can't say it won't have an impact. We have *no* idea what the impact will be on retention, on morale, on combat capability. What do you do with the 19-year-old guy with fundamentalist Christian roots who just wants to be a warrior – and he gets this social experiment?

It scares me. The biggest squabbling will be in the grunts [infantry units]. Support units may be more open to this kind of behavior. We're supposed to treat everyone with dignity and respect because they stood on the yellow footsteps and earned the title 'Marine.' But at the small unit level – there's going to be problems.

Younger people have grown up with this...exposed to Hollywood and TV versions of what's supposed to be normal. Laws change and policy changes, and we get this training and they say, 'We're not here to change your beliefs. Chaplains can still preach 'It's a sin.' Now what are we supposed to do? Are we *endorsing this?* What people do in private – I don't wanna know and don't care. Don't ask, Don't tell was fine just the way it was.

Yes – some have said they would retire or leave the Corps over this. It's counter to their religious beliefs.

(A Master Sergeant) This transition to gay sh*t - It's all about 'I'm a victim. Look at *me!*' My answer is 'It's not about you; it's about being part of something bigger than yourself.' Now the majority has to assimilate to the minority. The argument is that we're intolerant, not inclusive. But this issue is divisive. Honestly – I don't care. I just don't want to know about it...and they don't want to know what goes on in my bedroom or the back seat of my car. The biggest impact is going to be on small unit cohesion.

Technology

I left this open – as technology, broadly, has impacted communications in many ways: computers, cell phones and satellite phones; weapons systems, intelligence collection, production and dissemination; in uniforms; in influences on social interaction and much more.

(A Master Sergeant) For both Marines and the Corps, the changes have been phenomenal – in positive ways. In weapons, comms [communications], clothing and equipment, improvements have been ten-fold. Our boots are the best we've ever had. When I came in – I had a [transistor] radio. Now I have Skype. We have significantly improved quality of life; for junior Marines and Marines with dependents – the barracks and housing are over the top. We work 'em hard – but now they have all the amenities. Better than a college dorm. With housing contracts, if we don't fill [military] base housing, the single Marines can apply to live in homes on base instead of the barracks.

We discussed my 1990 observation/admonition regarding small unit cohesion and the impact of moving Marines – particularly junior unmarried Marines – into 2-, 3- or 4-man rooms and out of "squad bays" that could accommodate 20 Marines in bunk beds, with "wall lockers" as area dividers. Squad bays were common around the Marine Corps well into the 1970s, and in some areas into the 1980s.

(The Master Sergeant) We don't need squad bays and barracks for unit cohesion. If they work enough…work together hard enough during the day, they get cohesion. After that – they need some space. Unit cohesion is really a leadership issue, not a geography issue. I see the Commandant and Sergeant Major [of the Marine Corps] as the spiritual leaders of the Corps in this great journey. It's like a religion and we need those leaders.

(Master Gunnery Sergeant) As far as technology's impact on the Corps, when I started out we had MARS radio (the Military Affiliate Radio System[ccxlvi]). On ships we had "sailor phones" for morale calls [to family, ashore] but they barely worked. When we deployed, the bases weren't as built up as today.

Consider the contrasts over two generations: Marines and soldiers going "forward," or deploying to combat zones during World War II, Korea, and even during Vietnam, were lucky to have a tent, clean water, and an occasional letter from home. And although combat is no less brutal, some (not all) Marines and Soldiers deploying to Afghanistan or Iraq since 2001 or 2003, if deployed to a Forward Operating Base, or "FOB," have been greeted by built-up bases with trailers (2 to 4 Marines per 12X15 room, depending on seniority), hot showers, an MWR operation (Morale, Welfare and Recreation) with e-mail and Skype connectivity to "home," chow halls with steak, ice cream and fresh vegetables, and more.[ccxlvii]

(Master Sergeant) In Iraq, what was irritating was the sat-phone [satellite telephone]. I had a staff sergeant whose priority was "parking" on that sat-phone – even though it had terrible connectivity; I wanted my people to focus on the mission (outside the wire). I did see one company-level unit at Haditha Dam that had good connectivity for telephone calls to the US and an Internet café. My guys could go to the Dam and get on the internet. But one guy found nude pictures of his wife all over the internet. He killed himself over that. MWR is important, but it's also distracting. The mission is more important.

Technology across the [Military] Services, broadly – it's insane. If "necessity is the mother of invention," we have a pile of inventions. A guy can hold ten custody cards. (*Marines sign a custody card acknowledging responsibility for sensitive, pilferable or high-dollar equipment.*) For example, a guy might have binoculars, a PEQ-18 tac light, a compass, a GPS, an M4 (rifle) with an M203 grenade launcher, a range-finder…it's insane. The uniforms are better. The

CVC suit – combat vehicle crew flight suit or "frog gear" is flame retardant. The boots are better. The SAW [squad automatic weapon] is awesome; nothing spits out rounds like a SAW. And the Javelin (anti-tank missile) has two modes; it's "fire and forget," and the optics are f***ing incredible.

Young Marines are still wowed by the technology. They watch those shows – *Tactical to Practical, the Military Channel.* They're prepped for it; that's how they think. Some people don't give the infantry much credit, but they're not "cannon fodder." Even down to the corporal level, you gotta make decisions. You've got to think. *Tactics* are an option, an opinion. *Doctrine* helps, but Marines aren't making doctrine decisions in combat; they're making tactical decisions, under pressure.

Women in previously all-male domains

(Female Lieutenant Colonel) I'm on the fence, but generally against women in full combat roles. Some of my peers disagree with me. But I'm a traditionalist. Conservative. You can see a schism in the officer ranks, but that breaks at field grade – from captain to major. Men, male Marine officers, come to respect female officers at major. They come to realize – you're doing the combat rotations, command and staff college, and taking care of a family. They respect the family unit.

Think about it. I've had two children. Women lose bone density; there are hormonal changes; physical changes. Very few women could do the infantry thing into their 40s. If I were an infantry officer as a lieutenant colonel, I should have a battalion command – at 5-foot-4 and 115 pounds? With 80 pounds of gear? Maybe in the next generation – those women who have no kids, aren't married – but not many. Women have to work harder to outshine their male counterparts, and still in OCS [officer candidate school] you see attrition is still high – about 50 percent.

(Master Gunnery Sergeant) In the counter-intelligence/human intelligence (CI/HUMINT) community, there has been push-back from the men. In general intel, we need that role – women in the combat AORs [areas of responsibility], but there have been laws to prevent putting women into contact with the enemy. There are things women can do that men can't do – like talk to the women in Afghanistan. It's value added. It will take time for the CI/HUMINT community to see FET and CI/HUMINT as two different things.

"FET" stands for Female Engagement Teams. This program, in operation in Afghanistan, and still evolving, is worth a book in itself. For the purposes of this book, the notion of deploying women in combat zones has been a contentious issue and culturally – a sea change for the Marine Corps. In an Islamic country like Afghanistan, where it is culturally wrong for male Marines to engage Afghani women, the FET program employs women Marines, with some cultural awareness training, as "junior anthropologists." This is no slight to the women; the Army and Marine Corps have both employed Human Terrain Teams – with PhD sociologists and anthropologists – with mixed success. The HTT program itself has taken some heat and drawn scrutiny from Congress. But HTTs and FETs are different beasts.

Although my original work completed in 1990 was not the driver for either program, both reflect my recommendation (or observation) that ethnographic discovery skills could be used to better understand terrorist organizations. With HTTs and FETs, however, the application is more focused on understanding the cultural environment of non-combatant populations. In a COIN (counter-insurgency) conflict, insurgent elements (read: Taliban, for example) seek to displace or supplant an existing government. Insurgents seek to influence the broader population to accept the insurgent shadow government as legitimate – either by providing services the elected puppet government cannot (security; food, water and basic necessities; dispute resolution (via shariah)), or through terror and intimidation. _Understanding_ that cultural space – Human Terrain – is the domain of trained anthropologists.

Women serving in FETs receive basic training and education in the cultural sensitivities of communicating with Afghan women. HTT team members gather deeper narratives. Both programs have credibility issues and are evolving. Challenges include: leadership and oversight of the programs; field commanders' lack of understanding in how to employ these teams or what to expect from them; the professional credibility of some of the team members. In addition to the challenges inherent in the military placing civilian anthropologists and female engagement teams in combat zones, the practice of applying anthropology or ethnography to understanding civilian populations in a war zone has drawn fire from the professional academic community. For one view of this discussion search for "human terrain" at: _http://zeroanthropology.net/_

Further confounding the kinetically focused military understanding of this domain is the employment of HUMINT Exploitation Teams: HETs. (An "-INT" in the intelligence community indicates the way intelligence information is collected. COMINT is communications intelligence; SIGINT is signals intelligence. HUMINT indicates that intelligence is derived from direct human interviews or elicitation.) Bringing women Marines into the Counter-Intelligence/HUMINT community and affording them of the same lengthy, demanding education and training as their male counterparts yields a far different capability than the FETs. They are different missions. A single phrase in a Marine Corps public affairs story succinctly explains the FET role:

"It is good news for us," said Sgt. Shokorunnah, a soldier with the ANA [Afghan National Army]. "The female Marines came and talked to the women and found out their problems. I am very happy."

Before the all-female team can even enter a compound, they must first talk to the owner, generally a male who is not used to interacting with Marine females.[ccxlviii]

A PhD anthropologist colleague who is also a Reserve Woman Marine major with two combat tours, points out that Afghan women don't quite know what to make of these women in uniform. They tend to view the FET practitioners as a *third gender.*

(The Master Gunnery Sergeant continues:)

Policy makers need to know the difference. FET teams in a combat zone does not mean women in combat. You can't put a FET member in charge of a rifle platoon. Women in the infantry? The first problem with that idea is physical. We'd have to hold them to the same standards as men. Second is the environment. Are we going to send our daughters – one or two women who really can handle the physical demands – out on a patrol or to an isolated outpost in a platoon of Marines?

The real question is: Is this a necessity, or are we trying to be "fair?" Is someone [in Congress] trying to speak for a segment of society? I think women should be able to be fighter pilots – fly Cobras (helicopters) and F-18s (fighter/ attack jets) in combat. They already do. But not infantry. Think about it: How many women are going to sign up for it? Then you get that one woman…she's in a squad at some remote outpost. Why do we want the added stress? They – the policy makers – have no military experience.

If some think tank study could prove it would enhance our combat edge, then OK. They should ask *all* of the women in the armed forces if they want to do this. This isn't a weekend thing. They need to be ready to make deployments (six to seven months, to year-long combat assignments). Is America ready to see this?

Chapter Summary

This section is far from scientific. I acknowledge that. The perspectives of these veteran Marine officers and Staff NCOs are representative of others in the Marine Corps – but of how many is impossible to say without in-depth research. Conversations with hundreds of Marines since 2005 suggest that what I viewed in 1990 is valid in 2011: there are differences between generations of Marines. In this case, however, the younger generation of Marines has distinguished itself, collectively, in combat operations around the globe and the topic of gays serving openly in the military, or women in combat, are not conflicts brought to the Corps by the younger generation. These are external influences delivered to the Armed Forces by civilian policy makers who have virtually zero understanding of military culture and the demands of sustained combat operations.

Other analysts may see this differently, but in this quest to "bring the original dissertation current by 20 years," what the foregoing suggests to me is that Marines view three of these four influences as *distractions* from the genuine missions of the Marine Corps. Nowhere in Title X of the US Code does it say that the mission of US Armed Forces is to serve as a social experimentation laboratory. The veteran Marines' observations, above, suggest that while a younger generation is more accepting of gays in general, and the older generation of Marines will "deal with it," American society needs to prepare for the consequences.

The Commandant and Sergeant Major of the Marine Corps have delivered an order to implement the repeal of Don't Ask, Don't Tell. We are a "nation of laws," with civilian control of the military. It's a model that has, tritely, stood the test of time. Senior leaders challenge small unit leaders to manage problems at the unit level. What do we do when two lance corporals are assigned to a room in the barracks...and one "comes out" as a homosexual male...and he wants his significant other to come to his room? But the other roommate is straight and wants out...wants a different room, but the barracks NCO says there are no more rooms?

Expand this discussion anyway you like – these are not my

questions; these are concerns expressed by officers and Staff NCOs still in uniform. Will we end up with barracks that are secretly the San Francisco barracks, or the Key West barracks? There will be fights and there will be courts-martial. And at some point in the future – most of the turmoil will fade; the current "younger generation" of Marines will become the older generation and the problem won't be as much of a problem anymore.

As with acclimatization to other minorities (Blacks, Women Marines" *encroaching* on the "white, male "rod and gun club") time and proximity go a long way to desensitization. Senior Marines observe that most younger generation Marines are accepting or ambivalent, and while the senior (older) Marines are generally more conservative and not in favor of this change – they acknowledge the Commandant's reminder that we are a nation of laws and the armed forces report to a civilian government. They are, collectively, against the move but resigned to acknowledge "There's nothing we can do about it," and (more or less) "Leaving the Marine Corps, to make a point, for a job in the civilian world wouldn't change things anyway."

Likewise with women in combat. In the first place, women represent 5.8 percent of the officer corps (1200 of 20,600 total) and 6.4 percent of the enlisted ranks (11,700 of 182,000 total). Of the enlisted Marines, roughly 36,000 serve in infantry, although Marines with infantry MOSs may be employed in non-infantry assignments, like guarding embassies, or recruiting and basic training. As of 2010, there were no women assigned to tanks or artillery.[ccxlix]   Older generation Marines see the turmoil in terms of policy makers seeking to ensure the Armed Forces appropriately reflect the broader social demographic; that the Marine Corps and other services are "fair," and "inclusive;" that the majority change to accommodate the few. These are distractions. A New York Times article presents the conflicting views from *female* Marines, from a visit by Defense Secretary Chuck Hagel:[ccl]

One first sergeant objected strongly, saying that if women could add anything of value to combat infantry units, they would have been handed those missions long ago.

One staff sergeant worried that the Marine Corps' high standards would have to be lowered if women were assigned to combat. Other Marines in the group agreed, warning that women would not be accepted by their male counterparts living in spartan wartime conditions, or that family lives would suffer, especially for those female Marines hoping to have children.

One lieutenant, however, disagreed with anyone who argued that now is not the right time to start bringing women into combat roles, and several noted that the American armed forces often had led the rest of society, for example, in integrating minorities.

Each of the services has struggled with women in uniform for decades. Realistically – where there are men and women in the same geographic spaces, there will be some men and women who violate boundaries; some men who prey on women or other men; and some women who prey on men or other women. The problem of sexual assault or sexual harassment is not limited to the armed forces, but the impact on mission accomplishment is perhaps more severe than in the civilian community. A telling report, illustrative of the broader challenge, is the DOD assessment of sexual harassment at the academies (Army, Navy and Air Force academies).[ccli]

Early on in this book I noted that changes in the culture may have an internal genesis or be imposed on the organization from without. I started this project of "bringing the study current by 20 years" in 2010. Since then, Don't Ask, Don't Tell has been repealed. The Services are dealing with it. More recently is the mandate to determine the *if* and *how* of opening combat arms assignments to women. The Marine Corps, like the Army, Navy and Air Force, have a year or two to study the mandate, explore and report on the notion of "gender neutral" physical standards, and address the question of potentially excluded assignments, such as SEALS, Rangers and other Special Forces missions. It's a contentious issue:[cclii]

Publicly and privately, U.S. commandos are casting doubt on the sexual revolution looming over Navy SEALs, Army Rangers, Delta Force and Green Berets.

The Pentagon staged a press briefing to announce a two-year study to refine combat physical standards and find the best way to install women in the male bastion of infantry, armor and special operations. A decision on which combat roles will be open to women is expected in 2015. It is the special "ops" group — with its secretive isolation in small teams where physical stamina matters most — that has commandos the most nervous.

"The only option now is to offer reasons why they can't do it," said an Army special operations veteran who believes U.S. Special Operations Command will cave to White House demands to include women. "I haven't heard that anyone has the courage to say they can't do it, either. Maybe the new [military occupational specialty] can be 18P — Special Forces camp follower. Is that PC enough?"

An Army Special Forces soldier said the qualification course at Fort Bragg, N.C., to earn the Green Beret is so demanding that the Army will have to lower standards for some tasks in order for women to succeed.

"The real outcry will begin if the current standards are significantly lowered," the soldier said. "Genderless standards will cause many SOF courses to completely reassess how they select the best candidates."

Most tests of strength and endurance, the soldier said, "currently rely on a candidate's ability to endure physical hardships as a fundamental aspect of their assessment."

While debates continue on "lowered standards," no one has yet answered the question of whether the Selective Service law will change – and require women to register for the draft (that has been inactive for 40 years) between the ages of 18 and 25, like their "equal" male counterparts.

As for technology: In general, inventions and innovations seek to improve the lives and survivability of Marines and militaries everywhere. The other side of this double-edged dagger is that the ability to easily communicate with loved ones back home, from a combat zone, can distract a Marine from his mission. (The problem is parallel to the distracted driver who causes a fatal traffic accident while texting.) This is another leadership challenge. Additionally – if we have tech, the bad guys have tech too. There's no turning back the clock on the Internet, and the likes of Anwar al-Aulaqi will continue to spew extremist Islamist ideology. This is a *national* leadership challenge.

And the increasing academic standards for enlisted Marines: This is seen broadly as a positive. Officers and senior non-commissioned officers agree that better-educated troops are more manageable troops, generally.

Chapter Nine

Display and Analysis of Ethnographic Data: 1990

This chapter remains as an ethnographic record of "where we were in the Marine Corps" as of 1990 (rather than relegated to an appendix). It is not comprehensive, and additions to this section have been presented in prior chapters.

Introduction

One goal of ethnographic research is to understand cultural themes. Spradley defines a cultural theme as "any cognitive principle, tacit or explicit, recurrent in a number of domains and serving as a relationship among subsystems of cultural meaning."[ccliii]

Understanding those cultural meanings is one of the main goals of this book. But Spradley also notes that the purpose of ethnography is to generate hypotheses. To arrive at cultural themes and to write an ethnography, thus displaying and describing a culture in such a way that the culture almost explains itself to the reader, the researcher must go through several steps. The ethnographer takes on a cycle of hypothesis, participant observation, analysis, hypothesis, participant observation, etc. The first of the major steps is to make very rough hypotheses about domains, or categories of symbols. This step was actually an ongoing process beginning concurrently with the formulation of the paper's working hypotheses.

Spradley writes: "all cultural meaning is created by using symbols." These symbols are the symbols, rituals and myths discussed throughout this paper. A domain then, is a category of symbols, or as

Spradley refers to symbols, they are words, artifacts, stories, rituals or gestures that belong to a larger group "by virtue of some similarity."

Spradley further explained that "all symbols involve three elements: the symbol itself, one or more referents, and a relationship between the symbol and the referent." And, "linguistic symbols form the core of the meaning system of every culture, and with these we can communicate about all other symbols in a culture."

Language allows the ethnographer to replace artifacts with the words a member of the culture associates with the artifacts, gestures with words implied by the gestures, and rituals with words for rituals. The referent is the symbol, ritual, myth, artifact or gesture to which the symbol (or word for the symbol) refers. Through the analysis of the words and phrases which represent symbols, the researcher classifies these words and phrases into domains.

To describe the culture, the ethnographer must "decode cultural symbols and identify the underlying coding rules. This can be accomplished by discovering (from the natives) the relationships among cultural symbols." The researcher must come to understand the relationships between elements in a domain, and to reach this understanding, he must accumulate enough data to produce a domain with its elements.

To paraphrase Spradley's definition of the structure of domains: One of the most important elements in a domain is a cover term (the names for the domains, or categories of cultural knowledge.) "All domains have two or more included terms...[and,] all domains have a single semantic relationship. Finally, every domain has a boundary."

Included terms – the words or phrases for symbols – can be organized into lists of terms, or taxonomies. Through analysis of taxonomies, the researcher searches for the internal structure of domains. Further analytical steps lead to theme analyses which get at the relationships between domains, and reveal the tacit or explicit cognitive principles of the culture. Spradley notes that the cognitive principles are the things people of the culture believe; they are guides to the actions, thoughts and emotions of members of the culture.

In my understanding these cognitive principles are the held truths, values and beliefs of a culture. They are the map or maze of understandings which guide behaviors as discussed in earlier chapters. The symbols form the Edifice and the truths or values provide the map through the Complex – or the mortar that binds and supports the *bricks* in the "structure" of the edifice.

Developing emergent hypotheses

To provide an example and to continue defining the direction of this chapter, recall that I began the paper while immersed in the culture. Thus it was impossible to be naive about the culture. For this reason, I employed a variety of social science research tools to gather data, make preliminary hypotheses and analyze findings. Ethnographic research techniques promised to elicit a wealth of information that would be useful in this study but could not be relied upon exclusively. I therefore formed a number of preliminary hypotheses before beginning ethnographic interviews. On-going research and analysis allowed hypotheses to take shape in the course of ethnographic interviewing.

One working hypothesis discussed from chapter to chapter has been that the formation of discipline within the Marine Corps, a cultural theme, may be undergoing changes. What I discovered is that discipline is indeed a theme undergoing changes, but not for the reasons originally suspected. Note that it was some three years between writing the original Chapter I and this chapter in 1990. Yet, the stability of this hypothesis will support the accuracy of the findings.

Further, an early hypothesis was that I would find some cultural themes in synonyms of the Marine Corps' written leadership traits or principles. The leadership traits are:[ccliv]

Integrity	Knowledge
Courage	Decisiveness
Dependability	Initiative
Tact	Justice
Enthusiasm	Bearing
Endurance	Unselfishness
Loyalty	Judgment

Table VIII

Or leadership principles:

1. Be technically and tactically proficient.

2. Know yourself and seek self-improvement.

3. Know your Marines and look out for their welfare.

4. Keep your Marines informed.

5. Set the example.

6. Ensure the task is understood, supervised and accomplished.

7. Train your Marines as a team.

8. Make sound and timely decisions.

9. Develop a sense of responsibility in your subordinates.

10. Employ your unit in accordance with its capabilities.

11. Seek responsibility and take responsibility for your actions.

Indeed some of these traits and principles figure prominently in the final chapters, but some are more on the order of domains or terms in taxonomies rather than broad cultural themes. In retrospect, the ethnographic process has been one of discovery; some emerging cultural themes have been surprises.

Spradley writes that one may "carry out a surface analysis of as many domains as possible...[or] conduct an in-depth analysis of a limited number of domains."[cclv] Spradley presents positive and negative aspects about each, and guidelines for accomplishing either.

During data reduction, analysis and writing, I decided to conduct analysis of a fairly limited number of cultural scenes, combined with in-depth analyses of enough domains to define cultural themes that support the hypotheses and accomplish the purpose of the study.

In the interest of brevity, I will present several levels of analysis concurrently. That is, I will display taxonomies with intermingled semantic relationships. Additionally, the on-going ethnographic analysis draws from data presented in earlier chapters and from other notes and new findings.

Ethnographic data and analysis

At this point, by far the largest domain deals with people and their relationships to others. The first domain includes several taxonomies, such as terms Marines have for other Marines. As noted above, several layers of ethnographic analysis will be presented concurrently.

In addition, definitions and cultural meaning will be included at many points for the reader (and serve as an appendix or glossary).

Domain: Names for classes of People

Taxonomy of names for Enlisted Marines   Cover term: Marine

Formal names; enlisted Marines	Abbreviation	pay grade
private	Pvt	E-1
private first class	Pfc	E-2
lance corporal	LCpl	E-3
corporal	Cpl	E-4
sergeant	Sgt	E-5
staff sergeant	SSgt	E-6
gunnery sergeant	GySgt	E-7
master sergeant	MSgt	E-8
first sergeant	1st Sgt	E-8
master gunnery sergeant	MGySgt	E-9
sergeant major	SgtMaj	E-9

Names for warrant officers

warrant officer	WO	WO1
chief warrant officer	CWO	CWO2
	CWO	CWO3

	CWO	CWO4
	CWO	CWO5 (added in 1992)

Names for officers

second lieutenant	2ndLt	O-1
first lieutenant	1stLt	O-2
captain	Capt	O-3
major	Maj	O-4
lieutenant colonel	LtCol	O 5
colonel	Col	O-6
brigadier general	BGen	O-7
major general	MajGen	O-8
lieutenant general	LtGen	O-9
general	Gen	O-10

Taxonomy:

Nicknames by position   Cover term: other Marines

recruit	Recruit
Boot	Recruit
Boot	one who is junior
prive	Private

lance coolie	lance corporal
gunny	gunnery sergeant
first shirt	first sergeant
Top	master sergeants, some master gunnery sergeants
Gunner	warrant officers
butter bar, brown bar	2nd lieutenant
platoon commander	(usually) a lieutenat
skipper	captain
light bird	lieutenant colonel
full bird	colonel
VIP (now DV – Distinguished Visitor)	colonel or above or equivalent civilian rank
the old man	commanding officer
the six, six actual	commanding officer
the boss, the CO	commanding officer
XO	executive officer
CMC	Commandant of the Marine Corps

Classes of People: Table IX

The first taxonomy is a list of all the formal names of Marines' ranks currently in use in the Corps. Several excellent historical texts delve into past and present names and their etymologies. This paper is concerned with the symbolism (meaning) contained in the use of these names. A number of semantic relationships appear between terms within these taxonomies.

For example:

Included term	semantic relationship	cover term
private	is a kind of	Marine rank

or:

a private	is junior to	a private first class
a pfc	is junior to	a lance corporal

or the opposite:

a staff sergeant	outranks	a sergeant
a sergeant	outranks	a corporal

Table X

and so on. Of course a staff sergeant outranks all others below his rank, and is junior to all others above his rank. Recruits not only must memorize the names of and relationships between the ranks, but learn through the indoctrination of boot camp some of the relative power of each. They must also learn to identify the tangible symbols (referents) of the rank's names as gold and silver officers' insignia, and enlisted chevrons or stripes. The distinction between officer and enlisted is a clue to saluting – a required form of military courtesy steeped in centuries of tradition. After learning Marine Corps ranks and relative cultural relationships, Marines will at some point learn Army, Air Force and Navy ranks; and then (perhaps) other services' rank insignia, relative power and relationships.

Cultural rules change after boot camp. Whereas during training recruits must address directly or refer to all who are not recruits by formal title in the third person, indoctrination or socialization after boot camp reveals which short names or nicknames are allowable. For example, during boot camp, a drill instructor who is a gunnery sergeant must be addressed directly as "drill instructor Gunnery Sergeant 'Smith.'" If the Marine returned to the training depot a few weeks after graduating, he would be allowed by custom to directly address the same drill instructor as *gunny*, although the private would almost certainly say *gunnery sergeant* to his former DI for two reasons. First, the new Marine still holds the indoctrination of boot camp and the new freedom will take some time to sink in, allow him to relax around other Marines. Second, Marines always seem to have a stronger measure of respect for their drill instructors.

The reason recruits address all others in the third person is also twofold. Analysis indicates that recruits are not allowed to think of themselves as Marines – because they aren't Marines (yet. They're recruits), and are not entitled to the privileges Marines have within their own society. Second, as with the first haircut, it is important for the recruit to sacrifice his identity in order to accept a Marine identity. Boot camp is a kind of purgatory where a recruit has no civilian or Marine identity. An exchange would be something like:

"Sir, the private requests permission to speak to Drill Instructor Gunnery Sergeant Smith."

"Speak."

"Sir, the private requests permission to make a head call, sir."

"Very well." (or "Carry on," or "Git," etc.)

Other rules are not so clear. After boot camp, master sergeants and some master gunnery sergeants accept the moniker *top*. But other master gunnery sergeants deny the name. One at Parris

Island often said, "I ain't no f***ing top; I don't sit on my head and spin!"

Occasionally, a Marine lesser in grade than staff sergeant uses *staff*, as in, "Hey, staff, we got to do this today?" Staff sergeants universally disallow this, responding with something like: "Do I look like some sort of infection (staph) to you?" (*I haven't checked, but I don't think this aberration is on-going in the 21st Century anymore.*)

Civilians who work in government service, or have GS ratings in other words, have rank in terms of their position and pay grade, and evaluate Marines on fitness reports in some relatively rare circumstances. Note that the president, vice president and secretaries of defense and the Navy are all civilians and are all in the chain of command. VIPs are *very important persons*, just as in the civilian community. (Now "DV" or distinguished visitor.)

Another sub-domain similar to that above includes taxonomies of names used by Marines in particular jobs. Following are categories of terms used by recruiters and drill instructors.

Terms used by recruiters   Cover term: prospect

terms for prospects	applicants
females only	Queens
usually only males	
Desirable	high school grad; PT animal
Undesirable	non-grad
	Rock
	Cat-4

	Mama's boy
	Thieves, Hoods, Junkies
	pukes on the streets
other terms	
Retreads	(have prior service)
already enlisted	Poolees

Table XI

Terms for recruits   Cover term: recruits
DIs once used

terms used to address (male) recruits		
ladies	Girls	sh*tbirds
maggots	pussy	Bitch
sh*thead	Pigs	Asshole
hogs	sweet pea(s)	bitch eyes
communist	Queer	

Table XII

Names for recruits' jobs in platoon   Job

king rat	supervised house mouses
house mouses	cleaned the DI's office
coffee bean (usually of Mexican extraction)	carried Thermos, carried coffee for DIs

scribe or secretary	kept platoon records
(platoon) guide	supervised squad leaders
squad leaders	supervised men in squad

Table XIII

General terms for recruits

	recruit
	Private
terms for platoon or groups of recruits	
	the mob
	the herd
Terms for recruits now officially enforced for use by DIs	
	(platoon) guide
	squad leader
	private; recruit
	scribe or secretary
Acceptable	good recruits
	problem recruit

Table XIV

The first set of terms in this category is not all-inclusive, but represents names drill instructors used when addressing recruits in the 1960s and until the middle 1970s for certain. As General Wilson and others observed, the names were not condoned by the Marine

Corps. These and others may have been used in the 1950s and before as well, but the research base for this paper is not broad enough to determine that. In any case, no DI interviewed during the 1980-1984 period would admit to addressing a recruit by anything other than "recruit," "private," or the private's last name or job title, other than nicknames like "preacher," (the graduate from Bob Jones University) "alphabet" (with a name like Boguslawski or some other too-hard-to-pronounce name), or "snaggletooth" (for someone with some sort of remarkable dental work). The key now is not to offend or abuse any recruit's ethnic heritage, religion, personal appearance, etc.

The use of abusive language carries its own meaning. When used in *command voice* in the context of a recruit having a discipline or motivation problem, the recruit's tacit understanding is that recruits are the lowest form of life, less than human, incapable of becoming U.S. Marines. The challenge (then) was to encourage recruits to *earn* the title Marine. Richard Stack, the former Marine photojournalist noted in earlier chapters, recorded DIs saying:

> *We don't mean that they are the worst things that walk the face of the earth. We call them these names because if they should ever become prisoners of war, somebody is going to call them worse names than we call them. So if they can't take it here, they won't be able to take it over there. This brings out self-discipline.[alvi]*

My purpose is not to debate the utility of name calling and vulgar language, verbal abuse or hazing, but to contrast the different sides of the issue. By way of opinion, there is merit in the idea that if a recruit cannot stand someone calling him vulgar names in training, he will have trouble with someone calling him names if he becomes a prisoner of war. The other side of the argument is that physical and mental discipline does not have to include abuses of civil liberties to instill the will to fight and the courage to withstand the rigors of combat (or of being a prisoner).

The era of change, clearly during the mid-1970s according to personal observation and the testimony of those interviewed, brought the external enforcement of cleaner language during basic training. Again, senior drill instructors and series officers tell recruits during their first week that they should not be verbally or physically abused, and if they are, they should report such violations. Further, series officers interview recruits before they leave training and ask if they have been verbally or physically abused.

Another category of names for people includes the taxonomy of terms for women.

Terms for women used by at least some male Marines (into the 1980s)	Cover terms
women; Women Marines	WMs
	BAMs; broad-assed Marines
	Wives; wife; old lady
(commander-in-chief)	CINC house (the wife)
other relatives	Mother; mom; sister
other women	Hogs
	susie rotten crotch
	dog tag sally
	Hookers; whores
	Bitches; babes

Table XV

In the distant past, the Navy used the term WAVE (Women Accepted for Volunteer Service) for women in the Navy. The Army used WAC for women in the Women's Army Corps. During World War I, *Marinettes* served in the Corps in a reserve status, but the term fell out of use. Through at least part of the 1950s, 60s and into the 70s, many male Marines referred to Women Marines as BAMs. (When I reported to Camp Lejeune in 1974 for duty with the 2nd Marine Division Band, I stopped my car at the front gate to ask one of the military policemen where the band barracks was. It was my misfortune that the duty officer, who was outside at the guard shack, was a Woman Marine. She thought she heard "BAM barracks," and promptly chastised me for the use of such a derogatory term, "We refer to our women as Marines here!")

Although male Marines do not generally want women in male roles, the apparent meaning in terms like **hog** might suggest to civilians that male Marines do not respect all women in general. The use of the term, however, brings out the meaning. A sentence may employ the term as: "Let's go pick up some hogs and go to the club." This conveys the meaning that hogs are dates. Men do not usually use hog to address women directly, but to refer to them. A *hog board* was a bulletin board for displaying pictures of women, girl friends, etc.

Perspective: It's the 21ˢᵗ Century and we are all aware that the use of any of these terms is not politically correct, and that these terms extend the exploitation of women (which is unfortunate and wrong on an enterprise scale. We are also aware in this open media 21ˢᵗ century that women use similar terms to refer to men, and exploit men.) We are also adults and realize that whether such terms are distasteful, they are, or were, part of the culture – and an <u>accurate</u> record of what people actually said – on their terms.

The Armed Forces are dealing with an apparent explosion in the number of sexual assault cases. It is unclear if this represents a genuine increase or an increase in reporting that account for the concept of "X number of cases were reported, but the number is likely much greater." Service Chiefs, including the Commandant of the Marine Corps, have been called to testify before Congress on the matter – and told to "clean up the act." "Experts" have opined, variously, that the problem is due to the stresses of a decade of combat, to the lack of respect for women because they are not viewed a full partners in uniform – because they have historically not been allowed into combat roles, and other variations. The Department of Defense Sexual Assault Prevention and Response website provides statistical information on the phenomenon dating back to 2004. One notable artifact in this data is the number of males who are victims of sexual assault. Most don't report it because of the stigma.[cdvii]

Susie rotten crotch and *dog tag Sally* were names used to refer to whores usually, but one Marine may also use one of the terms to refer to the girlfriend of another Marine. Use, thus meaning, depends on the Marine.

The armed forces pay women, like men, according to rank and time in service, so women are paid the same as their male counterparts in identical circumstances. However, women's roles in the military have changed over the past two decades, and even though the Marine Corps, in the name of national policy, has not allowed women in direct combat jobs (yet), women Marines have taken more and more assignments closer to the front lines of combat. In my observations and according to those interviewed for this study, men met the movement of women into historically male roles with resistance.

Well into the 1980s, many male Marines called women who drove 10-ton trucks lesbians, homosexuals or dykes (*diesel dyke, nuke dyke* – for perceived *degrees* of lesbianism). Male attitudes toward women in the military have evolved over the decades, coinciding with apparent changes in the civilian sector. However, the empirical evidence holds that women are seen as generally inferior to men, largely because the military is a male tribal culture. As the lieutenant colonel observed in the previous chapter, male attitudes toward women evolve during a career with more mature attitudes evident as men see women pursuing their careers, going to service schools and raising families, instead of as competitors.

If the Marine Corps were a smaller culture like some of the tribes of the Pacific islands or the American Indians described in early anthropologies, it would be easier to say *all Marines* call their friends "_____." But with some 200,000 Marines there is a wide range of types. Some Marines choose not to use what is commonly called vulgar language, either because of religious upbringing, personal choice or for some other reason. The following taxonomy, although not organized along classic ethnographic semantic lines, is a logical grouping of many other terms Marines either use or universally recognize as being names for other Marines:

Terms for other Marines

term	is (are):
the guy next to you	another Marine
a hat, DI	a drill instructor
the heavy	a DI whose job is to act more strictly than the other DIs on his team
the senior	senior DI on a team of three or four; usually a staff or gunnery sergeant
CDI	chief drill instructor
Infantry marine	ground pounder, grunt, 03

inspector	the base, depot, station or other command-level representative of the commanding general whose duty is to inspect and report violations of orders or regulations
the duty	duty NCO, duty Hat; one who is on duty, on watch
airdale, wing wiper	an aviation Marine
remington raider chairborne raider; office poag; 01	a Marine who works in an office, in administrative jobs;
career planner	an in-service recruiter, often likened to a used car salesman, tries to get Marines to reenlist
buddy, drinking buddy	a friend, the Marine one goes out drinking with

Table XVI

Terms for other Marines

dark green Marine	Black Marine
light green Marine	White (Caucasian) Marine
feather merchant	a light-weight Marine
fat body	an overweight Marine
bad guy on the block	a Marine who thinks he is tough
brown-bagger	a married Marine, brings his lunch to work

man, dude	anyone, as in "Hey, man…,"
mess chief, mess sergeant	the Staff NCO or NCO who works in or operates the mess hall
brother, bro	usually, not exclusively used by black Marines as in "bro"
bra'	Marines who served in Hawaii
Joe-sh*t-the-rag Man	
Joe schmuck; Joe schmuckatelli	anyman (like John Doe)
Alphabet	a person whose name is hard to pronounce
slime bag, dirt ball, skate, malingerer whale sh*t gold brick, scum bag	Marines who don't hump their share of the load
SNM	subject named Marine
enlisted pigs, swine, pukes	sometimes used sarcastically by enlisted Marines (self-referentially) discussing their relationship to officers
brass	general term for officers
top brass	senior level officers
Officers	neutral term for officers and warrant officers
They	unseen outside forces, as in:

	"They ordered this mess."
personnel, people troops, men	general terms for Marines
NCO	non-commissioned officer (corporals and sergeants)
Staff NCO	staff non-commissioned officers: staff sergeants through sergeants major, master gunnery sergeants
Reservists	general term for Marines in the Marine Reserves
Lifer	a Marine who can't live without the Corps
career Marine	a Marine the Corps can't do without
R.O.A.D.	retired on active duty (lazy)
sea lawyer	one who gives free, but not necessarily accurate, advice
Hollywood Marine	(usually) a graduate of San Diego boot camp
poster Marine	a lean, handsome Marine esp. if used as an actual model for advertising posters
aide	aide de camp to a commanding general
"lieutenant" general	derogatorily used for a lieutenant serving as aide to a

	general, who acts as if he speaks with the general's authority

Table XVII

Historical Names

Soldiers of the Sea	
the old Breed	
Band of Brothers	
horse Marines	
old China hand	
sea-going bellhops	
Asiatic, Asian Marine	
Leathernecks	
Devil Dogs	
Additional terms	
former Marine	anyone once a Marine (never ex-Marine)
Retread	a Marine who got out of the Corps and returned
vet, veteran	retired or former Marine, or one who has been in combat, or who has experience
salt, old salt	a Marine who has been around

	a while
acting jack	(archaic) term for recruits who stayed after boot camp and acted as assistant DIs – acting corporals
PAO	Public Affairs Officer
Terms for legendary Marines	
John Wayne	"The greatest non-Marine who ever lived"
Chesty Puller	(deceased) LtGen Louis B. Puller, honored by all Marines as the greatest Marine who ever lived
Dan Daly	only enlisted Marine to win two Medals of Honor (neither posthumous)
Lou Diamond	legendary mortarman who could "drop mortars down the smokestacks of Japanese destroyers," fought hard, drank hard, etc.
chesty	the name often given to a dog who serves as a unit mascot, often a bulldog, thought of as one of the Marines in the unit

Doc	Navy hospital corpsman, an enlisted medical **expert** who takes care of some the medical needs of a Marine unit. Also thought of as one of the Marines when assigned to a grunt unit (on a doc by doc basis)
Padre	Navy chaplain; as with corpsmen, assigned to Marine units and authorized to wear Marine uniforms (with Navy insignia)
Terms for Units of Marines	
The Magnificent bastards	2nd Battalion, 4th Marine Regiment
The Walking Dead	1st Battalion, 9th Marine Regiment
The President's Own	the U.S. Marine Band
The Silent Drill Team	
Raiders	
Recon	

Table XVIII

(*As discussed, the Corps has added SOF Marines – Special Operations Forces. Marine Recon units have been absorbed into this command, based at Camp Lejeune, NC. and Camp Pendleton, CA. Again – the language and culture will continue to evolve, adding more terms and stories to the culture.)*

Tacit meanings in the words Marines use for each other fall into several categories. The first is rank relationships. Although a prospect for enlistment begins to see and perhaps understand well the meaning in the differences between ranks, he is not affected by the differences. He can observe, but he is not ordered to do anything, and Marines have no real control over him. Poolee meetings may be "mandatory," for example, but recruiters cannot order him to attend as a Marine would order a subordinate to perform some task.

There is a message that emphasizes rank relationships within the propaganda of boot camp indoctrination. During the 10 weeks of training, recruits internalize the tacit and explicit meanings inherent in rank. Recruits react to symbols of rank – enlisted chevrons and gold or silver officer's collar devices. Recruits learn that all enlisted Marines salute all officers. There is a body of knowledge that surrounds the saluting rituals. One salutes before the officer gets to six paces but not more than 30 paces away; salutes are not rendered indoors or while in civilian clothes; and several other regulations.

Recruits also *brace*, or stand at attention when other Marines enter the room (such as their squad bay or barracks). After boot camp, enlisted Marines are supposed to come to attention when an officer (but not an enlisted Marine) enters a room, in certain settings.

The Recruit Training SOP notes that one certain end result of turning recruits over from receiving barracks to their platoon DIs is to "Establish the authority of the drill instructor over each recruit." During the first several days in training there is no question how much authority a drill instructor has. Recruits quickly learn that authority is related to rank.

The chain of command is also related to knowledge and internalization of the values and reactions associated with rank. Recruits learn the chain of command from day one in training, but can actually memorize the upper part of the chain (the President, Vice President, Secretary of Defense, Secretary of the Navy, Commandant of the Marine Corps, etc.) as poolees. Explicit understanding is that the chain is never violated. One must keep intermediate commanders and other responsible people informed. However, after training Marines learn that there are variations in the chain. One of the variations is an informal network, an NCO *mafia*, or *good old boys* network of staff NCOs who can get things done more efficiently without formal channels or paperwork.

An example from my experience in working the informal chain comes from public relations. When an unannounced tour group, 40 Boy Scouts and their leaders in a chartered bus on one occasion, showed up at Parris Island, unannounced, looking for a tour and a place to eat, I called the mess chief, a master sergeant who was my neighbor in government housing, at one of the mess halls and fed the group without having had any of the required paperwork submitted in advance. The mess chief knew the paperwork would be submitted later and back-dated if necessary, up my chain of command and down his chain of command. If anyone complained, we could write the problem off to *good PR*.

The saying before the fact is, "What can they do, shave my head and send me to Okinawa?" (or Korea or Vietnam). A different saying, with the same meaning, is: "It's easier to get forgiveness than permission."

Another variation in the chain of command is seen in non-combat or support units. The officer in charge of a data processing center is not in command, but is in the chain of command for Marines who work in his offices. But they also belong to a headquarters or service company in a headquarters battalion. When it comes time to promote a Marine in a data processing center, the Marine may or may not be given the choice of who will promote him – his officer in charge at the data processing center or his battalion or company commander. The lack of articulation between competing chains of command can sometimes stir jealousies between officers. The problem becomes more acute when the headquarters battalion publishes duty rosters for guard duty for Marines who must also fulfill duties in their own offices (data processing, public affairs, communications, etc.). Usually the higher ranking officer wins the competition; the enlisted Marines can only learn coping strategies.

Perspective: Years before the first consumer "desktop" computers came on the market in 1980-82, big companies and large government organizations had central computers – data processing centers – which handled supply and logistics, finance and accounting, manpower (human resources / personnel) and other data in large chunks on tapes and in the early 1970s and before - on 80-column cards. What the "data processing center" for an entire Marine Corps Base could handle in the 1970s or early '80s, a $500 laptop computer can process in 2010.

Other than informal chains of command or chains of working relationships, Marines are not supposed to go out of the chain of command. Excusable exceptions are when someone in the chain is demonstrably inept or is breaking some law or regulation, or in the case of life-threatening emergencies, dangerous situations, and so on. Lieutenant Colonel Oliver North was questioned on Capitol Hill about a perception that Admiral Poindexter or others might be giving him unlawful orders. The meaning was that North was not required to obey orders he knew to be unlawful. North said he did not question his superiors and did not believe the diversion of funds for the Contras was illegal.[cclviii]

Another element of tacit understanding in rank relationships regards pay and promotions. All Marines learn well their rank and relative position in the chain. They also develop expectations for promotions. Sergeants learn through stories, as well as formal channels, of course, how long one can expect to be a sergeant before promotion to staff sergeant. Marine Corps Times and other unofficial sources may print charts and graphs that depict the Marine Corps average time in grade for a particular rank, but a Marine often gets a better understanding of his chances for promotion from stories about promotions from other Marines in his MOS.[cclix]

Pay, power and prestige are tied to promotions as well. An explicit understanding is that more senior Marines can afford newer, more expensive cars. A cultural given is that more senior Marines are able or expected to drive newer, more expensive cars, or wear more expensive clothes or live in bigger houses. This is generally *not* the case, as more mature Marines – officer and enlisted – start understanding what it means to save and invest for retirement, and also start putting their children into college. It is common, in fact, to see that the commanding officer *and* sergeant major of a Marine unit drive Honda Civics, Toyotas, or small American cars, and the unmarried sergeants or even corporals (flush with cash) drive fairly new Corvettes, BMWs, Mercedes or Cadillacs – well into the 21st century.

An oft-heard expression from junior Marines is: "If I were commandant or the commanding officer, or even the top or the sergeant major, I'd fix this or that problem." The power associated with rank leads to the perception that more can be accomplished within a particular pay grade. Having seen both sides, as an enlisted Marine and as a commissioned officer, what I see enlisted people not being aware of is that a few officers make decisions based on a measure of *paranoia*, fearing for their fitness reports, their next promotions and their careers. Every Marine is outranked by someone, even if the Commandant must answer to the Joint Chiefs of Staff, secretaries of the Navy and Defense, and to Congress.

Enlisted people hear of *politics* in the officer ranks, learning that social functions are mandatory, and that officers must pay for their share of social functions whether they attend or not. This is not always the case, and the extent to which a commanding officer evaluates his subordinate officers on the level of their social activity varies from commander to commander. Such problems are apparently less evident in the 1980s than in the past. *(In hindsight, and based on experiences since 2005, this phenomenon depends entirely on the leadership style of the commander.)*

As for some specific terms, such as *butter bar*, the tacit understanding in the culture is that second lieutenants are inexperienced, are ignorant of the Marine Corps or are *wet behind the ears*. A second category of tacit understandings is that which allows Marines to group other Marines into good and bad, productive and non-productive, gung-ho or lazy, ethnic groups, hard jobs and easy jobs, etc.

Some terms conjure a wealth of stories, such as *the duty*. When a monthly duty roster is posted (or for Marine officers, promulgated), Marines groan when they see they have duty on Fridays or weekends. Some Marines *sell* the duty, meaning they are actually paying someone else to either take the spot on the roster or trade with them. Duty rates varied from unit to unit, from $5 a weekday and $10 a weekend day, to $20 for a weekday and $50 for a weekend day (into the 1980s).

Standing duty varies from job to job, but may include guard duty or manning an empty office, after work hours and through the night, while on *phone watch*. When talking about someone else having the duty, Marines know they *do not mess with* the duty (the duty NCO) because he can *write you up*. No matter how much one complains, once in a duty position, a Marine assumes a new identity. He represents the commanding officer and must enforce the unit's regulations, including all upper echelon regulations. A Marine on (guard) duty has no friends.

But a Marine on duty may have interesting or unusual experiences: While serving as the assistant officer of the day (assistant to a captain, who was "officer of the day") for Marine Corps Recruit Depot, Parris Island, one Saturday in 1981, two Women Marine second lieutenants in dress green uniform (Service Dress "A") rang the buzzer to the front door of the depot headquarters building. The duty clerk admitted them and escorted them to the duty officer's room on the second deck. In unison the two women (about 22 to 24 years old) announced that they wanted to see the commanding general.

The captain looked at me and smiled knowingly yet imperceptibly. "Why is that?" he asked.

They replied that they had just graduated from the Marine Officer's Basic Course at Quantico, Virginia, and their orders read: "Report to the Commanding General, MCRD, Parris Island, not later than 1700 – on that date."

The captain tactfully explained that the terminology did not mean that one reports *directly* to the commanding general, but to his duly appointed representative, in this case the captain. We were both amused. Stories like this are flexible, and can be dusted off during story telling sessions to illustrate truths about Women Marines, second lieutenants, officers, or standing the duty.

Hearing such stories repeated time after time adds to the socialization of Marines after boot camp. No immediate response, other than another story, is called for, but the internalization of tacit understandings, cultural givens, should cause one to act in a particular way given the right cues. One may believe second lieutenants are ignorant, but does not usually express that belief in the presence of second lieutenants or act in such a way that expresses that belief in their presence. The higher rank an enlisted Marine has the easier it is to teach or indoctrinate new officers. Experience tells that sergeants, staff sergeants and gunnery sergeants take the time to help indoctrinate lieutenants more than other enlisted ranks, but it varies. Junior Marines are less sure of their footing in such matters and some senior enlisted Marines seem to have little time or inclination to train *butter bars.*

One of the terms applied to Marines who lose the motivation to perform is *short timer.* Although the term can be applied in a neutral sense by others, usage suggests meaning, as in: "He has a short timer's attitude." (In the Philippines or on Okinawa, a *short time* is also a one-night stand with a hooker, and is not necessarily reserved for one who is soon to depart the island or the command.)

Expressions telling others how soon one is due to depart a command or get discharged from the Marine Corps are many and varied: On car windows at Camp Lejeune in the 1970s, *short* Marines would paint "6 and a hook" (or 7, 5, etc.) on the rear window of their cars. Often the word *hook* would be symbolized by a fish hook. The meaning is "Six days and the day I leave the Corps." Equivalent expressions are "Six and a sea bag drag," or "Six days and a wakeup."

To define how short one is, a Marine goes to work and says, "I'm so short I had to rappel down out of my rack this morning," or, "I'm so short, I had to use a step ladder to make a head call." Most Marines recognize that no one is shorter than the Marine who says, "I'm not short; I'm next." A genuine aficionado of short timer's culture might maintain a short timer's calendar, such as the outline of an airplane with numbered blocks to check off or color in.

When counting down, one claims to be a *two-digit midget* when there are 99 and fewer days left on the tour; a *one-digit midget* when there are 9 days and fewer. Those who work around the short timer know if he is just leaving the command and going to a new duty station or taking his discharge and leaving the service. Perceptions vary, but a Marine leaving the service with bad experiences, and perhaps a bad attitude, is worse for morale than one making a move within the Corps.

Other terms, such as *salty*, *John Wayne*, and *gung ho* carry double meanings. Marines do not speak of themselves with these adjectives, but refer to others with them. Usage carries meaning. Gung ho, loosely from the Chinese *to work together*, may still be used in the sense it was first introduced to the Corps, probably during the late 1930s. But one Marine referring to another as being *gungy* (from gung ho) may indicate that he thinks the other works too closely to regulations, tries too hard or does not allow room for personal initiative. Junior Marines who act as if they have learned all there is to learn of the Corps may be described as too salty by peers or seniors.

John Wayne is respected as one of the more admired silver screen ersatz Marines, for roles like that in *The Sands of Iwo Jima*. When a Marine is seen in the field with a helmet on and doesn't have his chin strap snapped, another Marine may ask, "What are you, John Wayne? Button it!" Just because *The Duke* did it in the movies does not mean the troops can do it. *A John Wayne* (or P-38) is also a small, metal can opener once issued with canned combat rations, or "C" rations.

Since "C" rations have been replaced by freeze dried foods called "MREs," (meal, ready-to-eat,) the coming generations of Marines may learn only of "'C' rats" and John Waynes in the history books. However, between my own time in boot camp and early experiences in the field, and the time when MREs were first issued, the John Wayne came to be called *the Clint Eastwood*.

As stories lead to more stories, recall an earlier example of the recruit who supposedly wrote home to his mother: "Dear Mom, I'm writing from a burning tank." Another recruit wrote home while he was in the field that he was eating *sea rats* ("C" rats). His mother made several telephone queries to find out what the Marine Corps was feeding her son.

Getting in trouble, attitudes, the environment

Other domains include words and phrases about how people relate to each other, and how they relate to their surroundings – the Corps and places in the Corps. One category includes taxonomies of "getting into trouble." There is a thin line between explicit and tacit knowledge, or formal and informal use of some of the following terms:

Domain: getting in trouble
Taxonomies of terms about getting in trouble

formal law	Uniform Code of Military Justice (UCMJ)	
	types of non-judicial punishment proceedings	office hours, Article 15
	(equivalent terms)	(of UCMJ), NJP (non-judicial punishment), on the carpet
	judicial proceedings	summary, special and general courts martial
getting busted, losing a stripe	types of punishment	loss of rank, reduction in rank
		loss of pay
		getting fined, forfeiture of pay and

		allowances
	Detention	going to jail, going to the brig, confinement, restriction, extra duty EMI (extra military instruction)
	Discharges	Administrative, DD (dishonorable), BCD (bad conduct), six, six and a kick (forfeiture of six months' pay confinement for six months and a discharge
	terms for more commonly violated article of UCMJ	fraudulent enlistment
		desertion
		unauthorized absence
		absent without leave,
		AWOL, UA (unauthorized absence; unauthorized anything)
		missing ship or movement
		disobedience of orders

		maltreatment
		unlawful disposition of government property theft, destruction
		drunken or reckless driving
		drunk on watch, leaving post without proper relief
		Assault
	the General article, article 134	the catch-all article
		regarding scandalous conduct or conduct prejudicial to good order or discipline (covers fraternization, off-duty employment, etc.)

terms for getting caught, in trouble		a Marine:
medical	short arm inspections getting the clap, drip	leaves fingerprints on the pipes
testing	going UNQ (unqualified)	fails a physical or rifle qualification

	Drinking	getting f***ed up, totaled, wasted, commode-huggin' drunk sh*t-faced
	making mistakes	falling on your sword stepping on your dick, shooting yourself in the foot
punishment	physical discipline	PT them, exercise them, bend and thrust them, drop them (to do pushups), up and shoulder arms, run their dicks in the dirt, run 'em, mountain climbers, incentive PT, pit call, make 'em dig
	send (recruits) to	motivation platoon, the mote' ditch, one-day moto
maltreatment	thumping	hazing, smack, grab, hit, thump, hit upside the head, butt stroke, thrash, tighten up
	counseling	hammer, reprimand, stress,

		stress him out
working	Cleaning	scuzzrag (the barracks polish, spit shine, shine)
getting out of work	a non-performer	skates, slides, hides, goldbricks
threats	I'm going to:	rip (tear) you a new asshole, tighten your ass up you won't be able to sh*t for a week

Table XIX

This rather loose set of taxonomies relating to punishments and getting in or being in trouble is a small sample of the terms Marines used in stories and routine conversation. Some of the terms relating to recruits and maltreatment may fall out of use as pressure continues to be applied to drill instructors to not abuse recruits. Likewise, unauthorized names once used for recruits have all but passed into history, according to the DIs I interviewed.

The meaning inherent in vulgar language in an all-male setting parallels locker room talk in most other all-male settings: athletic teams, for example. Some men posture and emphasize bravado or toughness by using vulgar language. Or, "There are no women around, we can swear." The Marine Corps officially emphasizes that it is unbecoming for a Marine to use vulgar language, and it is in fact against the Uniform Code of Military Justice and the recruit training SOP:

The use of vulgar, obscene, profane, humiliating, or racially or ethnically degrading language to address or refer to a recruit directly or indirectly is prohibited. A recruit will be addressed only by his last name, his rank, or word 'recruit.' The exceptions are that a guide, squad leader, fire team leader, or secretary may be referred to by title.[cdx]

Perspective: Maybe I'm just getting old (and too conservative) – but I am a trained observer. From the experience of serving with a battalion in Iraq on a routine deployment, with some 20 women in the battalion, to working in combatant command headquarters, with a significant percentage of women (military, civil service and civilian contractors) in the office spaces – not only do the men swear comfortably and regularly, but the women do too.

A Marine's environment changes from duty station to duty station and MOS to MOS. Grunts train in the field, remington raiders work in offices. But there are givens that allow a Marine moving to a new duty station to use key words or phrases, not all necessarily unique to the Corps, to find his way around. (For the under-30 crowd, *Remington* was the brand name for a typewriter. For the under 20 crowd, a *typewriter* was a predecessor to a computer. The hard drive was in your head.)

For example, from the taxonomy below, a Marine could ask: "Where is the headshed?" and be directed to the highest echelon headquarters building on the base. At large bases there is usually a central area where are located the headquarters, PX (post exchange), commissary, and many other support units and organizations. Within the PX, or nearby, Marines can expect to find a barbershop, a snack bar (slopchute) where one can buy junk food (pogey bait or gedunk), and so on.

Other givens not listed include: the PMO (provost marshal's office, or military police), the education center and library, the bowling alley, theater and Special Services (usually in or near the gymnasium), where one can check out athletic equipment and make arrangements for tours, or buy tickets for ball games and concerts. (*Now called MWR – Morale, Welfare and Recreation.*)

Certain areas once were *hallowed ground*, such as the married officers housing area: officer country. Enlisted Marines did not drive through the area in years past, partly because most did not have cars.

Now there are signs posted: "Do not enter. Private drive for residents and guests only." There are two points: the signs are often ignored and common knowledge (tacit understanding) should segregate the officers' living areas from the enlisted. Not only do such areas seem to be less segregated now, some bases have all-ranks clubs and swimming pools.

One may argue the lack of enforcement of segregation between officers and enlisted Marines, coupled with the greater mobility of enlisted Marines and the encroachment of civilian communities have had a hand in creating fraternization problems between officers and enlisted Marines. Allow it to be noted that of all the services, the Marine Corps has the strictest prohibitions against relationships between officers and enlisted Marines, and between Marines of different pay grades in the same chain of command or those in student-instructor relationships.

Domain: Places Marines go

Taxonomies of terms for places Marines go	names for the base	places on base
	the base, post, station, depot, camp	PX, barbershop,
		gym, the club, NCO club, Staff NCO club,
		shop, brig, jail, the correctional facility,
		rifle range, parade deck, grinder, head shed
	terms for places at	200-, 300-,500-yard

	the rifle range	line, the butts, the tower, downrange
	terms for living quarters	barn, hootch, the "Q," BOQ (bachelor officers "Q") BEQ, barracks, home, the crib, the house, base housing
	terms for parts or places in a building	deck, port, bulkhead, below, overhead
		the head, pisser, sh*tter,
		ladder, topside, the overhead (ceiling)
		scuttlebutt (drinking fountain)
	terms for the field	the boonies, in the field, in the rear (with the gear), in country
terms for places off base		(back) on the block, out the gate, in the 'ville
	terms for the United States	the world, the real world, stateside, CONUS
	places or duty not in the USA	overseas, PI (the Philippines (also RP), Subic (Bay) Oki,

		Okinawa, the Rock, Gitmo, Guantanamo Rosey Roads, Roosevelt Roads, Puerto Rico, sea duty, embassy duty
	terms for duty stations in the United States	29 Stumps (29 Palms) PI, Parris Island, "Q" Town, Quantico, OCS, boot camp, Triangle, TBS (the Basic School, 8th and "I", D'ego, San Diego, Headquarters, Marine Corps
	in front of everyone	right out in front of God, Corps and country

Table XX

In addition to the knowledge Marines have of their environment, there are certain expectations associated with most duty stations. Marines know that 29 Palms, California, is *in the middle of nowhere*, in the desert. Liberty is not good; one must drive hours to get to Los Angeles, Las Vegas, or other major cities. Likewise, Camp Lejeune, North Carolina, and Yuma, Arizona, are not known for having good off-base liberty, but it depends on what a Marine likes to do with spare time. Some Marines stationed at Camp Lejeune buy boats and go fishing or scuba diving off the coast of North Carolina.

Perspective: With the brief experience of Desert Storm in 1990-'91 and the past ten years in the Global War on Terror, Marines and the other services have added many more place names, like Fallujah, Haditha, Hit, Kabul, Ramadi, Anbar, Kandahar, the Perfume Palace, the Sand Box, and so on. Additionally, Marines have added phrases from the local languages – as noted in previous chapters: emir, shura, jihad, jirga, and many more.

But *good liberty* means different things to different Marines; some prefer hunting and fishing and some prefer the nightclubs of larger cities. Marines receiving orders to Quantico, Virginia, expect to salute "all those new 2nd lieutenants" going to the Basic School. Duty at Headquarters, Marine Corps and in Hawaii are "good if you can afford it," and assignments to Norfolk, Virginia, or coastal California "aren't too bad." But these are broad generalizations, and each duty station has plusses and minuses.

Nautical terms such as *head, port, starboard* and *deck,* etc., emphasize the birth of the Marine Corps mission: providing marksmen aboard ships in the Revolutionary War. Marines have been called *sea-going bellhops* (referring to manner of dress and seeming lack of things to do at sea) and *soldiers of the sea,* but are never soldiers. Soldiers are in the Army. The *Handbook for Marine NCOs* points out: "Never feel self-conscious about using Marine terms. Require that subordinates use them. Accept no substitutes."[cclxi]

During the 1980s junior Marines seemed to be using fewer and fewer nautical terms. *The Edifice Complex* was not designed to quantify this apparent phenomenon.

Domain: Attitudes

Taxonomy of expressions of satisfaction and dissatisfaction	
Observations	
There's a right way, a wrong way and the Marine Corps way.	

We've done so much for so long with so little that now we can do anything with nothing forever.		
First to go, last to know.		
Nobody likes to fight but somebody has to know how.		
Uncle Sam's Misguided Children (USMC)		
descriptive terms expressions	Good	squared away, sh*t hot, sierra hotel (S.H.), ichi ban (number one), career enhancing
	OORAH, or arrugah	compared to the primal scream, a war whoop, an expression of satisfaction OORAH-ish, gung ho or gungy, John Wayne (pronoun) sometimes used sarcastically to describe one who is too squared away but has no quality or substance
	happy	fat, dumb and happy happier 'n a pig in sh*t

	bad	f***ed up, fouled up trashed, wasted, bad attitude, short timer's attitude, doesn't give a sh*t (f***, rat's ass), short, ten percenter unsat, doesn't have a military bone in his body
	belligerent	You confuse me with someone who gives a sh*t
	fear	scared sh*tless
	throwing something away or turning in	survey it, trash it, sh*tcan it
	turn someone in	drop a dime

Table XXI

Taxonomy of parts and places

body parts	head	brain housing group between the running lights (eyes), upside the head

	Neck	Stackin' swivel, grab you by the stackin' swivel
	Teeth	snags, fangs, brush your snags
	hands	meat grabbers, dick skinners, paws
mythical parts, places or things		headspace, flight line
taking things from original owner		cumshaw, borrow, rip off, midnight requisition, relieve something from its owner
take out or open something, put things away or stop		break out (a cold beer, a flag), stow it, stash it, can it

Table XXII

Although a search for etymologies is not a specific purpose of ethnography, it is interesting to note in the above several taxonomies a blend of words and phrases from several subcultures including the native Marine Corps. *Cumshaw* is said to mean something extra or free, from the Chinese words *kamsia* (meaning grateful) and *sia* (meaning thanks). The association between Marines (old China hands) and China (approximately 1898 to World War II) also led to the adoption of *gung ho*. If someone says to *cumshaw* something, he does not want to know where it came from.

Ichi ban, or Japanese for number one, tells of a later association between Marines and Japan following World War II. The relationship continues today with Marines stationed on Okinawa and mainland Japan. Many Marines who have served in the Far East say *domo* or *arigato* for thank you, or *dozo* for please.

Upside the head and *drop a dime* probably find their roots in Black American dialect, and tell of the integration of the Marine Corps in 1942. Millett notes:

> "Blacks were even less welcome than women in the Corps, the Marine Corps having been (unlike the Army and Navy) an absolutely segregated organization."[cclxii]

But as they joined in rising or diminishing numbers throughout the decades, *Dark Green Marines* have helped shape Marine folklore, bringing unique language with them. *This term is not as apparent in everyday language in 2013. A prior Sergeant Major of the Marine Corps recommended the term's retirement, as all Marines are just that: Marines.*

The point of this discussion is that language is pliable, flexible. Almost any culture interacting with another is open to influence from the other. Evidence of this can be found throughout history, especially in the development of American English.

A large part of what contributes to a Marine's self image is his uniform. One of the more recognizable Marine uniforms, known as dress blues, is often seen on posters or in television advertising. Lieutenant Colonel North's appearance during the Contragate hearings also introduced many uninitiated Americans to the service dress green (Winter and Summer service "A") uniform.

To the untrained eye, Marine and Army combat uniforms may appear identical (in the 1980s), yet Marines and soldiers recognize that soldiers wear shoulder patches, slightly different rank insignia, embroidered name tags and "U.S. Army" sewn above their pockets. Soldiers call their combat fatigues **BDUs**, or battle dress uniforms. Marines call theirs *cammies*, short for camouflaged utilities.

Perspective: One could write a book on uniforms alone. Marines and soldiers no longer have "virtually identical" combat utility uniforms. The most notable changes in the past 20 years came about largely as a result of duty in the First Gulf War. Through a series of experiments, and based on recommendations from both Marines and soldiers serving "in the sand box" (with temperatures exceeding 120F), Marines and soldiers have more realistic, more comfortable, camouflage combat utilities as well as "rough out" boots that don't need to be shined. (Oo-rah!)

In 2002, the Marine Corps adopted the digital pixel "MARPAT" or Marine Pattern camouflage combat utilities, in both desert and green. Other services followed with digital patterns, and in 2013 – Congress and the media are asking: "Do we really need 10 different uniforms for the nation's armed forces?"

One symbolic element of Marine uniforms that may also be unrecognized, or not considered by those who are not Marines is that the khaki shirt is the same color as the Navy officer's and chief petty officer's khaki summer working uniforms. Marine trousers are green (although not the same shade of green as current (1980s) Army uniforms). The intentional or unintentional symbolism is that Marines have an amphibious mission, as heralded in the Marine's Hymn: "in the air, on land and sea."

Taxonomies of daily routines

chow, food	where Marines eat	the chow hall mess hall, in the field, the dining facility at home, at the slopchute McDonald's or	in the field, Marines eat: rations, "C" rations, MREs tray

		Burger King, NCO club	packs chow
	where to buy food	slopchute geedunk, PX, commissary	food: chow geedunk, junk food, pogey bait, munchies
Time	military time		0001 is midnight, 0100 is 1 a.m., etc. through1300 is 1 p.m., 1400 is 2 p.m.
	telling time		time on deck is, chow time, chow call, liberty call, on leave, basket leave
	response time		immediately (if not sooner), instant willing obedience to orders, yesterday,
	wasting time		screwing off, talking, flapping your jaws, skating, sluffing off, running your mouth
	officially wasting time		reinventing the wheel, going on a boondoggle, going TAD (temporary

		assigned duty), putting on a dog and pony show
	official time	Commander's time, commander's call
	Financial	fiscal year, also said "physical" year by the uninformed
	Seniority	time in grade, time in service
	old, salty, a long time	since Christ was a corporal
	time on station or tour, duration of duty assignment	short, short timer two-year tour, etc. short tour one, two, etc., days and a hook, ...days and a sea bag drag, I'm so short I had to walk under paint
sleeping	Taps	hit the rack, crash, sleep, "the rack monster got me..."
war		when the balloon goes up when the war starts, when the sh*t hits the fan

pay call	NPD	no pay due
	LES	leave and earnings statement
	BP	base pay
	rats, BAS comrats commuted rations	rations, allowance for subsistence, food
	BAQ (now BAH)	basic allowance for quarters, housing
	hazardous duty pay, combat pay	
	DD	direct deposit
	SRB	selective reenlistment bonus
	pay day	when the eagle sh*ts
	Money	okani, scratch, taksan okani (lots of money)
	loans (between Marines)	40-for-50, 50-for-75
transportation, movement	Vehicles	jeep, six-by(-six), my ride (personal car), POV, military air, MAC flight (military airlift

		command), a hop, HUM-VEE gamma goat, the boat
	Moving	shove off, swoop, depart the area, going ashore
	Parades	troop the line, troop and stomp, romp and stomp
	boarding a vehicle	embark, debark, disembark

Table XXIII

In addition to the topics suggested in the above taxonomies, Marines talk about or tell stories about their jobs, cars, liberty, wives and families, or girlfriends, sex, money (pay raises), and promotions. In earlier taxonomies were listed duty stations and a variety of other topics also open for discussion. Again, hearing a story may not cause any immediate reaction other than another *can-you-top-this* story, but adds to the body of knowledge learned in part through stories. Knowledge prepares the Marine to act later; it predisposes him to accept elements of the story as legitimate symbols or cues to action.

Stories do not have to be true or completely true. Belief is more important than truth. If a Marine believes the Corps is older than the Army, no soldier can convince him otherwise. (*The Army was created in July 1775; the Continental Navy in October 1775. The Continental Marines were formed with a resolution of the Continental Congress, dated 10 November 1775.*) There is no taboo against using someone else's story and embellishing it, even claiming it as one's own. Marines exaggerate.

Stories are used to teach, and may include messages or meaning in leadership principles or traits, or illustrate values or model characteristics such as self-discipline. Junior Marines may learn that they do not tell stories about boot camp or drill instructors in the presence of saltier Marines because the older Marines will scoff them or upstage them. New boot camp stories are less impressive than old boot camp stories, and neither compares to combat stories.

Even when telling stories, conversations will often include a wide variety of uniquely Marine slang or folk terms unintelligible to many civilians but generally decipherable to other militaries.

In addition to presenting the guiding tenets of ethnographic research methods, this chapter's main purpose has been to give the reader a cross section of the Corps' folklore through taxonomic and domain analysis. The domains presented are some of those central to the Corps' culture but are certainly not all of the domains that could be presented. Nor are the taxonomies exhaustive. (*And the symbols, rituals and stories added since the start of combat operations in Afghanistan and Iraq have been filling books and other literature since.*)

The following chapter – the final original chapter – stands as a historical view of the recommendations I made based on my findings. Some of those recommendations have changed – influenced by conversations with other Marines. An update from 2013 follows.

Chapter Ten

<u>Conclusions and Recommendations: 1990</u>

The rationale for presenting theme analysis in this chapter follows from the relationship between the emerging themes and the conclusions of *The Edifice Complex*. The ethnographic process of analyzing taxonomies and domains revealed many terms that are not uniquely Marine, or nautical or military. Some terms suggest civilian, regional or ethnic influence and many of them support the hypothesis that certain elements of the Corps' culture are changing (*a 1989 observation; more on this below.*)

Distinctions might be drawn between regional differences: between a *country* Marine and a *city* Marine (or "*redneck*" Marine and "*Hollywood*" Marine), for example, and differences between a civilianized Marine and a *real* Marine. No matter where a Marine was reared he may be susceptible to indoctrination in the Corps' values. Yet, those who shun most of the influences of the civilian world and accept the military as a calling are far different in their values than those who come to the Marine Corps and stay for the pay or the bonuses.

Some evidence of the conflict between Marine values and civilian values came up in literature review. Some terms uncovered in theme analysis provided additional evidence; and still others surfaced in the search for the causes of change. Preliminary findings presented in the foregoing two chapters led to two sets of important conclusions. Theme analysis, which will be presented first, draws conclusions from ethnographic findings and supplies answers to

377

many of the research questions. An additional, important set of findings may be divided into two sets of grounded theory. Change will be discussed in theme analysis; causes and effects are discussed in theory, following.

<u>Theme analysis</u>

This study of Marine folklore has yielded a number of cultural themes. Some of them recur in two domains; some cover several. I identified the following major cultural themes from each of the domains selected for analysis, from the content analysis of literature about Marines, and through the application of the various research methods detailed in prior chapters:

Concern for authority by senior Marines

Concern for careers by officers

Concern with getting in trouble by junior Marines, including concern for laws or regulations

Time and Money

Women Marines and other minorities

Mission accomplishment

Masculinity, physical prowess, "tough" roles and aggression

The display of discipline and self-discipline

Freedom

<u>Concern for authority</u>

Marines who voiced strongest concern for authority were those who served in Vietnam, or any significant time in the Corps before 1975. Those Marines who served as drill instructors prior to 1975 in particular expressed concern for the perceived authority of the DI. Specifically, there was a perception of dissolution of authority and erosion of trust by seniors in the abilities of non-commissioned officers and staff NCOs.

The concern about rules and regulations points to a parallel observation by those interviewed that the increasing numbers of rules, as in the Standard Operating Procedures for Recruit Training, seem to be imposed to serve the purpose of leadership – replacing individual judgment and decisiveness.

These observations may or may not be quantifiable, or necessarily valid, but they represent the reality of those interviewed. When one feels threatened – in this case, when a Marine feels his authority to command or make decisions is threatened – the principles of cognitive dissonance and justification tell that one must rationalize or justify the end result. One explanation for the imposition of rules perceived by active duty Marines as too restrictive is that if enough rules are written down, those who write the rules "will have everything covered."

According to many of the drill instructors interviewed in 1984, the number of regulations guiding recruit training "multiplied dramatically" after the Ribbon Creek incident, and "multiplied again" following the McClure incident in the mid-1970s. The two reasons given by all drill instructors who discussed the proliferation of regulations were organizational concern for public image and organizational concern for the Congressional action that might be taken if the Corps did not more tightly govern or control recruit training.

The increase in the number of regulations and the drill instructors' attitudes about the changes brought by the new regulations fall into two of the categories of change presupposed in this paper's hypotheses. First is internal planned change as the result of perceived needs. The Ribbon Creek incident was said by many older Marines, drill instructors notably, to have caused the Corps to begin limiting the power of drill instructors.

The *Smokey the Bear* hat (cover) was evidently offered as a symbol of leadership to the brotherhood of drill instructors, emasculated by regulations which severely limited their authority after the Ribbon Creek incident, according to those interviewed.

The second type of change is external planned change. Although not always in response to a perceived need for change, directly or indirectly Congress has imposed or allowed changes that limit decision-making authority of individual Marines. Congressional interest in the Ribbon Creek and McClure incidents did not cause the imposition of new regulations directly. However, interviews with drill instructors and personal experience in Public Affairs at Parris Island tell of the concern for Congressional interest through Congressional investigations, or *congrints*, as they are called by Marines who must respond to them.

A Congressional investigation often ensues after a recruit writes home that he feels he has been wronged. Many recruits are so shaken by the first weeks of boot camp that they are afraid to talk to anyone in their chain of command about a perceived wrong. *This has likely ebbed in the past generation as officers and senior drill instructors now explain to incoming recruits that they are not to be hit or otherwise abused – and to report such incidents if they happen.* Congressional representatives' offices and senior Marines in the chain of command investigate legitimate complaints about such things as hazing or physical abuse. Sometimes recruits' letters home are just misunderstood, even humorous.

Other letters may draw attention to issues that are not real problems, out of a single private's innocent letters – resulting in a regulation that drill instructors see as unnecessary. Examples may include regulations that require recruits to get a certain amount of time to read mail, specifying how many times a day a recruit needs to brush his teeth, how long a meal should last or the prescribed limits of incentive physical training for recruits.

Such regulations limit the drill instructor by denying initiative. The recruit's training day is so tightly planned, in fact, that an unavoidable delay in one training event can delay the rest of the day's activities. Some drill instructors cut corners (use initiative) to make up for lost time. The prevailing attitude at Parris Island in 1984 was that there were so many regulations controlling the drill instructor that one could not help but run afoul of at least one regulation or another in a two-year tour.

Concern for getting in trouble

Many Marines and former Marines pointed to the death of Private McClure in 1975 and the Ribbon Creek incident of 1956 as landmark years leading to the creation of new laws governing recruit training. This cultural knowledge or feeling may be true in part, but did not answer all of the questions about cultural change. Themes relating to masculinity (which may incorporate the use of vulgar language and the tendency to view women as incompatible with military life), aggression and discipline seem to be common to militaries worldwide, especially those considered elite or which consider themselves elite, and notably among enlisted men.

The expansion of regulations and laws, whether from internal or external sources, evidently causes some of the concern for getting in trouble. Regulations and laws also cause a similar reaction in some small number of officers, which is referred to as Concern for Careers, or careerism. As these unknown numbers of officers display this concern, they practice crisis management, micro management or other leadership styles that hinder enlisted leadership and cause enlisted Marines to have concern for getting in trouble.

In summary, the mistakes of some Marines in the past are

major causes of the growth in regulations. These (planned) changes in response to the need to prevent similar mistakes cause changes in the culture and folklore of the Corps—the concern for getting in trouble by enlisted Marines and concern for careers by officers.

(A parallel in the private sector – and government – is the question of whether and how much to regulate banks, private industry, insurance and so on. Some believe less regulation will allow competition and spur positive economic growth; others believe the quest for profits will harm consumers and damage economic growth.)

Concern for careers

Although I did not interview Marine officers (in the 1980s) for the most part, some clues about their images of the Corps did surface. For example, whereas officers may also express masculinity, aggression and discipline in their folklore, there seems to be just as much or more concern among some officers for their careers and personal financial matters, as well as the expression, affectation or articulation of gentlemanly qualities and intelligence.

The literature and interviews suggest officers are expressing serious concerns with careers and career patterns. Far-reaching legislation in the 1980s years dramatically altered how officers view their careers, chances for promotions and choice assignments. Notable concerns are that the *professional soldier* has been replaced by a government functionary who fills a job, instead of a career or a calling. One source of this change in officer attitudes is DOPMA, or the Defense Officer Procurement and Management Act, which dictates when officers must leave the service if not promoted, among other things.

Some view the *up or out* policy of DOPMA as a hindrance to maintaining a seasoned officer corps. One answer to this is that the program ensures that the services aren't bogged down by officers who do not progress, improve or qualify for promotion. The resulting concern for careers is good on the one hand, as it causes officers to continue to try to improve themselves and groom for promotion and command. However, some officers allow their quest for success to get in the way of accomplishing unit missions, or prevent enlisted Marines from exercising leadership at their levels. This concern was included because of its effect on the enlisted culture, which in its manifestation is an unplanned internal change.

Time and Money

As for Time and Money, this theme as an end result of research seems to be reflective of genuine change in Marine Corps culture. Changes in the ways Marines view time and money also seem to be causes for other changes – in attitudes of allegiance to the Corps, competition between the Corps and family, personal life, etc.

As previously discussed, Marines have more disposable income today than did Marines of generations past, and enlisted Marines in particular seem to be concerned with how to spend their incomes – often on cars – and their time, usually off base. The phenomenon of civilian communities crowding Marine Corps and other services' bases means that it's now a short drive out the gate to liberty in a civilian community.

Parris Island, for example, was once connected to the South Carolina mainland only by barge or ferry. Now there is a bridge, and the usual motels, convenience stores, fast food restaurants, night clubs and pawn shops within five minutes of the gate to Parris Island.

From 1775 to about World War I, enlisted Marines did not earn more than $100 a month. Privates in 1990 earned nearly $700 monthly and senior enlisted Marines earn more than $2500 a month. Bonuses for reenlistment in certain job skills could exceed $20,000 in a career.

Base pay for a private in 2013 is $1516 per month. Top pay for a *master gunnery sergeant or sergeant major (E-9) is $7435 per month (at 40 years of service). Many Marines who hang on to military life as a first career will retire (go on retainer) between 20 and 30 years. Monthly pay for E-9 retiring at 30 is $5057. Bonuses: Most Zone A Bonuses are capped at $40,000. Zone A bonuses are for Marines who (at the time of reenlistment) have between 17 months and 6 years of service. The Marine Corps pays their reenlistment bonuses in a lump sum. Reenlistment bonuses are subject to taxes unless the member reenlists in a tax-free combat zone (Certain "low density/high demand jobs," such as explosive ordnance technicians, nuclear power technicians (in the Navy), and cryptologic technicians can qualify for as much as $90,000 in reenlistment bonuses. In 1973 – a king's ransom.*[cclxviii]

Time and Money as a theme, spoken in the words and phrases of everyday life, is the result of unplanned evolutionary change. The desire to increase standards of living is commendable, but the challenge to maintain an All-Volunteer Force in the face of competition for recruits from industry and higher education has led to an almost mercenary service.

Combine the increase in pay with closer civilian communities and the lost practice of requiring liberty cards for junior enlisted Marines and the end result is a generation of Marines who seem to view their time in the Corps as a job that one leaves at the end of the work day. Older Marines claim they were Marines 24 hours a day, they did not leave base even for entertainment, and developed a closer small unit camaraderie – an important factor in fighting as a team when they went into combat. The resulting cultural changes were unplanned, stemming from both internal and external causes.

Women Marines and other minorities

There is also evidence of a separate, fully defined cultural theme regarding attitudes toward women, but the evidence is neither clear nor complete in this study. However, male Marines now seem reluctant to discuss women Marines. The notion that women do not belong in the culture is strong, but is evidently waning somewhat because of similar relaxing attitudes about women in the civilian sector. Again, the numbers of Women Marines are proportionately small compared to other armed forces. Women seem to be accepted on a case-by-case basis, shop to shop, unit to unit. When a woman proves herself, she is accepted. The prevailing undercurrent, however, still suggests that some men believe women do not belong in the armed forces.

Personal observation and the findings of this study reveal that non-white racial ethnic groups, especially Blacks, have been largely assimilated into mainstream Marine Corps culture. The animosity evident through the later 1960s and into the mid-1970s seems to have dissipated measurably. Racist undercurrents did not surface during this study, but reports of Marines and soldiers stationed at bases in North Carolina participating in Ku Klux Klan rallies represent a very small percentage of Marines, reflective of the American culture as a whole.[cclxiv] This does not suggest that personal and cultural prejudices are nonexistent, but more than ever, Black Marines, for example, are just "dark green Marines," or just Marines, rather than "Blacks," in contrast to the 1960s. (*Keep in mind that this was the prevailing language of the culture when I collected data through the 1980s.*)

The introductions of women and Blacks into Marine Corps service were both planned external changes. Contrary to the other types of causes and effects, these planned external changes probably had the most observable effect on the informal folklore of enlisted Marines, even though the changes altered the formal structure of Marine Corps culture. As in civilian society, the acceptance of women and Blacks into white, male roles has not been an easy transition. Indeed the transition is not complete, for either women or Blacks.

Mission accomplishment

As a cultural theme, mission accomplishment must be

mentioned, even though it is more rightly a theme belonging to the formal culture rather than having emerged from the study of informal culture. Recall however that senior officer and enlisted Marines are seen as representing the official culture of the Corps; they are the Marines who express most concern for accomplishing the mission.

A mission, like a goal, may be divided into many small segments (*tactical* elements as part of *operational* plans – within broader *strategic* plans). Junior Marines accomplish small missions, and working together are responsible for the collective accomplishment of larger missions. But the *idea* of a mission is large. Senior Marines, drill instructors, for example, talk about training recruits as a mission. Junior Marines usually talk in terms of their *job*, although a mission may indeed be as small as guarding a post.

The concept of *mission* was spoken of many times by drill instructors who felt they were restricted from accomplishing their mission of recruit training by suffocating regulations and the consequential threat of punishment for not accomplishing the same mission. Those who had been in combat felt that on the smaller scale, their mission in Vietnam was clearer – to kill Viet Cong and North Vietnamese regular soldiers – than training recruits.

Masculinity and aggression

In the film *Anybody's Son Will Do* is a segment about recruits at pyrotechnics class during field training week. The drill instructor talks about *Susie rotten crotch* and blood, guts and death. Many instructors will add graphic descriptions of how to kill the enemy in order to fire up a class of recruits, with phrases like, "Rip out his eyes, slit his guts open, slash him, kick him, cut him a new smile, etc."

The result is usually a cheering, yelling crowd of temporarily blood-thirsty 18-year-old boys, many of whom have never even been in a fist fight. One effect is to keep recruits awake in class. Another effect is getting Marines inured to killing or the taking of human life in the cause of freedom. Epithets against the enemy, cultural and military patriotism and the constant exposure to the ways and purposes of infantry combat accomplish this desensitizing.

The daily concern with masculinity and aggression is often displayed on the T-shirts Marines wear while in civilian clothes. The lists above tell just some of the epithets related to physical strength, war, death and destruction. But Marines are as diverse as their civilian counterparts: some Marines are gentle, Bible-toting, mother-loving and quiet. They may even be infantry Marines. Men like them fought in past wars, many bravely to be sure.

A number of related circumstances lead many Marines to continually display their own physical masculinity. One is the understandable requirement by the Marine Corps for Marines to remain physically fit. But the tacit understanding that Marines are *supposed to be* big and strong leads many Marines to athletic teams, body building and weight lifting for off-duty activities. I would propose that probably a higher percentage of Marines take part in organized athletics, including martial arts, running (5k through marathon, ultra-marathon and triathlons), weight lifting and body building than a random civilian organization of the same size. (*Although as the master gunnery sergeant noted in an earlier chapter, this is likely diminishing as younger Marines enter the Corps with a penchant for social media and spend more time on Facebook and video games than in the gym.*)

Display of discipline and self-discipline

In virtually all daily routines, the concept of discipline is a theme guiding personal attitudes and actions. If one gets in trouble, he did not exercise self-discipline; he must be disciplined by someone in authority. When one has a mission to accomplish, self-discipline (perseverance) is the motivating force. Whether in parades or just walking across the street a Marine is expected to demonstrate military comportment, a function of the discipline of training. The concept is broad, coloring a Marine's every waking hour.

The change in the 1980s seems to stem from the flowing and ebbing tide of liberal civilian attitudes, the informality of the *call-me-Jimmy* Carter presidential administration. Although drill instructors claim recruits are no longer fully disciplined in boot camp – "as they once were" – one can be sure that senior enlisted Marines and officers will stop junior enlisted Marines who do not display proper military courtesies or who are slack in their attitudes about military bearing, wearing of the uniform, and so on.

With Commandant General Gray, there seemed to be a continuing reversal of the lax attitude of the late 1970s. The changes in discipline are evolutionary, unplanned, internal changes which result from other planned or unplanned internal or external changes. In general, however, the increased concern over discipline by senior enlisted Marines is directly related to the perceived decreased control over enlisted Marines in boot camp and later. Decreased control is tied to the increase in free, uncontrolled time enlisted Marines have after work, their money and mobility, and the encroachment and influence of civilian communities.

Perspective: That was 1987. Consider this look back on Gray from civilian authors in the realm of organizational development:

When Alfred M. (Al) Gray Jr. became commandant (the highest-ranking officer) of the U.S. Marine Corps in 1987, most knowledgeable observers believed that the Corps's fabled "warrior spirit" culture was already damaged beyond repair. During the Korean and Vietnam Wars, the Corps had grown from its historic level of 75,000 regulars to more than 200,000, and its values and discipline had eroded. It would have been easy for Gray to blame the damaged organizational culture for the problems he inherited, and to launch a formal, full-scale change initiative. But instead, he began to praise and seek out elements of the old Corps culture, such as its ethic of mutual respect. For example, he regularly slipped into the mess halls without insignia, so he would be served the same meals as the privates. To this day, Al Gray is the only Marine Corps commandant portrayed in battle fatigues in his formal portrait in the Pentagon. He is one of the most respected leaders in the Marines' 250-year history.

Leaders like Gray understand the value of an organization's culture. This can be defined as the set of deeply embedded, self-reinforcing behaviors, beliefs, and mind-sets that determine "how we do things around here." People within an organizational culture share a tacit understanding of the way the world works, their place in it, the informal and formal dimensions of their workplace, and the value of their actions. Though it seems intangible, the culture has a substantial influence on everyday actions and on performance.[cdxv]

Freedom

If there is a cultural theme that comes close to being universal in the Marine Corps, it's *Freedom*. Young men (and presumably some women) enlist to be free of dad and mom, of the small town life, of the decision to go to college. Recruits can't wait to get free of boot camp and their drill instructors. Marines can't wait to get free of a day's work so they can tend to their wives, girlfriends or cars.

But Marines also speak grandly of freedom in Mission Accomplishment: to keep the world free for democracy, for freedom and the American way. An earlier discussion presented the idea that Marines fight for freedom from the horrors of combat.

It is a natural instinct of man to want to belong to a group. It is just as natural for man to fight to defend his personal freedoms in their many forms. Parallel to the conflict in *The Edifice Complex* – that conflict between older and younger Marines – is the conflict between wanting to belong to a group and wanting freedom. After a Marine has drawn the boundaries around himself and included himself *within* the Marine Corps, he may then remember the sayings presented in other discussions in this book: "For those who fight for it, Freedom has a flavor the protected will never know," and "The more you sweat in peace, the less you bleed in war."

Analysis

As Spradley suggests, cultural themes connect domains. Elements from the theme of Discipline recur in the themes of Time and Money, Concern for Authority and Getting in Trouble. That is, a Marine can be disciplined by taking away his time (freedom) or his money, or both. Authority and discipline may seem to have a simple cause-effect relationship but the evidence separates them.

First, Marines tend to view themselves as having moved from discipline to self-discipline, which follows from the informal hypotheses in prior chapters – suggesting that training should lead one through externally imposed discipline to self-discipline. Second, authority is not just the responsibility to administer discipline, but encompasses the rights of initiative and decision making.

If a Marine errs and is seen as needing discipline after boot camp, the perception is that a lack of self-discipline caused the infraction. Another view is that committing an offense represents a disregard for authority. But, respect for authority is only one expression of self-discipline. The two are therefore presented as separate themes.

Other domains interlinked within themes include *Places Marines go, Getting in Trouble* and *Attitudes*. When asked "What are some places Marines go?" Many Marines included *the brig*. Someone "goes to the brig," or "goes to jail." Discipline and Authority link the two. In Attitudes, someone who is *unsat* is seen as undisciplined (usually) and should eventually be discharged.

Marine Corps time and money are also paired. Many senior enlisted Marines and officers sign custody cards when taking responsibility for government property. There is an overriding concern with the fiscal year (and dollars) when transferring people and ordering supplies (when does this year's money run out?). Marines frequently discuss time in rank and time in service, pay scales, bonuses and pay raises. And, although many civilian organizations and businesses transfer people to new assignments occasionally, the military services always transfer people after two to four years in a particular assignment. Transfers often coincide with promotions, prevent Marines from stagnating in one job or location, and provide opportunities for breadth and depth of experience.

Aggression and the expressions of masculinity also recur in several domains. Because additional themes would probably emerge through additional research, there is little doubt that large complex matrices could be drawn showing recurring themes across many domains. The case has been made, however, and leads to other conclusions of this study.

Research Questions

Originally I worked under the hypothesis: "The influx of new recruits is the major cause of cultural changes and cultural conflicts in the Marine Corps." In-depth research proved this wrong, but led to research questions:

- Are there other ways civilian society causes change in the Corps' culture?
- Are there other external causes of change in Marine Corps culture?

Each of these has been answered in the affirmative through the presentation of evidence in previous chapters. As I reviewed the raw data collected for *The Edifice Complex* over a three-year period in the mid- to late 1980s, cause-effect relationships between folklore and culture were more narrowly defined. That is, folklore reflects culture, thus cultural changes cause changes in folklore.

I support the concept that folklore serves as a behavior shaping tool. But folklore is handed down within the Corps, and changes in folklore are not generally seen or felt by outsiders. Civilians would not recognize that elements of folklore express diminishing trust in the authority of officers and staff non-commissioned officers, for example. Marines, however, have expressed feelings or opinions that there is something to demonstrate that the Marine Corps has changed. The hypotheses of *The Edifice Complex* identify *that something* as folklore. The taxonomies and domains include dozens of terms that indicate many changes, as suggested in the cultural themes listed.

Perspective: While this surfaces in other areas of the book, one most important, tangible difference between the late 1980s and 2013 is that the Marine Corps was not engaged in combat in the late 1980s. When there's no war to fight and the armed forces are perceived as "sitting around like an enormous insurance policy," it seems like there's nothing for officers and staff NCOs to do except to focus on training, deployments, staff work and inspections. Now that we've been engaged in combat operations for more than 10 years, combat serves as its own training venue and senior Marines don't have to worry about whether junior Marines have shined their boots. The raison d'etre that comes from serving in combat has erased the ennui of the 1980s.

For example, Marines use terms such as *my room*, or *my ride*, in the 1970s and '80s. These are symbols of independence, rather than terms like *the squadbay*, or *our barracks*, where many junior Marines lived together in one large room, depended on each other in the past and trusted each other for the security of their few valuables. Cars (a ride or a *set of wheels*) have increasingly filled parking lots around enlisted barracks during the most recent generations, but it was uncommon for especially junior enlisted Marines to own cars in the 1950s and 60s.

Marines do not use liberty cards (a pass to get off and back on base for free time after work) anymore. When work is over now, many Marines drive out the gate for entertainment or to go home. It is as if the Marine Corps is just a job. (*remember: a 1989-'90 observation...*)

To return to what civilians do not see, it is as if folklore supplies *public service announcements* as window dressing to the Edifice. The window dressing, or public perception of the Corps, is usually shaped by the Marine Corps. The edifice (the outside view looking in) changes slowly compared to the changes actually occurring within the culture, thus the mystique of Marine recruit training has survived despite major changes in the Corps since the 1940s. Civilian images of the Marine Corps in the late 1980s have probably remained fairly stable compared with public perceptions of the Corps in the 1920s or '30s, with some notable exceptions.

First, with the Korean War, then to a far greater degree during Vietnam, the unpopularity of the on-going military conflict and civilian demonstrations in opposition to the war shaped public perceptions of the military. Through the political coincidences and accidents of history, the United States has not been in a declared war since World War II. Widespread use of television, then satellite communications followed World War II. Television and satellite-transmitted news stories and photographs told Americans at least as much about Vietnam as they wanted to know. Both later wars, in Korea and Vietnam, were fought far from the spiritual and ethnic homeland of most of America's ancestry – Europe.

So whereas it may be moot whether mass communication, the location of the conflicts in Asia or the judgments of civilians of the justness of the Vietnam War swayed public opinion, it may be argued that Marines and soldiers were not highly regarded; enlisting voluntarily was not a widely accepted career option during Vietnam. Civilians saw the ugly realities of war; they heard stories, and whether the war in Vietnam was right or wrong, the news about friendly and enemy body counts and deaths of Vietnamese civilians overshadowed the Corps' advertising. A story about enlisting 90 percent high school graduates would have been lost on the back page of the newspaper in 1968. Much of what civilians saw of Marine Corps folklore was that which civilian reporters gave them via television.

War is no longer something Marines can conduct on their own private battlefields far away. Experiences in Lebanon in the early 1980s have again proved that. Reporters travelled freely to the Marine compound in Beirut. This time the enemy was *the ragheads*, equating to Iran, Iranian and other Muslim-backed enemies of peace in Lebanon, the capture of Americans and the desecration of the embassy in Tehran in 1979. Although Marines remain generally a-political through time, the vengeance of the loss of lives and the national humiliation of the military formed a natural enemy. Middle Easterners were different enough from the cultural European ancestry to help popularize the Marines' efforts in Beirut.

The Reagan administration's coup in Grenada was to keep the assault secret from civilian journalists, but in the end a pool of journalists was created so civilian media could cover future conflicts to which American forces are deployed. Again, public opinion was generally favorable because the mission was to ward off communism; and, it was successful.

Sergeant Lonetree's fiasco in the embassy in Moscow, in which he was court-martialed for fraternizing with Soviet women, not reporting contacts with suspected KGB agents, and reportedly allowing Soviet citizens' access to sensitive areas of the American embassy, died a relatively quiet death in the media. The story gained less attention than it might have because there was evidently no significant compromise of classified information and Lonetree's trial came when LtCol North's Contragate testimony was being broadcast live across the United States. Whether North's story offset Lonetree's is immaterial insofar as Lonetree's errors blemished the Corps' reputation.

Marines in public affairs still have an impact on how civilians view Marines and the Corps. It is often the case that the ones who make contact with civilian media through public affairs are the ones who are in a position to protect the interests of the Corps. A newspaper story will illustrate:

These guys are the front line, and they know it to their souls. They're young, ready for a fight, for combat, macho. They're trained to keep the peace and, with a fire the other services don't have, they learn how to kill. They're the Marines, they're the Corps. For some of them, the Marine image is a matter approaching fanaticism. They believe mystique, pride and honor must surround the Marine mission, and they're basking in the patriotic warmth sparked by Lebanon and Grenada. But for the Corps, as for its brother services, the first decade of an all-volunteer force was a trying experience that was seldom kind to that spit-and-polish image. [cclxvi]

This macho image of the Corps is easy for the Corps to feed to a civilian reporter, especially in the aftermath of positive public attitudes about the United States in Grenada and Lebanon. The generally positive civilian attitudes and media attention gave the Corps an opportunity to point to its recruiting successes while it was in the spotlight. When reporters make contact with Marine Corps public affairs, the Marine is not likely to discuss the fact that enlisted Marines do not use liberty cards anymore, or that some Marines tend to think of the Corps as a job (and the variety of other conflicts and changes discussed in this study). Reporters may also discover that new barracks are being built, with three- and four-man rooms and lounges with cable television, but would not be aware of the sociological impact of the new housing. *Honestly – I don't think*

Marines use the word "macho" much in 2013.

In all fairness it must be noted that in the 1980s many Marines lived in barracks built in the late 1930s and 1940s; their barracks have needed refurbishing or replacement for decades. The point made in this study is that moving Marines into small rooms divides small units into clusters of young men who then seem to show less unit esprit or individual responsibility for their fellow Marines – relative to the small unit camaraderie of a generation past.

(On the other hand: It's 20 years later and Marines are engaged in combat. The successes of Marines and Marine units in Iraq, Afghanistan and other hotspots around the globe, on a tactical level, suggest that "small unit cohesion" is alive and well. I would attribute this to successful leadership – by non-commissioned officers in particular, but senior NCOs and officers generally. The positive aspects of providing Marines with "dormitory rooms" and a measure of privacy have apparently overcome most of the negative aspects of losing "the barracks." The master sergeant introduced in earlier chapters suggests that repeated deployments and solid leadership provide ample "small unit cohesion," and that the amenities of 2-man rooms offer a much needed break from "the sandbox.")

Crichton's story also quotes enlisted Marines and officers referring to the recruit deaths of Ribbon Creek and 1975 and 1976 as part of the reason for horror stories about boot camp. The purpose of the story, however, seems to be to illustrate how the Marine Corps is changing or has changed – for the better – because of the input of a large percentage of high school graduates. But the issue of the value of a high school graduation is not clear. Those who direct the enlisting of new Marines tend to insist that having completed high school serves as an indicator of tenacity and trainability. Those who train Marines – DIs – generally agree, but also feel that in the past 10 to 15 years (1975-90) their authority over recruits has been diminished by burdensome regulations.

Perspective: On a deeper level, this issue/concept/discussion gets to organizational psychology and the questions of freedom and control. More freedom (less regulation) leads to greater innovation and the possibility of results far beyond what may have been possible in a "regulations restricted" environment. Some may be wildly profitable; some may be disastrous.

Take this a step further. Without allegory or a stretch of the imagination, if as a parent of teenagers (lots of Marines are teenagers) I impose NO restrictions and offer only the most cursory of guidelines – the potential results are unpredictable. Some succeed wildly; some are average; some fail. And the real question gets to my personal evaluation of how well I have educated, trained, influenced my teens before I cut them loose with little supervision and ample opportunity to innovate. I have three teenagers at home.

Because of the push for Marines with higher technical proficiency, the Corps will continue to advertise for high school graduates; the diploma will continue to serve as a symbol of trainability. It will be up to the internal pressures of the Corps, centered in the echelons of enlisted leaders, to regain the prestige and authority of the drill instructor.

Further, a diploma symbolizes education and intelligence, whereas the values of the old Corps center on combat, discipline and self-discipline, initiative and unselfishness. The strongest values of the old Corps focus on brotherhood, as evidenced in the value placed on saving another man's life by awarding medals. The Medal of Honor, the United States' highest military honor, is awarded for acts of heroism that directly or indirectly save other men's lives.

Many older Marines pointed out that the changing character of war and the so-called softening ("wuss-ification" in 2013) of civilian society combine to produce Marines who may not be able to withstand a protracted war. The changing character of war was realized in Vietnam, during which Marines were sent overseas for a year-long tour of duty. Some returned to Vietnam voluntarily, but for many getting the tour out of the way was a ticket to a stateside tour for the remainder of the war.

Prior to Vietnam, Marines trained and fought in both small and large units that remained together as units for the duration. Esprit de Corps was evident on many levels. It is not unusual to find an older Marine veteran who served in just one Marine division for his entire career. During the 1980s, the Corps recognized the relatively positive effects of keeping units together and began a unit rotation system that transferred entire battalions from Camp Lejeune, North Carolina, to Okinawa, Japan; or from Okinawa to Camp Pendleton, California.

Considering the positive bonding effects of small unit cohesion, one must also recognize that all Marines who fought in World War II and Korea lived through the Great Depression of the 1930s. Older Marine veterans point out that those who endured the hardships of the Depression were far better prepared for combat and military life in the 1940s and '50s than the teenage boys of this generation.[cclxvii]

The older Marines question: "How many of today's young men entering the service have worked a day in the fields? On an oil rig, in a quarry, a foundry, or steel mill? How many have gone a day without a meal, without shoes, without a shopping mall, a Pepsi or a video game?

Older generation Marines see a disparity between the old Corps and the values of young Marines in the mid-1980s. Very few of that decade's younger Marines had been in combat, and certainly not for sustained periods. The Marine mission remains combat. At the Russell Conference on Leadership (1981), Lieutenant General Carey quoted Army General Douglas MacArthur in his welcoming address:

Duty, Honor, Country: The code which these words perpetuate embraces the highest moral laws, and will stand the test of any ethics or philosophies ever promulgated for the uplift of mankind. Its requirements are for the things that are right; and its restraints are from those things that are wrong. Your mission remains fixed, determined, inviolable—it is to win wars.[cclxviii]

General Carey does not indicate that a Marine's mission is to get a high school or college education, although the Marine Corps is keen on individual Marines continuing their education in civilian and military studies. A military force that is effective in combat has always had strong leadership and strong unit identity. Increasingly over the past several decades, the ways to win wars have included the use of complex weapons systems. Insofar as the statement "every Marine a rifleman" holds true, the need for a high school diploma is not essential; infantry Marines with rifles have in the past been able to operate without a high school diploma. *(But because the Corps can enlist virtually 100 percent high school grads – it's a bonus.)*

The Corps as a culture has heretofore been ultimately successful in indoctrinating its men and women with the will to fight a perceivable enemy in the name of symbols: the man in the next foxhole, mom and apple pie; truth, justice and the American way, the flag. This indoctrination cannot be lost while seeking to recruit and train Marines who are proficient in an ever-more technically oriented battlefield. The missions of the Corps are still to deter aggression, and fight and win wars if necessary. Because of the changing character of war, the trend for individual Marines in 1990 may be toward seeing their mission as operating a piece of equipment. For as long as Marines can remember, the calling card of the Marine Corps has been that "every Marine is a rifleman."

It remains imperative for the Marine Corps to continue to indoctrinate and socialize Marines in the cultural mindset of "every Marine a rifleman." Training men for combat requires redefining them, legitimizing them, making them *not civilian*. For Marines, redefinition is equivalent to making them unique. Based on the evidence in this paper, Marines could be losing their uniqueness.

Perspective: Maybe…not so fast. The Marine Corps – Marine folklore and culture – have staying power. Resilience. I don't have the details, but some years ago "someone" thought it would be a grand cost-cutting idea to have Marines and soldiers all wear the same camouflage uniforms. They did – for a while. The Army (four times larger than the Marine Corps) put their soldiers in brown skivvy shirts. Marines moved from white to green skivvy shirts. "Someone" in Washington pushed the Corps into brown skivvy shirts. For a while. And eventually all of this dissolved when the Marine Corps fielded its own trademarked "Marine Pattern" (MarPat) camouflage pattern (with green skivvy shirts).

Too – as noted earlier, the Corps has once again been sucked into the role of being America's second army, with Marine units rotating in and out of Iraq and Afghanistan on (usually) repeated seven-month deployments. The current presidential administration's promise to end the war in Afghanistan (and the mounting economic burden of American debt) will undoubtedly have the Marine Corps facing cutbacks in end-strength (reported in the neighborhood of 180,000 to even 150,000 – down from about 205,000) and working to re-define our mission into the coming decades of the 21st Century. As for the perceived differences between Marines of a past generation and today's Marines, today's Marines are doing just fine.

Changes in the technical landscape of the battlefield always come with the next war – the Gatling Gun in the Civil War, the airplane and chemical warfare in World War I, the submarine, radar, sonar, aircraft carriers and atom bombs in World War II, jet aircraft in the Korean War, drones in Yemen, Afghanistan, Iraq and elsewhere. Despite the gradual removal of the soldier from the battlefield, there remains a need for infantry troops who can face the enemy and fight as a team. We may have Predator drones, but eventually – someone will need to kick in someone's door. If it's not Special Forces teams, it's often United States Marines. In a sense, the Corps takes teenagers from a technological society and molds at least the grunts, the foot soldiers, in principles of war little changed in hundreds of years.

On the one hand, the Corps cannot avoid reflecting civilian society because its recruits come from the larger society, are trained to protect it and is controlled by a civilian government in this society. On the other hand, the Corps must maintain, and be allowed to maintain, its own values, but within tolerances acceptable to the larger society, in part to make service life attractive to recruits. It is recognized inside and outside the Corps that the military is not, cannot and should not be a democracy, that people lose some civil rights when they enlist (or are drafted).

In a final essay in the proceedings of the Russell Conference, Major General Schulze wrote:

> *The act of disobeying a lawful order in a combat situation is dreaded by professional military people because it is a fatal breakdown in discipline. It reflects the collapse of an individual's subordination to authority and the ultimate undermining of unit cohesion....If people are taught to think of service as just another job through the use of materialistic inducements they must inevitably shift their outlook toward it from one of self-sacrifice to one of self-service.*[cdxix]

It is natural for young Marines to display symbols of their macho subculture, but the older generation of Marines was concerned about how the coming generation would carry themselves in combat. Senior enlisted Marines and officers who were willing to discuss these concerns recognize the changes discussed in *The Edifice Complex*, such as the apparent breakdown in unit cohesion brought by hotel-style barracks, the diminishment of authority, initiative and control over discipline because of changes in regulations, the potential to view the Corps as a job because of higher pay, bonuses, increases in enlisted marriages and the encroachment of civilian communities near military bases.

Older Marines who toe the party line of good news in the interest of public relations and recruiting mask the problems with stories about percentages of high school graduates enlisted, new barracks, or the creation of jobs for civilians in the defense industry.

In the interests of the Corps' culture, the high school graduate cannot be allowed to see his place in the Marine Corps as just a job. Even in peace time, drill instructors have been able to inspire belief in the Corps and its missions in recruits. Marines must continue that belief with the same fiery determination to win wars and accomplish missions after boot camp, and shun the 9-to-5 attitude. Those who leave the service after three, four or five years will return to a civilian "normalcy" as countless thousands have done in generations past.

Conclusions

Folklore as a behavior shaping tool

Consider Marine recruit training in strictly behavioral psychology terms: A recruit steps off the bus and stands "like a civilian," says, "yeah" instead of "Yes sir," looks directly without deference into the eyes of the drill instructor and says, "you" and "I" several times. All are faults because the slovenly civilian who thinks he wants to be a Marine is a "poor excuse for a human being" and "has no right to an identity." All such behaviors and attitudes must be extinguished and replaced by a Marine identity with respect and deference for rank and authority, and with military bearing. Errors lead to punishments.

Drill instructors effectively use psychology to extinguish unwanted civilian behavior; such behavior is no longer reinforced as it was by peers in the civilian society. A variety of punishments and rewards serve to replace civilian behavior with acceptable military behavior.

Negative reinforcement works with indoctrination when recruits strive to perform at their best to avoid aversive ingredients such as displeased drill instructors, "incentive" physical training or some other aversive ingredient.

Positive punishments work with negative reinforcement throughout training, but particularly in the first phase or first three weeks, as drill instructors scream at recruits to extinguish unwanted civilian behaviors. (*Positive* indicates an aversion is *added* to the environment. Negative indicates something, like free time, is removed.) The DIs interviewed for this original study acknowledged they are putting on an act, screaming, during the manic first week of training, but are quite effective in getting recruits to stop referring to themselves as "I," and the drill instructor as "you;" slouching, and other unacceptable behaviors. And they don't actually believe the private is a "poor excuse for a human being" with "has no right to an identity." The concept is used to shock recruits into paying attention to what will be demanding, stressful training.

Positive reinforcement takes hold in training when correct behaviors and responses earn grudging approval or acknowledgment from the drill instructor. For example, a drill instructor will acknowledge only perfection in a drill step, a well-made *rack*, a properly folded shirt, etc. Early in training the only external reinforcements a recruit seems to experience are punishments and the reward of avoided punishments. Internally the recruit faces cognitive dissonance – the "Why am I here, what am I doing?" thoughts that must go through a large percentage of recruits' minds. But the acquisition of symbols by the platoon (always as a team first) begins to shape the platoon. Resolution of cognitive dissonance for the recruit must come as part of a team. The answer to "Why am I here?" comes in a form of: "To help the platoon avoid doing incentive PT, or to avoid the drill instructor's wrath." "Why am I here?" is replaced with "Why are *we* here?"

At first the platoon has a number, thus an identity. Recruits discover their DI has a tough reputation among recruits in other platoons, so they are seen as tougher by proximity. They are allowed a *body count* or *sound off*: The DI says, "Sound off!" and the platoon responds with something like, "Sir! 65 Hiiiiighly Motivated, Hiiiiighly Dedicated, screaming, teaming, steak-fed, beer-cooled, rompin', stompin', blood- thirsty, little green amphibious monsters – SIR!" The purpose is for the DI to keep track of how many recruits he has in his charge.

At the rifle range, recruits make a range flag with symbols of death, superior marksmanship and the Marine Corps. If they fail as a team, their drill instructors may take away their flag (their identity). Taking away symbols serves as a negative punishment.

Boot camp is a school of behavior modification through operant conditioning. Whereas recruit training may also be viewed in other psychological constructs—cognitive, psychoanalytic, gestalt— each in its own way is incomplete in explaining the causes for changes in behavior or predicting the consequences of behavior modification.

Social and behavioral psychology combined

By combining social and behavioral psychology, one comes to understand changes in the Marine psyche during the past 40 years. Principles of social psychology have been discussed. As for behavioral psychology, Skinner offered the following principles which, to me, *complement* social psychology:

1. The very substitution of positive reinforcement for aversive control is at the heart of the struggle for freedom.

2. A second principle in improving the control of people is the avoidance of contrived reinforcers.

3. Behavior which consists of following rules is inferior to behavior shaped by the contingencies described by the rules.

4. Control of people by people is likely to be disturbed by 'noncontingent' reinforcers.

5. A social environment is extraordinarily complex, and new members do not come prepared with appropriate behavior.[cclxx]

Positive reinforcement

Regarding the first, the struggle of recruit training is a recruit's struggle for freedom. The principles of cognitive dissonance suggest that peer pressure and justification (internal and external) and the hard facts of a legal contract prevent most recruits from giving up the quest to *get out the gate*. While temporarily abandoning that larger freedom, the recruit is fighting day by day for small freedoms – positive reinforcement to replace the aversive control of the drill instructor.

The life or death fight for freedom in combat is not just a fight for freedom and the American way, but a fight for personal freedom from the aversions of combat – death. Recruit training is supposed to reflect combat; it is combat training in the most basic form. Evidence suggests that older Marines view recruit training as less and less a reflection of combat. Boot camp must prepare the man mentally to react instinctively in combat; the Marine must be self-disciplined; he must respect authority. Even in garrison, Marines are expected to conduct themselves with evidence of self-discipline and respect for authority; it becomes a way of life.

Contrived reinforcers

Second, primary contrived reinforcers in the Marine Corps

are money, time and awards such as ribbons and medals that have little material value but some intrinsic value. Money has been discussed; time can be earned as in a **96**, or a 96-hour liberty (a four-day weekend).

An example of the growing glut of awards is the ribbon for service overseas for Navy and Marine Corps personnel. American Marines and sailors have been serving overseas since 1775; that's what they do. One can imagine former Marines shaking their heads in amusement or displeasure. The practice of awarding a Marine an end-of-tour medal, such as the Navy Achievement Medal, is seen by older Marines as becoming too common. Marines who do not ascribe to the practice note that the award is given because the Marine did his job right, and feel that medals and other awards should be reserved for genuinely meritorious service. The main idea is that respect for authority and control over Marines should not be gained by the perception that contrived reinforcements will follow *standard* performance.

Skinner noted: "The behavior of the production line worker which has no important consequence except a weekly wage suffers in comparison with the behavior of the craftsman which is reinforced by the things produced."[cclxxi] The same findings are told again and again in *Corporate Cultures* and *In Search of Excellence*.

I took these same lessons into the private sector, working as an independent consultant and teaching corporate leadership in the petrochemical, aerospace and other industries. A paycheck is delayed gratification; a four-day weekend for all hands – regardless of individual job performance – is a reinforcement not contingent on performance. The most effective rewards, incentives, motivations, in uniform, industry or government, are the personal satisfaction of a mission accomplished.

<u>Contingency-shaped behavior</u>

The third principle, that "behavior which consists of

following rules is inferior to behavior shaped by the contingencies described by the rules," closely parallels Perrow's observations about first-, second- and third-order controls discussed in Chapter Four. The Marine drill instructors are not the only Marines (or other servicemen) who have observed the burdensome increase in rules in the military over time. The recruit training SOP is but one example.

Contingencies are the latitudes or suggestions offered by a small number of rules. *That is, the discretion of a leader who knows his job and ethically exercises a range of positive leadership traits and principles should be able to replace a long list of regulations.* When regulations become restrictive, the leader is either prevented from doing his job with a measure of initiative, or is fearful of making a mistake in the performance of his duties, or both. The perception of many Western analysts is that the Russian military is thus strangled by limiting the initiatives of the middle and lower echelons of command.

Marines with the determination to avoid the burden of regulations fight them overtly, or skirt them discreetly. Few Marines attain the rank or power to rewrite or discard useless or initiative-hindering regulations. Quality in leadership is maintained by the leader who uses regulations to *guide* rather than proscribe his actions.

In the Marine Corps, propaganda and folklore in several forms offer contingencies. From stories, Marines learn contingencies for settings yet to be encountered, such as how to salute when boarding a ship, examples of leadership, how to react in chemical warfare. Socialization prepares enlisted Marines for interaction with officers. Many examples can be recalled from the study.

Non-contingent reinforcers

Of the fourth principle, Skinner wrote further:

Non-contingent reinforcers are characteristic of both affluence and welfare. By reducing the level of deprivation, they preempt many possibilities of reinforcement....The results are sometimes productive. More often, however, they are stultifying and wasteful—as when we turn to alcohol or drugs....or turn to violence as an escape from boredom.[cdxxii]

Although Millett (1983) was quoted regarding the indices of indiscipline, the Marine Corps' fight against drug and alcohol abuse has not been well-documented in this paper. But the evidence strongly suggests that Marines in lower ranks have too much time on their hands, too much freedom and too much money. The money alone is not necessarily a problem; the basic pay scales for men and women in the military cannot and probably should not be cut back. But far more than subsistence pay for single Marines, virtually unrestricted free time after work, transportation and civilian communities close to the gate equate to a reduced level of deprivation. It is not that they have money, but little constructive guidance during unrestricted free time with the money.

Non-contingent reinforcers are those for which one does not work. Free cable television in the unmarried Marines' barracks is another example. By comparison with past generations of Marines, today's enlisted Marines live a life of luxury when they are not in the field, and relatively few train in the field. The comparison is important because it is a change in military lifestyles, not a comparison between military and civilian lifestyles. (1985-1990.)

As for other changes, the Naval services have formalized stricter civilian dress codes in on-base establishments – clubs, the PX, the commissary, etc., during the 1980s. It took laws or regulations rather than peer pressure to forbid men from wearing an earring or T-shirts and belt buckles with symbols of marijuana – acceptable standards in civilian society.

Indoctrination in appropriate behaviors

Nowhere, it seems, is the fifth principle (new members do not come prepared with appropriate behavior) more evident than in application to recruit training. New recruits simply do not come prepared with appropriate behavior. Skinner suggested that "programmed sequences of contingencies, in the hands of skillful teachers and counselors, can lead effectively to the complex repertoire demanded by a social environment." The programmed sequence exists in recruit training, but considered within the frame of the other principles, it is clear that the level of deprivation of recruits has been lessened over time, and the restrictions of rules, laws and regulations prevents the drill instructor from completely training (disciplining) recruits.

In the absence of reduced deprivation, some recruits may fail to completely internalize the values of the Corps. Cognitive dissonance is not so severe as in the past, and the resulting perceived lack of discipline in newly graduated Marines is felt in the Fleet Marine Forces by older Marines who then must continue training the younger Marines. The relaxation of control over Marines in their first two to four years of service after recruit training is yet another change. Both periods – boot camp and the first enlistment – are the periods when a Marine must be moved from discipline to self-discipline. The conflict resurfaces: older Marines question the ability of the new generation to perform in combat or other situations requiring self-discipline.

Purpose of the study

The foregoing prologue of conclusions regarding discrete elements of the study allows for a discussion of the achievement of the study's purposes. Recall that the main purpose was:

To describe the causes and effects of cultural changes and conflicts in the Marine Corps during an approximately 30-year period (from the mid-1950s to the mid-1980s).

Contrary to the impression that may have been given thus far, it appears that much of Marine culture has remained fairly constant over time and is actually quite resistant to change. The successes of generations of Marines in and out of combat have established the Corps as a preeminent fighting force respected by allies and feared by enemies around the world. That reputation remains today by all visible accounts (including personal observation through interaction with members of the militaries of Japan, the Republic of Korea, Australia, Canada and Great Britain, and through readings of Soviet literature, some of which was noted earlier in the study).

Symbols

Tangible and intangible symbols are the most durable of the folklore elements (as compared to rituals and myths). Symbols are passed from generation to generation, and those which truly can be called folklore are passed by example or word of mouth, as in the teaching of values.

Language is by nature volatile. Some words fall out of common use and the meanings of other words change. Uniforms change from generation to generation, ever so slightly it seems. But today's uniforms hearken symbols from generations past: The **quatrefoil** used to decorate the tops of officers' barracks covers is a recollection of the markings on Marines' hats in the Revolutionary War; the red piping on enlisted dress blue uniforms and the *NCO* **blood stripe** are storied to have originated as memorials to blood shed at various battles – although some historians have discounted these claims, ascribing their use to the fashion of the day when originated. The high stiff collar of the dress blue uniform gives Marines the name **leatherneck**, from the original composition of the collar on earlier uniforms. The officer and NCO swords, ceremonial accoutrements now, find their histories in the 19th century.

Many symbols have endured for generations even though the original meaning or purpose has changed. The quatrefoil was used to mark U.S. Marines so marksmen would not shoot their own; the sword is now ceremonial. The leatherneck collar, however, not only protected a Marine's neck from the enemy's sword, it kept the chin erect, as it does today. The causes of change in symbols are often unplanned, but because they are uniquely Marine, almost always change from within the culture. The Marine Corps emblem evolved into its present form in 1868; the phrase Semper Fidelis has been altered, but by Marines. Heroes, as symbols, are made in the Corps, usually in combat. Myths, as symbols spoken in the values of propaganda, likewise evolve in the Corps.

External influences, planned or unplanned, have relatively little control over symbols, as symbols are hardest to change and are closest to Marines' hearts. Intangible symbols encompass values, traits and characteristics. Discipline and self-discipline, initiative, teamwork, the eliteness of the Marine Corps and a host of other intangibles are still held in high regard by Marines, particularly those who stay long enough to make the Corps a career, a way of life.

Myths and Rituals

Myths as stories and rituals, more than symbols, are reflective of changes in the Corps' culture. The phenomenon of telling stories has endured, and perhaps the types have remained common, but the stories change from generation to generation.

Many rituals survive as ceremonies, and may be seen as archaic by civilians. Parades and saluting are examples. Rifle marksmanship training has become ritualized in this century and until the succession of command by Commandant General Gray in the late 1980s, survived relatively unchanged since World War I. The principles of rifle marksmanship and artillery have survived hundreds of years, but now carry on into advanced computerized weapons systems. Even training with the rifle is aided by infrared hit indicators worn by Marines (*and the use of virtual reality simulators in the 21ˢᵗ Century*).

Structures and Processes

Changes in the culture told through folklore, tell that changes have taken place in the structures and processes of the Marine Corps. Major changes in the structures and processes in the past 40 years include the relationships between the Corps and the industrial base – the military-industrial complex, with the civilian communities surrounding Marine bases, and internal structural reorganizations because of legislation: accepting draftees in lieu of Army service, accepting Blacks and increasing numbers of women, allowing malpractice suits against military doctors, changes in enlisted rank structure, the formalization of the Marine Corps status in public law and the imposition of the Uniform Code of Military Justice. The latter two are the direct results of massive reorganization of the military services following World War II. Structural and procedural changes in Corps culture suggest that the Corps has been largely changed by outside forces. What is important is understanding the effects of internal and external forces acting together. This phenomenon will be summarized below.

Those who control rules and regulations control changes in formal structures and processes. Some changes in informal structures and process represent coping strategies to deal with other changes and may be initiated by any generation.

In effect there are two or more cultures growing farther apart, one for the elders of the society and one for the younger Marines. The elders control the structure of regulations, and can usually impose decisions on the spot to deal with issues that are not yet covered by formal regulations: When junior Marines wore pictures of marijuana leaves on their T-shirts after work (approximately the mid-1960s to mid-1970s), there were at least two distinct cultures. Older Marines could spot a *doper* or *hippie*: he parted his hair in the middle, wore wire-rim glasses (instead of plain, black plastic frames issued by the government) and probably had a moustache. Many of these *"hippies"* and *"dopers"* were taken to the barbershop for a *real* haircut, were ordered outright to get regulation glasses, although civilian frames were allowed if conservative, and were harassed until they shaved their moustaches.

Many planned internal and external changes in the past few decades have been made in the name of troop morale. My view is that some changes have been good for morale without having a negative impact on indoctrinating or socializing Marines in the Corps' values. These changes include improvements in morale, welfare and recreation, or MWR, and improved living conditions. The older generation is responsible for these changes, but is then also partly responsible for decreases in the organization's control over junior Marines.

Control as a function of Corps size

The Marine Corps remained large after Korea (over 175,000), and the organization took on the burden of supporting much larger numbers of troops in peacetime, eventually forcing many to live on the civilian economy as more and more junior ranking Marines started families. Bases had not been well-suited to housing large numbers of married junior enlisted Marines before the Korean War. The Corps never had more than 17,500 men in uniform before World War I, and after a high of about 75,000 officers and men during World War I, decreased to and remained at fewer than 30,000 until World War II. Again, after a peak of more than 500,000 Marines during World War II, the Corps decreased to fewer than 90,000 until the Korean conflict.[celxxiii]

The old breed's poetic hymns about "We few, we proud, we band of brothers…" were a reflection of a truly small Corps. The national trend to maintain the size of the military is a 20th century phenomenon brought on in part by the Cold War. One cannot attribute changes brought on by fluctuations in Corps size, or its effects, to any generation of Marines, but perhaps influences by the older generation can counteract them. The resulting larger Marine Corps has made it impossible for the Commandant to know all of his officers, as he once could do. Enlisted Marines will only know the Marines in their unit on a first tour, and even after a few tours, will still only ever meet a handful of fellow Marines. Marines may tend to feel like they do belong to a bureaucracy, that the service treats them like numbers, that regulations standardize things to the point that their leaders don't give them personal attention.

Control and peer pressure

The Marine Corps has lost its complete hold on the Marine. The contributing factors – hotel-style barracks, urban expansion and dramatic increases in pay – have been discussed. The major fault, however, and one of the most important conclusions of *The Edifice Complex* is that the Corps has allowed itself to lose control of the Marine after work. Of the many causes, the Marine Corps has the least control over urban expansion. Building new bases in remote areas would be an expensive proposition, but is not the only way to control Marines and the effects of civilian society.

The hotel-style barracks damage the feelings of small unit identity and brotherhood. Peer pressure, which is most supportive of self-discipline, is undercut by the *removal* of peers by putting up walls, and figuratively giving them car keys and opening the gates. Peer pressure and third-order controls could overcome much of the change brought on by the various external influences discussed in *The Edifice Complex*.

Recommendations for the Marine Corps (1990)

Reinstate the use of liberty cards for non-rated Marines (E-1 through E-3), with inspections in civilian clothes prior to liberty. Off-base liberty should not be automatic after work.

With this change, the Marine Corps must provide constructive activities for non-rated Marines, including unit athletics, civilian and military education, and occasional inspections. Supervision should be conducted by NCOs on a rotational basis – duty NCO type responsibilities. Non-rated Marines could still earn liberty for exceptional performance. The outcome should be a stronger indoctrination during the first two years, decreases in indiscipline indices, greater respect for authority and stronger reliance on peer pressure and other third-order controls.

Make non-commissioned officers and staff NCOs more accountable for their subordinate Marines.

In these days of hotel-style barracks, when the gates are open and many junior enlisted Marines are married, some of the principles and traits of leadership are forgotten – "know your men," for example. It is more difficult to "stop by and see the men," when they live in 15 or 20 different rooms in the barracks, or off base. Leaders can be encouraged to better know their men and get more involved in the personal, professional and educational improvement of their troops. This recommendation follows from the first, in that the NCO needs to earn the respect of his men. To do that he has to learn his men, set an example and take an active role in leadership beyond the hours of a routine work day.

Related to the first two recommendations: Turn the hotel-style barracks into office spaces and return to the use of Quonset huts or open squad bays. Or tear down the walls and make open squad bays.

The results would be many: Theft in the barracks would virtually stop, Marines would know their fellow Marines and their problems, Marines in the barracks would protect the unit's integrity, the unit would function better as a unit.

Require non-rated Marines to have their commanding officer's permission to marry. This use of discretion by commanding officers could prevent many enlisted Marines from entering the economic burdens of marriage and taking on the responsibilities of a family while they are still in an indoctrination phase (two to three years) and comparatively immature.

Disallow living off-base for married sergeants and below (and build adequate housing on base for them). This action would keep junior Marines closer to the military environment. Of course, there should be a range of entertainment and other activities to entice them to stay on base and within the social context of a military community.

The result should be that socialization continues for NCOs – the corporals and sergeants; they remain closer to the Corps and feel greater allegiance to the Corps for the fulfillment of their needs.

Gradually decrease the dollar amount of reenlistment bonuses to about half of their present scales. Reduced contrived rewards will be replaced by non-monetary incentives, or indirect bonuses such as educational assistance funding beyond base-level GI Bill funding.

Acquire or build new training bases in isolated areas, or send Marines to training at such places as 29 Palms more frequently. The result would be that the Corps exercises greater control through geography and reduces the influences of civilian encroachment.

Get Marines with non-combat MOSs into field training at least twice a year for one to two weeks. The Marine Corps claims all Marines are riflemen first.

Such a training regimen would remind office poags and remington raiders that they are Marines, that they are riflemen; it would prevent the de facto creation of two Corps—one technical and one combat.[cclxxiv]

A colleague suggests deferred income for junior enlisted Marines. Many 17-, 18- and 19-year-olds have trouble even keeping a checking account, let alone knowing how to save or invest their income.

Putting a portion of the junior Marine's income into a trust for the first few years would benefit both the Marine and the Corps; the Marine would not have the excess money that now serves as a contrived incentive to work. Combined with liberty cards and other reasonable controls, the junior Marine would be adequately controlled during his first, critical enlistment.

Internal problems

In addition to the recommendations offered by Heinl, which are still valid:

Do not let Poolees visit the recruit training depots; such visits reduce the mystique of boot camp.

Rewrite the recruit training SOP: Begin a careful review of the SOP by senior enlisted Marines who have served at least two tours on the drill field and by officers who have the talents and knowledge of training and manpower needs to create a workable guide. The end result should be a smaller SOP that allows discretion for the drill instructor. This suggestion would also require a review of all intermediate commanders' regulations interpreting the SOP. Consider prohibiting regimental, battalion and company directives or regulations that alter or further restrict the DI.

Take corporals off the drill field. Based on several sets of evidence, DIs should be sergeants over age 22 who can pass the psychological screening.

Reduce the stress on the drill field by cutting the hours worked by DIs. The official position is that DIs work about 80 hours a week. Drill instructors interviewed assert that the DI who has a first or second phase platoon works about 100 hours a week. One reason for the longer hours is the fluctuating number of DIs not working directly with recruits, while being investigated for allegations of abuse – often petty crimes like swearing in the presence of recruits. Other DIs must then fill the gaps with longer hours.

Extend time-in-grade requirements for promotions: The services are going to face serious problems in recruiting in the coming years as the pool of available recruits shrinks. The demographics studies presented earlier indicate the services will have to enlist a greater percentage of just those who are interested in the military in coming years. The end result of extending time in grade minimums would be to allow retention of more people and the (re)creation of a truly professional career Marine. This would also reduce annual enlistment quotas.

Scrap the All-Volunteer Force. It costs too much to maintain in advertising and enlistment and reenlistment bonuses. When the economy is healthy and drawing on the pool of young men and women and the numbers of men and women available for military service decreases, the draft will again become a necessity. This observation is made with regard to the size of the defense establishment during the cold war, "pre-perestroika" days before 1989 and 1990. The changing character of Europe and the apparent diminishing threat may cause a drastic reduction in the size of the armed forces during the 1990s. If the Marine Corps and other branches of the service are reduced in size, they should then be able to maintain manpower with the All-Volunteer Force.

(The Global War on Terror has changed this imperative; the advent of global recession and rising unemployment in the US will continue to make the military an option for years to come – even as the Obama administration will seek to claim victory in Iraq and Afghanistan and look for deep budget cuts throughout the federal government, including the armed forces.)

In addition to the dissolution of the brotherhood of

significant others, personal observation and other indications show that Marine officers have sometimes been thwarted in their attempt to discipline Marines under their control. Because the power base for the exercise of individual authority and decision making has been diluted by a large body of laws, discipline too is weakened. Another slogan in the Marine Corps, trading off of President Nixon's campaign to win the hearts and minds of the Vietnamese people, is: "Once you have them by the balls, their hearts and minds will follow." Staff NCOs and officers cannot seem to get Marines "by the balls," for fear of violating their civil liberties or constitutional rights.

The informal folklore of coping strategies is passed from Marine to Marine, generation to generation, on how to get past unnecessary, ambiguous or restrictive regulations. Thus folklore serves as indoctrination in the skillful application of legal training and discipline methods.

In 1984, the Marine Corps had more lawyers than infantry platoon commanders. According to Armed Forces Journal (1984), there were then 394 lawyers in the Marine Corps (for 357 lawyer billets) with some lawyers filling secondary MOS duties, in keeping with the Marine philosophy, First a Marine (an infantryman). At the same time, there were 243 infantry platoon leaders. The article asks, "Has Congress passed so much legislation micromanaging the US defense establishment that it takes half a battalion of lawyers to make sure the Marine Corps' work to defend our country does not violate one law or another?"[cclxxv]

This observation may or may not present logical or valid inferences for comparisons about the number of lawyers in the Corps compared to past generations, but it does express the excessive concern about laws. Further study could quantify and compare not only the number of lawyers in today's Marine Corps with past generations but also the number and type of laws and regulations. One would have to evaluate the sources of the laws and regulations.

The impression seems to be that most new laws have been originated by Congress, but further study would have to determine which Marine Corps regulations originated within the Corps and which actually trace back to laws imposed by Congress.

Before moving to recommendations for further study, several analytical points can be summarized in the following excerpt from an essay by retired Admiral James B. Stockdale, a Navy pilot who spent seven years as a prisoner of war in Hanoi, North Vietnam. Stockdale wrote as senior research fellow at Stanford University's Hoover Institution:

What our military needs is men and women whose sense of duty overrides personal concerns, whose sense of honor allows them to make do with less, and whose sense of country transcends ethnic or family allegiance. Just how can these people be attracted to the military when service requires not only meeting standards far above those of the common citizenry but also long hours, frequent separation, financial hardship and little recognition?

First, by telling it like it is. Make it clear that there is a very real possibility that there will be combat, perhaps in a foreign country with which we have no clear ties. People, civilian as well as military, may be wounded or killed.

Prisoners will likely be isolated and tortured.

Moreover, when the chips are down there can be no more carrot and stick—no enticements, no perquisites, no easy way to opt out. Our warriors must rely on themselves and their fellow Americans. Looking out for No. 1 loses its validity very quickly when everyone is looking over the precipice, staring at the bottom of the barrel, together.

Second, by appealing to that better man or woman who lives inside every person. Low-order enticements are short term and cannot match the higher order commitment to duty and country. Contemplation during my years in solitary confinement led me to conclude that a good life is one that accumulates high-quality memories. Can memories of comfort and a workaday life, even a workaday life spiced with financial coups compete with memories of bold strokes of service which one knows in his gut really mattered in the course of history? For what, in his old age, would one trade his lifetime memories of uplifting comradeship in times of shared danger? For what, in his old age, would one trade that flush of comfort in knowing that he has paid his dues as he listens to the band strike up the National Anthem?

Third, by underscoring the historic roots of this nation's freedom. We've fought wars around the globe in freedom's name and have paid a terrible price for our most fundamental national belief. All must be clear on the fact that those in uniform may someday sacrifice their lives for this country and the freedom for which it stands.[cdxxvi]

Stockdale says in few words what much of this paper discusses, that the military services are in danger of creating a welfare society that caters to the civil rights of men and women in uniform. They are, or will become, little more than mercenaries, who, as Stockdale observed: "do not win wars or maintain deterrence. People committed to their country and bound by a common duty do."

It is agreed that there are many emotional, impossible-to-quantify topics at issue here, some of which will be debated for years. But a parallel between one sociological truth, that the common good of the whole outweighs the needs of the individual man, and a military axiom – the mission before the man – shows that it is possible and in fact necessary to maintain a professional military establishment.

The Edifice Complex has shown that changes in Marine culture, discovered through the investigation of folklore, can be traced directly to trends in American society that threaten to dissolve not only the traditional concept of what is military, but the capabilities of the military to perform it mission. There is no question that a military that is not bound by some civilian control and restrictions is a danger to the country it defends. Yet there has been no military coup in this country's 200-plus year history because the founding fathers built checks and balances and civilian control of the military into the original concept of government for the United States. Rather than becoming too strong, over the past 40 years especially, the military has become weakened by regulations and paperwork. What is military has been diluted.

In all fairness to the Marine Corps, it is certain that the Corps' leaders have fought, with some success, against the bureaucratization of their service; Marine recruit training is still perceived as more demanding than the other services; and the Marine Corps more deeply and effectively indoctrinates its recruits in the folklore of its service than do the others. Many Marines, officer and enlisted, will not agree with the recommendations of this study, but those who recognize the problems uncovered herein will recognize that some have been voiced before.

The ability of the Marine Corps to perform its missions is probably not in danger in this decade. One wonders, however, about less-than-successful missions such as the rescue of the Mayaguez off the coast of Cambodia in 1975, the attempted rescue of hostages in Iran in 1980, and in some measure, the Vietnam War. A point of view is that much of the blame for failure can be laid on war by committee, emanating from civilian policy makers in closed spaces in Washington, D.C. – not on the Marine Corps.

Ultimately, senior Marines at many levels (officer and enlisted) are responsible for preserving Marine Corps values and culture. If younger generation Marines have caused changes in the Corps' culture, older generation Marines have allowed them to happen. The commandant alone cannot be responsible. Officers do need to demand to be treated like officers, but must earn the respect they demand. NCOs must have authority and instill respect for authority in non-rated Marines.

Marines in all ranks can preserve their language and traditions. Staff NCOs must instill the Corps' values in NCOs, and NCOs must continue the indoctrination of junior Marines as they report to new duty stations after boot camp.

The Edifice Complex in other organizations

As for generalizability to other services or to civilian organizations, it is clear that many points apply across the entire Defense Department. There are common themes in all the armed forces: pay scales and monetary concerns are the same, discipline is a common theme; encroachment of civilian communities affects many bases of all services. As for further study, there is an Edifice Complex in each of the U.S. armed forces. *The Edifice Complex's* methodology can be applied to similar studies and analyses of other military services. With lessons learned in this research, additional studies can be conducted with more efficiency and more specific results.

This study of the Marine Corps should be narrowed in scope, with a search for more stories and folklore that support the following hypothesis, grounded in this study:

Hypothesis

The ability of the military services to perform their missions is in danger of being weakened by regulations which restrict commanders from exercising appropriate control over service members. Control through discretionary leadership has been replaced in many cases by de jure and de facto control through civilian laws and military regulations, civilian values, the civilian courts, Congress, and the Civil Liberties Union, for example. The loss of control by commanders and relaxed liberty policies, urban encroachment and pay increases have allowed Marines to recivilianize after training. The end result is another danger: non-contingent rewards (the easy life) threaten to devalue the traditions of the service and dramatically change the Marine Corps way of life.

This argument is not *my* rallying point, but is presented on behalf of the findings of the research, based on the realities of the generations of Marines interviewed. Many of the changes discussed have already taken place; the effects may not be fully understood until the next ground war when Marines are again tasked to fight.

To apply this study to other services, one may follow the same course, with an ethnography. I still support the idea that an ethnography can be done from within the culture being studied. Skilled ethnographers quickly learn indigenous language, customs, folklore and meaning – and their target populations develop translation competence. However, it is apparent that this study has evolved into two: a search for folklore and the search for the causes of change in folklore. Similar results may be found in the other services. In joint assignments, soldiers in particular have voiced similar concerns about changes in the Army during and since Vietnam. A tentative observation about the Navy is that many traditions have held ground because of the amount of time sailors spend out of the United States – at sea especially. Sailors are less affected by urban encroachment, liberty policies and civilian influences while at sea.

Chapter Eleven

Conclusions and Recommendations

a 2013 View

Chapter Preview

If I had not conducted this research…if someone else had written this original text some 20 years ago, and then I picked it up in 2010 with a critical eye, I would disagree with many of the recommendations above. I suspect others will too. But there are explanations.

It is apparent in hindsight, for example, that many of the concerns expressed in the late 1980s by Marines a half-generation older than me were a reflection of the "what do we do now?" attitude between wars. *This is the most important element of these findings.* Although the Corps saw its share of action – in Beirut, Somalia, Liberia, Panama, Grenada and other operations – most of these were comparatively smaller scale operations and the "rest of the Marine Corps" was still seeking validation post-Vietnam.

Additionally, from a cultural point of view, I interviewed Marines who had served from the 1960s into the 1980s. They rather proved my point, my hypothesis, that older generation Marines yearn for the good old days. In concrete terms, that meant they felt that today's Marines should make less money, have smaller bonuses, live in squad bays with 20 other Marines in their platoon, have permission to get married (if below the rank of corporal), and live in base housing if they are married. Most of these concerns about time, pay, small unit cohesion, authority, and discipline are reflective of the cultural narrative of the day almost 30 years ago. All expressed concern that basic training – boot camp – had "gone soft" and recruits were not enduring the same kind of "tougher" training they had gone through – up to the eve of Desert Storm. If cultural decay – social entropy – is inevitable, it's hard to imagine what the United States and the US Marine Corps will be battling culturally, internally, in order to accomplish their 'national security' missions - 20, 30, 50 years from now. The only comfort is that a generation from now, those seeking to enlist in the Marine Corps will have been born into and come to see as 'acceptable' a country and a Corps unrecognizable to Marines and other citizens of the 20th Century. We'll all be dead.

Officers and Staff NCOs still have concerns about their junior Marines, but these concerns are expressed in different ways in a different time. All whom I interviewed in 2010-2011 agree that small unit cohesion in the Marine Corps is healthy and that concern about breaking up platoons with 2-man rooms is overcome with solid, responsible leadership. All of these concerns are erased by the experience of packing up, shipping out, and working together to defeat a recognizable enemy.

Contemporary senior enlisted Marines may still suggest their boot camp was tougher, more demanding – but are quick to explain or rationalize that training and indoctrination continue well after boot camp. Small-unit pre-deployment combat training, the process of deployment, combat experiences, and the process of retrograde…returning from deployment…are all rites of passage and generally serve to bond small units and reinforce the Corps' values.

The psychology remains the same. If anything, the Marine Corps has continued to improve – from recruiting through basic training to career retention. The Crucible program, initiated at the recruit training depots in 1996, brings together all that recruits have learned in boot camp, focuses on teamwork and underscores the rites of passage in earning the title "Marine."

I don't see liberty cards, permission to marry, deferred income, squad bays or restrictions on junior Marines driving out the gate coming into discussion in the coming years. The barracks are just another "where" for junior Marines. Control may be symbolic – in terms of holding on to the car keys or putting Marines in squad bays – but the real control is imbedded, internalized ideology, and for grunts and *fobbits* alike, that ideology is fined-tuned in multiple deployments to Iraq or Afghanistan. I can't find the reference, but a relatively recent Commandant of the Marine Corps issued a directive in the past 20 years, requiring junior Marines to get permission to get married (for specifically the reasons cited above), but was shot down. Mainstream media made an issue of the whole affair and the office of the Secretary of Defense (and presumably the White House) erased the notion of the Marine Corps stepping back in time by 40 years. We still have the Uniform Code of Military Justice, but even as we go to press, battalions of lawyers are self-abusing over specific UCMJ articles dealing with "adultery" and "sodomy" as the repeal of Don't Ask, Don't Tell begins to impact the armed services.

Retention bonuses: Just as recruiters are in sales, operating the Marine Corps in today's economy is "big business." It's a far different business than a Fortune 500 corporation, and it's a unique culture, but the Corps – like any organization – needs to attract and retain the best possible talent with a variety of tangible and intangible incentives. For that reason, I don't see the bonuses going away. (Federal debt and deficit issues, however, may impact pay raises, bonuses, retirement plans, the cost of government-provided health care and other related factors.)

As for the veteran drill instructors and other Staff NCOs of the mid-1980s and their concerns about "getting the attention of" or "keeping a hold on" junior Marines, and the concept of self-discipline in those young Marines: the unholy war has done that.

That high school diploma the recruiters are looking for in a "prospect" does not convey discipline (or courage); it's important, but it's merely an indicator of tenacity. The Corps isn't looking for quitters. Are there selfish, undisciplined Marines in the ranks? Of course. Every organization has them. But the partnership of recruiters, drill instructors and FMF non-commissioned officers, the professional NCOs and Staff NCOs, accomplishes in 2013 pretty much what their predecessors have done for the past 238 years.

With the guidance and leadership of an officer corps (which includes a significant percentage of prior-enlisted Marines), it is that NCO backbone of the Corps that will "deal with" the externally imposed challenges to the Corps: the social experiments of women in the infantry, gays serving openly in uniform, and the distractions of YouTube, Facebook, Skype and other social media.

A final word on pay (I realize I have covered this in some measure): For the uninitiated, enlisted Marines serve on contracts, typically 2- to 4-year enlistments, but are paid the equivalent of a salary, as are officers. In other words, all men and women in the armed forces are roughly equivalent to the "exempt employees" in the private sector who are exempt from the National Fair Labor Standards Act, and thus are not eligible for overtime pay. Routine accounting in the private sector considers a business year for pay purposes to be 2080 hours. Once again: If a private in 2013 is paid $1516 monthly base pay, dividing a year of that by 2080 equals roughly $8.75 an hour – roughly in keeping with national minimum wages ($7.25), and appropriate for an entry-level job. If the *reality* of 18-hour days in a combat zone were multiplied out, a 6-month deployment works out to 3240 hours; a year-long deployment is 6480 hours. (Fallujah, Baghdad, Kabul, Kandahar ... have no weekends.)

The private serving in a combat zone on a year-long deployment ($18,192/6480 hours) is earning $2.80 an hour. Even 12-hour days, seven days a week adds up to 4,380 hours in a "work year."

A staff sergeant with 12 years of service earns $40,500 a year in base pay. Deployed rotation after rotation ($40,500/6480 hours), that staff sergeant is making about $6.25/hour. They're not doing what they do for the money.

A Brief Summary of the Book

As discussed in the Preface, my primary purpose in this text has been to discuss the premise that most of the fundamentals of social psychology, as those fundamentals pertain to indoctrinating warriors, are common to all cultures.[cclxxvii] Several elements are key to this concept: A "culture" may be:

- as narrow as an isolated tribe,
- as broad as a nation's military – like the US Marine Corps,
- or specified by a movement or religious ideology, and embedded and reverberated through the global network of social media, hard drives, cell phones and mosques, like radical Salafist Sunni Islam.

At the core of this premise is the global population of mostly men (roughly) 15 or 16 years old to their mid- to late 20s. Various factors pass over most women and diminish the numbers of men in their late 30s, or 40s, 50s and beyond. Some generals hang on into their late 50s and 60s as senior strategists and leaders, but they're not on the front line, pulling the triggers. Young men seek a sense of belonging, a sense of relevance or purpose, validation in a peer group. Young men want jobs. Some of these young men want to get married (and need the money to support a family); most seek leadership. Some are drawn to violence; most are drawn by a sense of adventure.

Socialization of future warriors, in any culture, begins at home and can begin as early as 2 or 3 years old (reference the video links in a previous chapter). This socialization process is not just about "going to war" or as Coker put it in the first chapter: "(...why) young men (are so) susceptible to what the writer Luis Borges called 'the moral and ascetic charms of war.,'" but to war for a specific cause. *Most* young men and women socialized in an American Judeo-Christian world (whether they are Judeo-Christian or not) are not signing up to fight for al-Qaida; and *most* young men schooled in Saudi-funded madrassahs are not knocking on the doors of US Marine recruiters. And, as discussed in previous chapters, some percentage of civilians in each population supports the military efforts of its culture – with good wishes, votes, or financial contributions, but not with active military service.

Almost every discussion in this book about Marine Corps recruitment advertising, basic training and follow-on indoctrination and acculturation applies to al-Qaida, the Taliban, Hamas, Hezbollah and the rest of the irhabists. Apart from some converts, the vast majority of these radical Islamists are reared in a culture which lays the foundations for their recruitment to war (or whatever version of *jihad*). They take their reality for granted just as much as a British member of parliament takes his reality for granted, or a Japanese businessman or a pharmacist in Argentina. They respond to the calls of their own priests and politicians; their peer groups provide symbols, rituals and stories – their narratives – and help newcomers conform to, identify with and internalize the values of their organizations. They endure training in physical fitness, combat and religion. The Marine's religion is his Corps' history.

Based on this fundamental premise, discussed throughout the text, each culture consciously and subconsciously engineers its indoctrination (and radicalization) so that when young men and women reach an age of majority, 17 with a parent's signature in the US, some small percentage of the population actively seek to join a military organization or willingly respond to a recruiter.

As militaries – US Marines, al-Qaida or any other more- or less-organized unit – seek to attract adherents, they pitch their wares. Some folklore includes symbols, or rituals and stories or cultural myths with symbolic value, calculated to invoke emotional response. A typical response is "I have been…" or "my people have been violated." The US Marine response may be based on a reaction that US territorial sovereignty has been violated; American citizens have been murdered, including large numbers of civilian citizens. The Radical Salafist Sunni response is that Westerners – Americans – have violated their holy spaces; that Americans support apostate governments that usurp Allah's rightful sovereignty on Earth (e.g., Saudi Arabia, Kuwait, Egypt, ad nauseam), and Muslims deserve to re-establish their caliphate and impose shariah over all the earth. There are more reasons, as discussed in bin Laden's declaration of war fatwa, like the wailing and gnashing of teeth over Palestine, the excess spending of wealthy Arab leaders, and the embarrassments of Arab peoples in various wars.

Not only are these two perspectives at stark odds with each other, but within each corporate whole there are internal discords. In al-Qaida, we have seen, as discussed in previous chapters, disagreement between Zawahiri and Zarqawi over the rectitude of killing unarmed Muslim civilians. More than one organized element of Islamists has split internally over interpretations of the Quran, Sunnah and hadith.

Humans have a knack for not fully understanding their own religion and for pulling quotes out of their own *and* others' scriptures, often out of context, to make a point. The debate continues in Africa, in the Islamist insurgent groups that unsuccessfully sought to overthrow the Algerian government and came to align with al Qaida in the past decade.

There are voices in the *ummah* – the community of believers in Allah – who decry the barbaric actions of bin Laden's al-Qaida. They may in principle agree with General Mattis and Dr. Kilcullen that al-Qaida and its franchise terrorist organizations have robbed Islam of its "good name," that they are not jihadi but irhabi and takfiri. But those voices are not mobilizing armies of "the faithful" to rise up against al-Qaida, either, and missteps by US armed forces, such as at abu Ghraib in Iraq, civilians killed ("collateral damage") in Predator drone strikes, and so on, don't help our cause.

As discussed earlier, we are not just demanding radical Muslim extremists change their behavior; we're demanding they change what they believe. Behavior follows belief. So imagine a real *War* on Terror, in which the same numbers of American Marines, soldiers, sailors and airmen as fought in all of World War II – more than 15 million – were to take on "radical Islam." Can't be done...at least it can't be done exclusively through kinetic warfare. It's also not going to be a change brought on by external forces.

While Sunni and Shi'a battle each other in Syria, while Egypt roils in revolution, while Iran pulls the puppet strings in Iraq and so on, what Islam is waiting for is the next Saladin (Salah al-Din Yusuf ibn Ayyub) or Ataturk (Mustafa Kemal Ataturk) – a leader – but in this era, a strong, charismatic, unifying leader with a *moderate* voice. The civilized world might hope for that kind of leader to be a realist, in addition to being strong, charismatic and moderate, and unifying enough to get the ummah to accept getting along with the rest of the planet. Someone over there has to realize there are 5.5 billion *NON*-Muslims.

In the Marine Corps, as in Islamist organizations, we see a rolling tension between generations. I picture it like this: If the hundreds of thousands of Marines were placed on an "assembly line of time," and we selected samples of, say, 19-year-old lance corporals out of several points in time over the past 50 years, we would see a number of differences and many common themes as well. Of the common themes, we would see lance corporals who just a year or so earlier were recruits in boot camp, seeking freedom their "crazy" drill instructors while still fighting to earn the title "Marine." A year later, many of those lance corporals have found ways to express their individuality – perhaps with tattoos, or motorcycles. Some of them would also be combat veterans and well into the process of internalizing the culture but still relatively immature and in the age group of "prone to rebel against authority and get into trouble."

Meanwhile, if we pulled gunnery sergeants with, say, 12-16 years on active duty from several points along this 50-year assembly line, we would see other common themes. One of those themes typically is the expressed belief that the younger generation isn't as disciplined or hasn't endured training as difficult as when those gunnery sergeants were recruits. And yet, somehow, the organization maintains its effectiveness; adds, modifies or discards cultural symbols, rituals and myths; and absorbs externally imposed changes such as admitting women to formerly all-male domains.

On both sides of this equation: in the Marine Corps and the "armies" of radical Salafist Islam, landmark events and charismatic leaders become the "priests and politicians" referenced by Coker in this book's first chapter. Each passing year offers up a new population of "military age" men and women as the corresponding population of elders matures past the prime target range of 17 to 24 years. In the US, that rolling 17- to 24-year-old age group was roughly 30,600,000 in the 2010 census,[cclxxviii] or just under 10 percent of the total US population.

According to that Pew Research study on the military-civilian gap referenced in the first chapters, at any given time over the past 10 years, roughly .5 percent of the total US population has been on active duty, compared with 9 percent at the height of World War II.[cclxxix] At the end of calendar year 2011, regular active duty Marines numbered roughly 203,000 to 205,000. Their adversaries in this unholy war come from almost any country on Earth, including the United States, and their exact numbers are undefined. However, more important than quantifying a *human order of battle* is understanding the social psychology of war.

<u>Final Recommendations</u>

Some writers (and President George W. Bush) have referred to the ongoing war on terror as World War III. The October 5, 2011, Pew study on *War and Sacrifice in the Post-9/11 Era* is insightful in how today's men and women in uniform view the conflict. Pew reports, for example, that only a third of veterans in this post-9/11 period say that the wars in Iraq and Afghanistan have been worth fighting. "About half (54 percent) say that relying too much on military force to defeat terrorism creates hatred that leads to more terrorism."[cclxxx]

The Pew study carries 150 pages of excellent, must-read information on the apparent or perceived gaps between the armed forces and our host civilian nation: GIs are proud of their service, the nation appreciates their efforts, significant numbers (over 40 percent) have experienced personal and family stress as a result of their service – but most are resigned to that notion that "it comes with the territory of life in the military."

As previously discussed, the Post-9/11 Commission report, Lawrence Wright's book *The Looming Tower* and a variety of other source documents suggest that we might have had a chance at preventing the attacks of 9/11. We failed for "a lack of imagination." But we also failed, corporately, for a lack of inter-agency cooperation, among other reasons. Many of those failures have been targeted, internally, for repairs and better protocols.

Given the established links between al-Qaida and the Taliban, and the known AQ training bases and hideouts in Afghanistan and bordering Pakistan, the American and coalition invasion of Afghanistan in 2001 (Operation Enduring Freedom) could be seen as justifiable – whether clearly thought through or not. But while the Taliban was initially defeated and the war in Iraq (Operation Iraqi Freedom) morphed into a counter-insurgency, we were left to fight two wars, and over time… the Taliban scratched its way back to relevance. Since then, the Taliban has been severely bloodied, again, but is a long way from being irrelevant in Afghanistan, and we're finalizing plans during 2013 to "bring the troops home" and declare_____ what? Obama's "victory?"

The invasion of Iraq, in contrast, can easily be seen as an emotional response. It *wasn't* clearly thought through. History tells that we either had bad intelligence or misused existing intelligence. Washington (Vice President Dick Cheney and Secretary of Defense Donald Rumsfeld, both Cold War throw-backs), delivered a shock and awe blitzkrieg, designed to defeat "the 5th most powerful army in the world." Done and done. What about the collateral damage and the insurgents? The US did not demand capitulation of a central government. Saddam Hussein went on the run like cornered vermin. We bombed the hell out of infrastructure that we would need American tax dollars to rebuild, including oil, rail, electric and water systems – in order to lay foundations for a stable Iraq.

By 2006, we had a full-blown insurgency on our hands. The 1920 Revolution Brigade, the remnants of the Ba'ath Party and other elements sought to dislodge both the puppet (read: Shi'a) government of Iraq – seen as installed by the US, but also propped up by Iran – and to rid the country of Western invaders. Neo-Crusaders. And at that point, we had precious little understanding of the broader culture of Iraq or the tactical-level understanding of the tribal culture of the country either. Al-Qaida's real presence in Iraq was small in 2003 compared to 2006-'07; the more troops we sent, the more justification for recruiting more al-Qaida foot soldiers.

In 2007, then-Lieutenant Colonel Paul Yingling (US Army) authored a paper for the Armed Forces Journal: *A Failure in Generalship*.[cclxxxi] (I had to check, wondering if this kind of bold criticism of the US Army's general corps might have ended this fellow's career. No. Yingling was eventually promoted to colonel, and as of August 2011, was on active duty as professor of security studies at the George C. Marshall Center in Germany.) Yingling' article (http://www.armedforcesjournal.com/2007/05/2635198) compares Iraq to Vietnam:

"For the second time in a generation, the United States faces the prospect of defeat at the hands of an insurgency. In April 1975, the U.S. fled the Republic of Vietnam, abandoning our allies to their fate at the hands of North Vietnamese communists. In 2007, Iraq's grave and deteriorating condition offers diminishing hope for an American victory and portends risk of an even wider and more destructive regional war."

And who's commanding the AQ forces seeking to topple Assad's Alawite Syria? The not-quite defeated head of al-Qaida in Iraq. Yingling's main indictments are that the generals paid lip service to the concept of *transformation* after the first Gulf War, focused almost entirely on expensive, high-tech solutions, did not adequately prepare for "the next war" or account for the prospect of an insurgency in a post-war Iraq, and allowed the military to enter into this fray with half the troops needed to adequately finish the job:

Given the lack of troop strength, not even the most brilliant general could have devised the ways necessary to stabilize post-Saddam Iraq. However, inept planning for postwar Iraq took the crisis caused by a lack of troops and quickly transformed it into a debacle. In 1997, the U.S. Central Command exercise "Desert Crossing" demonstrated that many postwar stabilization tasks would fall to the military. The other branches of the U.S. government lacked sufficient capability to do such work on the scale required in Iraq. Despite these results, CENTCOM accepted the assumption that the State Department would administer postwar Iraq. The military never explained... the magnitude of the challenges inherent in stabilizing postwar Iraq.

After failing to visualize the conditions of combat in Iraq, America's generals failed to adapt to the demands of counterinsurgency.

Counterinsurgency theory prescribes providing continuous security to the population. However, for most of the war American forces in Iraq have been concentrated on large forward-operating bases, isolated from the Iraqi people and focused on capturing or killing insurgents. Counterinsurgency theory requires strengthening the capability of host-nation institutions to provide security and other essential services to the population. America's generals treated efforts to create transition teams to develop local security forces and provincial reconstruction teams to improve essential services as afterthoughts, never providing the quantity or quality of personnel necessary for success.

After going into Iraq with too few troops and no coherent plan for postwar stabilization, America's general officer corps did not accurately portray the intensity of the insurgency to the American public.

What do we do about this?

To put this in perspective: the Berlin Wall came down in 1989. An officer graduating from college and accepting a commission as 2nd lieutenant in 1987 to 1991 or so would have been a student of the Cold War; that's what the curriculum of officer candidate school, command and staff colleges and the war colleges provided. The evil Communist threat had a zillion tank divisions, fourteen zillion infantry divisions, three to five zillion combat air wings and four or five hundred zillion submarines, cruisers, destroyers, and fast attack boats, *AND* two hundred and twenty three million zillion nuclear warheads in submarines, Bear and Badger long-range bombers and land-based *first strike strategic ballistic missile* systems. Awesome! And all of their soldiers and sailors were 10 feet tall...

How do we defeat "a threat" in 1991? We line up zillions and zillions of tanks, infantry divisions with 11-foot-tall Marines and soldiers, strategic and tactical air wings, strategic and tactical navies, and strategic and tactical..........

By 2001 little had changed. There was still little or no

mention of different religions, different cultures, niqabs and burqas, chai tea and village elders, sheikhs and emirs, shuras and jirgas. This other stuff is all *order of battle stuff*, and there is virtually no mention of sociology, psychology, anthropology or ethnography coming into Afghanistan or Iraq. There have been pockets of excellence since 1991 – including independent papers out of the Army War College Peacekeeping and Stability Operations Institute at Carlisle Barracks, Pennsylvania; Countering Terrorism Center (CTC) at the US Military Academy, the Marine Corps' Center for Advanced Operational Cultural Learning and Marine Corps University and Marine Corps Intelligence Activity at Quantico, Virginia; and the Navy Post-Graduate School at Monterrey, California, from RAND and some others. But still…

We have battalions of officers on active duty who were commissioned in 1986 through 1991 or so. Some are colonels, a few are general officers. Many are lieutenant colonels who can remain on active duty past 20 years of active duty without having been selected to the rank of colonel. Some of those lieutenant colonels are gate-keepers who ensure three- and four-star generals get the "right" information in their daily and weekly briefings Some of *those* lieutenant colonels are still fighting the Cold War. According to Yingling, some of the colonels and generals were fighting the Cold War too, at least as of 2007.

What we're doing right

More than ever, since 9/11, Marines work in an inter-agency environment. The level of cooperation between and amongst the Department of Defense and US Government agencies (FBI, DIA, CIA, NSA, NGA, Homeland Security, State Department, USAID, Commerce, Treasury and several others) has never been better. Cooperation needs to improve – a lot – and continue to improve. To the extent that one agency needs to "get credit" for a bust, or another agency has "equities" on a particular target…we need better communication. Beyond learning to work in a joint environment, with the US Army, Navy and Air Force, Marines in intelligence, strategy and operational planning, in particular, need to learn the authorities, capabilities, limitations and cultures of these other government agencies.

We now have automated intelligence systems that suck in data from a range of countless other intelligence systems. The volume of raw data from all sources is staggering. Mainstream liberal media and Washington think tank wonks who hope to cut "10 percent per year for three years" from government contracts have no idea what they're asking for – particularly in the face of rising nations like Brazil, Russia, China, India, and Iran, not to mention growing partnerships of convenience between radical Islamists and narco-terrorists. It's not that any of these pose extant threats to the national security interests of the United States, but where we fail to establish relationships with potential partner nations – Russia, China, Brazil, Iran and others have, and will continue to do so. In other words – we lose influence.

Training for both junior officers and entry-level enlisted Marines, Soldiers, Sailors and Airmen has never been better. That tiny percentage of Americans who volunteer for service in uniform are more than aware that the United States has lost nearly 7000 men and women in combat deaths, and tens of thousands of wounded, in both Iraq and Afghanistan, the majority to improvised explosive devices (IEDs). They get it, and they sign up anyway. And, we export our training to other countries – with the goal of teaching other nations to defend themselves.

Our technology is the best on the planet. It's so good, in fact, that other countries, including allies and "friends," do their best to either steal it or copy it so they don't have to replicate it from scratch.

Despite some of my griping early on in this text, the United

States still has the best deal on the planet. The basic structure of the Republic is intact and we have a more or less healthy balance between Conservatives and Liberals. We don't need more of one or the other; we DO need more civility. In this context we have a base of elder statesmen – upon whom we need to rely. We need to ensure that primary and secondary education does not lean too far to the left.

What we don't have and are not doing

This will likely never change, and we know it, but as discussed in more than one scenario, above, little boys and girls who grow up realizing they are destined for military service will seldom if ever think in terms of anthropology or social psychology (or finance and accounting, logistics, public relations, etc.). They start to learn of violence and war from cartoons and video games. It doesn't matter if it's *Tom and Jerry* cartoons or *Mario Brothers, Pokemon, HALO* or *Black Ops*, some kids grow up shooting. They don't grow up solving social and psychological problems. I do *not* see a commercial future for cartoons or children's books that deal with cognitive dissonance or justification theory.

So?

What we can do better

1. Professional development in the profession of arms begins in basic enlisted and officer training. Some of this formal training occurs before young men and women are "on contract" to the armed forces, but in broad strokes, we can educate the coming generations in *all* phases of armed conflict. Phase Zero is that period before conflict. With our partner nations we are intensely focused on fragile states and faltering democracies. These are inherently State and Commerce Department, USAID, and SOF missions. Yet, "general purpose forces" need to understand these Phase Zero missions too.

Starting with enlisted boot camp, and the service academies,

ROTC (reserve officer training corps in college) and officer candidate school for officers, military education and training needs to address the complexity of the generational conflict we face as a nation. Even though they may never engage with a village elder, manage a village water or electrical system, train a local constabulary or establish a community health clinic, all men and women in uniform need to understand these missions as part of the larger whole. Marine boot camp is approximately 70 days. Enlisted infantry Marines receive an additional 60 days of infantry-specific training; non-infantry specialties get 30. All should be getting an additional 60 days of education and training beyond that in global politics, regional conflicts, socio-cultural dynamics, religious extremist agendas, nation-building concepts and the like. An additional 60 days of 8-hour training days equates to roughly 12 college courses (of 40 hours each), or roughly a master's degree. The opportunity cost would be expensive; the return on investment would be enormous.

Does an 18-year-old infantryman need a master's degree to go into combat? No. Just like World War II we continue to pull kids right out of high school, train them in basic infantry skills, add physical fitness and military fundamentals and ship them off to the combat zones as more-confident young men and women. And they've performed superbly. But this isn't World War II. Our adversaries are not "the Japanese Imperial Army" holding an island in the Pacific, or "a Nazi panzer division enveloping a city on the Rhine." Our adversaries are global and mercurial, and the manifestation of their ideology assumes different guises when superimposed on different indigenous populations. Mali is not Iraq. Iraq is not Afghanistan. Somalia is not Honduras. Al-Qaida is not Hezbollah.

The Marine Corps has in fact started a regional studies program. Officers and enlisted Marines are assigned a region of the globe for the duration of their careers. They are obligated to take on both formal and self-paced language and cultural awareness training.

This is a step in the right direction. The other services should be investigating this model if they aren't already. Even though a Marine may be assigned "out of his region," the Corps will know how to find those specialists who speak Farsi, Spanish and Portuguese and who understand the regional politics of Iran, Argentina and Brazil, for example.

2. Professionalize the anthropology corps. Oops – there is no anthropology corps. In addition to 60 additional days of education and training for "the troops," the armed services need a professional cadre of PhD anthropologists, high-risk ethnographers, and social-psychologists. The Human Terrain System was a great idea. It's had problems (lots of problems) and, with plenty of assistance from Congress, HTS is being evaluated. The Women's or Female Engagement Teams, or Cultural Support Teams fold into this bigger picture. In countries where religious or cultural taboo prevents male soldiers from engaging directly with women, FETs or CSTs can provide an enormous advantage – but they have to be properly trained and equipped and the infantry commanders need to understand what they aren't as much as what they are. (And they are *not* certified Human Intelligence (HUMINT) collectors.)

These programs need better leadership; their operations need to be held closer to the vest. Displaying images, with names and locations, of the women who interview and who are interviewed in Afghanistan and other locations puts both populations at risk. Broadly, this uniformed cadre of professionals in socio-cultural dynamics needs to continue developing already existing relationships with civilian academic professionals. The universities already are the credentialing base anyway. The European community of ethnography wizards is more than a generation ahead of us. They have already reached into villages and valleys we don't yet know we will eventually need to understand.

3. Fix America's propaganda machine. There's a military side

and a US government side to this. Wikipedia notes:

The Voice of America has been a part of several agencies:

> *From 1942 to 1945, it was part of the Office of War Information, and then from 1945 to 1953 as a function of the State Department. The VOA was placed under the U.S. Information Agency in 1953. When the USIA was abolished in 1999, the VOA was placed under the Broadcasting Board of Directors, which is an autonomous U.S. government agency, with bipartisan membership. The Secretary of State has a seat on the BBG.*

> *VOA's parent organization is the presidentially-appointed Broadcasting Board of Governors (BBG). The BBG was established as a buffer to protect VOA and other U.S.-sponsored, non-military, international broadcasters from political interference. It replaced the Board for International Broadcasting (BIB) that oversaw the funding and operation of Radio Free Europe/Radio Liberty, a branch of VOA.*[clxxxii]

Translation: the federal government doesn't know where to put the propaganda engine because most politicians don't understand it. Government agencies typically have public affairs offices and "strategic communications" experts, but as with military psychological operations (PSYOP) we need to understand the psychology behind existing attitudes *before* we try to influence a given population, and I don't see that coming out of Washington.

In concert with PSYOP, America's ideas engine must get in front of extremist ideology in order to defeat it. This unholy war is an ideology war, and far from being a rag-tag bunch of "camel jockeys and rag heads" with a can of spray paint, al-Qaida's media machine, as-Sahab, operates a sophisticated enterprise rivaling 5th Avenue ad agencies, with radio, TV, magazine and internet publications. They are quicker to the punch line (that we have screwed up (true or not)) because they don't have to deal with the molasses of American "authorities, permissions, and approvals."

The Secretary of Defense changed the name of military

PSYOP to "military information support operations" in 2010. MISO. Again, there seems to be a fear in Washington associated with influencing populations in other countries. It's unethical to "mess with their minds," but cleaner and more antiseptic to point a predator drone at a verified target? Really? Why can't we do both (and actually understand when and how to use PSYOP)? Corporate America and politicians use psychology in their messaging all the time, through advertising. Presidential administrations of both parties use propaganda in both overt public affairs messages and clumsily disguised advertising.[cclxxxiii]

The general military population, and commanders in particular, need to understand what Information Operations *is* and *is not*. Enduring a weekly "intelligence and operations" brief and hearing a colonel comment about some target with, "We need to get some IO on that..." (when it's clear he means PSYOP specifically) is like *night of a thousand fingernails on a chalk board*. Information Operations *includes* PSYOP, as well as computer network defense and attack, operational security (OPSEC) and so on. Theorists need to come to grips with memetics, crowd-sourcing and flash mobs, understand influence in a virtual world, and devise state-of-the art strategies to be able to lead, not follow, in this new sand box.

4. From the sum of this book's research, the next study should evaluate *why people leave the military*, apart from death, injury or infirmity and age. Over the course of 40 years, I've had countless conversations with men and women who are either departing the uniformed existence at something less than 10 years or retiring at 20 years and a day. In a few of those conversations are the same kind of tidbits one would hear in the private sector (and I've been a hiring manager in the private sector over 17 years): I hate my boss; I didn't get the job, location or assignment I wanted; the work wasn't what I expected it to be; I'm away from my family too much; my heart isn't it; the organization is corrupt; I got no support from the company;

my boss took credit for my work; and so on. These numbers are actually rather small in the military. That Pew survey noted above indicates that some 96 percent of post-9/11 veterans are proud of their service. The adage *Once a Marine, Always a Marine* suggests that even Marines who were "un-promotable" and eventually discharged (such as for weight control) likely retain pride in being a Marine.

The point is that if 16- to 25-year-old jihadis, irhabists or radical Islamists have a lot in common with their Western counterparts with regard to seeking what recruiting propaganda has to offer, they likely have a lot in common with the reasons men and women leave the military in these Western countries as well. In other words: What can we do to make their view of al-Qaida turn sour? Part of the answer lies in discrediting the ideology, the movement, and part of that is a PSYOP mission.

When American corporations wither, like Montgomery Ward, Woolworth, TG&Y, some part of that dissolution is due to brand dilution. Kodak is on the ropes, having missed too much of the digital revolution. They might claw back to survive. Enron's iconic leaders claimed to the very end that what they were doing in the derivatives and risk markets was legal because it hadn't been declared illegal; that the real reason Enron failed was because of a loss of confidence. Enron stock was over $90/share when I started work there in August, 2000; the closing prices at the end of November 2001 hovered around 10 cents a share.

Undercutting al-Qaida's "market cap" includes drying up their sources of funding and decapitating their leadership. Literally. Social psychology fits in all of these: confidence in the cause, pattern of life assessments on leaders, predicting financial strategies through a better understanding of human motivation, and so on.

5. I listened to a news radio report in September 2011 about the lawyers who are preparing transvestite rights briefs for the

military in the wake of the recent repeal of Don't Ask, Don't Tell. In that repeal, the LGBT *community* is generally supportive, but transgender service members are not afforded the same freedoms as the openly gay. The concept that the military should be a reflection of the general population is okay as far as it goes; the idea that hiring practices should not discriminate based on race or religion is great. The idea that the armed forces' hiring practices should be "fair" to all groups is insane. Most lawmakers in Washington have zero understanding of the demands of military service or combat; using the armed forces for social experimentation is more than a distraction.

5.a. Just as the armed forces need to understand cultures in other nations, we need to understand subcultures in our own nation. "LGBT" is not a community, and *Transgender* citizens do not necessarily vote for the same issues as lesbians, gays and "bi" citizens.

5.b. *Community* or not – lesbians, gays, bi-sexuals and transgenders need to get on board with the critical distinction between their version of *diversity* and *enriching* a culture and the existing culture's assessment of disruption or destruction. More on this, succinctly, in the epilogue.

5. c. Gays are more or less accepted in many communities within the United States (but not in some of the countries where our armed forces operate). Accommodating gay, straight and transgender service members with separate bathrooms and shower facilities, including alterations on ships and submarines as well as barracks and headquarters office buildings, would be a multi-billion dollar enterprise – in the name of equality. That equality has not been demonstrated to either improve national defense nor to demonstrate that it would not distract from national defense.

6. Finally, we need to better understand our own organizations. In the core of this book, in my original analysis, I

wrote of the concept of "an Edifice Complex." The organization's symbols, rituals and myths – as building blocks – form the façade, edifice or structure of the organization's folklore (or culture). That façade serves as the "storefront window" to the outside world. What goes on behind that façade, behind that storefront window, is never quite the same as what the public face suggests.

Behind that storefront window, it's human motivation. Some people are motivated by a national mission, a combat mission or a higher calling. Some are motivated to seek power, recognition or wealth. Some are selfless and seek to defend their brothers in arms or their families. Discerning what motivates the private or sergeant, captain or colonel, what drives our colleagues in those government agencies, universities, corporations or NGOs would go a long way toward understanding our adversaries. The ideologies behind the motivators may be different; the processes are the same. My premise was; my conclusion is: we are not fighting an army; **we are fighting an ideology.**

K2

Epilogue

Everyone gets a voice – in America. It's a First Amendment thing and it's my book. Disagreement is allowed, and disagreement is one thing; trying to shut down *politically incorrect* dissent smacks of something insidious: American *dhimmitude*.

So that there is no stone unturned, the following essay wraps up thoughts on women in tactical infantry units and gays in the military. These thoughts are rooted in philosophical and academic pursuits, in teaching and consulting both in uniform and the private sector, and a wide range of experiences over 40 years.

In 1990, *The Edifice Complex* allowed me to pull the Marine Corps into the academic world for examination and inquisition. I'm thankful for the opportunity, on the GI Bill. When I retired after 22 years, I took what I had learned into the private sector, and when recalled to active duty in 2005, I bundled the entire mess for another round of examination, with new data, and retired from the Marine Corps again in 2008. I now straddle the armed forces, the private sector (as a government contractor) and the academic community.

The following essay is one chapter in another of my books, informed by this entire 40-year process, and deals with organizations managing the challenge of their cultures being diluted by external influences. I promise to wrap up the commentary with a few paragraphs after the following essay.

Peeling the allegory:

From CONVECTION to CONVICTIONS

Reassembling my favorite two-page newsletters from the past 10 years (2002-'12) – I realize I must have had a temporary fascination with Social Entropy. Thermodynamics is a natural fit in the Grilling Studio; but social thermodynamics may seem a stretch.

What these hypotheses get to is my 2nd Law of Social Thermodynamics. In classical thermodynamics, the 2nd Law describes the tendency of a closed system (like a barbecue grill – <u>roughly</u>), with different pressures and temperatures, to move toward equilibrium over time. Turn *off* the gas to a hot grill and place a frozen rack of ribs on the grill with an internal temperature of 300 degrees; the internal temperature of the grill will drop. The rack of ribs will warm. Leave the ribs and the grill alone in your back yard for a day – without a heat source – and the entire "system" will reach equilibrium. Thermodynamics tells us that this process is *irreversible*; it is impossible in this system to maintain the internal 300-degree temperature without an external heat source like charcoal, or propane and those 6 burners – defined as *work*.

Social Entropy

Imagine, for example, you decide to start a new business – or even a new country (or a "Marine Corps"). You surround yourself with four or five like-minded people because you like working together. You're all the same age and have a common, but not necessarily identical, understanding of history; all of the same religion; same gender; same political persuasion; virtually identical academic credentials from the same university (all MBAs or all engineers for example). You all speak English as a primary language, hail from a common racial heritage and share common tastes in music, culture, food and spirits.

You've surrounded yourself with yourself. You write a charter, or constitution, and all agree on your organization's vision, mission and goals. But! Your company is so successful you eventually need to hire another full-time employee. Or, your organization is so inviting – knocking at your country's door are some other country's "tired… poor… huddled masses yearning to breathe free, the wretched refuse of someone else's teeming shore." Try as you might, you can't find another clone; another qualified You. Now what? Any negotiation on race, gender, age, academics, music, language, religion, politics or culture has the *potential* to dilute your organization's culture. Some will insist this will enrich your culture. That's part of the challenge. Again – the question is: what's *rock-solid core* to your organization, your country? What *values* are enduring?

If you're all men, and hire a woman – she might start angling for maternity leave. If you're all women, and hire a man – he might turn out to be a creep. If you're all conservatives and hire a liberal, you run the risk of Monday morning acrimony at the water cooler. If you're all middle age and your best qualified candidate is a teenager – you may have initial doubts about his or her work ethic...and he or she may have misgivings about your choices in music. People live by heuristics. Our nation has absorbed those huddled masses for longer than we've been a nation. We even face the same general kinds of compromises in our marriages. What, exactly, is negotiable?

The theory of Social Entropy suggests that organizations expend enormous amounts of capital in maintaining their organizational cultures, acknowledging that change, once it has occurred, is irreversible without enormous expenditures of calories, capital or consternation. What is it they are *un* willing to compromise on?

The lesson, through Pork Ribs on the Grill, comes from Social Psychology. The reason we keep those ribs together in their early leadership development is because, amongst all of the reasons humans justify their behavior, on or off the job, the realization that "everyone else is doing it" is one of the strongest. Our peers reinforce, validate, confirm and justify our beliefs and behaviors – in any society. Military Psychological Operations (PSYOP), Religion, Education and Advertising all base their premises on the need to create, proselytize to and maintain a group of people who are *psychologically unified*. This is the core of the mechanics of propaganda.

As you train your junior leaders, and as you teach them the fundamentals of creating Vision, Mission and Goals statements for your organization – lead them to William Bennett's *The Book of Virtues: A Treasury of Great Moral Stories*; to the US Constitution's *Bill of Rights*, and the *Ten Commandments*. Ask junior leaders to consider the underlying meta-truths in these and similar documents. Challenge them to reveal what they believe to be their own and their *organizations'* unbending values...[end of the essay]

So?

Many Marines I've worked with or interviewed for this book spoke in terms of the notion of *belonging to something bigger than themselves*. Most of these Marines are severely offended by these new or pending policy changes (exactly to the point of the generational conflict examined in my dissertation in 1990), some to the point of leaving the service without retiring, or to retire earlier than planned so they wouldn't have to deal with the changes. They acknowledge the changes are likely irreversible, short of generations. This leaves "the ball in your court," select few women and gays. (Not "lumped together," but coincident in time.) It will be up to you to prove yourselves and blend in to a society that has existed for 238 years, without disrupting the Corps' missions – which are larger than your individual, personal, civil rights missions. There will be Marines who will never be "predisposed to be psychologically unified" with what you view as your rights.

For the Marine Corps: "Giving in" does not mean acquiescence. Bring all candidates, gay or straight, in to the training and indoctrination environment (For this generation – we don't have a choice.) and focus them on "something bigger than themselves." Intensely. Some gay will make it and some will fail. Some straight will make it; some will fail. The "straight" boys and girls of the 21st century, for the most part, don't give a damn. Women in the infantry? Same drill. Don't relax standards. The Two Percent of female warriors who can demonstrate not just the upper body strength but all of the rest of the requirements should be admitted. Those who make the grade are more than aware of the potential consequences. In a generation – let the nation decide.

As it was in the age of DADT, the goal is still to avoid having the conversation be about who's doing who in the back room. The conversation is supposed to be about national defense and those who would do us harm.

Gay soldiers and female warriors: Just as with my study in 1990, you seek to be part of "something," but by joining, that something is no longer what you sought...in the eyes of the veterans who built what you seek to join. (The same thing is happening with immigrants, including illegal aliens, entering the United States, seeking to partake of something amazing. Some of them contribute substantially; some dilute, disrupt, diminish – subtly or substantially.[cclxxxiv]) The Commandant and the Sergeant Major of the Marine Corps can't fight the President, the Secretary of Defense or Congress, so the policies are what they are, likely for a lifetime. We do indeed work for a civilian government. So in (tempered) Marine Corps Staff Sergeant terminology: **"You got what you asked for; Don't *screw* it up."**

In this context, read Robert Pirsig's *LILA*, in which one of America's most profound philosophers explores Quality on the levels of inorganic, biological, social, and intellectual *quality*. Read and understand the whole book. If you get it, you will realize that your biological rights are subordinate to your nation's social and intellectual rights to defend itself. If your rights diminish or distract the Marine Corps and the Republic from its larger missions, then your experiment is a failure. Our enemies are internally fractured over one ideology (interpreting Islam) and we are internally fractured over sex, sexual orientation and individual rights as an ideology.

If one takes Pirsig's understanding of evolutionary ethics – from inorganic to biological, thence to social and intellectual – what's missing (because of Pirsig's own limitations) is a fifth level, "spiritual." This is important because even if I would disagree on many personal or professional levels with any version of Islam, or *holy war* based on any version of Islam, (pursued by "pure" jihadis or not) – radicalized Muslim extremists root their ideology in Islam, even if bastardized. Islam is recognized globally as a major religion. Whether I believe it is a false religion or not is beside the point; someone on the other side of the battlefield believes there are spiritual foundations in their terrorism. They believe it is a religion, and the rift between Sunni and Shi'a is based on spiritual canon.

What's the point? If those who seek to enter the culture of the US Armed Forces, or to enter the combat arms, would point to, for example, the US Constitution and the Bill of Rights, those individual rights are at the biological level and therefore subordinate to the intellectual and spiritual rights of the nation to defend itself in order that all citizens may enjoy the broadest ranges of rights.

One of the lawsuits enmeshed in this debate comes from an Army Colonel Ellen Haring, of the U.S. Army War College in Carlisle, PA. Haring and a Command Sergeant Major Jane P. Baldwin, as complainants, filed a lawsuit in May 2012 in U.S. District Court in Washington, D.C., demanding the U.S. Department of Defense allow women on the front lines. A portion of the law suit text suggests some women agitating for the opportunity to serve in hand-to-hand combat assignments seek the changes for personal opportunity: "The Military Leadership Diversity Commission Report concluded that the combat exclusion policies constitute a 'structural barrier' that limits women's abilities to pursue careers in the military that are "associated with promotion to flag/general officer grades" and other "career-enhancing assignments." And: "These are the precise occupations that the DoD and Army Policies formally close to women *for no rational reason*."cclxxxv (my emphasis.) Whose version of "rational," Miss Haring? Col. Haring serves as a civil affairs officer. <u>Male</u> civil affairs officers also do not have a path to flag/general officer promotions – because there are no generals in civil affairs. (There may be one general, as of 2010.) The same is true in military information support operations – the old "PSYOP." Haring's argument rings disingenuous. And Haring and Baldwin, at colonel and command sergeant major, are almost certain to NOT deploy with rifle platoons. Compared to the privates and corporals who fill the ranks of rifle companies, both are Army dinosaurs – pursuing a burn-our-bras agenda and neither (in ample press coverage) have supplied statistics indicating what percentage of female enlisted or officer patriots in uniform are agitating to smash heads and drill bullets into enemy combatants. Haring and Baldwin are likely in their 40s. Neither will ever pick up an M-16 in armed combat, side-by-side with an 18-year-old private. Whom do they represent? *All* American 18-year-old high school girls who should now be running to register for the draft?

Colonel Haring is appalled that rewards for valor "celebrate killing," but that peace-keepers who calmly and rationally convince our adversaries to put down their weapons are not afforded the same respect. While there is always room for those can appease and influence without armed conflict (civil affairs and PSYOP for example), there also always will be a need for grunts, those prepared kill in the name of their nation. Recall this passage from much earlier in the book and consider what percentage of women fit this career path (Our nation doesn't know the answer):

The basic principles of military training have changed hardly at all in thousands of years. It takes ritual aggression of young males infected with the warrior ethic and converts (perverts?) it into the disciplined killing reflex of the soldier. Aggression happens between individuals, and is often turned aside by gestures of submission; military killing is an impersonal skill that has to be taught....The cultural norms that encourage aggression and gang behavior amongst teenage males are probably several million years old. They are designed to produce warriors, which is what was needed for the old inter-tribal warfare...As anybody knows who has been through it, basic training is a primitive form of brainwashing, intended to produce a new and highly artificial set of 'military instincts.'[cdxxxvi]

What all of this leads to is this: If the social psychology of creating warriors is common to the Marine Corps and the Radical Muslim Extremist Terrorists of Salafist Islam, the path to destroying the Radical Muslim Extremists' ability to harm our Republic derives also from the preceding argument: insert distractions into their narrative and dilute their jihadi, takfiri ideology.

Or better yet – when moderate or secular Muslims insert dilutions and distractions, our nation needs to stand back and allow Radical Salafist Islamists to spend enormous capital managing their own internal entropy, as in Tunisia, Algeria, Egypt, Saudi Arabia, and so on. Let Syria diminish the ranks of the Salafists without the loss of more American blood and treasure – which certainly will be needed on a front that threatens America's vital national security interests.

So to hearken back to the essay above, What I predict will happen is this: The Corps will continue to be the kick-ass, medium-weight fighting force the country needs for centuries to come, but will also expend enormous capital (more lawyers and wasted energy that have nothing to do with national defense) to fend off organizational entropy. Instead of just half a battalion of 400 lawyers or judge advocates – we could see the 7th Marine Judiciary *Division* in the future. But the Marine Corps will continue…

The Corps is healthy and has remained healthy, culturally, by weathering a range of internal and external storms. Those who wish to participate in the cultural wealth of the Marine Corps are not unlike those immigrants in the United States who wish to participate in the financial wealth of the Republic. Does one seek to be a Marine or soldier (with access to the combat arms) so one can retire as a 4-star female general, or does one seek to be a Marine or solider to serve our country? Is it good for you or good for the Corps? One must be prime and there is no 'means justify the ends' argument.

K2

Author's Bio

Karl Klicker began his career as a musician in the Marine Corps in 1973, then transferred into print journalism and public affairs. After 12 years as an enlisted Marine, Karl was commissioned as a Naval Intelligence Officer in 1985 and served at Joint Forces Command in Korea; on board the USS Nimitz in the Persian Gulf theater; and as an instructor in electronic warfare. During the brief months of Operations Desert Shield and Desert Storm, Karl transitioned back to the Marine Corps, as a captain, and served four additional years – with 2d Marine Aircraft Wing (did not deploy to Desert Storm) and a final assignment as 'dean of academics' at the Navy and Marine Corps Intelligence Center in Virginia Beach. Karl holds a BA in English (Texas A&M University); MS in Education (University of Southern California); MS in Entrepreneurship in Applied Technologies (University of South Florida – Dec. 2013); and Doctor of Education (Ball State University). He has taught as an adjunct professor for more than a dozen colleges and universities since 1983. Between retirement from the Marine Corps in 1995 and a recall to active duty in 2005, he served as a training manager at General Motors in Detroit (via Hughes Aircraft); as a training manager supporting astronaut training at NASA's Johnson Space Center in Houston (via Raytheon); and as a training manager at ENRON (through ENRON's collapse in 2001). Karl is employed with a global engineering firm, serving as a principal military strategist in support of a large US government organization with transnational interests. He aspires to retire into publishing children's books, and currently spends his nouns and verbs with his wife and three teens in Tampa, Florida.

K2

Appendix I

Additional Sources: Review of Related Literature

(Informed this study, but not directly cited.)

Topics evaluated by the Countering Terrorism Center (CTC) at the US Military Academy (West Point) reviewed and reported on by other outlets:

"Jihadis Shift Attention to War in Afghanistan"
Christian Science Monitor

"Indonesia Tries Deradicalization"
Middle East Times

"Afghanistan's 'pristine jihad' draws in outsiders trained in Pakistan"
The Times Online

"Influx of al-Qaida recruits entering Afghanistan"
Newsday

"Al-Qaida draws more foreign recruits to Afghan war"
The Associated Press

"Why Some Terrorists Make the Choice to Leave al Qaeda"
US News

"Why Terrorists Quit"
Wired.com

"Yemen struggles against multiple challenges"
Reuters

"The Military's Internet Civil War"
The Washington Independent

"Pakistan Will Use Army to Combat Terrorism Threat, Gilani Says"
Bloomberg News

"No Political Solution in FATA Likely Anytime Soon"
Daily Times (Pakistan)

"NATO Is Troubled by Pakistan Peace Talks With Taliban Militants"
Bloomberg News

"Troops Shouldn't Become Reliant on Technology"
MSNBC

"No political solution in FATA likely anytime soon"
Daily Times (Pakistan)

Video: Al Qaeda Online
CBS Evening News

"The Risks of Defeating Al Qaeda in Iraq"
U.S. News and World Report

"Al Qaeda Claims Its Space On The Web"
CBS Evening News

Musharraf Says Tribal Bombing Aimed at Ruining Peace Process
Bloomberg News

"Jihad Industry"
Daily Times (Pakistan)

"Pakistan A 'Hotbed' For Terror"
National Post (Canada)

"Pakistan Takes Control of Swat Valley From Militants"
Bloomberg News

"Rehabbing Militants in Saudi Arabia"
Los Angeles Times

"Inside Qaeda's 'MySpace' Internet Sites"
New York Sun

"Logbuch Al-Qa`ida"
Der Spiegel (Germany)

"Pakistan Needs Political Accord With Tribal Leaders, U.S. Says"
Bloomberg News

"Analysis: U.S. Military Aid to Philippines"
United Press International

"Qaeda Said to be Pursuing N-Weapon"
Daily Times (Pakistan)

"Analysis: Saudis Aim to Reform Jihadis"
United Press International

"Al-Qaeda Directing Terrorist Groups on Afghan Border, U.S. Says"
Bloomberg News

Jihadica.com blog threads

Afghanistan	Islamic Party of Turkestan	Recruitment
Al-Qaida on the	Islamic State of	Retractions

Arabian Peninsula	Iraq	
Algeria	Islamic War Doctrine	Russia
AQ Central	Israel	Saudi Arabia
AQ in Iraq	Jaysh-e-Mohammed	Shi`a
AQ Leadership • Mustafa Abu al-Yazid • Zawahiri	Jihad culture	Somalia
AQ in the Islamic Maghreb	Jihadi book club	Sport and recreation
Arab Media	Jihadi journals	Strategy
Art	Jordan	Suicide bombings
Australia	June Ansar Allah	Sweden
Bin Laden	Kenya	Syria
Chechnya	Kuwait	Tactics
China	Lebanon	Taliban
Conspiracy theories	Libyan Islamic Fighting Group	Technology
Converts	Mauritania	Terrorism
Dreams	Messianism	Terrorism Trials
Eastern Turkestan	Morocco	Training

Islamic Movement		
Egypt	Motivations	Training camps
Europe	Muslim Brotherhood	Travel routes
Foreign fighters	North Africa	Turkey
France	North Caucasus	U.K.
Germany	Nuclear	Uncategorized
Hamas	Obama	USA
Hezbollah	Oil	Uzbekistan
Ideological Trends	Oman	Western Analysts
Indoctrination	Operational Material	Western Books
Indonesia	Pakistan	Western Media
Iran	Palestinian Territories	WMD
Iraq	Penetration	Women
Islamic Army in Iraq	Poetry	Yemen
Islamic Jurisprudence	Propaganda	

Table XXIV

K2

Appendix II

Additional Sources: Review of Related Literature

(Informed this study, but not directly cited.)

Atran, S. Who becomes a terrorist today? Perspectives on Terrorism, Vol. II, Issue 5, March 2008. http://www.terrorismanalysts.com/pt/index.php?option=com_rokzine &view=article&id=37&Itemid=54. Retrieved 12 July 2010.

Horgan, J. From profiles to *pathways* and roots to *routes*: perspectives from psychology on radicalization into terrorism. Annals, AAPS, 618, July 2008. Retrieved 12 July 2010.

Filiu, J. The brotherhood vs. al-qaida: a moment of truth? Current Trends in Islamist Ideology: The Hudson Institute. http://www.currenttrends.org/research/detail/the-brotherhood-vs-al-qaeda. Retrieved 9 June 2010.

Carnes, L. and Dale, H. Public diplomacy and the cold war: lessons learned. Backgrounder: Published by the Heritage Foundation. No. 2070, September 18, 2007. Retrieved from www.heritage.org/Research/NationalSecurity/bg2070.cfm.

Murphy, C. Jihadi dispute points to deeper radicalism among youths. The Christian Science Monitor. Retrieved 22 December 2009 from www.csmonitor.com/layout/set/print/content/view/244213.

U.S. Government Counterinsurgency Guide. Contributions from Departments of State, Defense, Justice, Treasury, Homeland Security, Agriculture, and Transportation; U.S. Agency for International Development, and Office of the Director of National

Intelligence. Printed January 2009. Retrieved from www.state.gov/t/pm/ppa/pmppt on 21 December 2009.

Fradkin, H., Haqqani, H. and Brown, E., eds. Current Trends in Islamist Ideology. Vol. 1. © 2005 by Hudson Institute, Inc., Center on Islam, Democracy and the Future of the Muslim World. Retrieved from http://www.currenttrends.org/myhudson/ December 2009.

Fradkin, H. Recent statement of islamist ideology: bin laden and zarqawi speak.

Paz, R. The impact of the war in iraq on the global jihad.

Whine, M. The penetration of islamist ideology in britain.

Gunaranta, R. Al qaeda's ideology.

Current Trends: Vol II (© 2005)

    Kazmi, N. A virulent ideology in mutation: zarqawi upstages maqdisi.

    Bar, S. Sunnis and Shi`ites: between rapprochement and conflict.

Current Trends: Vol III (© 2006)

    Wahid, A. Right islam vs. wrong islam.

    Elad-Altman, I. Democracy, elections and the egyptian muslim brotherhood.

    Bar, S. and Minzili, Y. The zawahiri letter and the strategy of al-qaeda.

Current Trends, Vol IV. (© 2006)

Vidino, L. Aims and methods of europe's muslim brotherhood.

Paz, R. Salafi-jihadi responses to hamas' electoral victory.

Kazmi, N. Zarqawi's anti-shi`a legacy: original or borrowed.

Current Trends, Vol VI. (© 2008)

Fradkin, H. The history and unwritten future of salafism.

Kepel, G. The brotherhood in the salafist universe.

Mneimneh, H. The islamization of arab culture.

Johnson, Ian. The brotherhood's westward expansion.

Haqqani, H. The politicization of american islam.

Baran, Z. The muslim brotherhood's u.s. network.

The Long War Journal: http://www.longwarjournal.org/

The Washington Institute for Near East Policy. Presidential Task Force Confronting the Ideology of Radical Extremism. Rewriting the narrative: an integrated strategy for counter-radicalization. © 2009 by the Washington Institute for Near East Policy, Washington, DC.

National Security Strategy. May 2010. Retrieved 22 December 2010 from http://www.whitehouse.gov/sites/default/files/rssviewer/national_security_strategy.pdf.

K2

References (1990)

A Marine legend. (1983, November). Marines, pp. 20-23.

Alberto, P. A. & Troutman, A. C. (1982). Applied behavioral analysis for teachers: influencing student performance. Columbus, OH: Charles E. Merrill Publishing Co. pp. 75-78.

Alvarez, E. (1984). Where it all begins. Blountstown, FL: Gayle Publishers.

American Forces Information Service. (July, 1981). Defense 81. (GPO jacket no. 281-488/S 101). Washington, D.C.: U.S. Government Printing Office.

American Forces Information Service. (September, 1983). Defense 83. (GPO jacket no. 381-338/302).Washington, D.C.: U.S. Government Printing Office.

Aronson, E. (1976). The social animal (2nd ed.). San Francisco: W. H. Freeman and Company.

Bishop, R. A. (1984, May). Memories [Letter to the editor]. Leatherneck, pp. 4, 8.

Burlage, J. (1987, August 10). Military not giving North, Poindexter blind support. Navy Times, pp. 6, 8.

Campbell, J. & Moyers, B. (1988). The power of myth. (pp. 3-36). New York: Doubleday.

Clark, B. R. (1970). Organizational saga in higher education. Administrative Science Quarterly, 178-184.

Commandant of the Marine Corps Posture Statement highlights (FY 85). (1984, February). Division of Public Affairs, Headquarters, Marine Corps, Washington, D.C.

Crichton, D. (1984, January 4). Marine Corps' mystique remains despite changes. Richmond Times-Dispatch, pp. 1, 3.

Deal, T. E. & Derr, C. (1983). Toward a three-way contingency theory of change. In: The Stanford-Berkeley Symposium, United States National Institute of Education.

Deal, T. E. & Kennedy, A. A. (1982). Corporate cultures: The rites and rituals of corporate life. Reading, MA: Addison-Wesley Publishing Company.

Department of the Navy, Headquarters, U.S. Marine Corps. (1980). Program of instruction for male recruit training (SOP, Marine Corps Order 1510.13C). Washington, D.C.

Duncan, H. G. & Moore, W. T., Jr. (1980). Green side out. Clearwater, FL: D&S Publishers, Inc.

Duncan, H. G. (1981). Brown side out. West Palm Beach, FL: Gayle Publishers.

Dyer, G., Bryans, M. & Kramer, J. (1980, August). War. Proposal for a series of films. Montreal: National Film Board of Canada.

Ellul, J. (1966). Propaganda: the formation of men's attitudes. New York: Alfred A. Knopf.

General visits hospital: Purple heart awarded to 18 wounded Marines. (1983, October 26). Indianapolis Star, p. 8.

Heinl, R. D., Jr. (1970). Handbook for Marine NCOs. Annapolis, MD: United States Naval Institute.

Heinl, R. D., Jr. & Ageton, A. A. (Eds.). (1967). The Marine officer's guide (rev. ed.). Annapolis, MD: United States Naval Institute.

History of the friday evening parade. (1984). Press release. Division of Public Affairs, Headquarters Marine Corps, Washington, D.C.

Holcomb, T. H. (1983, November). Reprinted extract of an address by Holcomb, Commandant, U.S. Marine Corps, 1936-1943. Marines, p. 31.

House of Representatives, Committee on Armed Services, Subcommittee on Military Personnel. (1976, May 26, June 9, August 9). Hearings on recruiting practices and abuses in recruit training. L. N. Nedzi, presiding. Washington, D.C.

Janowitz, M. (1982). Consequences of social science research on the U.S. military. Armed Forces and Society, Summer, 507-524.

Janowitz, M. & Little, R. W. (1974). Sociology and the military establishment. Beverly Hills, CA: Sage Publications.

Kamens, D. (1977). Legitimating myths and educational organizations. American Sociological Review, 42 (April), 208-219.

Katz, D. & Kahn, R. (1975). Organizational change. In J. V. Baldridge & T. E. Deal (Eds.), Managing change in educational organizations (pp. 35-74). Berkeley, CA: McCutchan Publishing Company.

Kerlinger, F. N. (1979). Behavioral research: a conceptual approach. (pp. 128-143). New York: Holt, Rinehart and Winston.

Klicker, K. D. (1982). Propaganda cycles in the U.S.Marine Corps. Unpublished master's thesis, University of Southern California, Los Angeles.

Lindsay, R. G. (1956). This high name: public relations and the U. S. Marine Corps. (Ch. 5). Madison:University of Wisconsin Press.

Manning, P. K. (1979). Police work: The social organization of policing. (Ch. 2). Cambridge, MA: MIT Press.

Marine Corps Association. (1977). Guidebook for Marines (13th ed.). Quantico, VA: Author.

Marine Corps Development and Education Command. (1981, August 25). Proceedings of the Major General John H. Russell Conference on Ethics and Leadership. Record of the Conference conducted at Quantico, VA.

Marine Corps Institute. (1983). The United States Marine: Essential subjects. Arlington, VA: Author.

Martz, L., Parry, R., Clift, E., DeFrank, T. M. & Thomas, E. (1987, July 20). Ollie takes the hill: The 'fall guy' becomes an American folk hero. Newsweek, pp. 6-10, 12, 14.

Millett, A. R. (1980). Semper fidelis: The history of the United States Marine Corps. New York: MacMillan Publishing Co., Inc.

Millett, A. R. (1983). The U.S. Marine Corps: Adaptation in the post-Vietnam era. Armed Forces and Society. Spring, 363-392.

National Film Board of Canada (Producer), & Cowan, P. (Director). (1984). Anybody's son will do [Film]. Montreal.

Oliver, M. (1984, April 16). I was a nobody before. I respect myself now. Birmingham News, p. A1.

Peters, T. J. & Waterman, R. H., Jr. (1982). In search of excellence. New York: Harper & Row, Publishers.

Pinch, F. C. (1982). Military manpower and social change: Assessing the institutional fit. Armed Forces and Society, Summer, 575-600.

Schwab, G. (1946). Gods and heroes: myths and epics of ancient Greece. (pp. 230-245). New York: Pantheon Books.

Scott, W. R. (1961). A case study of professional workers in a bureaucratic setting. Unpublished doctoral dissertation, Department of Sociology, University of Chicago.

Skinner, B. F. (1978). Reflections on behaviorism and Society. Englewood Cliffs, NJ: Prentice-Hall, Inc.

Spradley, J. P. (1979). The ethnographic interview. (p. 13) New York: Holt, Rinehart and Winston.

Stack, R. L. (personal letter to General Leonard Chapman. July 8, 1971). Archives, History and Museums Division, Navy Yard, Washington, D.C.

Stack, R. L. (1975). Warriors. New York: Harper & Row, Publishers.

Stockdale, J. B. (1981, September 29). Fighting fools, thinking cowards? Our military enticement system ignores duty, honor, country. San Diego Union, p. 9J.

Sumner, W. G. (1971). On in-groups and out-groups. In M. Truzzi (Ed.) Sociology--the classic statements (pp. 285-289). New York: Random House. (original work published 1906)

The president's own: United State Marine Band. (1984). Press release. Division of Public Affairs, Headquarters Marine Corps, Washington, D.C.

Thompson, J. Walter (company). 1980. 6th Marine Corps district recruitment advertising plan FY81. Atlanta, GA: Author.

Thompson, J. Walter (company). (1983). Awareness and attitude tracking study (Wave XIX). Research and Planning Dept. Washington, D.C.: Author.

U.S. Marine band history. (1984). Press release. Division of Public Affairs, Headquarters Marine Corps, Washington, D.C.

USMC has more lawyers than infantry platoon leaders. (1984, May). Armed Forces Journal, p. 126.

Waxman, N. (personal letter to General Louis H. Wilson, November 21, 1975). Archives, History and Museums Division, Navy Yard, Washington, D.C.

Weaver, C. G. (1983, March 18). Art Buchwald: Humorist recalls 'good times' in boot camp. Parris Island: The Boot.(newspaper) p. 4.

Wilkins, A. (1980, June). Stories which control the organization. Unpublished manuscript, Brigham Young University, Graduate School of Management, Provo, UT.

Wilson, L. H. (personal letter to Nahum Waxman, December 29, 1975). Archives, History and Museums Division, Navy Yard, Washington, D.C.

Notes

[i] ...as well as Army Specialist Vince Pomante. We were not acquainted. Fumento, Michael: "While most journalists heading into Ramadi require no PAO escort, for some reason on December 6 both McClung and Patriquin, plus 22-year-old Army Specialist Vincent J. Pomante III decided to jump into a Humvee to accompany Oliver North and his crew from Fox plus some journalists from *Newsweek* downtown. A tremendous blast from an improvised explosive device (IED) ripped apart their truck, killing all three. Mercifully, it appears all died instantly. I heard about Patriquin [from] his cousin, then left a message for McClung asking for verification and offering her my condolences. Then I found out about her. McClung has the dubious honor of being the first female Marine officer and highest-ranked female officer overall killed in the war." http://www.fumento.com/weblog/archives/2006/12/maj_megan_mcclu.html . Retrieved June 30, 2013.

[ii] Ellul, J. *Propaganda: The Formation of Men's Attitudes*. Alfred A. Knopf, New York. 1965. Randall Bytwerk, Professor of Communication Arts and Sciences at Calvin College in Grand Rapids, Michigan, writing on German propaganda (http://www.calvin.edu/academic/cas/gpa/faq.htm) digs past Ellul's textbook definition of propaganda to the interplay between propagandist and "propagandee" in the next cited paragraph. Of Ellul, Wikipedia notes: "**Jacques Ellul** (January 6, 1912 – May 19, 1994) was a French philosopher, law professor, sociologist, lay theologian, and Christian anarchist. Ellul was a longtime Professor of History and the Sociology of Institutions on the Faculty of Law and Economic Sciences at the University of Bordeaux. A prolific writer, he authored 58 books and more than a thousand articles over his lifetime, many of which discussed propaganda, the impact of technology on society, and the interaction between religion and politics. The dominant theme of his work proved to be the threat to human freedom and religion created by modern technology. Among his most influential books are *The Technological Society* and *Propaganda: The Formation of Men's Attitudes*." (en.wikipedia.org; September 3, 2013)

[iii] Tajfel, H., & Turner, J. C. (1986). The social identity theory of intergroup behaviour. In S. Worchel & W. G. Austin (Eds.), Psychology of intergroup relations (pp. 7–24). Chicago, IL: Nelson-Hall.

[iv] http://en.wikipedia.org/wiki/Tawfik_Hamid. Retrieved August 14, 2013.

[v] Personal correspondence with Tarek Hamid; August 6-14, 2013.

[vi] Wright, L. *The Looming Tower: Al-Qaida and the Road to 9/11.* © 2006 Lawrence Wright. Vintage Books, New York, 2007. A Pulitzer Prize winning essay examining the rise of Osama bin Laden and al-Qaida, and the story behind the plot to attack the American homeland.

[vii] International Affairs 84: 5 (2008) 908-914. p. 903.

[viii] Alberto Manguel. *A reading diary: a year of favourite books* (Edinburgh: Canongate, 2005), p. xi.

[ix] International Affairs 84: 5 (2008) 908-914. p. 904: As Coker discusses in brief, "the theory that much of human social evolution is based on the differential spread of units of culture called memes (a notion originally proposed by Richard Dawkins in his 1976 book *The Selfish Gene).*

[x] However: "The Internet is not magic "freedom juice." As Evgeny Morozov documents in his new book The Net Delusion, the Internet can be used by authoritarian regimes to manipulate, censor and monitor their citizens in subtle and sophisticated new ways. Radio was used powerfully by Josef Goebbels to disseminate Nazi propaganda, and just as powerfully by King George VI to inspire the British people to fight invasion." Internet wasn't real hero of Egypt. The author of this CNN online article notes that the real heroes of revolutions…are the people. People like Ghonim and countless others who were willing to risk their jobs, go to jail, face torture or death for the sake of their ideals. Without a critical mass of flesh-and-blood people willing to take life-and-death risks, connectivity on its own is not enough to bring down the kind of ruthless dictatorship that allows its police to bludgeon innocent people to death on a regular basis in order to stay in power. By Rebecca MacKinnon, Special to CNN, February 12, 2011 2:13 p.m. EST. Retrieved February 14, 2011.

[xi] I got an IMDB credit out of it: http://www.imdb.com/

[xii] National Film Board of Canada, *Anbody's son will do.* Cowan, P., Dir., written and narrated by Dyer, G. 1983.

[xiii] Richard Dawkins. *The Selfish Gene,* Oxford University Press. 1976.

[xiv] Klicker, K. Propaganda Cycles in the United States Marine Corps, University of Southern California. Unpublished master's thesis. June 1982.

[xv] According to Pulitzer Prize winning Lawrence Wright (*The Looming Tower*, Knopf Doubleday Publishing Group, 2006), At the time, the Grand Mosque was being renovated by the Saudi Binladin Group in what was the most prestigious construction contract in the Islamic world. An employee of the organization reported the seizure to corporate headquarters before attackers cut phone lines. A representative of the Binladin Group was thus the first to notify King Khalid.

xvi See: George Crile, *Charlie Wilson's War: The Extraordinary Story of the Largest Covert Operation in History*, Atlantic Monthly Press, 2003.

xvii Filiu, Jean-Pierre. *Could Al-Qaeda turn African in the Sahel?* Carnegie Endowment for International Peace. Washington, DC. Middle East Program. Number 112, June 2010. p. 2.

xviii Klicker, K. *The edifice complex: a study of the causes and effects of conflict between generations of marines, and of cultural changes in the united states marine corps.* Unpublished dissertation, Ball State University, © Karl Klicker, 1990.

xix It's as if they don't realize Saudi Aramco actually sells oil on a global market and makes a profit – rather than the notion that Americans slip in under cover of darkness and load oil tankers without leaving a tip. Take it up with the House of Saud.

xx *Marathons:* © Karl Klicker, 2009.

xxi Start the e-mail now. I don't give a sh*t about political correctness. Not one woman in that battalion had boots bigger than mine.

xxii http://www.iusafs.org/moskos/moskos.html. Retrieved February 9, 2010.

xxiii "History is full of the shipwrecks of nations and empires; manners, customs, laws, religions…and some fine day that unknown force, the hurricane, passes by and bears them all away…" *Les Miserables,* Victor Hugo, 1862. I was not the first to think in these terms, nor – likely – was Victor Hugo. But I came across this passage on my Samsung tablet in June 2013 on the English Language version of Les Mis… page 661, Chapter IV., decades after I penned the comment.

xxiv With an apologetic nod to the venerable Toys "Я" Us, that "Я" (pronounced "ya") is the Cyrillic / Russian letter for the nominative "I" corresponding to the objective "me."

xxv xxv Kilcullen, David. *The Accidental Guerilla: Fighting small wars in the midst of a big one.* Oxford University Press. New York. 2009.

xxvi Truespeak.org. Defining and Defeating the AQ and Taliban Narratives. October 2, 2010. http://truespeak.org/contents/view/defininganddefeatingtheaqandtalibannarratives. Retrieved November 19, 2010.

xxvii Bandura, A. (1990). Mechanisms of moral disengagement. In W. Reich (Ed.), *Origins of terrorism: Psychologies, ideologies, theologies, states of mind* (pp. 161-191). Cambridge: Cambridge University Press.

xxviii Latos, Allison, *Marine Speaks After 2011 Video Scandal.* Charlotte (NC) WSOC-TV (wsoctv.com) July 15, 2013. Retrieved July 18, 2013. RICHLANDS, N.C. — American Marines were captured on camera and in combat uniform urinating on the bloody bodies of Taliban fighters in Afghanistan. Sgt. Joseph Chamblin was one of them. The incident happened in 2011 and he is speaking about what happened. Chamblin said the sniper team he led was on a mission to stop the Taliban insurgents making roadside bombs. "These were the same guys that were killing our family, killing our brothers," he said. One of the brothers, Sgt. Mark Bradley, was killed by an IED blast days before the incident. "We're human," Chamblin said. "Who wouldn't (want to get revenge) if you lost your brother or mother? Wouldn't you want revenge?" After a gun battle in enemy territory, Chamblin said nearly a dozen Taliban insurgents were dead and he and his colleagues were ordered to recover the bodies, which is when the incident happened. "It's not like it was a conscious thought or decision but one was like, 'You know what, (urinate) on these guys.' And some said, 'Yeah, (urinate) on them,'" Chamblin said. "Do you want the Marine Corps to be a group of Boy Scout pretty boys or do you want guys that will go out and kill the people trying to take advantage of your country and kill Americans?" Chamblin said. "Which do you want? Because you can't have both." Chamblin was court-martialed and pleaded guilty in December to urinating on the bodies and dereliction of duty for not stopping junior Marines. The Marines fined him $500 and demoted him. After 15 years of service, Chamblin will soon enter civilian life, retiring in September without regrets. "I didn't do it to be appreciated," he said. "I did it because I love my country and what America stands for. I don't regret my service." [Chamblin is correct and the emotions are understandable; yet there are still laws of armed combat and the Geneva Convention. It remains difficult for the United States to take and hold the moral high ground.]

xxix John 15:12-13. The Holy Bible: New International Version. © 1973. International Bible Society. American Standard Version. Revised 2001 by the Zondervan Corp, Grand Rapids, MI.

xxx *Conservatives are Single Largest Ideological Group.* Lydia Saad; June 15, 2009. Retrieved from www.gallup.com April 20, 2010.

xxxi Pew Research Center, author. *War and sacrifice in the post-9/11 era.* October 5, 2011. Washington, DC.

xxxii The fractured "world of Islam" lost its *caliphate* in 1924, in some measure because of decisions leading to the Ottoman-German alliance of 1914 and Germany's defeat in World War I. This serves as a background story, and adds to Islamic anomie and Osama bin Laden's list of complaints. The modern state of Turkey emerged and westernized; with a Muslim majority – Turkey is on bin Laden's list of illegitimate, *apostate* governments.

xxxiii Brannan, D., Esler, P., and Strindberg, N. T. *Talking to Terrorists: Toward an Independent Analytical Framework for the Study of Violent Substate Activism.* Studies in Conflict and Terrorism. 24: 3-24, 2001. © Taylor & Francis. Brannan et al write that "…the theoretical deficiency within the terrorism studies community is merely a symptom of a more serious intellectual predicament….an attitudinal predisposition and framework of analysis – prevalent in the terrorism studies community – that has the researcher approaching his or her subject antagonistically, as a threat, with a view to facilitate its defeat….taints the validity of the research itself…..The close collaboration of the terrorism studies community with the Western counter-terrorism agencies is mirrored by a profound reluctance to engage in dialogue with "terrorists." …an enemy to be engaged in combat rather than a social phenomenon to be understood. Terrorism studies vilify sociopolitical out-groups and perpetuates their images as "dangers…" (and so on.) We didn't really refer to al Qaida in Iraq as "socio-political out-groups" when they were leaving bodies in the streets of Ramadi and Fallujah, or dismembered heads on pikes in family neighborhoods (its own kind of propaganda).

xxxiv Retrieved July 17, 2013: From Benghazi to Boston: The state of the jihad. By Peter Bergen, CNN National Security Analyst. July 16, 2013. *Benghazi and Boston don't alter reality about jihad. [Bergen]* says al Qaeda central is in trouble and that it offers no solutions to regional problems…says some affiliates of al Qaeda show life but don't pose major threat yet to West. – Every July in the lush, green mountains of Aspen, Colorado, many of the top present and former U.S. national security officials and other experts gather to discuss how the war against al Qaeda and its allies is going. – Ahead of last year's Aspen conference, I wrote a piece for CNN provocatively titled "Time to declare victory: Al Qaeda is defeated." Since last year's Aspen conference, a group of men only very loosely aligned with al Qaeda attacked the U.S. Consulate in Benghazi, Libya, killing four U.S. diplomats and CIA contractors. And in April, the Tsarnaev brothers whose family originated in the Caucasus -- one an American citizen and the other a US resident -- were accused of detonating pressure-cooker bombs in Boston that were based on a design that al Qaeda's Yemeni affiliate had widely distributed on the Internet. – the bombing killed three and wounded more than 250 and brought ordinary life to a screeching halt in one of the nation's largest cities. – certainly the attacks in Libya and Boston were victories for "Binladenism," the ideological movement that al Qaeda has spawned. – However, the attacks in Libya and Boston don't really change the prognosis that al Qaeda, the organization that attacked the U.S. on 9/11, is going the way of the VHS tape Al Qaeda "Central," in short, remains on life support.

xxxv Democracy in this sense would suggest dispersed "power vested in the people" with direct impact on governing. In our Republic, however, people rule indirectly through representation, with representatives (theoretically) responsible to the people.

xxxvi The challenge with this, of course, is that Mohammed and his companions lived 1400 years ago. Some regions of the world were just emerging from the late Iron Age. The disconnects from the 7th Century and the 21st century are apparent, and reflect what Samuel P. Huntington and Bernard Lewis in the early 1990s referred to as "The Clash of Civilizations."

xxxvii http://www.missionislam.com/mission/index.htm. Retrieved June 6, 2010. This website presents what may appear as an innocuous introduction to the basics of Islam. One internal link – Muslim Kids Club – reads like a simple Disney-esque series of games, stories and "color the cartoon characters."

xxxviii MEMRI TV. www.memritv.org. retrieved June 6, 2010. In the December 4, 2009, episode of the children's television show "Pioneers of Tomorrow," on Hamas's Al-Aqsa TV, program host Saraa Barhoum and teddy-bear character Nassur discuss the "values, morality, and good manners" promoted by "education in Islam," as opposed to the hatred for and killing of Arabs taught by the Jews. (To view this clip on MEMRI TV, visit http://www.memritv.org/clip/en/2291.htm)

xxxix *Nina Shea is director of the Center for Religious Freedom at Freedom House.* (Freedom House, like all camps, has its own agendas. Caution to the reader to read with balance.)

xl Nina Shea. Retrieved June 6, 2010. © 2006 The Washington Post Company http://www.washingtonpost.com/wp-dyn/content/article/2006/05/19/AR2006051901769_pf.html

xli Retrieved June 29, 2013 http://www.hudson.org/files/publications/SaudiTextbooks2011Final.pdf.

xlii http://www.nationalreview.com/corner/338569/very-very-quiet-diplomacy-religious-freedom-nina-shea. Retrieved June 29, 2013.

xliii Hezbollah started life as the *Islamic Jihad Organization.*

xliv Folklore also suggests that the conflict between the Judeo(Christian) and Muslim ancestors dates to the sons of Abraham – Ishmael and Isaac. See Genesis 16 and Judaism 101: ttp://www.jewfaq.org/origins.htm

xlv Bufano, Michael P. A reconsideration of the Sunni-Shi'a divide in early Islam. Master's thesis, Clemson University, May 2008.

xlvi *A Brief History of The Fourteen Infallibles.* Qum: Ansariyan Publications. 2004 Southern Baptist Convention. cbn.com.) [and] "Kairos Journal, which seeks to equip church leaders as they engage the culture for Christ and has several leading Southern Baptists on its editorial team, has taken a look at Iranian President Mahmoud Ahmadinejad's fascination with the return of Shiite Muslims' messiah and what that means if Ahmadinejad is armed with nuclear weapons. "Ahmadinejad belongs to the mainstream of Shi'a Islam, known as 'Twelvers,'" an article posted at www.kairosjournal.org stated.

"They recognize a historical succession of Imams, connected by family ties, commencing with Muhammad and concluding with the 12th Imam."
"President Ahmadinejad seems to think that the time is ripe for the 12th Imam's reappearance and that, as president, he should play a role in opening the way for his return," the journal said. "He is reported to have said in one of his cabinet sessions, 'We have to turn Iran into a modern and divine country to be the model for all nations, and which will also serve as the basis for the return of the 12th Imam.'" Like Bernard Lewis of Princeton, the Kairos authors said Ahmadinejad seems to believe "that the hand of God is guiding him to trigger a series of cataclysmic events which could precipitate the return of the 12th Imam." Only time will tell if this is his true conviction; but if he does hold such a view, his possession of nuclear weapons is a particularly scary prospect."
http://www.cbn.com/spirituallife/onlinediscipleship/understandingislam/12thimam_baptistpress060817.aspx. (retrieved June 29, 2010).
[xlvii] Egypt's Muslim Brotherhood initiated Hamas in 1987, at the start of the First Intifada, an uprising against the Israelis in Palestinian Territories.
[xlviii] From the Seventh Century until the early 1920's, there was little effort to define the countries we today think of as Saudi Arabia and Kuwait, Jordan and Iran, Iraq, Yemen, Syria, etc. – as countries. Each of these Arab or Persian lands was the center of or contiguous with one empire or another: The Rashidun Caliphate, followed by the Umayyad Caliphate in the early Middle Ages (including the caliphs ruling on the Iberian Peninsula); the Abbasid and Fatimid dynasties and a succession of others stretching into the Middle Ages and the Medieval era. Overlapping and intertwined with Arab Muslim rule, Persian (Iranian) caliphates held sway from the 9th to the 11th centuries, and so on through late Medieval and Early Modern periods, ending with the collapse of the Ottoman Empire in the 1920s.
[xlix] Sunnah – from which Sunni derives – applies to the habits, beliefs, words or actions of the prophet Mohammed... in other words, living within the practice of Islam according to the example of the prophet. Taken in modern context, this led to (stories of) al-Qaida extremists in Iraq killing an ice merchant (because Mohammed didn't have ice)(when all they were really after was the merchant's money).
[l] The Muslim Brotherhood mantra: http://www.ikhwanweb.com/articles. retrieved September 26, 2010.
[li] The stated intent of the Muslim Brotherhood in the United States is to conduct an "organizational jihad" in order destroy the U.S. from within. Last year the Hudson Institute published Steven Merley's *The Muslim Brotherhood in the United States*. It is an impressive research monograph with the following synopsis: The leadership of the U.S. Muslim Brotherhood

(MB, or Ikhwan) has said that its goal was and is jihad aimed at destroying the U.S. from within. The Brotherhood leadership has also said that the means of achieving this goal is to establish Islamic organizations in the U.S. under the control of the Muslim Brotherhood. Since the early 1960s, the Brotherhood has constructed an elaborate covert organizational infrastructure on which was built a set of public or "front" organizations. The current U.S. Brotherhood leadership has attempted to deny this history, both claiming that it is not accurate and at the same time that saying that it represents an older form of thought inside the Brotherhood. An examination of public and private Brotherhood documents, however, indicates that this history is both accurate and that the Brotherhood has taken no action to demonstrate change in its mode of thought and/or activity. Among the tentacles of the Muslim Brotherhood in the United States discussed by Merley are the Islamic Society of North America, the Muslim American Society, the Council on American-Islamic Relations, and the Muslim Student Association. Retrieved September 27, 2010. http://www.powerlineblog.com/archives/2010/03/025798.php..

[lii] Abou El Fadl, Khaled, *The Great Theft: Wrestling Islam from the Extremists*, Harper San Francisco, 2005, p.298

[liii] Alexei Vassiliev, *The History of Saudi Arabia*, Saqi Books, London 1998

[liv] Maulana Maudoodi wrote an article titled *Fitna-i Takfir* ('The mischief of calling Muslims as *kafir*') for his magazine *Tarjuman al-Quran* in its May 1935 issue. It can be found in the collection of his writings published under the title *Tafhimat*, Part II (eleventh edition, Islamic Publications, Lahore, March 1984, pages 177–190). An English translation of this article…was done by Dr. Zahid Aziz and first published in *The Light & Islamic Review*, dated November–December 1996. The Lahore Ahmadiyya Movement: presenting Islam as peaceful, tolerant, rational, inspiring. Retrieved from http://www.muslim.org/ movement/maudoodi/art-takfir.htm; October 6, 2010.

[lv] Kilcullen, David. *The Accidental Guerilla: Fighting small wars in the midst of a big one*. Oxford University Press. New York. 2009. Kilcullen is a former Australian Army officer, "leading expert on guerilla warfare, past special advisor to Secretary of State Condoleeza Rice and Senior Counter insurgency Advisor to General Petraeus…"

[lvi] Wagemakers, Joas. "A Crash Course in Jihadi Theory." Posted September 21, 2010 at www.jihadica.com. *Jihadica* is a clearinghouse for materials related to militant, transnational Sunni Islamism, commonly known as Jihadism. Retrieved October 10, 2010.

[lvii] http://www.guardian.co.uk/books/2002/jan/12/books.guardianreview5

[lviii] *Jarhead: Welcome to the suck*. 2005, Universal Pictures, Red Wagon Productions, Neal Street Productions. Directed by Same Mendes. Screenplay by William Broyles, Jr. Book by (Marine) Anthony Swofford. Stars Jake Gyllenhaal, Jamie Foxx and Lucas Black. (IMDB http://www.imdb.com/ title/tt0418763/) Like any other Marine's story – some Marines will say "this isn't the way it happened at all…" Those who did not pan the film agree, to one extent or other, that the movie depicts some level of reality of the boredom of being in a combat zone – without combat, and the natural aggression (and frustration) of young men who have trained for war, left girlfriends and family behind to live in an inhospitable environment and "just want to do what they trained for." One "user review" includes the comments: "Many people may think that the obscenity of some of the interactions was overdone for effect. But whatever anyone's personal judgment of that behavior, that is the closest portrayal of Marines (or soldiers) being themselves I have yet seen on screen. Marines are vulgar. They do watch porn. They do fight among themselves. They do both hate, and love, the Marine Corps. There is an omni-present anti-war conspiracy theorist. They do say ridiculous things. There are some who are over the line. The reality of the Marine Infantry is that things happen there every day that are well beyond conventional sensibility, and which strain credibility to the average civilian. It's all true. I love the Marine Corps and I am still serving - I don't have an axe to grind. It just happens to be true."
[lix] (Schwab, 1946, 230-245)
[lx] Webster's Seventh New Collegiate Dictionary (1972, p. 585)
[lxi] This concept of wanting to join the organization because it is a shit-hot organization…but unknowingly changing the organization as a result of joining, is an essential concept in this book. Be alert for discussions on this concept in the final chapters.
[lxii] While I am trying to leave this portion of this chapter intact – this observation relates directly to the experiences of NASA employees: civil service and government engineers employed at Johnson Space Center in the months and weeks before the Columbia tragedy of 2002. In my close-in and personal observation, the informal laws embedded in that culture were far more powerful than the written dictates of engineering sciences.
[lxiii] Ellul, J. (1966). Propaganda: the formation of men's attitudes. (Ellul, 1973, English translation, New York; Alfred A. Knopf. p. 61)
[lxiv] NASHVILLE — "If you want to know what a member of the military thinks about repealing "Don't ask, Don't tell," you could start by asking how old they are. Generational differences appear to play a big role in how soldiers, Air Force personnel, Marines, and sailors feel about repealing the policy that has barred gays from serving openly since 1993 but faces a

possible court-ordered end. Age may also influence how a change is implemented, if the courts or Congress ultimately lift the ban. "Younger soldiers wouldn't have a problem with it, but older soldiers are the ones that enforce Army regulations," noted Jason Ashley, 43, a former Army first sergeant who served with the Army's 101st Airborne Division, which is based at Fort Campbell, Ky. Details on the findings [of a comprehensive survey of military-wide views of gays in the ranks] were still scarce. But in conversations with troops and veterans, the idea repeatedly emerges that younger recruits, who make up the bulk of combat troops in Afghanistan and Iraq, are indifferent while older ones, including many officers, don't want the ban lifted."

[lxv] Sumner, W. G. (1971). On in-groups and out-groups. In M. Truzzi (Ed.) Sociology--the classic statements (pp. 285-289). New York: Random House. (original work published 1906)

[lxvi] Ibid. Sumner, (p. 287)

[lxvii] Ibid. (pp. 288-289)

[lxviii] Ibid. (p. 289)

[lxix] Ibid. (p. 289)

[lxx] Wilkins, A. (1980, June). Stories which control the organization. Unpublished manuscript, Brigham Young University, Graduate School of Management, Provo, UT.

[lxxi] Cited in Wilkins: Wilkins, A. (1980, June). Stories which control the organization. Unpublished manuscript, Brigham Young University, Graduate School of Management, Provo, UT.

[lxxii] Wilkins (p. 2)

[lxxiii] Geertz, cited in Wilkins. p.2.

[lxxiv] Clark, B. R. (1970). Organizational saga in higher education. Administrative Science Quarterly, 178-184.

[lxxv] Wilkins, p. 5.

[lxxvi] Kamens, D. (1977). Legitimating myths and educational organizations. American Sociological Review, 42 (April), 208-219.

[lxxvii] Ibid. Kamens. (p. 209)

[lxxviii] Ibid. (p. 209)

[lxxix] cf: Bruner and Tagiuir in R.J. Sternberg (Ed.), Handbook of intelligence, 2nd ed. (pp. 359-379). Cambridge, U.K.: Cambridge University Press, 2000.

[lxxx] Ibid. Kamens. (p. 215)

[lxxxi] DOD Evaluates Sexual Harassment and Prevention Response Efforts at the Military Service Academies. Wednesday, December 15, 2010. <http://www.defense.gov/releases/release.aspx?releaseid=14141.

[lxxxii] Pacific Stars and Stripes, February 25, 1980, p. 2. (Sergeant) Bambi Lin Finney said "...she thought being in Playboy was 'the essence of being

pretty' so she sent the magazine a picture and a letter. It got her into the magazine but out of the Corps.

lxxxiii http://www.thedailybeast.com/articles/2013/06/04/seven-misconceptions-about-military-sexual-assault.html. Retrieved June 22, 2013.

lxxxiv Allen, David. Stars and Stripes. March 2, 2008. Okinawa Marine accused of rape is released by Japanese police. Staff sergeant in military custody after 14-year-old drops complaint. Retrieved January 6, 2011.

lxxxv Perry, Tony. Los Angeles Times. March 27, 2010. Marine to face court-martial in killings of 24 Iraqi civilians. A judge at Camp Pendleton refuses to throw out charges against Staff Sgt. Frank Wuterich, the last of eight Marines accused in the 2005 deaths. Charges were dropped against six and one was acquitted. Retrieved January 6, 2011. In this and the previous endnote, part of my perspective is informed by my experience as an independent consultant (2002-2005) delivering leadership seminars to middle managers in Houston, TX. One of the vignettes I would discuss was the situation in which I asked my students to imagine going to a retail store – Sears, Home Depot, The Gap – and interacting with "the clerk behind the counter," who likely earns around $10 an hour...in sharp contrast to the CEO of the corporation whose annual salary is likely in the millions. The customer probably never sees the CEO of any of these corporations and in the experience of interacting with "the clerk behind the counter," that clerk represents Sears, Home Depot or The Gap to the customer. The most important person at the point of sale is not the president, CEO or COO of the corporation – but the clerk.

lxxxvi Manning, P. K. (1979). Police work: The social organization of policing. (Ch. 2). Cambridge, MA: MIT Press.

lxxxvii General visits hospital: Purple heart awarded to 18 wounded Marines. Indianapolis Star, October 26, 1983, p. 8.

lxxxviii F. Carr, personal communication, August 2, 1984

lxxxix Manning, chap. 2.

xc Campbell, J. & Moyers, B. (1988). The power of myth. (pp. 3-36). New York: Doubleday.

xci Ellul, J. (1966). Propaganda: the formation of men's attitudes. New York: Alfred A. Knopf.

xcii Ibid, Moyers and Campbell.

xciii Clark, B. R. (1970). Organizational saga in higher education. Administrative Science Quarterly, 178-184.

xciv Ibid, Clark, p. 180.

xcv Millett, A. R. (1980). Semper fidelis: The history of the United States Marine Corps. New York: MacMillan Publishing Co., Inc.

xcvi Ibid, Clark, p. 179.

[xcvii] Millett, A. R. (1980). <u>Semper fidelis: The history of the United States Marine Corps</u>. New York: MacMillan Publishing Co., Inc. pp. 528-532.

[xcviii] For days, news of the death of the man whose actions caused an overhaul of Marine Corps basic training - some say the demise of the "Old Corps" - has circulated by word of mouth and e-mail throughout the Marine Corps community. <u>http://www.popasmoke.com/notam2/archive/index.php/t-4011.html</u>. Retrieved October 21, 2010.

[xcix] "Close order drill" is that ceremonial practice, with a rifle, of performing "RIGHT SHOULDER ARMS, PORT ARMS, LEFT SHOULDER ARMS, and PRESENT ARMS" on command. In a sadistic point of view – it would be funny to watch. But recruits end up with bruised heads and smashed fingers. If it were recorded on video and release to the modern *YouTube*, it would have gone viral and drill instructors would have been court-martialed.

[c] Millett, A. R. (1983). The U.S. Marine Corps: Adaptation in the post-Vietnam era. <u>Armed Forces and Society</u>. Spring, 363-392.

[ci] Ibid, p. 363.

[cii] Ibid, p. 364.

[ciii] Ibid, p. 364.

[civ] Ibid, p. 378.

[cv] American Forces Information Service. (September, 1983). <u>Defense 83</u>. (GPO jacket no. 381-338/302). Washington, D.C.: U.S. Government Printing Office. p.183.

[cvi] <u>http://siadapp.dmdc.osd.mil/personnel/MILITARY/rg1011.pdf</u>. Department of Defense Active Duty Military Personnel by Grade/Rank, November 2010. Retrieved January 8, 2011.

[cvii] Millett, A. R. (1983). The U.S. Marine Corps: Adaptation in the post-Vietnam era. <u>Armed Forces and Society</u>. Spring, 363-392.

[cviii] American Forces Information Service. (September, 1983). <u>Defense 83</u>. (GPO jacket no. 381-338/302). Washington, D.C.: U.S. Government Printing Office.

[cix] Ibid. p. 380.

[cx] Clark, B. R. (1970). Organizational saga in higher education. <u>Administrative Science Quarterly</u>, p. 180.

[cxi] Ibid. p. 182.

[cxii] Clark, B. R. (1970). Organizational saga in higher education. <u>Administrative Science Quarterly</u>, p. 183.

[cxiii] Dyer, G., Bryans, M. & Kramer, J. (1980, August). <u>War</u>. Proposal for a series of films. Montreal: National Film Board of Canada. p. 11.

cxiv Dyer, G. (1985, 2005). WAR: The lethal custom. New York: Carroll & Graf Publishers, an imprint of Avalon Publishing Group, Inc. Original Copyright Gwynne Dyer, 1985.

cxv Millett, A. R. (1983). The U.S. Marine Corps: Adaptation in the post-Vietnam era. Armed Forces and Society. Spring. p. 389.

cxvi Millett was a Reserve Marine colonel (presumably a retired Reserve colonel now) and teaching history at The Ohio State University. It's been 20 years… and we've never met, but an Internet search suggests he is Professor Emeritus of History at The Ohio State University and Director, Eisenhower Center for American Studies, National World War II Museum. Millett served on the doctoral committee of one of my colleagues at the early stages of my original research.

cxvii Janowitz, M. & Little, R. W. (1974). Sociology and the military establishment. Beverly Hills, CA: Sage Publications.

cxviii Janowitz, M. (1982). Consequences of social science research on the U.S. military. Armed Forces and Society, Summer, 507-524.

cxix Janowitz, M. & Little, R. W. (1974). Sociology and the military establishment. Beverly Hills, CA: Sage Publications. pp. 27-27.

cxx Pinch, F. C. (1982). Military manpower and social change: Assessing the institutional fit. Armed Forces and Society, Summer, 575-600.

cxxi Janowitz, M. & Little, R. W. (1974). Sociology and the military establishment. Beverly Hills, CA: Sage Publications. pp. 27-27.

cxxii Janowitz, M. (1982). Consequences of social science research on the U.S. military. Armed Forces and Society, Summer, 507-524.

cxxiii Janowitz, M. & Little, R. W. (1974). Sociology and the military establishment. Beverly Hills, CA: Sage Publications. p. 60.

cxxiv Additionally, for an appreciation of the type of social psychology research which seeks to understand how some people may act beyond reasonable limits when placed in a position of authority, see the citations behind the Wikipedia entry on Stanley Milgram's shock experiments: "The Milgram experiment on obedience to authority figures was a series of social psychology experiments conducted by Yale University psychologist Stanley Milgram, which measured the willingness of study participants to obey an authority figure who instructed them to perform acts that conflicted with their personal conscience. Milgram first described his research in 1963 in an article published in the *Journal of Abnormal and Social Psychology*, and later discussed his findings in greater depth in his 1974 book, *Obedience to Authority: An Experimental View*. Retrieved July 21, 2013, from: "http://en.wikipedia.org/wiki/Stanley_Milgram_shock_experiments.

cxxv Klicker, K. D. (1982). Propaganda cycles in the U.S. Marine Corps. Unpublished master's thesis, University of Southern California, Los

Angeles.

[cxxvi] Ellul, J. (1966). Propaganda: the formation of men's attitudes. New York: Alfred A. Knopf.

[cxxvii] With the opportunity to return to active duty 10 years after I originally retired in 1995, I've had more exposure to Marines serving alongside Army, Navy and Air Force service members. And in my 3rd (or 4th) career, serving as a defense contractor at both US Central Command and US Special Operations Command headquarters, I work in a joint (Army, Navy Air Force, Marine Corps) and combined (US Forces and Coalition partner) environment – with British, Canadian, Australian and many others. The American armed forces penchant for ethnocentrism brings out (good-natured) chiding comments about Air Force servicemen and women doing their "physical fitness" tests on the golf course, or in a Lazy Boy recliner with beer, popcorn and a football game. The competition is never ending; and the Marines always win.

[cxxviii] Aronson, E. (1976). The social animal (2nd ed.). San Francisco: W. H. Freeman and Company.

[cxxix] Pinch, F. C. (1982). Military manpower and social change: Assessing the institutional fit. Armed Forces and Society, Summer, 575-600.

[cxxx] Ibid. Pinch, p. 579.

[cxxxi] Commandant of the Marine Corps Posture Statement (FY85), pp. 2-3.

[cxxxii] Dao, James. With Recruiting Goals Exceeded, Marines Toughen Their Ad Pitch. New York Times, September 18, 2009. Dao writes: "Calvin Klein it's not. The advertisement shows men crawling through mud and under barbed wire, being smacked in the head with padded fighting sticks, vomiting after inhaling tear gas and diving, boots and all, into a swimming pool…The new approach is a result of recruiting successes, General Milstead (Maj. Gen. Robert E. Milstead Jr., who heads the Marine Corps Recruiting Command) said. Thanks in part to the weak economy, the Corps is ahead of its recruiting goals not only for this year but for the next three as well. And so the high command has concluded that it can be pickier about new recruits. The Corps is not the only service meeting its goals. As is typical when job markets are weak, all the services have been meeting or exceeding their targets, including the Army, which struggled just a few years ago when the economy was strong and the Iraq war was sending home large numbers of casualties. General Milstead said that in 2008, the Corps had its most bountiful recruiting year since 1984, bringing in about 42,000 new Marines. He also noted that the quality of recruits was higher: nearly 99 percent this year are high school graduates, up from 95 percent in 2007. (sic, sic, sic…Marines always capitalize "Corps," and if the New York Times used the Associated Press Style Guide, they would do the same.)

[cxxxiii] Aronson, E. (1976). The social animal (2nd ed.). San Francisco: W. H. Freeman and Company.

[cxxxiv] House of Representatives, Committee on Armed Services, May 26, 1976, p. 509

[cxxxv] Personal communication, E. Alvarez, August 15, 1984.

[cxxxvi] Gunnery Sergeant Young, personal communication, October 26, 1984.

[cxxxvii] Ibid.

[cxxxviii] J. Walter Thompson, 1980, p. 2.

[cxxxix] Ibid. JWT, pp 2-3.

[cxl] Ibid. JWT, pp 7-8.

[cxli] In the case of radicalization in Islam, family, media and peers have significant influence, but it is the imam, study group leader or face-to-face recruiter who levies the critical radicalizing influence on the future irhabist.

[cxlii] Ibid. JWT, p. 8.

[cxliii] Klicker, K. D. (1982). Propaganda cycles in the U.S. Marine Corps. Unpublished master's thesis, University of Southern California, Los Angeles.

[cxliv] Ibid. Klicker, pp. 34-39.

[cxlv] Aronson, E. (1976). The social animal (2nd ed.). San Francisco: W. H. Freeman and Company. p. 88.

[cxlvi] Peters, T. J. & Waterman, R. H., Jr. (1982). In search of excellence. New York: Harper & Row, Publishers. p. 279.

[cxlvii] Ibid. Peters & Waterman, p. 269.

[cxlviii] Ibid. Peters & Waterman, pp. 4-15.

[cxlix] Deal, T. E. & Kennedy, A. A. (1982). Corporate cultures: The rites and rituals of corporate life. Reading, MA: Addison-Wesley Publishing Company. p. ii.

[cl] Ibid. Deal & Kennedy, pp. 6-7.

[cli] personal communication, June 28, 1984. (Telephone conversation.)

[clii] Deal, T. E. & Derr, C. (1983). Toward a three-way contingency theory of change. In: The Stanford-Berkeley Symposium, United States National Institute of Education, Finance and Productivity Division. p. 50.

[cliii] Ibid. Deal & Derr, pp. 54-55.

[cliv] Ibid. Deal & Derr, p. 55.

[clv] Think in terms of buying a car. If I have harbored a negative attitude directed at Cadillac for five decades, based on my father's and grandfather's indoctrination toward a more favorable appreciation for Lincolns – but the local Cadillac dealer sends me a personal offer to buy a new (2011) Cadillac CTS for $5000 (with no catch), I would likely buy the Cadillac despite my attitudes. (Justification theory takes hold however, and if the car performs, I may change my attitudes as a result. Those who work in PSYOP are well-

versed in this phenomenon. I need to shift my attitude from "I bought the Cadillac for financial reasons" to "I own a Cadillac because it's a fine car." Real car dealers and others with "something to sell" do this all the time.) It's easier to change behaviors than attitudes or beliefs.

[clvi] Klicker, K. D. (1982). Propaganda cycles in the U.S. Marine Corps. Unpublished master's thesis, University of Southern California, Los Angeles.

[clvii] *Talking to Terrorists: Toward an Independent Analytical Framework for the Study of Violent Substate Activism.* Studies in Conflict and Terrorism. 24: 3-24, 2001. © Taylor & Francis.

[clviii] Clark, R. and Knake, R. Counter-terrorism issues for the next president. CTC SENTINEL, vol 1, issue 3, February 2008. pp. 1-3. Mr. Clark is chairman of Good Harbor Consulting, LLC, a homeland security and cyber security consulting firm. His perspectives are informed by 11 years of service in the White House, under three presidents, variously as Special Assistant to the President for Global Affairs, National Coordinator for Security and Counterterrorism, and Special Advisor to the President for Cyber Security. Clarke's bio on the CTC Sentinel article indicates that prior to his White House service he served 19 years in the Pentagon, the Intelligence Community and the US State Department. Knake is a Director at Good Harbor, with a master's degree in international security studies at Harvard University's Kennedy School of Government.

[clix] At least two reasons exist for the lack of a more powerful influence effort: First, even the professionals in military PSYOP (MISO) have a difficult time in quantifying the effects of influence operations. PSYOP is focused on people and psychology – fuzzy and difficult to predict. Second – combat arms warriors have always led armies, and we *can* quantify ships sunk, aircraft shot down, tanks destroyed, and human body counts. As a result, four-star generals and admirals will primarily rise through the ranks of infantry (including special forces/SOF), tactical and operational aviation and naval warfare; there are no "PSYOP generals." As a career field, colonel is the exit point (unless the warrior changes branches). And psychological operations are not the only influence operations at our disposal. Similar career paths await officers in Civil Affairs. SOF operations in foreign internal defense (FID), security force assistance (SFA) and other "presence ops" gain influence as well.

[clx] http://www.drtomoconnor.com/. O'Connor's site clearly identifies itself as *not* an official site of Austin Peay University, but as his personal web site: Mega Links in Criminal Justice. He teaches a range of courses in criminal justice, homeland security and terrorism. O'Connor indicates that his primary offices are located at the Army Education Complex, Fort Campbell,

KY. His bachelor's degree was in anthropology/sociology; master's in social justice (criminal justice); and PhD in criminology.

clxi O'Connor, T. Last updated December 30, 2010. Retrieved January 17, 2011 from http://www.drtomoconnor.com/3400/3400lect04asecure.htm.

clxii Ibid. O'Connor.

clxiii O'Connor presents a quote (from WorldNet Daily) from Omar Ahmad, the founder and chairman of CAIR – the Council on American-Islamic Relations (which bills itself as a peaceful entity): In 1998, Omar Ahmad, founder and chairman of CAIR spoke before a packed crowd at the Flamingo Palace banquet hall in Fremont, California, urging Muslims not to shirk their duty of sharing the Islamic faith with those who are "on the wrong side." Muslim institutions, schools and economic power should be strengthened in America, he said. Those who stay in America should be "open to society without melting (into it)," keeping mosques open so anyone can come and learn about Islam, he said. "If you choose to live here (in America) ... you have a responsibility to deliver the message of Islam," he said *"Islam isn't in America to be equal to any other faith, but to become dominant. The Koran, the Muslim book of scripture, should be the highest authority in America, and Islam the only accepted religion on Earth."* [original emphasis]

clxiv Ibid. O'Connor.

clxv http://www.jihadica.com. Jihadica's web site provides a listing of principal contributors to their blog, including "The founder of *Jihadica*, William McCants, [who] is also co-founder of Insight Collaborative, a DC-based company that provides education and expertise on Islamism. He has a PhD from Princeton University and is the editor of the *Militant Ideology Atlas* and the author of various other publications and translations related to Jihadism. He is on indefinite leave from *Jihadica* and Insight Collaborative but hopes to return." (and) "Thomas Hegghammer [who] is a fellow at Harvard Kennedy School and a senior research fellow at the Norwegian Defence Research Establishment (FFI). He has a PhD from Sciences-Po in Paris and is the author of a forthcoming book entitled *Jihad in Saudi Arabia*." Over the past three years or so, Hegghammer has been the principal host, often commenting on guest blogs from other scholars.

clxvi As a footnote (end note) to the "Islamic State of Iraq," my team of the "meritorious non-commissioned officer" noted in my dedication, the female gunnery sergeant (now master sergeant) a female corporal, and a civilian contractor who were responsible for monitoring "Open Source" intelligence in Iraq in 2006 and 2007, found the very first expression of the Islamic State of Iraq by way of an unclassified Associated Press video from downtown Ramadi (provincial capital of Anbar) clxvii www.jiadica.com. February 1, 2010 — reposted from Better Know a Forum, Jordan. Retrieved from http://www.jihadica.com/?s=conflict January 17, 2011.

clxviii *Obama Relieves McChrystal Over Critical Remarks, Names Petraeus as Replacement.* Published June 23, 2010, FOXNews.com. Retrieved January 17, 2011. "President Obama said Wednesday he feels no "personal insult" from Gen. Stanley McChrystal but accepted his resignation as the commander of U.S. forces in Afghanistan because he couldn't abide scathing comments by McChrystal and his aides that appeared in an article out this week in Rolling Stone magazine. The conduct represented in the recently published article does not meet the standard that should be set by a commanding general. It undermines the civilian control of the military that is at the core of our democratic system. And it erodes the trust that's necessary for our team to work together to achieve our objectives in Afghanistan," Obama said. At the center of this is civilian control of the military – a hallmark of America's strength – and McChrystal's alleged lack of respect for the seniors in his chain of command. Lots of lapses in judgment here…especially from McChrystal's advisors.

clxix Stewart, Scott. A Revolt Within the al Qaeda Movement - Security Weekly, STRATFOR, June 20, 2013: http://www.stratfor.com/. Retrieved July 5, 2013.

clxx http://www.jihadica.com/?s=conflict. Al-Qa'ida and the Afghan Taliban: "Diametrically Opposed"? Beginning with a statement from Mullah Omar in September, the Afghan Taliban's Quetta-based leadership has been emphasizing the "nationalist" character of their movement, and has sent several communications to Afghanistan's neighbors expressing an intent to establish positive international relations. In what are increasingly being viewed by the forums as direct rejoinders to these sentiments, recent messages from al-Qa'ida have pointedly rejected the "national" model of revolutionary Islamism and reiterated calls for jihad against Afghanistan's neighbors, especially Pakistan and China. However interpreted, these conflicting signals raise serious questions about the notion of an al-Qa'ida-Taliban merger. The trouble began with Mullah Omar's message for 'Eid al-Fitr, issued on September 19, in which he calls the Taliban a "robust Islamic and nationalist movement," which "wants to maintain good and positive relations with all neighbors based on mutual respect." Mullah Omar further stated that he wishes to "assure all countries that the Islamic Emirate of Afghanistan … will not extend its hand to jeopardize others, as it itself does not allow others to jeopardize us." A week later, Abu Muhammad al-Maqdisi, one of the most influential living Salafi jihadi ideologues, released an angry rebuke to these "dangerous utterances" of the Taliban amir, pointing out that they were of the same order as Hamas leader Khaled Mashal's statement that the Chechen struggle is a Russian "internal matter." For a person of Maqdisi's stature to equate the Taliban with Hamas, especially in light of the recent jihadi media onslaught against Hamas for its "crimes" against the Jund Ansar Allah, is an extremely serious charge. Maqdisi ends his statement with the hope that he has misunderstood Mullah Omar's message and that some clarification from the Taliban leadership will be forthcoming. (More follows at Jihadica.) Retrieved January 17, 2011.

clxxi http://www.jihadica.com/the-jihadis-path-to-self-destruction/. Retrieved January 17, 2011. I look forward to adding this to my library. Note the reference to "takfiri" reflexes. This is that phenomenon I discussed earlier in regard to the work of Dr. David Killcullen and Maulana Maudoodi (see end notes xxxvii and xxxviii, above.)

clxxii http://www.jihadwatch.org/about-robert-spencer.html. Retrieved January 17, 2011.

clxxiii Lambert, S. Y: The sources of Islamic revolutionary conduct. Center for Strategic Intelligence Research, Joint Military Intelligence College. Washington, DC. April 2005. (With the cooperation and support of the Institute for National Security Studies INSS) and the USAF Academy, Colorado Springs, CO.

clxxiv Ibid. Lambert. p. vii.

clxxv Ibid. Lambert, p. viii.

clxxvi http://www.biblestudytools.com/history/creeds-confessions/luther-95-theses.html. Martin Luther's 95 Theses. Retrieved July 19, 2013.

clxxvii Ressentiment: deep-seated resentment, frustration, and hostility accompanied by a sense of being powerless to express these feelings directly

clxxviii Ibid. Lambert, p. 121.

clxxix OnLine News Hour with Jim Lehrer. The… text is a fatwa, or declaration of war, by Osama bin Laden first published in *Al Quds Al Arabi*, a London-based newspaper, in August, 1996. The fatwa is titled "Declaration of War against the Americans Occupying the Land of the Two Holy Places." Retrieved February 17, 2010. http://www.pbs.org/newshour/terrorism/international/fatwa_1996.html.

clxxx Ibid. Lambert, p. 9.

clxxxi Ibid. Lambert, p. 9.

clxxxii Ibid. Lambert, p. 131.

clxxxiii Jenkins, B. M. (2007). Building an army of believers: jihadists radicalization and recruitment. Testimony presented before the House Homeland Security Committee, Subcommittee on Intelligence Sharing and Terrorism Risk Assessment on April 5, 2007. © The RAND Corporation: Santa Monica, CA. http://www.rand.org.

[clxxxiv] Hofstede, Geert (1984). "The cultural relativity of the quality of life concept". *Academy of Management Review* 9 (3): 389–398. Retrieved February 12, 2011.

[clxxxv] Maslow, A. Motivation and personality. Harper and Row New York, New York 1954. Maslow's hierarchy has in fact been criticized as being ethnocentric – written from the perspective of an "individualistic" society (American), and not taking the societal (cultural) differences of "collectivist" societies into account. See also: Cianci, R., Gambrel, P.A. (2003). Maslow's hierarchy of needs: Does it apply in a collectivist culture. Journal of Applied Management and Entrepreneurship, 8(2), 143-161. No matter how needs are depicted or ordered on a scale – they exist as the normal baggage of being human, and serve as drives or motivations. It would benefit the broader community to apply a range of lenses and perspectives (including psychology and motivation) to the understanding of our enemy's "culture."

[clxxxvi] Ibid, Jihadica.com. Prucha, N. 24 January 2011. Retrieved January 26, 2011.

[clxxxvii] http://www.ctc.usma.edu/imagery/imagery_introduction.asp. Retrieved January 29, 2011.

[clxxxviii] Ibid, Jenkins / RAND. p. 3.

[clxxxix] Elliot, Andrea. A Call to Jihad, Answered in America. http://www.nytimes.com/2009/07/12/us/12somalis.html?pagewanted=all. Retrieved October 8, 2011.

[cxc] Ibid: Elliot.

[cxci] http://abcnews.go.com/Blotter/american-jihadi-samir-khan-killed-Aulaqi/story?id=14640013. Accessed on October 8, 2011.

[cxcii] http://en.wikipedia.org/wiki/Adam_Yahiye_Gadahn. Accessed October 8, 2011.

[cxciii] http://en.wikipedia.org/wiki/Boko_Haram. Retrieved October 8, 2011.

[cxciv] As of mid-2011, Marine Corps end-strength is 203,000; Army – 560,000; Navy – 325,000; Air Force – 331,000. As a percentage of size, one might infer from the registered TWS numbers that Marines are more active in maintaining the social bonds created in their *Band of Brothers*. There may be other factors at work, however, including the relative age distribution: there are fewer officers per enlisted Marine (therefore enlisted Marines are a higher percentage of the service), and enlisted Marines in the most junior ranks – private through sergeant – are comparatively younger than in the same ranks or pay grades of the other services. In other words, if tech-savvy younger Marines log on because they are tech-savvy younger Marines.... there will be a higher percentage of Marines.

[cxcv] http://www.leatherneck.com/forums/view_aboutus.htm. Retrieved August 22, 2011.

cxcvi http://usmilitary.about.com/od/marines/a/tattoo.htm. About.com's military web site, with information (and advertisements) directed at men and women in uniform. This story discusses the Marine Corps policy on tattoos in April, 2007. Maj. Tinson's remarks are from August 2011. Tinson notes that the Army's policy on tattoos is less restrictive than the Corps' and as recruiters in the same office suites will sometimes cooperate on prospects, a Marine recruiter with an otherwise-qualified prospect who is ineligible because of visible tattoos might send the lad or lady "across the hall" to the Army recruiter. (The author served with Tinson in Fallujah in 2006-'07.)

cxcvii http://www.leatherneck.com/topsites/list.php. accessed August 27, 2011.

cxcviii Accessed September 3, 2011. http://en.wikipedia.org/wiki/List_of_films_featuring_the_United_States_Marine_Corps.

cxcix Ibid, Millett. 1982. p. 7.

cc Ibid, Millett, 1980, pp. 13-15

cci Lindsay, R. G. (1956). This high name: public relations and the U. S. Marine Corps. Madison: University of Wisconsin Press. p. 19)

ccii Ibid, Millett. 1980. p. 324.

cciii Ibid, Millett, 1980. p. 324.

cciv Ibid, Lindsay. p. 43.

ccv Ibid, Millett, 1983. p. 365.

ccvi Burlage, J. Military not giving North, Poindexter blind support. Navy Times, August 10, 1987. pp. 6, 8.

ccvii http://en.wikipedia.org/wiki/Oliver_North. Most lieutenant colonels retire from the spotlight, get a job as a government contractor, start a consulting business or teach high school ROTC – and mow their own lawns. Like any good American opportunist handed the brass ring, North grabbed it and has remained active in conservative politics. He writes, appears on television, and has a Wikipedia presence: Oliver Laurence North (born October 7, 1943) is a retired U.S. Marine Corps officer, political commentator, host of War Stories with Oliver North on Fox News Channel, a military historian, and a New York Times best-selling author.

ccviii Ibid, Burlage. p. 6.

ccix Buchwald died January 17, 2007. (New York Times, January 28, 2007. Obituary: Art Buchwald, columnist who delighted in the absurd – Americas – International Herald Tribune. Retrieved February 5, 2011, from http://www.nytimes.com/2007/01/18/world/americas/18iht-web.0118buchwaldcnd.4252394.html?_r=1, NYT writer Richard Severo writes: "Art Buchwald, who poked fun at the follies of the rich, the famous and the powerful for half a century as the most widely read newspaper humorist of his time, died Wednesday night in Washington. He was 81....

With the outbreak of World War II, Buchwald, still in high school, ran away to join the Marines, hitchhiking to North Carolina. "The Marine Corps was the first father figure I had ever known," he wrote. Assigned to the Fourth Marine Air Wing, he spent most of his tour on a Pacific atoll cleaning aircraft guns and editing his squadron's newsletter while earning a sergeant's stripes. After the war, Buchwald went to the University of Southern California in Los Angeles under the G.I. Bill and became managing editor of the campus humor magazine. But he neglected to tell U.S.C. that he had not finished high school. When officials found out, they told him that he could continue to take courses but that he could not be considered for a degree. (Thirty-three years later, the university gave him an honorary doctorate.)

[ccx] Weaver, C. G. (March 18, 1983). Art Buchwald: Humorist recalls 'good times' in boot camp. Parris Island: The Boot (newspaper), p. 4.

[ccxi] Ibid, Weaver, *The Boot.* p. 4.

[ccxii] Fleming, K. Personal correspondence, August 9, 1984.

[ccxiii] House of Representatives, Committee on Armed Services, Subcommittee on Military Personnel. (1976, May 26, June 9, August 9). Hearings on recruiting practices and abuses in recruit training. L. N. Nedzi, presiding. Washington, D.C.

[ccxiv] Several, personal communication and interviews, Parris Island, 1984.

[ccxv] Article 15, Uniform Code of Military Justice. The maximum reduction by a lieutenant colonel is one pay grade – one "stripe" for sergeants and below. Staff sergeants and more senior staff non-commissioned officers may not be reduced in rank, through Article 15, for disciplinary charges.

[ccxvi] Ibid, Stack, 1975.

[ccxvii] Parris Island drill instructors, personal communication, August 10-15, 1984.

[ccxviii] As it turns out, Paul Cowan and I maintained contact through these past 28 years, mostly through Christmas cards. Paul contacted me via e-mail while I was deployed to Iraq in 2006-'07, seeking support for a film – a retrospective from the point of view of the recruits and drill instructors depicted in *Anybody's Son Will Do*. With support from other researchers, we sent hundreds of e-mails, made countless phone calls, scanned social networking sites (e.g. *Together we Served, Facebook*), queried veterans organizations, and even visited Parris Island's photo archives in what sadly has become a futile attempt to locate more than one or two recruits from that filming in 1982. We did track down one drill instructor, one of the series officers and two recruits. As if this writing – I am assuming the project is "on hold."

[ccxix] Dyer, G., Bryans, M. & Kramer, J. (1980, August). War. Proposal for a series of films. Montreal: National Film Board of Canada.

[ccxx] A "mustang" is prior enlisted, then commissioned.

[ccxxi] Personal communication, Marine officers, 1984-1986.

[ccxxii] Carr, F., personal communication, August 7, 1984.

[ccxxiii] Thompson, J. Walter (company). 1980). 6th Marine Corps district recruitment advertising plan FY81.Atlanta, GA: Author. pp. 4-5)

[ccxxiv] Thompson, J. Walter (company). (1983). Awareness and attitude tracking study (Wave XIX). Research and Planning Dept. Washington, D.C.: Author. p. 6)

[ccxxv] Ibid, JWT, 1983, p. 6)

[ccxxvi] Thompson, J. Walter (company). 1980). 6th Marine Corps district recruitment advertising plan FY81.Atlanta, GA: Author. p. 72)

[ccxxvii] Ibid, J. Walter Thompson, 1983.

[ccxxviii] Ibid, JWT, 1983, pp. 7-8

[ccxxix] Ibid, JWT, 1983, p. 26.

[ccxxx] Ibid, Millett, 1983. p 365.

[ccxxxi] Department of the Navy, Headquarters, U.S. Marine Corps. (1980). Program of instruction for male recruit training (SOP, Marine Corps Order 1510.13C). Washington, D.C. pp. 5-4 to 5-7.

[ccxxxii] Navy Times, 28 February 2011. Additionally during this evolution, there has been some agitation over command and control of MARSOC. The end result is this comparatively small (2500 Marines), specialized unit reports to Special Operations Command as does Navy Special Warfare Command (the SEAL teams), for example. Although they are *special operators*, they are still Marines. The Corps has since created new MOSs, or occupational designators, and those who earn the MOS will stay in the MOS for the balance of their career in the Marine Corps.

[ccxxxiii] This article from: A Future for the Young. Options for helping Middle Eastern Youth Escape the Trap of Radicalization. Cheryl Benard. WR-354 / September 2005. RAND's Initiative on Middle Eastern Youth: 3. The Dark Side of jihad: How young men detained at Guantanamo asses their experiences. Introduction ; From November 2003 to July 2004, the author was assigned to Guantanamo Bay Detention Center and tasked with reviewing the interrogation transcripts of approximately 600 young men held at that facility. [1] In addition to the factual materials that were at the core of that assignment, this review also elicited some significant patterns that emerged from the anecdotal and narrative content of the interviews. These patterns pertain to the mechanics and the motives of recruitment; the experiences of the young men while in their training camps, in combat situations, and during their subsequent flight; and perhaps most

significantly, to their shifting attitudes and mindsets as their venture into jihad unfolded and – ultimately – began to fall apart. These observations are shared here in the belief that they reveal opportunities to deter, reclaim and in some cases reintegrate young men such as the detainees described below. [ccxxxiv] The Marine Corps Division of Public Affairs official web site offers this explanation of the PAO practitioner's duties: "To accomplish their mission, Public Affairs Marines must have a sound understanding of the organization, tactics and equipment used in war and other conflicts. They must be ingrained within the Commander's battle staff and must train side-by-side with the warfighting units. In peacetime and in war, the Public Affairs mission is to inform America's citizens about what their Marines are doing."
[ccxxxv] http://www.marines.mil/unit/iiimef/Pages/band.aspx, accessed 5 September 2011. "On October 1, 1978, the First Marine Aircraft Wing Band of Iwakuni combined with the Third Marine Division Band of Okinawa to create the III Marine Amphibious Force Band. It was assigned to Camp Foster on December 1, 1978, and later re-designated as the III Marine Expeditionary Force Band, the only Expeditionary Force Band in the Marine Corps. This unique attribute exemplifies its versatile nature as a military organization comprised of professional musicians that are also competent and effective Marines."
[ccxxxvi] http://www.jwt.com/#!/content/424910/united-states-marine-corps, accessed September 4, 2011.
[ccxxxvii] JWT June 16, 2011, Author. Marine Corps Recruiting Command Long Range Strategy Conference: Generational Overview: Contemporary Views of Service among Millennials and their Parents. (via e-mail from Randy Shepard, JWT, August 9, 2011.
[ccxxxviii] http://www.marines.mil/unit/marsoc/Pages/default.aspx. Accessed September 5, 2011. "In October 2005, the Secretary of Defense directed the formation of a Marine component of U.S. Special Operations Command. It was determined the Marine Corps would initially form a unit of approximately 2,500 to serve with USSOCOM. On February 24, 2006, MARSOC activated at Camp Lejeune, NC. MARSOC initially consisted of a small staff and the Foreign Military Training Unit, which had been formed to conduct foreign internal defense."
[ccxxxix] Ibid JWT June 16, 2011. Page 21.
[ccxl] Accessed September 9, 20011
http://www2.marines.mil/news/publications/Pages/CONCEPTSPROGRA MS2008.aspx. The Marine Corps enlists some 30,000 (active duty) recruits a year to maintain an "end strength" of roughly 187,000 enlisted Marines (…in 2010-2011 numbers. These totals will decline in the coming draw-down of the surges for Iraq and Afghanistan and America's fiscal

irresponsibility). That's 30,000 out of 22 million – a little over 1/10th of one percent of the sliding population of 16- 24-year-olds (every year, 15-year-olds become 16-year-olds; 24-year-olds turn 25 and while everyone gets a year older, this segment of the population remains relatively constant – shrinking or expanding gradually.

[ccxli] http://ni-u.edu/prospective_students/criteria.html. Accessed September 9, 2011. NDIC offers a Bachelor of Science in Intelligence, and Master of Science in Strategic Intelligence and MS and Technology Intelligence. Enlisted Marines who meet the requirements for graduate programs (virtually unheard of in the 1970's), may apply to the graduate programs.

[ccxlii] Non-rates are "non-rated" because they are not yet Non-Commissioned Officers. NCOs in the Marine Corps start at the rank of corporal. During times of war, with comparatively rapid promotions, an enlisted Marine could be promoted to corporal in less than two years and at the age of perhaps 20, have exponentially more responsibility than a civilian counterpart at the same age. With deaths in combat in prior wars, it was possible that a corporal might temporarily be the senior Marine in a unit and serve as a platoon commander. Some received "brevet" or field commissions to the rank of lieutenant.

[ccxliii] The Marine Corps physical fitness test includes a 3-mile run (18 minutes or better is 100 points); pull-ups (5 points each – with 100 points for 20); and crunches (1 point each – with 100 in two minutes to reach a maximum score). A max'ed run and crunches (200 points) with 16 pull-ups, for example, would yield a score of 280 points – darn good for a 47-year-old, and likely better than a significant percentage of the Marines half his age (who are not PT-focused infantry Marines).

[ccxliv] Pub.L. 103-160 (10 U.S.C. § 654). Accessed via wikipedia.org on September 10, 2011:
(http://en.wikipedia.org/wiki/Don%27t_ask,_don%27t_tell). The policy prohibits military personnel from discriminating against or harassing closeted homosexual or bisexual service members or applicants, while barring openly gay, lesbian, or bisexual persons from military service. The restrictions are mandated by United States federal law. The policy prohibits people who "demonstrate a propensity or intent to engage in homosexual acts" from serving in the armed forces of the United States, because their presence "would create an unacceptable risk to the high standards of morale, good order and discipline, and unit cohesion that are the essence of military capability. The act prohibits any homosexual or bisexual person from disclosing his or her sexual orientation or from speaking about any homosexual relationships, including marriages or other familial attributes, while serving in the United States armed forces. The act specifies that

service members who disclose that they are homosexual or engage in homosexual conduct shall be separated (discharged) except when a service member's conduct was "for the purpose of avoiding or terminating military service" or when it "would not be in the best interest of the armed forces." Following mandated reviews by Department of Defense and individual Service Chief, Secretary of Defense and the White House, this law is set to be repealed effective September 20, 2011.

ccxlv McMichael, W., and McGarry, B. *How troops really feel about gays serving openly.* Army Times, February 15, 2010, pp. 10-11.

ccxlvi MARS radio was originally an "affiliate" radio patch communication network, operating over HF, SSB (single side band) or shortwave radio, offering military members deployed overseas an opportunity to "patch" a call from a MARS radio station in Okinawa, Japan, (for example) through operators in Guam, or Wake, or Hawaii to a stateside operator –who would then patch the radio call to a landline telephone and call the Marine's family for a "morale and welfare" call at no charge to the Marine. In the 1970's – well before the advent of Skype, Voice Over Internet Protocol (VOIP) and rapid e-mail exchange – one 5-minute international telephone call from Japan to California might cost $25, while the base pay for a private was about $175 per month. As of 2009, the "Affiliate" status was changed to "Auxiliary," placing the program in parallel to the Coast Guard Auxiliary and Civil Air Patrol (Department of Defense Directive 4650.02).

ccxlvii It was the MWR contractors in Fallujah and al-Asad Air Base who helped Major McClung and me organize and operate the Marine Corps Marathon in October 2006 and Houston Marathon in January 2007.

ccxlviii Henderson, D. Lance Corporal. Regimental Combat Team 7: *Female engagement team helps establish connection between Marines and Afghan women.* http://www.marines.mil/unit/iimef/2ndmeb/Pages/Female. accessed September 16, 2011.

ccxlix

http://www2.marines.mil/news/publications/Documents/U.S.MarineCorps ConceptsandPrograms020103.pdf.

ccl http://atwar.blogs.nytimes.com/2013/07/19/marines-share-frank-views-with-hagel-on-women-in-combat/. Retrieved July 20, 2013.

ccli DOD Evaluates Sexual Harassment and Prevention Response Efforts at the Military Service Academies <http://www.defense.gov/releases/release.aspx?releaseid=14141> accessed September 16, 2011.

cclii Scarborough, R., Special Ops Worried About Adding Women. Washington Times, p. 1. June 28, 2013.

ccliii Spradley, J. P. (1979). The ethnographic interview. (p. 13) New York: Holt, Rinehart and Winston. p. 186.

ccliv Guidebook for Marines, pp. 27-31.

cclv Ibid, Spradley, p. 133.

cclvi Ibid, Stack, Warriors, 1975.

cclvii http://www.sapr.mil/index.php/annual-reports. Retrieved June 30, 2013.

cclviii Newsweek, July 20, 1987, pp. 8-14.

cclix Navy Times, founded in 1951, was originally published by Army Times Publishing Company (Army Times was founded in 1940; Air Force Times in 1947.) Gannett bought the group in 1997 and launched Marine Corps Times that year.

cclx Marine Corps Order 1510.13C, para. 203, 1980.

cclxi Ibid, Heinl, 1970, p. 98.

cclxii Ibid, Millett, 1980, p 375.

cclxiii http://usmilitary.about.com/od/marinebonuses/a/zoneabonus.htm. Retrieved 12 February 2011.

cclxiv Nightline, AFKN, August 9, 1987. (Armed Forces Korea Network Television).

cclxv Excerpt from an article written by Jon Katzenbach and Ashley Harshak for strategy+business magazine. https://ffbsccn.wordpress.com/tag/alfred-m-al-gray-jr/. Retrieved February 12, 2011.

cclxvi Crichton, D. (January 4, 1984). Marine Corps' mystique remains despite changes. Richmond Times-Dispatch, pp. 1, 3.

cclxvii In his book on the Ribbon Creek Incident, Gene Alvarez observed that drill instructors in the 1940s and '50s referred to their recruits as "men." Though the incoming recruits were the same age in the late 1950s and into the '60s and 70s, (combat veteran) drill instructors gradually began to refer to recruits as "boys."

cclxviii Marine Corps Development and Education Command. (August 25, 1981). Proceedings of the Major General John H. Russell Conference on Ethics and Leadership. Record of the Conference conducted at Quantico, VA. At the Russell Conference on Leadership, Lieutenant General Carey quoted Army General Douglas MacArthur in his welcoming address. p. 25.

cclxix Ibid Russell Leadership Conference, p. 84.

cclxx Skinner, B. F. (1978). Reflections on behaviorism and Society. Englewood Cliffs, NJ: Prentice-Hall, Inc. pp. 11-13)

cclxxi Ibid, Skinner, pp. 11-12.

cclxxii Ibid, Skinner, p. 13.

cclxxiii Ibid, Millett, 1980, p. 628.

cclxxiv Lombardo, T. *For Grunts Only?* Marine Corps Times, March 14, 2011, pp. 20-21. Although off the front pages, an undercurrent of controversy surrounds the concept of "every Marine a rifleman." Social media (and anonymity) has allowed *grunts* to post the notion that only infantry Marines (in the 03XX MOSs should be allowed to wear the crossed rifles that are part of the enlisted rank insignia from lance corporal through master sergeant. Lombardo's Marine Corps Times story illuminates some of the dialog, including a response to the open debate from the Sergeant Major of the Marine Corps: "MOS does not make a Marine." The debate will continue. Marines and soldiers who fight "outside the wire" are in more danger, face more of the horrors of war, than do those who remain within the relative security of "the FOB." Unremarkably – the same debate continues in the radical Islamist extremist camp as well.

cclxxv (p. 126)

cclxxvi Stockdale, J. B. (1981, September 29). Fighting fools, thinking cowards? Our military enticement system ignores duty, honor, country. San Diego Union, p. 9J.

cclxxvii A quick check at dictionary.com turned up this discussion of "culture:" Students arriving at college [in the Fall of 2011] were greeted, as usual, with plenty of *culture*. For example, a few course titles in one catalogue: "Theorizing Culture," "Transnationalism and Culture in the Americas," "Conceptual Process for Visual Culture as Curricula." In college classrooms, it seems, the word is everywhere. But what does it mean? Merriam-Webster's definition of *culture* includes a couple of senses relevant to the academic use: the integrated pattern of human knowledge, belief, and behavior that depends upon the capacity for learning and transmitting knowledge to succeeding generations: the customary beliefs, social forms, and material traits of a racial, religious, or social group; also : the characteristic features of everyday existence (as diversions or a way of life) shared by people in a place or time. Beyond that, exploring the range of this word is partly what student life is about. *Culture* comes from Latin: "to cultivate land."

cclxxviii http://www.census.gov/prod/cen2010/briefs/c2010br-03.pdf

cclxxix Pew Social and Demographic Trends, author. *War and sacrifice in the post9/11 era.* Retrieved from www.pewsocialtrends.org on October 6, 2011.

cclxxx Ibid, Pew.

cclxxxi http://www.armedforcesjournal.com/2007/05/2635198

cclxxxii http://en.wikipedia.org/wiki/Voice_of_America

cclxxxiii U.S. House of Representatives, 111th Congress, Committee on Oversight and Government Reform. *Analysis of the first year of the obama administration: public relations and propaganda initiatives.* August 9, 2010. This is a <u>must read</u> for anyone interested in domestic propaganda and message manipulation. The report discusses both Obama's and George W. Bush's administrations.

cclxxxiv If the reader is genuinely adventurous, read up on "Schrödinger's Cat" and related thought experiments. Previously – openly serving gays were external to the military. Now serving openly, gays are a social *experiment* (as would be women in special forces and in the infantry). For the gays to look in on… to participate in… the experiment, they would have corrupted the findings.

cclxxxv Case 1:12-cv-00832-RMC Document 1 Filed 05/23/12, District Court for the District of Colombia. Command Sergeant Major Jane P. Baldwin and Colonel Ellen L. Haring, plaintiffs, v. The Honorable Leon Panetta, et al. Retrieved August 8, 2013.
http://www.law.virginia.edu/pdf/combat_exclusion_policy_complaint.pdf.

cclxxxvi Ibid, Dyer.

K2